W9-ACV-411

MARVELLOUS THIEVES

MARVELLOUS THIEVES

SECRET AUTHORS OF THE ARABIAN NIGHTS

PAULO LEMOS HORTA

Cambridge, Massachusetts, and London, England

2017

Printed in the United States of America

First Printing

LIBRARY OF CONGRESS CATALOGING-IN-PUBLICATION DATA

Names: Horta, Paulo Lemos, author.
Title: Marvellous thieves : secret authors of the Arabian Nights / Paulo Lemos Horta.
Description: Cambridge, Massachusetts : Harvard University Press, 2017. | Includes bibliographical references and index.
Identifiers: LCCN 2016017325 | ISBN 9780674545052 (alk. paper)
Subjects: LCSH: Arabian nights—Authorship. | Arabic literature—European influences.
Classification: LCC PJ7737 .H67 2017 | DDC 398.22—dc23
LC record available at https://lccn.loc.gov/2016017325

CONTENTS

A NOTE ON TERMINOLOGY

The story collection that is the subject of this book goes by different titles. Because my focus is on the new tales and material added by European translators to the original collection, I refer to it primarily by the English title most commonly used for these translations: *Arabian Nights.* When referring to Arabic versions that preceded the European translations, or to translations into languages such as Urdu, I use *Thousand and One Nights,* a title that is closer to the original Arabic title, *Alf Layla wa-Layla.*

I refer to the characters by the names that were established in eighteenth-century European translations, such as Aladdin, Ali Baba, and Prince Ahmad, or by the names that appear in recent scholarly editions by Hussain Haddawy and Malcolm Lyons, such as Shahrazad and Shahriyar.

Arabic words and proper names are transliterated without diacritical marks.

MARVELLOUS THIEVES

INTRODUCTION

On May 8, 1709, there were riots over food shortages in the Paris neighborhood where Antoine Galland lived, but he made no note of this in his journal. Instead, the first French translator of the *Arabian Nights* reported that he had received a story that day—"The Story of Aladdin and the Wonderful Lamp." This famous tale follows Aladdin, its young protagonist, from an impoverished life in an unnamed Chinese city through the wonders of a magical cave to a palace more spectacular than that of the sultan himself. This extraordinary palace, created by the jinni of a magical lamp in one night for Aladdin and his new wife, Princess Badr al-Budur, inspires awe in its first visitors. Within its spacious halls, lit with innumerable candles and filled with the sounds of the most melodious instruments, the couple feast from an extraordinary banquet set on plates of solid gold, surrounded by ornaments and decorations of exquisite craftsmanship. Even the sultan is convinced that no palace on earth can rival its riches. He is particularly struck by a chamber whose twenty-four windows are decorated with screens studded with diamonds, rubies, and emeralds, and he tries in vain to help Aladdin complete the last window of this chamber with his own jewels.[1]

The story of Aladdin and his wondrous palace has become a standard part of the collection known in English as the *Thousand and One Nights,* or perhaps more popularly as the *Arabian Nights.* Behind the familiarity of this story, however, lies a persistent riddle. Where is this palace located? Traditionally, the tale is set in China, but this is a distinctly Islamic China, for it must accommodate the cosmology of the jinn—the magical beings who drive this rags-to-riches story. A setting in Central Asia might solve this problem—but does "Aladdin" really take place in the Orient at all? Where does this story come from? And how did it become part of this fascinating book of tales?

Galland included the tale of Aladdin and the equally famous story of "Ali Baba and the Forty Thieves" in his French edition of the *Arabian Nights,* even though he did not find these stories in the Arabic manuscript that he used as the principal source for his translation. Entries in Galland's diary reveal that these "orphan tales" were told to him by a Syrian traveller named Hanna Diyab in Paris in the spring of 1709.[2] Scholars of the *Arabian Nights* have assumed that Galland drew from his own travels in the Levant to turn the outlines from these storytelling sessions with Diyab into the rich characters and elegant prose of the tales in French.[3] However, Aladdin's palace bears little resemblance to the residence of the Ottoman sultans at Topkapi Palace in Istanbul. Instead, this marvel of the jinni's magical powers appears distinctly European.

It might be simple to credit Galland alone for the apparent resemblance between Aladdin's palace and the baroque residences of European monarchs, but the recent discovery of the memoir of Diyab, long neglected in the collections of the Vatican Library, offers an intriguing counterargument. Providing the first glimpse of Diyab's own remarkable journey from his home in Aleppo to the palaces, cathedrals, and opera houses of Paris, this document suggests that the tale of Aladdin was strongly imprinted by the European marvels seen by the young Syrian during his months in France. Before the discovery of this manuscript, Diyab had only a shadowy existence in literary history as the mysterious Maronite who related "beautiful stories" to the more famous French translator. Diyab's memoir now reveals a talented storyteller in his own right, and it prompts us to ask just how much he contributed to some of the most famous tales of the *Arabian Nights.*[4]

Galland was not the only translator of the *Arabian Nights* to utilize the narrative talents of others. *Marvellous Thieves* examines three of the most influential European translators of the story collection with reference to their unacknowledged reliance on other storytellers, translators, and cultural insiders. Among the innumerable versions of the story collection in French and English, the translations produced by Galland, Edward William Lane, and Richard Francis Burton still retain their power to define these tales in the Western imagination, and each has played an important role in analyses of Orientalism as a framework for understanding the Middle East. This study examines how these translations were created within a literary context in which practices of imitation, forgery, and plagiarism flourished. I trace the process by which the tales of Shahrazad were claimed as a territory of European authorship by an erasure of the many collaborative relationships that made these three versions of the stories so distinctive. Writing the lost chapter of these cross-cultural exchanges, this book seeks to uncover the storytellers, the treasure hunters, the booksellers, the translators, the poets, and the local linguists who made their own contributions to the creation of this most famous of story collections.

✦ ✦ ✦

The history of the *Thousand and One Nights* reveals the remarkable capacity of this Arabic story collection to take on new forms and absorb new influences over the course of centuries. Its origins are murky, but an argument can be made that it begins with an act of translation—the passage of the frame tale of King Shahriyar and his wife, Shahrazad, from Persian into Arabic sometime in the second half of the eighth century CE. This frame, in which Shahrazad narrates ever more marvellous tales in a bid to save the lives of the young women of the kingdom from her husband's murderous designs, became the creative stimulus to add story upon story, transforming the collection over time. The result was the emergence not of a single text, but of a vast ensemble of texts that, according to Aboubakr Chraïbi, the leading scholar of the *Thousand and One Nights* in Arabic, represents both a new literary genre and a mass literary phenomenon.[5]

The *Thousand and One Nights* in Arabic must be understood not as a singular work but as an array of texts, coexisting with a large number of variants and analogues and constantly interacting with other literary models as it circulated within a diverse region of Arabic speakers.

The manuscript that Galland finally translated into French at the beginning of the eighteenth century was a product of a long period of development in which the *Thousand and One Nights* absorbed elements of a popular oral storytelling tradition and responded to classical Arabic texts. The addition of the technique of *'ajā'ib*—story elements capable of evoking wonder or astonishment—encouraged the expansion of the story collection, and over time it integrated ever more amazing tales of magic and adventure. The result was not exactly popular literature, but it certainly was not classical literature either. The tales of the *Thousand and One Nights* were written in Middle Arabic, and they belong to a category of "middle literature" associated with the major cities of the Arabic-speaking world and the middle class of tradesmen and merchants who resided in them.[6]

From the perspective of the Arabic scholar, the *Thousand and One Nights* lacks the features of an authoritative text. It is authorless; it exists in multiple variants; it is not written in a "noble, imposing style"; and it does not require commentary to help the reader interpret the language of the text. The Moroccan author Abdelfattah Kilito argues that, unlike the treasured manuscripts of classical Arabic, the *Thousand and One Nights* was a text that begged to be translated. This is a particularly powerful comment coming from a literary critic who has expressed his deep distrust of translation and perceives it as a form of epistemic violence. His stance reflects not only an awareness of the power differential that lies within such linguistic exchanges, but also a tradition of resistance to the translation of sacred texts. Drawing on authorities such as the ninth-century scholar al-Jahiz, Kilito makes a strong claim for the untranslatability of Arabic poetry, which becomes merely "a web of banalities" when stripped of its metrical structure. He also expresses doubt about the translatability of classical Arabic prose texts, for these are seen as inextricably linked to the scholarly commentaries that illuminate their meaning. In this context, the apparent accessibility of the *Thousand and One Nights* to appropriation in another language is exceptional.[7]

The unique qualities of the *Thousand and One Nights* in Arabic offered enormous freedom of action to the scholars and translators who made it part of world literature in French and English. Beyond a core of forty tales and 282 nights, there is no clear and consistent canon of the *Thousand and One Nights*. Each Arabic manuscript of the story collection betrays the distinct cultural milieu in which it was produced and the workshop atmosphere of its compilation, which often entailed borrowing whole sequences of tales from rival story collections. Versions of the *Thousand and One Nights* often contain repetitions of a particular story type, suggesting that scribes added stories that they believed to be similar in spirit or form to those already in the collection. However, the *Thousand and One Nights* is by no means homogenous. Later recensions gather together a bewildering range of genres—love stories, trickster tales, historical epics, tales of the supernatural, animal fables, and tales of heroic journeys to foreign lands. The collection often contains traces of several different historical moments and some of the key cities of the Islamic world—Baghdad, Damascus, and Cairo.

The *Thousand and One Nights* entered European literature at the beginning of the eighteenth century as Orientalist scholars began to turn their attention to the collections of vernacular tales that had arrived in manuscript form during a period of intense commercial exchange with the Levant. For the history of the *Thousand and One Nights*, the most important of these early acquisitions was the "incomplete" manuscript used by Galland, which is dated to the middle of the fifteenth century.[8] Other famous manuscripts also played their part in generating new versions of the story collections: the eighteenth-century manuscript brought from Egypt by Edward Wortley-Montague, a British diplomat and eccentric who converted to Islam; a manuscript covering 281 nights brought to England by the Scottish herpetologist Patrick Russell, who served as a physician to the British merchants of Aleppo; and an Egyptian manuscript carried by a British officer to India, where it became the basis of a new Arabic edition in the nineteenth century. Perhaps the most fascinating story of the "transmission" of a manuscript version of the *Thousand and One Nights* involved Joseph von Hammer-Purgstall, an interpreter for the Austrian consulate in Constantinople. On the orders of the Habsburg ambassador, he procured a manuscript copy of the *Thousand and One Nights* in Egypt from a British traveller. The manuscript was lost in a shipwreck, but Hammer-Purgstall somehow acquired an identical manuscript and translated it into French in

1804–1806. Unfortunately, both this manuscript and the French translation were also lost, but a German translation of Hammer-Purgstall's French text had already been prepared, and this survived to become a part of the rich textual history of the *Thousand and One Nights* in nineteenth-century Europe. Such attenuated processes of transmission make a mockery of any notion of an "authentic" original of the story collection.[9]

The discovery of the *Thousand and One Nights* led to efforts to compile new versions in Arabic, further blurring the lines between the authentic and the counterfeit. European editors and publishers acted like the Middle Eastern scribes before them by gathering tales from various manuscripts, some of dubious value, to make up the fabled 1,001 nights of tales. The Breslau edition is typical in this regard. Associated with its editor, Maximilian Habicht, this Arabic edition of the *Thousand and One Nights* appeared in twelve volumes from 1825 to 1843 and was based principally on the manuscript used by Galland, but the German Orientalist also added stories from a series of manuscripts copied, collated, or forged by a group of Arabs living in Paris—including the so-called Tunisian manuscript that we now know was invented by Habicht's assistant, Mordecai ibn al-Najjâr. Just as there was no singular Arabic version of the *Thousand and One Nights,* the many manuscripts and printed editions of the story collection circulating among European Orientalists in the nineteenth century were a result of much creative embellishment.[10]

The status of the *Thousand and One Nights* as an authorless text, and the many variants in which it was available, offered countless opportunities for cross-cultural appropriation, whether through translation or the kind of creative imitation that has been termed *pseudotranslation.* The imitation of foreign texts through translation was as acceptable as pillaging foreign treasures in the age of mercantilism. Usually these texts were easily incorporated into local literary culture through a process of domestication. In Britain this desire to assimilate foreign texts within the comfortable certainties of a home culture is often traced to the example of the seventeenth-century poet John Dryden, who famously claimed, "What I bring from Italy, I spend in England: here it remains, and here it circulates; for, if the coin be good, it will pass from one hand to another. I trade both with the living and the dead, for the enrichment of our native language."[11] Galland's translation of the *Arabian Nights* into French has been seen in a similar light, and the success of the first volumes in 1704 quickly spurred efforts by other translators to deliver stories on this model. Translators would turn to manuscript sources in Arabic, Persian, or Turkish, or simply manufacture their own version of the "oriental tale." Galland's work was thus quickly followed by François Pétis de la Croix's *The Thousand and One Days* (1710), which claimed to be a translation of a Persian manuscript, and Jean-Paul Bignon's *The Adventures of Abdalla* (1712–1715), a pseudotranslation of an Arabic manuscript.[12]

Even as Romanticism gave birth to a notion of authorship based on individual genius and personal authenticity, the foreign-language text was still a common source of inspiration for French and English writers. The recognition of the author's rights in copyright law—the result of the 1710 Statute of Anne in Britain and the Civil Code in France—applied only within the boundaries of a national literary culture, and this was a license for a flourishing industry based on pirating foreign literary works—sometimes through translation and sometimes not. Right after its publication, Galland's French version of the *Arabian Nights* was used as the basis for a series of English versions of the story collection. Most were cheap bootleg editions, some just one story long, produced with a popular audience in mind and with little concern about the accuracy of the translation. Others, like that of Jonathan Scott, claimed to be translations from Arabic but were really English versions of Galland's text with the addition of some stories from other manuscripts. The expanded capacity of print capitalism supported a rapid proliferation of popular versions of the *Arabian Nights*, so that by 1800 there were already eighty English editions, none of which was a direct translation of the story collection from an Arabic source.[13]

Galland's version of the tales has become a prime example of what can be gained in translation, placing this French edition of the story collection firmly within the definition of world literature.[14] Praising Galland's creative reworking of his material, critics argued that the Arabic original was merely raw material that required the literary intervention of the French master to take its place on the shelves of the French *bibliothèque.* This act of elevation through adaptation was key to the retrospective recognition of Galland as the "author" of the *Arabian Nights* in French. In stressing an intervention more akin to rewriting than translation, literary critics elevated the French Orientalist from a field ultimately defined by its derivativeness. Translations often resemble forgeries, for they need to disguise the impossibility of fidelity to an original, and the textual history of the *Arabian Nights* might be taken as an extreme example of this phenomenon.[15] Certainly, Galland valued elegance of expression over fidelity to an original text, and the wide array of translations that drew parasitically on this work had an even more tenuous connection to any Arabic original.

A retrospective claim for Galland's status as an "author" of a literary text depended on manufacturing a direct relationship between his distinctive experience of the Orient and the additions he made to the original. Scholars would point to his service as a member of the French embassy to Istanbul in 1670 and his subsequent role as collector of manuscripts and antiquities for the collections of King Louis XIV. Galland's edition of the *Arabian Nights,* comprising twelve volumes (1704–1717), was seen as the natural culmination of his engagement with the "Orient"—from his exploration of the book bazaars of Istanbul in the 1670s to his achievement of a professorship in Arabic in 1709. His fabled immersion in Istanbul was such that French scholars long believed him to be the subject of Philippe de Champaigne's *Portrait d'un Turc* (ca. 1660–1663), clothed in robes of gold brocade and sporting the turban and sword of a member of the Ottoman elite. This painting is now known to be the image of a French botanist, but the temptation to see Galland in the rich dress of the professional Orientalist remains.[16]

In Britain, where the *Arabian Nights* circulated in the eighteenth century primarily as imitation and adaptation, translators would have to make a similar claim to authority through their distinctive experience of the Orient. Portraits of Lane produced by his artist brother Richard portrayed him as a scholar at home in the exotic Egypt of ancient ruins and strange superstitions. His two residencies in Cairo (1825–1828 and 1833–1834) and his ethnography on the "manners and customs" of Egypt seemed to provide a privileged vantage point from which to produce the first substantial English translation of the story collection.

Philippe de Champaigne's *Portrait d'un Turc* (ca. 1660–1663) was long presumed to be a representation of Antoine Galland during his immersion in Istanbul in the 1670s, and it was reproduced as the frontispiece of the 2011 edition of Galland's diary. When the Huntington Library recently acquired the painting, it identified the subject not as Galland, but as the naturalist Jean de Thévenot. The sitter, the Huntington notes, "bears little resemblance" to Galland.

When Lane turned to translating the *Thousand and One Nights*, he did so under the assumption that it had been composed in Cairo two and a half centuries earlier and was therefore integrally connected to the city in which he had lived. His edition—published in three volumes in 1838–1840—is infused with a romantic nostalgia for a distinctly Egyptian world where piety survived and miracles were possible. As Argentine modernist Jorge Luis Borges asserts, in Lane's Cairo real life was blotted out by the angelic.[17]

Richard Burton (1821–1890) was an even more consummate self-mythologizer, thrilling his contemporaries with accounts of his pilgrimage to Mecca and his explorations of the source of the Nile. During his long career he took on the roles of soldier, ethnologist, linguist, and diplomat, and he was famous for his ability to travel in the guise of a Persian merchant named Mirza Abdullah. Burton claimed to speak thirty languages and stated that it was the devil who drove him on his endless travels through India, Arabia, Africa, and the Americas. His charisma was legendary. "As he talked," Bram Stoker wrote, "fancy seemed to run riot in its alluring power; and the whole world of thought seemed to flame with gorgeous color."[18] Perhaps Burton's greatest feat of self-invention was to persuade his contemporaries that he had translated the *Arabian Nights* in ten volumes in a single year (1885) at his consular residence in Trieste. Penned in a strange, archaic style with a distinctive "foreign" rhythm, this version of the story collection was often interpreted as evidence of Burton's intimate knowledge of the "pure" culture of Arabia. In fact, the sprawling corpus of the *Arabian Nights* gave Burton the opportunity to demonstrate that he could move effortlessly through diverse cultural realms by mastering different languages and social conventions. Burton's most radical claim to authorship of the work came in the notes he attached to the stories and the terminal essay he added to the last of his original ten volumes. In these additions, Burton assumed a series of cultural identities, displaying the cosmopolitan spirit identified in him by the philosopher Kwame Anthony Appiah.[19]

A close analysis of these early European translations of the *Arabian Nights* reveals the many acts of literary appropriation, and outright piracy, that lay behind the successful construction of the myth of the Orientalist translator. Both Lane and Burton assumed the mask of otherness, but behind these impersonations lay a series of other figures whose contributions were vital to the acts of translation and commentary for which these men were lauded. Taking my cue from recent work on translation, I seek to expose the way in which these texts are "a site of translational or editorial labor" rather than a "stable object owned by a single author."[20] I direct attention to the ways in which authorship was asserted over the *Arabian Nights* in the rewriting of the stories of others and the construction of elaborate commentaries through which the translator assumes the identity of local informants or hijacks the text for a performance of subversive authenticity. Most importantly, I try to highlight the contributions of other intermediary figures to a text that remains a potent source for continued gestures of imitation.

A close examination of the translations produced by Galland, Lane, and Burton reveals the degree to which each was a "collaborative event," resulting in the production of a polyvocal literary text.[21] In each case, new voices were integrated into the *Arabian Nights* through the practices of imitation and appropriation that flourished under the broad umbrella of the original story collection. Under pressure to produce 1,001 nights of tales, Galland would be challenged to radically alter his practice of "translation" when he recorded the stories told to him by the Syrian traveller Diyab in 1709. However, Diyab is only the first of many storytellers whose words were appropriated to fill out the mythical sequence of 1,001 tales. Other voices lie hidden within the commentary added by Lane to his English translation. Here Lane channelled the insights provided by friends like the Scottish former slave Osman Effendi and the Cairo bookseller Sheikh Ahmad, who both guided the Englishman through the confusion of nineteenth-century Cairo. The tales of the *Arabian Nights* were thus glossed by the anecdotes of local informants who shared their lives and their fantasies along with coffee and tobacco in Lane's living room in Cairo. The oddly pitched third-person narration that Edward Said identified in Lane's ethnographic work is the result of this attempt to replicate the apparent neutrality of a literal translation in commentary meant to convey the authentic experience of the Orientalist interpreter.

The transformation of the *Arabian Nights* in the hands of its English translators offers an ideal opportunity to explore the neglected role of

Translators of the *Arabian Nights* relied on language teachers, friends, and informants. This sketch by Edward Lane shows him receiving a guest at his home in Cairo, most likely the bookseller Sheikh Ahmad, his most frequent caller.

collaboration within the practice of translation. Hidden within the pages of these multivolume works are the many contributions of teachers, guides, and translators who often were as adept as Lane or Burton in navigating the cross-cultural exchanges of literary production in the eighteenth and nineteenth centuries. These include not only storytellers like Osman and Sheikh Ahmad, but local language experts who provided the models for the commentary added to the tales by Lane and Burton. Lane's translation proves to be deeply indebted to Arabic traditions of scholarship in Cairo, where the student was taught the text along with a commentary that explained its more obscure passages. Adapting this strategy in his translation of the *Thousand and One Nights,* Lane employed an Arabic scholar, Sheikh Muhammad Ayyad al-Tantawi, to provide an annotated copy of the text before he applied himself to the translation process. Many of his notes are a verbatim record of his collaborator's words. Burton developed his philosophy of translation in colonial India, where he relied on *munshis*—local scribes and translators—to produce a basic translation of the source text, which he would then elaborate with his own characteristic flair. When he set out to produce his translation of the *Arabian Nights*, he would find another way of delegating what he called the "ponywork" of translation.

An analysis of the versions of the *Arabian Nights* produced by all three of these figures reveals the porous boundary between translation and theft, and between imitation and ventriloquism, and in the case of Burton it exposes a chain of plagiarism that has only been hinted at until now. Within the vast literature on Burton and his varied career, one of the least discussed facts is that he actually translated very little of his version of the *Arabian Nights*. Continuing the practice of translation that he had adopted in colonial India, Burton was content to rework the translations of others—including the versions published by John Payne, a Pre-Raphaelite poet, and Henry Torrens, a member of the colonial service in India. Burton's distinctive foreign style—marked by a rhyme and rhythm that many have associated with the Arabic language of the original—was actually imposed on a text largely appropriated from other English editions.

The translations of Torrens and Payne prove to be crucial links in the cycle of plagiarism and adaptation that produced the impressive edifice of Burton's story collection. Both seem to represent a philosophy of translation more akin to that of Romanticism, allowing room for the foreignness of their text while still trying to capture its apparent universalism. Both men took on the challenge of rendering the "untranslatable" poetry embedded in the tales, and both treated the sexual content of the stories with an unusual degree of frankness for their time. However, these translations were embedded in very different cultural environments. Torrens undertook his translation in Simla on the eve of the First Anglo-Afghan War, and it bore the unmistakable signs of a campaign to foster a new empire of English within the polyglot environment of South Asia. Payne produced his translation in the cosmopolitan precincts of bohemian London, and the literary effects that he achieved were the result of translating and rewriting other versions of the stories in European languages rather than devoting himself to translating the Arabic text.

Seen within this framework, Burton's famous version of the *Arabian Nights* opens up to reveal a rich assortment of source texts beneath its strangely exotic style, praised by theorists as a model for a subversive practice of translation capable of disrupting the stale conventions of a literary tradition.[22] In his *Arabian Nights,* Burton copied, rewrote, and annotated, but translating the Arabic manuscript of the tales was not a high priority. He added his distinctive rhyming prose to texts that he was encountering largely in English, and, following Lane's model, he focused on notes and commentary essays as the principal realm of originality for the "translator." Burton's version of the *Arabian Nights* reflects his love of taking on a multiplicity of identities, creating the overwhelming impression of a man with no homeland. In this remarkable syncretic story collection, he found a convenient receptacle for the provocative opinions generated outside the confines of a single culture. In his commentary on the *Arabian Nights,* he becomes his own informant, imparting his own controversial opinions on the failures of empire and the repressive sexual conventions of his time.

✦ ✦ ✦

As one of the key texts in the emergence of world literature in French and English, the *Arabian Nights* has provided some of the most widely circulated tales in European letters. To gauge its significance, Robert Irwin contends, "is a little like asking about the influence on western literature of that other great collection of oriental tales, the Bible."[23] European translators of the story collection navigated these strange worlds—both in reality and on the page—with significant help from others. Not infrequently, the creation of these distinctive versions was a product of these relationships. *Marvellous Thieves* mines new evidence to chart these forgotten chapters of cross-cultural encounter, collaboration, and theft. The long-neglected memoir of Diyab brings into focus the young Maronite traveller from Aleppo who told the stories of Aladdin and Ali Baba to Galland and whose account of his travels reveals a curiosity about social context and character that sets him apart from the French translator. A careful study of Lane's notebooks and correspondence reveals the importance of a series of intermediary figures who established crucial links between the social world of nineteenth-century Cairo and the European travellers and scholars who pursued its manuscripts and monuments. Newly identified drafts of Burton's translation of the *Arabian Nights*—written over the work of other translators—reveal the true method of his distinctive appropriation of the tales. Seen through this prism, these legendary authors of the *Arabian Nights* appear as masters in an unacknowledged workshop, or in some cases as little more than ventriloquists.

This story of partnerships and rivalries changes the way we understand the process of creating the *Arabian Nights.* The addition of tales and commentaries differs from the act of translation. The process by which texts are added, their meaning reshaped, and the literary significance of the *Arabian Nights* forged is particularly personal. It is an intimate process of storytelling, in which the tales themselves are intertwined with the lives and ambitions of the tellers. The elaboration of a particular literary style is not simply the result of a particular philosophy of translation. In some cases a distinctive style was chosen to conceal borrowings from another author or to cover up a lack of attention to the text itself. Borges imagined the translators of the *Thousand and One Nights* locked in a hostile dynasty as each sought to efface traces of their precursors from the story collection.[24] My evidence shows that, if these translators were animated by an anxiety of influence, that anxiety was generated by the lingering traces of their unacknowledged coauthors in their versions of the tales.

Against this backdrop of discord and suspicion, partnerships built on empathy for other cultures were rare but possible. In nineteenth-century Cairo, Lane did not consistently maintain the "cold distance" that Said attributed to him. If his relationship with the bookseller Sheikh Ahmad was a complex mixture of interest and manipulation, his friendship with his neighbor Osman was real, and so was his desire to believe in the existence of jinn and the possibility of magic in nineteenth-century Cairo. This impulse strongly influenced his *Arabian Nights* and is an important part of the impact of his work on writers like George Eliot and Borges.[25] For all his arrogance and self-confessed sins, Burton used his *Arabian Nights* to argue that Britain, as the greatest Muslim empire of the age, should govern its territories with sympathy for Arab and Muslim mores. Clothing himself in the garb of the stranger, he sought to appropriate this voice to ask vital questions of his own society. His commentary arguing for the tolerance of homosexuality—one of the key lessons that he believed could be carried from the Arab world to the imperial metropolis of London—would make him a legend in the gay rights movement of the twentieth century.

However, instances of such sympathy for another culture would prove the exception rather than the rule. More commonly, the *Arabian Nights* entered European literature in contexts of imperialism and conflict, and the asymmetrical relationships between translators and their collaborators reveal the limits of comprehension and translation across cultures. In this respect, the misunderstandings and mutual suspicions that pervaded many of the stories of Diyab also characterized his interactions with the story collectors of eighteenth-century France, as well as the process by which the English versions of the *Arabian Nights* were fashioned in Cairo, London, Calcutta, and Trieste. Within this larger narrative of deception and mistrust, the search for the secret authors of the *Arabian Nights* reveals the seemingly endless potential for Shahrazad's stories to grow through the voices of a multitude of storytellers.

1

THE STORYTELLER AND THE SULTAN OF FRANCE

On March 25, 1709, a visit by Antoine Galland to the Paris apartment of his friend Paul Lucas yielded a discovery that would shape the literary legacy of the first French translator of the *Thousand and One Nights*. Lucas, a collector of treasures for the court of Louis XIV, was well known for his travels in the Middle East, and his apartment was recognized as one of the marvels of the French capital. Listed in early eighteenth-century guidebooks as a place to view antiquities and other rare objects from Greece, Egypt, and Asia Minor, it drew scholars, collectors, and curiosity seekers of all kinds.[1] Over the course of his journeys in the Mediterranean and the Ottoman Empire, Lucas had amassed enough medallions, coins, engraved stones, and gems to fill six rooms. The *herbier* in his apartment contained some 3,000 varieties of plants taken from foreign locations, and the *droguier* was equally impressive. One visitor to the apartment in the 1730s described a remarkable sculpture of the goddess Ceres that Lucas had acquired in Athens forty years earlier. Ten feet tall, the figure was made of Oriental jasper and plated with bronze, and in Paris she enjoyed the company of many other bronzes from Greece, Macedonia, and the Levant, as well as two Persian sculptures of nude sages at prayer. Among such historically valuable pieces, stranger artifacts were scattered: petrified mushrooms, seahorses, and mummified birds encased in bronze.[2]

Arriving at this cabinet of curiosities in 1709, Galland found an even greater treasure awaiting him: a young Maronite traveller from Aleppo by the name of Hanna Diyab who, he reported, "[knew] some very beautiful Arabic tales."[3] While Lucas may have viewed Diyab as just another Oriental curiosity to be displayed at the French court, Galland saw in him a solution to a frustrating predicament. After translating all the stories in his incomplete Arabic manuscript of the *Thousand and One Nights,* Galland was in need of more, and he had now found a storyteller who could fill the gap. In a sequence of twelve meetings between May 5 and June 2, 1709, Diyab related sixteen fantastic stories to Galland, who chose to add ten of these to the final three volumes of his French version of the *Arabian Nights.* These storytelling sessions were the origin of some of the most famous of the *Arabian Nights* tales—including "Ali Baba and the Forty Thieves" and "Prince Ahmad and the Fairy Peri-Banu"—and represent a lasting contribution to a story collection that has taken its place in the canons of world literature.[4]

It was not the first time that Galland had benefitted from the curiosities collected by Lucas. Despite his lack of respect for Lucas's abilities as a scholar, Galland found his collection of coins very useful in his own numismatic research, and he tried to gain access to lists or drawings of these from common acquaintances when his younger colleague was unwilling to share. Just as Galland borrowed coins to add entries to his numismatic dictionary, he would borrow Diyab to add stories to his version of the *Arabian Nights.* Considering his impact on the first French edition of the Arabic story collection, the Syrian storyteller could be judged the most valuable curiosity Lucas ever brought back from the Levant.[5]

Since the publication of *Les mille et une nuits,* Galland's French version of the *Arabian Nights,* in twelve volumes from 1704 to 1717, Galland has been credited as the first "author" of the collection in European letters, and as a crucial contributor to the emergence of the "Oriental tale" in French. Not only did he translate the 282 nights of stories in his Arabic manuscript in elegant Parisian prose, but he is credited with making a more substantial contribution to the story collection by lovingly adopting and adapting the tales that he heard from Diyab in 1709.

These stories, called the "orphan tales" because (with one exception) they have no known Arabic manuscript source, are seen as central to Galland's achievement as a translator of the *Arabian Nights.* In this portion of his story collection, Galland's work was no longer simply translation or adaptation; it represented "creation."[6]

Jean-Paul Sermain, one of the editors of the most recent edition of Galland's *Les mille et une nuits* (2004), states the case most persuasively. He argues that Galland, working from his sparse notes on Diyab's oral performances, created tales of ordinary characters caught up in extraordinary predicaments. Drawing on French literary conventions, he invented dialogues and descriptions and gave narrative coherence to the tales. Characters were developed with more sympathy, and moral lessons were highlighted. In the hands of Galland, the orphan tales of Diyab spoke of the superiority of the hero of humble origins and the need to behave decently in difficult circumstances. To fill out his meager notes, the French translator drew on his scholarly knowledge and his own travels of the Orient to imagine the fabulous details of voyages, palaces, and magical objects. Sermain argues that these orphan tales teach the reader how to read the *Arabian Nights* as a whole. In the space between the French fairy tale and the Arabic story cycle, Galland seemed to fashion a new genre—that of the "Oriental tale."[7]

Within this narrative, the exact contributions of Diyab have remained a mystery. The most direct evidence of his involvement in the process of crafting the orphan tales—entries in Galland's Paris journals—presents difficult issues of interpretation. Do these notes accurately represent the voice of Diyab during his storytelling sessions with Galland, or are the journal entries already a reworking of the tales that the translator heard? Did these diary entries merely provide an outline for stories that Galland would later elaborate according to his own literary instincts, or were they a mnemonic tool used by the translator to reconstruct the details of Diyab's oral performance? The absence of information about Diyab himself has often led scholars to discount his contribution to the process of creating the orphan tales of the *Arabian Nights,* but the identification of his manuscript memoir in the Vatican Library has opened up a new vantage point from which to consider his distinctive life and talents.[8]

Diyab's date of birth is unknown, but his memoir suggests that he was about twenty years old when he told his tales to Galland in the spring of 1709 and therefore about seventy-five when he penned the memoir between 1763 and 1764. He was born at the end of the seventeenth century in Aleppo, into a family that belonged to the Christian Maronite minority in that trading city. His family was not wealthy, but it was situated within a social milieu that was closely associated with the European merchants residing in Aleppo. Losing his father early in life, Diyab spent his boyhood in the service of a French merchant named Rimbaud. As a teenager, he briefly contemplated another kind of life for himself and joined a local monastery. When this proved a failure, Diyab joined a caravan in which Lucas was travelling in 1707 and accompanied the Frenchman on his journey through Lebanon, Cyprus, Egypt, Libya, Tunisia, Italy, and France. After a series of adventures that included encounters with pirates and bandits, Diyab arrived in Paris with his French "master" with the understanding that Lucas could secure him a position as the librarian of Arabic in the royal collections. The appointment never materialized, but Diyab was presented to the king at Versailles, and his fateful meeting with Galland in 1709 led to the birth of the orphan tales.[9]

When his hopes for a position in Paris evaporated, Diyab decided to return to Aleppo in 1710, and, after a long journey, he was reunited with his family. Back in his hometown, he learned the textile trade from his uncle, and his brother Abdallah helped set him up with his own shop. The European trade in fine silks from Persia was in decline in the eighteenth century, but Aleppo was still the center of a flourishing regional market, and Diyab seems to have had some success. His name appears on a marriage contract in the registry of his parish in 1717, and a census conducted in 1740 suggests that he lived in one of the largest houses in the community, a household of six men and six women, including his two older brothers and his mother. Though his memoir is devoted almost exclusively to his youthful travels, these other historical records attest to Diyab's life within the Maronite community of Ottoman Aleppo.[10]

Diyab's talent for storytelling is richly evident in the memoir that he produced in Aleppo in his later years. Displaying features of both travel writing and autobiography from this period, this narrative reveals Diyab's ability to weave together a multitude of stories drawn from different cultural traditions. He displays a familiarity with the tales of saints and miracles that were popular within Maronite circles, the conventions of travel narratives, and the oral storytelling traditions of his homeland. On his return to Aleppo, Diyab claims to have told stories about the marvels of Italy to his fellow Maronites, and research conducted by Johannes Stephan suggests that after twenty-two years as a merchant he took up the role of book collector and author. The first pages of Diyab's memoir, which are missing, may have contained a clearer rationale for the creation of the manuscript, but there is little doubt that this narrative represents the self-assured voice of a mature storyteller. It is also vital evidence of the cross-cultural encounters that were critical to the construction of the *Arabian Nights* in European letters.[11]

In delivering a series of tales to Galland in the spring of 1709, Diyab was responsible for connecting the *Arabian Nights* to his own experience as a resident of Aleppo, a youthful traveller in the Mediterranean region, and a perceptive observer of eighteenth-century France. The mixture of different cultural traditions and narrative strategies within the text is the product not just of "translation" but of the reworking of stories by figures like Diyab, who already embodied the overlapping worlds of East and West. His memoir now reveals the fascinating life of the Syrian traveller and suggests ways in which the orphan tales may have been influenced not only by the stories that circulated within Aleppo but also by the perspective of a young man marked by the storytelling culture of the road and the marvels of Paris.

✦ ✦ ✦

When Galland is cast in the role of "author" of the *Arabian Nights* in French literature, significant emphasis is placed on his scholarly credentials as an Orientalist and his travels in the Middle East in the service of the French court. Bridging the sixteenth and seventeenth centuries, Galland's career exemplifies the particular dynamic of baroque Orientalism in France. Unlike the more aggressively imperialist practice of the nineteenth century, Orientalism in the time of Louis XIV was a relatively unsystematic project driven by a fascination with exotic commodities and the desire to accumulate manuscripts, antiquities, and mere oddities from the East. Louis XIV's powerful finance minister, Jean-Baptiste Colbert, was central to this enterprise of building collections of rare artifacts for the kingdom (and himself) by sponsoring the voyages of a series of travellers. By commissioning these expeditions to the Levant, Colbert hoped to build his own library of wonders and to ensure that the kingdom of Louis XIV did not fall behind the courts of Sweden, Germany, Holland, England, and Italy.[12]

Galland's first journeys to the Middle East had little to do with the Arabic stories that would lead to his lasting fame. Although he had begun to study Arabic in Paris, it was his excellent training in Greek and Latin that led to his appointment to the French embassy in Istanbul of Charles Olier, Marquis de Nointel, in 1670–1675. The goals of this diplomatic mission reflected the political, commercial, and religious interests of the French kingdom in this period. Nointel was to renegotiate the Capitulations (agreements with the Ottoman sultan that ensured special rights and privileges for French traders), to ensure the position of minority Christian communities within Ottoman territory, and to gather ammunition for the theological battle between Catholics and Protestants over the issue of transubstantiation.[13] Galland's principal duty in Nointel's embassy was to collect official statements from leaders of the Christian churches of the East that would provide "irrefutable" arguments against the Calvinist position on this theological issue. His linguistic skills as an accomplished classicist would be vital in gathering, recording, and translating these statements.[14]

Galland shared the deep investment in classical culture of Nointel, who filled his embassy with classical antiquities; however, Galland also found some time during this mission to study Turkish, Arabic, and Persian, and build the skills that would facilitate subsequent trips to the region as a collector of curiosities for the king's cabinet.[15] Beyond the confines of Nointel's embassy, Galland would experience the "enchantment" of the distinctive architecture and rituals of the Ottoman Empire. As the sultan departed from Edirne for a campaign against the Poles on May 7, 1672, Galland confessed that he was at a loss to communicate "anything that even approached the beauty [and] the splendor" of this procession. It would, he wrote, "demand an angelic intellect to communicate and understand this wonder." The "Grand Seigneur" himself provided the climax, for he "effaced all of the radiance and splendor of the ranks that had come before him," just like "the planets and the stars are deprived of all their radiance and brilliance when the sun is there." In contrast to the pagan Mars, "covered with blood and dust," this Turkish Mars, with "his air and apparel of a warrior together with the glittering brilliance of the large precious stones and pearls," produced a union of war and celebration that elicited "surprise, astonishment, admiration and enchantment" among its viewers. This record of the extravagance of Ottoman ceremonies in Galland's diary has led scholars such as Sylvette Larzul to argue that the French translator filled out Diyab's tales of Aladdin and Prince Ahmad with details from the processions and palaces he had seen on his journeys.[16]

Galland began to study and collect antiquities on his first visit to the Levant, but it was on subsequent voyages (1675–1676 and 1679–1688) that he really came into his own as a servant of Colbert, contributing to the burgeoning collections of rare coins and manuscripts that constituted the material basis of baroque Orientalism. His powerful patrons had a well-established interest in works written in Greek and Latin, but Colbert was also looking for manuscripts relating to medicine, history, and geography in any language as long as they were complete and in perfect condition. Galland could purchase Arabic manuscripts that met these stringent requirements, but he was explicitly prohibited from buying texts of the Quran, lives of the Prophet, or any works of Arabic poetry or fiction. Colbert believed that the king's library was already well stocked with these works.[17]

Despite the restrictions of his commission, Galland's third voyage to the Levant, in 1679, would thrust him into Istanbul's vibrant literary culture. In the seventeenth century, Istanbul was famous for its book trade, and Galland would be awed by the extraordinary number and variety of manuscripts from around the world available in the libraries and markets of the Ottoman capital. In Istanbul, he believed he could accomplish in a single year "what elsewhere it might take ten or twenty years" to achieve. Carried away by this enthusiasm, Galland began to borrow books from Turkish booksellers for use in creating an Oriental dictionary, but he was forced to abandon this project when he was reminded to prioritize the antique manuscripts and rare coins that his patrons most desired. In October 1682, Galland was unable to resist the opportunity to purchase a full private library of Arabic manuscripts after the death of its owner, despite his fears that it was not "in the spirit of Mr. Colbert." Aware of the tenuous legitimacy of such a purchase, he quickly composed a catalog of the library's works of history that could be seen as falling within the scope of his original charge.[18] Ironically, Galland's official commission would have precluded him from purchasing a copy of the *Thousand and One Nights,* not only because of the injunction against Arabic works of fiction, but because a "complete" manuscript of the story collection (containing 1,001 nights of stories) may have been impossible to find.

The constraints of Galland's commission make it difficult to determine his own intellectual interests in the Ottoman world. In his letters, he might wax lyrical over the purchase of medical histories, but he rarely mentioned literary manuscripts.[19] Galland was undoubtedly aware of the rich culture of oral storytelling in Istanbul. The booksellers of the Grand Bazaar would often lend their manuscripts to public storytellers who entertained evening crowds in the city's coffeehouses. Galland himself attended at least a few evenings of storytelling, and he did consider it worthwhile to record two isolated story summaries in his diary. Included among them was the intriguing tale of Cogia Muzaffer, who arrives in a foreign city and is crowned king based on a local tradition that dictates that the first man to enter the city after the death of the king would become its new ruler. Enthroned as king, Cogia Muzaffer finds that his luck has turned when his wife dies, and he learns of another distinctive tradition of the city: the burial of the living spouse with the deceased. Deposited in the grave of his wife, he meets a woman who has likewise been buried with her spouse, and together they survive to embark on a new series of adventures.[20]

In this fantastic tale, Galland had inadvertently stumbled on an analogue of Sinbad's fourth voyage, but there is no evidence that he recognized the connection between this tale and the Arabic story collection that had become popular in Ottoman literary circles and Istanbul coffeehouses. The tales had been translated into Turkish in the sixteenth and seventeenth centuries, and manuscript versions could be found in prestigious collections such as those of the Suleymaniye Mosque in Istanbul, but Galland would have had little incentive to track the story collection down at this point.[21] His patrons were more interested in Arabic manuscripts relating to science, philosophy, and history than in versions of the *Thousand and One Nights*.

As a collector of Oriental manuscripts for the royal library, Galland played an important role in building the material basis for early developments in French Orientalism, and he was also involved in the production of one of the key reference works of this period—Barthélemy d'Herbelot's *Bibliothèque orientale* (1697), the first encyclopedia of the Islamic world. This iconic work, which Galland finished editing after the death of its principal author, was the product of a lengthy process of collecting, but it was given a particular impetus by the acquisition of a bibliographic encyclopedia by the Ottoman scholar Katib Chelebi. Two manuscripts of this work—the *Kashf al-zunūn*—were sent back from Istanbul by French ambassadors, and a letter from Galland to his friend Jacob Spon in 1682 reveals his excitement in discovering a work that contained some 30,000 book titles. Galland's calculation of the number of titles was an exaggeration, but the importance of this work in shaping early Orientalist scholarship can be seen in the organization of d'Herbelot's work, which is arranged alphabetically under headings that are Oriental terms rather than Western categories.[22]

The network that connected Paris to the Ottoman Empire brought people as well as manuscripts, and as Galland sought to establish himself as an Orientalist scholar in the French capital, he initially encountered competition from a small group of Eastern Christians who served as key links within this broad web.[23] Determined to hold the chair of Arabic at the Collège Royal, Galland happily reported spiteful gossip that denigrated the Arabic skills of the holder of this chair, a Christian Maronite named Pierre Dippy, and kept a jealous eye on the role of Dippy's nephew as interpreter to the king. When he finally gained the coveted chair in 1709, Galland could relish his victory over the younger Dippy, who had made a claim to it. During this period when he was advancing his position as an Orientalist scholar, however, Galland's diaries reveal that he remained first and foremost a classicist, devoting his most productive hours to translating Greek or pursuing his numismatic research. During the month when he was meeting with Diyab to record the tales that he would later insert into the *Arabian Nights*, Galland's diaries are full of references to academic lectures on the Eleusinian mysteries and Homeric poetry.[24]

Strangely enough it would be the story of Sinbad, with its analogue of the tale of Cogia Muzaffer, that would draw the French Orientalist to the task of translating the *Arabian Nights* several decades after his initial travels in the Middle East. Sometime before 1701 Galland procured an Arabic manuscript of the voyages of Sinbad and began translating it into French. He seems to have been attracted to the tale by the parallels between the voyages of Sinbad and the wanderings of Odysseus. Referring to the tale as the "Arab Homer," Galland's translation did a certain violence to the text to ensure that the reader saw those parallels. In his third voyage, Sinbad encounters a ghoul, a supernatural man-eating creature of Arabic folklore. Although in the Arabic manuscript the ghoul has two eyes, Galland transforms him into a Cyclops in his translation, linking him to the Cyclops Polyphemus, who was bested by Odysseus in the Greek epic. It was a characteristic maneuver for a scholar more versed in classical texts than Arabic letters.[25] By affiliating tales like "Sinbad" with Greek literature, Galland saw himself as giving the *Arabian Nights* a universal value, and the parallels between Sinbad and Odysseus that he constructed in his version would linger in eighteenth- and nineteenth-century European readings of the tales as an "Arabian *Odyssey*."[26]

Galland claimed that he had completed his translation of "Sinbad" in 1701 from a manuscript acquired in Istanbul, yet he only published his version of the tale at the start of the third volume of the *Arabian Nights* in 1704. Remarkably, a rival Orientalist, François Pétis de la Croix, also translated "Sinbad" in 1701, and one cannot discount the possibility that knowledge of his work helped spur Galland's own translation of the *Arabian Nights*.[27] Making inquiries as to where he could find more stories like "Sinbad," Galland managed to acquire a manuscript containing 282 nights of tales through a Syrian friend in 1701. Galland would supplement his translations of these Arabic stories with his translation of "Sinbad" and additional tales drawn from other Arabic manuscripts.[28]

Galland's translations of the stories in his Arabic manuscript of the *Thousand and One Nights* can be understood in terms of a classical aesthetics in which imitation and adaptation of other texts were considered essential to the writer's art. The status of the *Thousand and One Nights* as an authorless work only increased the translator's freedom to transform it in accordance with the aesthetic sensibilities of his time. Galland followed the plot of the original stories relatively closely, but simplified the text by eliminating the division of the story collection into nights and by cutting and abbreviating the interpolated poetry. He lent greater coherence to the stories by smoothing the transitions within each tale and clarifying the motives behind the actions of the characters. In general Galland tried to reveal an order beneath the seemingly random play of events. For example, the appearance of a tree in a barren wilderness was explicitly attributed to the agency of "fortune," which had provided for a character's health. The stories were also enlivened by the insertion of dialogues in accordance with prevailing French conventions.[29]

In his foreword to the first volume of his *Arabian Nights,* Galland introduces the story collection as a source of edification for a reader willing to recognize in these tales "examples of virtues and vices," and throughout his version he seeks to guide the moral judgment of the reader. Heroic protagonists have been subtly reshaped to match Galland's own values, and subsidiary characters are conveniently introduced as a "good old man" or a "detestable old woman" in an effort to guide the reader through unfamiliar story patterns.[30] Following his stated principles of decorum and delicacy, Galland elides the more explicit sexual material in the tales, transposing and rewriting scenes to convey romantic force if not erotic detail. He is also willing to alter the original text in translation to ensure that the hierarchies of his own society were reflected in his *Arabian Nights.* For instance, the original "Tale of the Fisherman" ends with a virtuous fisherman receiving riches and marrying his two daughters to a king and a prince, but Galland upholds strict barriers between the social orders by eliminating these marriage alliances in his translation.[31]

Despite these adaptations of his material, Galland argued that his translation offered insights into the essential qualities of the Arab Islamic civilization represented in the stories. Drawing on his own knowledge, he added almost imperceptible glosses within the text to explain the "customs and manners of the Orientals." Characters in Galland's *Arabian Nights,* therefore, are presented as acting "in the manner of the monarchs of the Orient" or "following Arab custom" or behaving "as a good Muslim."[32] At the same time, specific details of the material world of the stories are often replaced by the abstractions that Larzul argues are a part of the classical aesthetics of Galland's time. The specific sociocultural environment of the tales might be referenced through the repeated mention of mosques and fountains, but beyond these clichés of an Oriental world, the stress is on a strangely imprecise "magnificence" and "splendor." The rich materials used to adorn the amazing palace, described in the original manuscript, are no longer specified. The tantalizing dishes on offer at the feast are replaced by bland references to ragout and cake. The paradisiacal qualities of gardens and the specific tropes of beauty in the Arabic original are sacrificed in favor of the familiar landscapes of Versailles and the generic charms of a lovely woman.[33]

By the time Galland met Diyab at the Paris apartment of Lucas in 1709, he had already published seven volumes of stories from his manuscript of the *Thousand and One Nights.* Translating and transforming the stories through the prism of French literary style and Orientalist simplification, Galland had hit on a winning formula that found receptive readers and inspired imitators. A new market for tales from the Orient was emerging in the early eighteenth century, and Galland found that rivals like Pétis de la Croix were ready to meet the demand. When Galland ran short of stories for his *Arabian Nights,* his publisher simply inserted two of Pétis de la Croix's translations of Turkish tales into the eighth volume of the collection (published in 1709). Galland's response on this occasion reveals the proprietary interest he felt in his creation. In anger, he demanded that the publisher insert a prefatory note explaining that the two tales "are not from the work *A Thousand and One Nights*" and "they have been inserted without the translator's knowledge."[34]

Responding to his publisher's desire to extend his translation of the *Arabian Nights,* Galland turned his attention to the tales that Diyab had told him in the spring of 1709 and integrated them into volumes nine

An illustration by Mirzâ 'Ali-Qoli Kho'i from "The Ebony Horse," a tale in which a sage gives to the king of the Persians a flying horse that can reach any destination in a day. Hanna Diyab told Antoine Galland this story in 1709. This illustration is from an 1855 Persian edition of the *Arabian Nights*.

through twelve of his version. With this step, the French translator made his own decisive contribution to the creation of a story collection in which translations of tales from Arabic mingle promiscuously with additions whose origins remain unclear. The orphan tales represented a new challenge for the French Orientalist. They did not require translation. Diyab could narrate his stories in French, and Galland was able to record them in this language. Among these stories only "The Ebony Horse" has been found in an Arabic manuscript source, and there is no evidence that Galland had access to a manuscript copy of any of the tales. In order to insert the orphan tales of Diyab into his *Arabian Nights*, Galland had to work from the notes he had recorded in his journal and his own memories of the storytelling sessions with Diyab.[35]

French scholars tend to assume that the orphan tales were produced according to the same logic as the translations in Galland's *Arabian*

Nights. They argue that Galland once again drew on his experience and scholarly expertise to create an "Oriental atmosphere." He connected the stories to an Islamic world by explaining the practices of prayer and inserting phrases that reflected Muslim submission to divine authority (such as "It is God's will, we must accept it" or "God did not consent to grant me this"). Drawing from the conventions of the French fairy tale, he added moral lessons to "Aladdin" and "The Enchanted Horse" to give the tales an edifying quality. However, other aspects of Galland's orphan tales depart from the tendency toward abstraction apparent in his earlier translations of the Arabic stories of his manuscript. Stereotypical details of an Oriental world appear much more frequently. Motifs that reoccur again and again include mosques, caravansaries, public baths, eunuchs, dervishes, and veils.[36] The orphan stories that can be traced to Diyab also contain more specific references to luxury and magnificence, more examples of precious jewels and rich fabrics, and more details of sumptuous ceremonies.

In some cases the specific details in the orphan tales can be attributed to borrowings from other sources. In the tale of Prince Ahmad, for instance, the description of Indian temples is clearly taken from the work of a Persian historian translated by Galland, and the description of the Sodge Valley is taken from d'Herbelot's *Bibliothèque orientale,* coedited by Galland.[37] These insertions are considered natural by scholars who emphasize Galland's scholarly expertise and his need to fill the gaps in the story outlines contained in his notes. The shift in Galland's approach in the orphan tales, however, requires some additional explanation. A closer look at Diyab's narrative style suggests that the greater emphasis on precious stones, luxurious materials, and elaborate ceremonies in the orphan tales might have been an attempt by Galland to reproduce the greater material detail of the stories related to him by Diyab.[38]

Scholars who see the orphan tales as a product of Galland's creative talents are reluctant to even consider the outlines recorded in his Paris journal as an authentic expression of Diyab's voice. Galland's biographer, Mohamed Abdel-Halim, argues that Diyab merely contributed "primitive" elements that were already acculturated and assimilated through their expression in the Orientalist's hand.[39] An examination of

Galland's pocket-size diary, however, suggests that there was more complexity to the process of capturing the stories told by the Maronite visitor. While Galland appears to have imposed a measure of order on some of these journal entries by inserting a designated lesson to be drawn from the tale, other notes seem to have been written in haste and are likely an attempt to record Diyab's storytelling at the moment of hearing. Fréderic Bauden, the editor of the diary, argues that some stories appear to have been transcribed from rough notes recorded elsewhere, while other stories are captured in rougher notation—with many strike-throughs, emendations, and grammatical mistakes. One scholar's analysis of the errors in these journal entries suggests that Diyab was telling these stories in French. The possibility that in some instances Diyab's words were being recorded relatively directly in a language that he shared with Galland must lead to a reconsideration of the status of these notes.[40]

An entry in Galland's journal of his travels in the Levant also suggests the tantalizing possibility that the notes in his Paris diary were more than mere outlines to be freely elaborated by the author at a later time. In his Istanbul diary, Galland mentions developing a method of note taking during his early journeys in the Levant that was meant to serve as an aide-mémoire to reconstruct the oral performances of storytellers.[41] It is certainly not a stretch to imagine that Galland might have used the same technique for the same purpose during his meetings with Diyab, and therefore that the orphan tales incorporated into the *Arabian Nights* were built on a more detailed reconstruction of Diyab's storytelling performances than has been previously acknowledged.

A closer examination of Galland's early travel journals might also call into question the belief that the orphan tales are primarily a product of the French translator's ability to add character and color to Diyab's outlines. While Galland's description of the Ottoman sultan's departure for battle in 1672 is memorable, Madeleine Dobie remarks that the "formless and dry" journal from this period actually contains very little information about local customs and conditions. Galland's diary demonstrates his interest in manuscripts and classical culture, but it "conveys little about the writer's personal impressions of Constantinople."[42]

Galland himself acknowledged that he was not a man of imagination but rather a sober recorder of scholarly truths. Describing his journal to Abbé de La Chambre, he wrote, "You will not find any of these adventures that engage the attention of readers. I was no doubt not born for these unusual things, and my personality inclines me even less to fictions."[43] In the face of this evidence, Galland seems an unlikely candidate to have contributed creatively to a series of tales that strongly engage with the marvellous, in the sense of both material riches and the supernatural. Content with his scholarly interests and his royal commissions, he is also less likely to have developed the psychologically complex characters that readers find in the orphan tales.

✦ ✦ ✦

Writing his memoir in Aleppo in 1763–1764, Diyab does not seem to have been aware of the significance of his contribution to the *Arabian Nights,* although by this date Galland's version of the story collection was well known among French readers. In a single passage of his memoir, Diyab recalls that an unnamed "old man" often visited his master, Lucas, and that this man was translating the *Thousand and One Nights.* "The book he translated was missing some nights," Diyab reported, "so I told him tales that I knew." At no point does Diyab claim that the stories he told Galland belonged to the *Thousand and One Nights.* In fact, his wording might suggest the contrary. He simply drew on stories that he knew—either narrating from memory or creatively combining elements to create new tales in the manner of a coffeehouse storyteller. According to Diyab, "[The old man] then finished his book by including these stories and was happy for my assistance."[44]

It is unlikely that the mixture of voices within the orphan tales will ever be disentangled by scholars, but it would be a mistake to assume that the storyteller from Aleppo did not make a decisive contribution to these stories because we do not have unmediated access to the storytelling sessions with Galland in 1709. The memoir that Diyab left behind provides ample evidence of his narrative skills: he deploys frame tales and embedded stories, captures colorful characters from a variety of social milieus, and exhibits psychological insight in capturing the emotional states of both his younger and his more mature self. The memoir includes a multitude of narrative themes that overlap with the content of the orphan tales: a fascination with the supernatural and the miraculous, an enthusiasm for the spectacle of wealth, and a concern for the struggles of youth and the plight of the socially marginal. The recovery of this manuscript thus justifies a reappraisal of Diyab as a crucial contributor to the networks of transcultural creativity that introduced the *Arabian Nights* to European literature.

Growing up in Aleppo at the turn of the eighteenth century, Diyab encountered a mixture of cultures, languages, and religions and learned to navigate the web of mercantile relationships that linked the city with Europe and other regional centers. Raised in a family of merchants and employed by a French trader in his early years, Diyab seems to have developed fluency in French, Provençal, Italian, and Turkish as well as Arabic. He was comfortable dealing with European merchants and familiar with Catholic religious culture through the well-established links between the Maronite community and the church in Rome. Entries in Galland's diary suggest that when he met Diyab in 1709, the Syrian youth possessed significant facility in a variety of languages and displayed knowledge of several story collections.[45]

Diyab's skill in weaving marvellous tales might be credited to the early years he spent in the rich storytelling culture of Aleppo. Situated in this regional center for trade, local storytellers had at their disposal not only Levantine folklore but also tales originating in India and China to the east and France and Italy to the west. In the city's more than sixty coffeehouses, storytellers held their audiences in thrall. Their stories were not merely narratives; they were a performance animated by the teller's actions as much as by his words. In this environment, the storyteller's most valuable skill was combining and adapting tales to appeal to the interests of a particular audience. In 1794, the Scottish physicians Alexander Russell and Patrick Russell famously described the ability of Aleppine storytellers to surprise their audiences by adapting familiar tales: "A variety of other story books, besides the Arabian Nights entertainment, (which, under that title, are little known at Aleppo) furnish materials for the story teller who, by combining the incidents of different tales, and varying the catastrophe of such as he has related before, gives

View of the city of Aleppo, with its citadel, from a travelogue by the British consul Alexander Drummond (1754). In the eighteenth century, Aleppo was a flourishing regional trading center with well-established links to European commerce.

them an air of novelty even to persons who at first imagine they are listening to tales with which they are acquainted."[46] At a moment of great excitement the storyteller would suddenly break off the tale and leave the coffeehouse, deferring the resolution of the story until the following evening and leaving the audience to debate possible endings no less hotly "than if the fate of the city depended on the decision." To hear the rest of the suspended tale, the listeners would have to return to the coffeehouse the next night.[47]

Coffeehouses were not the only places in Aleppo where people enjoyed stories, however, and professional storytellers were not the only ones skilled in spinning tales. Stories were told in gardens where Aleppines met to drink, eat, and listen to musicians and singers. This culture encompassed the Christians of Syria, along with their Muslim and Jewish neighbors, and its attractions were so strong that efforts were made at monasteries and among the laity to control indulgence in this pastime.[48] The oral storytelling culture of Aleppo was so pervasive that even servants astonished European travellers with their ability to recount amazing tales. Travelling to the Levant in the early nineteenth century, Ulrich Jasper Seetzen noted the formidable talent for storytelling displayed by members of the lower classes. Antoine, his nineteen-year-old servant, recounted tales of Harun al-Rashid and other stories, displaying an ability to present "very beautiful things in an interesting manner" and "an ardent love of a mordant satire." Seetzen concluded that Antoine's gift for storytelling was the result of listening to professional storytellers in coffeehouses, "where they can truly study how to agreeably entertain their audience." "In these cafés," Seetzen reported, "one does not only find the middle class, but also the most base, who for a cup of coffee which costs one *para,* spends an entire afternoon entertained and extraordinarily well."[49] One can imagine a young Diyab sitting in one of Aleppo's cafés, absorbing the storyteller's words and learning his tricks for enthralling his audience. Judging by the memoir he penned when he was in his seventies, Diyab learned the storyteller's lessons well and continued to hone this art throughout his life.

The tales recorded by Galland in his diary show that Diyab consciously participated in this Aleppine culture of oral storytelling and was capable of combining plots and motifs from Persian, Indian, and European literature. It is often assumed that the Maronite visitor provided Galland with "Arabic" raw material that the French Orientalist reworked from the vantage point of a Parisian sensibility. However, a closer look at Diyab's memoir reveals that he brought together the different strands of Occident and Orient in his own life and in his recounted stories. The memoir also demonstrates Diyab's ability to handle a complex narrative that mirrors the *Arabian Nights* in its use of framing devices and embedded tales. As he recorded his life story in the 1760s, Diyab clearly took pleasure in crafting it and repeatedly inserted tales and anecdotes into the main narrative that demonstrate a taste for the surprising and the strange—*'ajib* and *gharib,* in the Arabic tradition. Diyab does not seem to have taken notes during his journey; instead, his account is based on memories that crystallized over decades of telling and retelling. He may have made some mistakes in the details, but his ability to recall the impact of visiting the Palace of Versailles or surviving the harsh winter of 1708–1709 after fifty years is remarkable.[50]

Within the Ottoman world, storytelling, and indeed authorship, was no longer the preserve of an educated elite. New research has identified a series of travelogues and autobiographical texts generated at commercial centers like Aleppo and Damascus. These include a chronicle produced by a barber in Damascus and an autobiography produced by Hindiyya, a Maronite saint from Aleppo. Arab travel writing from this era—including the account of an Eastern Christian priest who travelled all the way to the Americas—demonstrates the particular mobility of minority Arabs within the Mediterranean world and beyond. The fact that these travellers saw fit to share their travels in written form testifies to what Dana Sajdi has called the phenomenon of "nouveau literacy" in the Ottoman Levant. Diyab shared the confidence of these other writers, and seems to have owned copies of other travelogues when he composed his memoir in Aleppo.[51]

Diyab's manuscript lacks an explicit explanation for its creation, but it displays features associated with both a travelogue and an autobiographical text during this period. His manuscript, likely written in his own hand or dictated to a family member, seems to have been composed for the benefit of his family or for a small circle of Maronite readers in Aleppo. Written in the first person rather than the third (as was customary for the genre of the travelogue in Arabic), it exhibits a highly personal and impressionistic style. Diyab did not aspire to scholarly refinement, and he avoided the citations, verses, and literary flourishes (such as *saj'* or rhyming prose) typical of the *rihla,* the classic travelogue of the educated Arab. Rather, Diyab wrote in Middle Arabic, an intermediary between classical literary Arabic and colloquial Arabic and, significantly, the register in which the *Arabian Nights* was written.[52]

The narrative as a whole is a collage of autobiographical episodes, descriptions of foreign lands, and entertaining anecdotes that Diyab heard or read along the way. Like many travel narratives from the

Ottoman period, his text can be seen as a particular mixture of fact and fiction that partakes of both Arabic and European storytelling traditions.[53] Diyab's knowledge of European languages and customs, acquired as a young apprentice to French merchants in Aleppo, allowed him to navigate territory from the Levant to Paris with relative ease. During his travels, Diyab exchanged stories with the people that he met along the way, and his memoir includes a number of embedded tales drawn from these encounters. Some of these are stories that circulated broadly within early modern culture, for instance the anecdote of the philosopher's stone and the tale of the woman buried alive. Both of these stories were part of the popular storytelling tradition during Diyab's time in France, and the last can also be found in Giovanni Boccaccio's *Decameron*.[54]

Diyab's memoir is particularly successful in capturing the naïveté and curiosity of his youthful self as he weaves a tale of exciting adventures and missed opportunities. However, even as the reader is drawn into this engaging story, the perspective of the successful Syrian merchant of his later years offers another layer to the narrative. Diyab not only chronicles the emotional states of his younger self, he also speaks in the voice of a mature narrator commenting in a more thoughtful, and sometimes regretful, way on the youthful choices that determined his path back to Aleppo. Diyab's journey to adulthood had many twists and turns. After losing his position with a merchant family in Aleppo, he made a seemingly impulsive decision to enter a monastery outside Tripoli. Perhaps he had hoped to use this avenue to escape his position at the bottom of the filial hierarchy, but on entering the monastery as a novice, he found himself in an even more uncomfortable position. Donning the habit of a monk, Diyab found he could not recognize himself and immediately regretted his decision. He reacted with revulsion to the skulls of deceased priests that lined the hall and watched with horror as the abbot of the monastery abused an elderly monk, turning him away from the dining hall with kicks and blows. The shock of the conditions in the monastery seems to have been too much for Diyab's spirit, and he was seriously ill during two of the three months he spent there. He finally obtained permission from the abbot to go home.[55]

It was after this false start that Diyab entered the service of Lucas, the collector of rare treasures for the French court. The memoir dwells on the following two years of travel through Syria, Cyprus, Egypt, Tunisia, France, Italy, and Anatolia, which clearly represented the most important experiences that Diyab sought to pass on to family and friends. However, within the many dramatic and amusing episodes of these years with Lucas, Diyab's identity as a Maronite remains clear, and he finds comfort in the common rituals of Catholicism that stretch throughout the Mediterranean world. As he travelled through new territories, he frequently sought out members of his own religious community. In this sense, he felt himself to be moving through a realm both familiar and unfamiliar, and he revelled in this opportunity to explore the marvellous qualities of his faith.[56]

One of the most powerful religious experiences recounted in the memoir occurred in Tunis, where Diyab encountered a visiting Jesuit priest who agreed to lead the local congregation on a weeklong spiritual journey. In a pitch-black church, the priest asked Diyab and other members of the congregation to walk with him into the realms of the afterlife. As they descended each rung of hell, the priest asked of the souls present there what sins they had committed to deserve such merciless torture for all eternity. Diyab describes being intoxicated, losing all sense of direction and falling into a faint. Still disconcerted by this experience, Diyab fell into a swoon again a day or two later while kneeling in deep meditation after attending mass. His companions found him unconscious in the church pew. By documenting the spiritual impact of these experiences, Diyab connects his story to the religious literature popular among his coreligionists in Syria.[57]

Many of the episodes related in Diyab's memoir reflect the influence of the hagiographic literature that circulated within Catholic communities in Syria. While the Maronite Church represented a distinct Eastern Christian tradition, it was also officially part of the Catholic Church of Rome, and the efforts of various religious orders had made miracle tales an important part of the life of Maronites like Diyab. When he describes his visit to the Church of Santa Madonna di Montenero, a popular pilgrimage site in the mountains outside Livorno, Diyab calls on these precedents. The location of the church is presented as the product of divine intervention—the result of the miraculous appearance of the icon of the Blessed Virgin of the Black Mountain three times. He also records many of the miracles attributed to the intercession of the Blessed Virgin: the voyager saved from a shipwreck by a dolphin, the man saved from a fall from a high ladder, and the condemned man saved from hanging when the rope breaks three times. These stories clearly left a strong impression on Diyab, and he explains that he brought them back with him to Aleppo and shared them with members of the Maronite community, inspiring them to donate funds to maintain the church in Italy. In narrating these stories orally and later recording them in his memoir, he combined the traditional explanation for the founding of the church—the miraculous appearance of the icon—with a common element of oral storytelling in Aleppo—the repetition of an event in threes. In embedded stories like this one, Diyab demonstrates his ability to combine story elements to craft a dramatic tale for his listeners, and his readers.[58]

Just as Diyab included episodes of supernatural intervention in the orphan tales that he related to Galland, he frequently drew from miracle tales in crafting the narrative of his own life. He confesses that he too turned to the Blessed Virgin of the Black Mountain for aid when he was robbed of 1,100 piaster coins. After Diyab prayed to the Virgin, the man who had robbed him confessed to a priest, and soon Diyab's money was returned through an intermediary. Arguably the most important episode of miraculous intervention described in the memoir occurred when Diyab fell ill in Italy and was in danger of being left behind by Lucas, who intended to continue his journey to Marseille without his faithful servant. Desperate to accompany Lucas, and perhaps distrusting his promise that he would wait for him in Marseille, Diyab turned to the Virgin Mary in prayer, and her intercession brought about his rapid recovery. More than this, Diyab claims that once this fever left him, he never suffered from it again. Within the memoir, this is only one of many episodes of miraculous healing—whether through divine intervention or the marvellous powers of amulets and secret potions. These examples echo Diyab's use of such motifs in orphan tales such as "Prince Ahmad and the Fairy Peri-Banu," where one of the princes manages to acquire a magic apple that can cure any illness. The record of Galland's diary reveals that Diyab told this story to the French Orientalist at a point when he believed Galland was relapsing into illness, and it seems to have been designed to lighten his mood.[59]

When Diyab describes his arrival in Paris in the company of Lucas, he dwells on the magnificent structures and elaborate ceremonies associated with religious life in the city. The immense size of Notre-Dame Cathedral evoked awe in the young traveller, as did the church bell that Diyab describes as the size of a small cupola. The Maronite narrator takes the time to explain this marvel to readers accustomed to the interdiction against the ringing of bells in Christian churches in the Muslim world. The bell of Notre-Dame, located on top of a "minaret," is likened to an "egg made out of iron" that is moved through an elaborate system of pulleys that requires a dozen men to operate. As he composed his memoir fifty years later, the sound of that bell still resonated strongly with Diyab. It was so powerful, he claims, that it frightened the people of Paris and could be heard at a distance of seven hours' travel.[60]

In Diyab's account, the French capital becomes the setting for striking ceremonies bursting with the material richness that so often appears in the settings of the orphan tales. Particularly remarkable is Diyab's reconstruction of the Corpus Christi procession that passed through the streets of Paris on May 30, 1709, which he viewed from the windows of Lucas's apartment. The shops were decorated with gorgeous fabrics; flowers were spread on the street; and the sound of prayers and hymns filled the air. Over 500 monks wearing blueberry-colored cloaks and carrying candles and golden crosses proceeded down the street, followed by the cardinal beneath a large canopy supported by twelve men. Diyab reported being blinded by the sight of the cardinal's monstrance, which contained the body of Christ. It shone like the sun as the light passed through it: "No one could stand the sight, so encrusted it was with jewels: diamonds, rubies, emeralds and other precious stones. It ravished one's sight."[61]

But even within this most Catholic of religious rituals, observers could spy evidence of the cross-cultural connections that had long drawn the worlds of Europe and the Orient together. While Diyab lost himself in the spectacle presented by the cardinal and his retinue, Lucas noticed the Arabic lettering embroidered onto the rich fabric above the cardinal's dais. "I was lost in contemplation, stupefied by this spectacle," Diyab writes, "when my master came to demand that I decipher the inscription above the dais."[62] Astonished, Diyab read the Islamic profession of faith that appeared in the midst of the splendor of the Catholic ceremony. Once Lucas was convinced of Diyab's accurate reading of the treasured artifact, he ordered him to go to the cardinal with what he knew. On further investigation, it was discovered that the offending cloth had been taken from banners seized as trophies in a French campaign against the Maghrebis. The banners would be burned, but the remarkable story of their discovery was recorded by both Diyab and Galland.[63]

In describing his time in the French capital, Diyab interweaves his own ambitions and frustrations with the stories of other members of the community of Eastern Christians in the city in a way that heightens the dramatic potential in the narrative. Diyab introduces his reader to Youssuf al-Jawharji, a Persian who dealt in gold, jewelry, and precious gemstones, and describes his attempts to secure a profitable marriage with a wealthy Parisian (despite his engagement to another woman). He also chronicles his friendship with Estephan al-Shami, whose rags-to-riches story is itself worthy of inclusion in the *Arabian Nights.* On his arrival in Paris, Estephan had convinced the cardinal to give him permission to beg at the doorstep of a prominent church, but he soon moved on to man a coffee stand in the market created to celebrate the feast of Saint Michael. After this modest beginning, Estephan became a successful café proprietor, consciously using his Arab identity to cultivate a clientele for this most successful of imports from the Middle East.

As Diyab searched for a more secure position in Parisian society, Estephan offered him both his daughter in marriage and the management of his café in Paris (since he was now focused on opening a second café in Versailles).[64] However, just as Diyab was considering the offer, he was arrested by the Paris police. The Syrian youth quickly discovered that he had been implicated inadvertently in the sordid drama developing around his friend al-Jawharji. After calling off one engagement to pursue a richer prospect, al-Jawharji had fallen into greater disrepute when his new engagement was challenged by a Chaldean man who rose when the engagement was announced in church to inform the priest that the intended groom was already married to a woman named Mariam Gebara in Aleppo. When al-Jawharji and some jewels disappeared, Diyab was arrested as a known associate and questioned for information on his whereabouts. Dragged through the streets to what he imagined would be a more forceful interrogation, Diyab was only saved by the intervention of Lucas, who explained that he had brought the Maronite from the Levant to serve as an assistant in the king's library of Arabic manuscripts.[65]

These dramatic tales of opportunity and disaster among the Oriental Christians of Paris not only testify to the particular challenges that Diyab had to negotiate as a foreigner in the French capital, but also demonstrate his substantial skills as a storyteller. The story of his arrest is related in his memoir as a sophisticated series of framing and embedded tales, not unlike those in the *Thousand and One Nights.* Borrowing the strategy of Shahrazad, Diyab builds suspense through frequent interruptions to the narrative, introducing a fascinating series of rogues and heroes against the backdrop of Enlightenment Paris. In these tales of Paris through the eyes of a Maronite traveller, the true value of Diyab to Galland's project of creating the *Arabian Nights* becomes clear.

As the embedded stories in Diyab's description of his arrest in Paris reveal, he was particularly attentive to the predicament of the social outsider trying to make his way in the world. The portrait of Paris that he paints in the travelogue reveals a fascination with the plight of the outcast and the economically marginal as the capital experienced the effects of economic crisis and harvest failure. The winter of 1708–1709 had been one of the coldest in recent memory, and by spring the people of Paris were suffering from food shortages. On May 5, 1709, as Diyab visited Galland to deliver the conclusion of the tale of Aladdin, there were riots in the market of the Abbey of Saint-Germain. Marie de Bailleul, Marquise d'Huxelles, recorded that one hundred men with axes, accompanied by a number of women, plundered the carts in the market, and that at least one man was severely injured as the police moved in to reestablish order.[66]

Galland, immersed in his beloved world of classical Greece as he pursued his translation of the *Arabian Nights,* makes no comment on the riots that occurred in his own neighborhood, but Diyab shows a lively interest in the fate of ordinary Parisians caught up in the intense tensions of this period. The famine that lingered from winter into spring features prominently in his portrait of the French capital. By the order of the governor, Diyab writes, a census was taken, and the rationing of bread was strictly enforced. Each person was allotted only enough bread to survive. In some places, the police would be called in to suppress rioting and prevent looting. Peasants from the villages poured into the city to beg, but, as Diyab recalls, no one would give them alms. Diyab would see them stretched out on the streets in the throes of starvation.[67]

Diyab's sympathetic portrait of Parisians caught up in tragic circumstances also includes the tale of a young man executed in a city square. He reports that at sunset he saw a young defendant with his arms tied in front of him being transported to the gallows in an open carriage, with a priest encouraging him by holding a crucifix in front of his face. Following this vehicle, Diyab found himself at the place of execution, where the young man was dragged up a ladder by the rope cord looped around his neck, accompanied by the priest. "The young man," Diyab recounts, "having the crucifix before his face, turned his eyes toward the window of his house and cried." Diyab's account suggests that he, like other members of the crowd, lamented the fate of the condemned: "The people cried for this young man who was in the flower of his youth. He was beautiful, luxuriously dressed in his wedding clothes. According to estimates, he was twenty-two years old. This is what bruised the heart of the people assembled there. One could hear the sound of their crying and lamentations as if each had lost their only beloved son."[68]

Diyab heightens his reader's investment in the fate of this young victim of execution by explaining the tragic circumstances that brought him to this end. An extremely rich merchant who had no children of his own entered the hospital of the bastards one day and saw among the children a beautiful, radiant youth who was bright and civil, and who surpassed all the others in his grace and modesty. He became attached to this young man, and asked to take him home to educate him. He made the youth his son and trained him in his own profession, and eventually the son opened his own shop. Some time later, however, there was a misunderstanding about some debt titles that the young man took from his father's shop to his own. When the father discovered the titles were missing, he brought the case to the police and a judge, not realizing that this would lead to the arrest of his adopted son. When the father found out about his son's predicament, he protested to the judge that he was his son and heir and that therefore the titles belonged to him as well, but the judge remained firm in his decision to send him to the gallows.[69]

These stories of everyday tragedies played out on the streets of Paris are characteristic of a memoir in which a young man's struggle to make his way in the world is marked by unexpected changes of fortune. It is a theme that appears prominently in orphan tales like "The Story of Aladdin and the Wonderful Lamp," but that is completely missing in Galland's journals. There is little in the writings of the French Orientalist that would suggest that he was capable of developing a character like Aladdin with sympathy, but Diyab's memoir reveals a narrator adept at capturing the distinctive psychology of a young protagonist, as well as recognizing the kinds of injustices and opportunities that can transform the path of any youthful adventurer.

✦ ✦ ✦

Diyab's description of his time in Paris makes it clear that he knew he was both a curiosity on display and a privileged observer of the Occidental curiosities presented for his appreciation. The mutual consumption of the experience of difference is first apparent in Diyab's descriptions of the arrival in 1708 of an Ottoman diplomatic envoy. Diyab describes the keenness of French dignitaries to show the Ottoman visitor the curiosities of Versailles, but a little later he uses the same term, curiosity, to describe the spectacle that the visiting ambassador and his entourage represented for the French men and women who came into contact with them.[70] Diyab's memoir reveals a clear awareness of the mutual fascination that shaped such cross-cultural encounters, and the efforts made in such instances to exaggerate cultural difference to elicit the thrill of the exotic.

Nowhere is Diyab's imaginative engagement with the consumption of the marvellous more evident than in his descriptions of his visit to the court of Louis XIV at Versailles in the company of Lucas. The use of Diyab as an exotic prop in a grand spectacle of Oriental wonders for the French court must have been Lucas's plan from the beginning. He had insisted that Diyab send for his most impressive Oriental costume soon after the Maronite joined his caravan in 1707. In his first voyage to the Levant, the French traveller had cast a young Istanbul slave boy named Pateque in a similar role—taking him to court to entertain an aristocratic audience with speeches on God and war, and singing and dancing *à la turque.*[71] In Paris, Lucas demanded that his servant prepare for the visit to Versailles by dressing in characteristically Oriental fashion. Diyab complied by donning a long tunic, baggy pantaloons, a headscarf of Damascene fabric, a precious belt, a silver dagger, and, at the insistence of Lucas, a fur cap from Cairo that bore no relation to his own festive robes from Aleppo. Suitably outfitted by his French master, Diyab was asked to carry a cage containing two curious creatures brought from Tunis for the amusement of the royal court.[72]

In his memoir Diyab evocatively captures the elaborate rituals and excessive luxury that accompanied his presentation to the "sultan of France" as one of the curiosities acquired by Lucas on his travels. Even from a distance, he felt the intense presence of Louis XIV as he approached the throne. The monarch's magnificence was such, Diyab writes, that no one could hold his gaze. The king's interest was immediately drawn to the creatures that Diyab refers to as "savage animals," but that were in fact jerboas, a variety of desert rodent related to the jumping mouse. Confounded by the king's questions about the animals, Lucas directed him to Diyab, and the Syrian youth wrote the name of the animal in both Arabic and French for the king. Louis XIV seems to have been intrigued by the young man in "Oriental" garb. After examining what Diyab had written, the king asked him who he was and where he had come from—extending the curiosity originally piqued by the animals to this other Oriental marvel.[73]

The mutual consumption of the experience of otherness is clearest in Diyab's description of his interactions with the women of the royal court at Versailles, who proved to be even more fascinated by him than by the jerboas. Abandoning the spectacle of the "savage animals," Diyab writes, they turned to examine his features and clothing instead. Some of the women reached out to touch him, lifting the folds of his clothing to get a better look at the garments and removing the Egyptian fur cap from his head. One princess asked why Diyab had a mustache, to which Lucas replied that it was the custom of his country. Diyab does not record what he felt when the laughing princesses treated him like a spectacle for their amusement. Was the young Diyab upset by their laughter? Was he embarrassed to be dressed in a strange ensemble of "Oriental" garments? Or was he flattered by the intimate attention of women dressed in their own regal finery?[74]

Whatever the young Diyab felt at that moment, the memoir that he recorded fifty years later describes his encounter with the ladies of Versailles in the style of a fabulous tale. When he entered the apartments of Lucas's patroness, the Duchess of Burgundy, he found the wife of the dauphin playing a game of cards with several princesses, with piles of gold coins arranged on the table in front of them. All wore dresses of precious silk embroidered with gold, but the duchess was attired with even greater extravagance and beauty than the rest. The princesses resembled stars, Diyab writes, and the servants seemed to orbit around them. Leaving the duchess's "palace," Diyab crossed paths with a lovely young woman wearing a diadem studded with diamonds, rubies, emeralds, and other precious stones who was surrounded by sumptuously dressed servants. So ravishing was she that Diyab imagined she must have been the king's daughter. Later, Diyab was summoned to the rooms of another princess whom he describes as beautiful, gracious, and surpassing all other women of the age. The princesses who clustered around her bed were dressed in splendid clothing heavily adorned with jewels and precious stones, and they appeared to shine with the brightness of stars.[75]

Diyab's descriptions of the radiant beauty and luxurious attire of the ladies of Versailles are reminiscent of the princesses in the tales like "Aladdin" and "Prince Ahmad and the Fairy Peri-Banu," which he related to Galland in 1709. Every one of the ladies in Diyab's account of the royal palace is beautiful and splendidly dressed, and as ravishing to the eye as the princesses in the fabulous tales of the *Arabian Nights*. Beyond the general hyperbole of Diyab's description, certain details of his Versailles princesses correspond to details in the tale of Prince Ahmad.

When Prince Ahmad first sees the fairy princess Peri-Banu emerging from her palace, she is adorned with the costliest of jewels. Her throne is covered with diamonds, rubies, emeralds, pearls, and other gems—a repetition of the precious ornaments of the diadem worn by the beautiful princess that Diyab assumed was the French king's daughter. The repetition of such details in Diyab's narration of his Versailles experience and his tale of Prince Ahmad suggests that Diyab was the author of more than just the bare outline of the orphan tale.[76]

In searching Diyab's memoir for clues about the creation of the orphan tales, the chronology of these events is striking. Diyab encountered the splendors of Versailles several months before he began telling Galland his tales in May 1709—opening up the possibility that the deep impression made by the ladies of Versailles shaped the stories that he contributed to the *Arabian Nights*. However, the influence may also have run in the other direction. When Diyab composed his memoir some fifty years later, he may have reused the stock phrases with which he had described fictional characters of ravishing beauty and wealth in tales like "Prince Ahmad" to describe the French princesses of Versailles. In this memoir, details of Diyab's fictional stories fuse with those of his account of the wonders of France.

The women of Louis XIV's court may indeed have appeared marvellous enough to inspire descriptions of a fairy princess, particularly in the imagination of a young man who had never seen such excessive luxury up close before. But Diyab's narrative of being received into the bedrooms of different princesses seems more like a fabulous tale than an accurate account. He recounts that he alone was invited into the private boudoir of a princess who was confined to bed rest after participating in the previous evening's hunt. When he saw her, she was lying in her bed covered with a precious brocade fabric. Such an audience seems unlikely, and Diyab's account grows more improbable when he relates that another princess glimpsed the silver dagger in his belt as he bowed and reached for it, thinking it was a saber. Diyab corrected her, raising his tunic to show her the weapon, and the princess immediately withdrew. Diyab explains in his memoir that a dagger that could be concealed and drawn in secret was considered much more dangerous in Louis XIV's court. Yet the princess kept silent, choosing not to give Diyab away to the guards. This episode of complicity within the intimate confines of Versailles reads like Aladdin's adventures with Princess Badr al-Budur, whom he steals away from her own bed on her wedding night through the jinni's power, and whose honor he gallantly preserves by placing a sword between them during the night.[77]

One can imagine that Diyab told the story of his audience at Versailles and his visit to the sultan's seraglio countless times upon his return to Aleppo. Perhaps he began adding details about his encounters in the private rooms of the ladies of the court to entertain his listeners and satisfy the ubiquitous desire for sensational stories of foreign cultures. By the time he wrote his memoir, the embroidered details had become part of the fabric of his account. In the middle of his tale of meeting the king, Diyab himself questions whether he could have remembered everything he saw and heard exactly after so many years, and he answers, "Certainly not!"[78]

As impressed as Diyab was by the magnificently dressed inhabitants of Versailles, he seems to have been even more struck by the palace itself. Diyab claims that as he approached the palace, he was dazzled by the light emanating from it, which could be seen a half hour's travel away. He confesses that he could not stand to look directly at the golden rooftops. Later, as they wandered the palace gardens together, Lucas would tell him the story of the construction of the palace, and Diyab would record it in his memoir in the breathless tone of an *Arabian Nights* tale. One day, Diyab reports with obvious fascination, the king commanded that a palace with gardens and promenades be constructed that would defy description—a palace that would have no equal on any continent and that would be celebrated throughout the Christian world. The king assembled all the master gardeners and artisans in his service and demanded that they divert the Seine River to water the new gardens of the palace, but the only solution the artisans could propose was to level the mountain separating the river's course from the palace. This solution did not satisfy the king because he wanted the water to flow down into the gardens from an elevated height. Embarrassed, the artisans told him this was not possible. Finally, one artisan presented himself to the king and told him he could make the water flow from the top of the mountain, but it would cost a great deal. The king replied that if the artisan accomplished this feat, he could ask for anything he desired and all his dreams would be realized. When at last the artisan was successful in his mission to build the "Machine de Marly," the king was able to order the construction of waterfalls and great stone basins for fountains.[79]

Diyab was fascinated by the aesthetic effects that could be produced in the grand settings of the French capital. His memoir gives particular attention to one fountain in the Versailles gardens that featured a large stone basin surmounted by lions with their jaws open wide. It bore a striking resemblance to a fountain that Diyab saw at an opera performance that he attended with the visiting Ottoman diplomat. This theatrical fountain was another wonder for Diyab, for a hidden mechanism caused water to gush from the open mouths of its two lions during the performance. The resemblance to the fountain at Versailles was no accident, according to Diyab, for the opera set was meant to be an exact replica of Versailles. For Diyab, this set turned out to be a marvel equal to the royal residence: "Everything that was on stage was raised into the air and in its place appeared a magnificent palace, with a high ceiling, with pavilions and salons, with glazed windows as well as other charms, the same as the palace of the Sultan of France." This palace disappeared and reappeared throughout the opera—much to the surprise of the Syrian viewer. Later Diyab's friends would explain the mechanism of hidden ropes and pulleys that could lift objects into the air in the blink of an eye, but Diyab's imagination was already captured by the vision of an elaborate palace appearing magically in front of the eyes of the audience.[80]

Elements of these wondrous settings reappear in the stories told by Diyab to Galland in 1709, suggesting certain continuities in the descriptive techniques used by the Syrian storyteller. In the tale of Prince Ahmad, for instance, the prince's father sets him a series of increasingly difficult tasks that he completes with the help of the fairy princess. The second of these tasks requires that the prince climb to the fountain of the lions and retrieve a goblet of its enchanted water without being mauled by its guardians, real lions rather than stone ones. The technical mastery exhibited in the fountains of Versailles, and the theatrical

This production of Jean-Baptiste Lully's opera *Atys* in 1709 was attended by Hanna Diyab during his stay in Paris. If the romance of Antoine Galland's time in Istanbul imprinted his *Arabian Nights,* so too did Diyab's experience of the marvels of Paris, which included these sets inspired by the gardens of Versailles. From a published score for the 1708–1709 run at the Royal Opera House in Paris.

replication of this effect in the Paris opera house, becomes a fantastic marvel in the tale crafted by Diyab.[81]

The tale of Aladdin possesses its own distinctive connections to the stories related decades later in the memoir of the Syrian traveller. Once Aladdin has won the beautiful Princess Badr al-Budur with the help of his magic lamp, he orders the jinni to build a magnificent palace for her next to her father's palace. Just as Louis XIV's Versailles was constructed to be without parallel in the world, so Aladdin's palace will be "the only wonder of the world, for nothing so grand, so rich, so magnificent has ever been seen before or since." The fame of Versailles is matched in this orphan tale by a palace that "the whole world must have been talking about ever since it was built."[82] The sudden appearance of Aladdin's palace over the course of a single night is a significant aspect of the plot. When the sultan rises in the morning, he is astounded to see a spectacular palace surmounted by a dome made of layers of solid silver and gold and embellished by twenty-four windows with lattice screens of diamonds, rubies, and emeralds. Like Diyab viewing the glimmering, gilded roof of the palace of Versailles, the sultan is amazed to see a palace shining in the light of dawn. Its sudden appearance is incredible, but even more marvellous is its sudden disappearance when a Maghrebi magician whisks it away to Africa with the princess still inside. Aladdin's fate rests on finding a way to make the palace magically reappear, along with the princess.[83]

Scholars have often seen the splendors of the palace in "Aladdin" as an Orientalist projection by Galland based on his experiences in Istanbul, but Aladdin's floating palace more closely resembles the Versailles palace described by Diyab than the Ottoman palace of Topkapi. Searching for a story to satisfy a European listener whom Diyab may have assumed shared the appetite for splendor visible at the French court, Diyab may have turned to the palace of Louis XIV as a model for the wondrous palace of Aladdin. The idea of an elaborate palace that appears and disappears in the blink of an eye may also have been inspired by the theatrical magic that Diyab experienced in the Paris opera house.

The magical palace of Aladdin is only one of the many examples of the heightened emphasis on luxury and marvels that scholars have seen in the orphan tales of Diyab. Larzul, for example, notices an increase in the superlatives that are scattered throughout these stories with their many examples of magnificence and excellence. When Aladdin presents jewels to the sultan in an effort to win the beautiful princess, for instance, the sultan is astounded by the richness of this treasure: "One could not describe how surprised and amazed the sultan was when he saw so many precious stones assembled in that vase, for they were so impressive, so magnificent, so perfect, so bright and so big in size that they did not resemble any of the gems he had seen before." While it is possible that Galland provided some of the details, the tone of these scenes is more likely a reflection of the wonder with which Diyab viewed the marvels of Paris than it is the perspective of the French Orientalist.[84]

When Aladdin finally wins the hand of the princess, he leads her to his fabulous palace in a splendid procession composed of richly attired slave girls, musicians, and columns of hundreds of soldiers. Four hundred of the sultan's pages hold torches, which shine so brightly they take the place of the sun. Though devoid of any Christian iconography, the grand processions in "Aladdin" are closely related to Diyab's account of the Corpus Christi procession, with its marching columns of hundreds and its crowds of thousands. The unnatural brightness of the torches takes the place of the cardinal's monstrance shining as brilliantly as the sun. In the memoir, the illumination offered by this monstrance is credited to an assortment of precious jewels that bear a striking resemblance to those that ornamented the beautiful princess of Versailles: "diamonds, rubies, emeralds and other precious stones."[85] Similar phrases recur in the description of the fairy kingdom of Peri-Banu in the tale of Prince Ahmad. While it is impossible to tell whether the experience shaped the story or the story shaped a later recollection of the experience, there is a clear family resemblance between the stories crafted by Diyab for both the readers of Aleppo and Galland, the French collector that he met in a Paris apartment in 1709.

✦ ✦ ✦

In the cover illustration of the first volume of Galland's published journals, the European traveller seems to embody all the romance of the Orientalist in the East. Many have seen this man, with his golden cloak and tasseled turban, set against a "dreamy pink- and blue-hued" background, as the true author of the *Arabian Nights* in French—discounting any contribution that might have been made by the Syrian traveller who first told the stories of Aladdin and Prince Ahmad. However, this contention is as questionable as the assumption that the man in the portrait is the French translator.[86] Galland's version of the *Arabian Nights* must be recognized as only the first of many episodes of collaboration that expanded and transformed the story collection as it circulated in French and English. In a repetition of the pattern established in the Arabic-speaking world, Galland's *Arabian Nights* created a space in which European storytellers could become the authors of their own Oriental tales by using manuscript sources from foreign lands, and incorporating their own experiences of travel or the stories they heard along the way.

The French translator's beautiful infidelities seemed to invite the creation of new tales through innumerable acts of imitation, adaptation, and forgery. In some cases, translators turned to manuscript sources in Arabic or Persian or Turkish; in other cases, they used the models provided by Galland and Diyab to create new stories in the spirit of the *Arabian Nights*. In the first of these gestures of imitation, Galland's rival Pétis de la Croix published *The Thousand and One Days* (1710–1712), which claimed to be a translation of a Persian manuscript given to him by a dervish in Isfahan in 1675. Like Galland, Pétis de la Croix had travelled in the East in his youth, and his knowledge of Arabic, Persian, and Turkish had earned him a position as a royal interpreter. His story collection was adapted from several sources—most importantly a Turkish manuscript of *Relief after Hardship* (*al-Faraj ba'd al-shidda*). The literary qualities of the final version of this translation were the result of a rewriting of the text by Alain René Lesage, a writer known for his translations and adaptations from Spanish. Galland was not impressed with the final product, for he "found in this work many things that deserved criticism from those who have some knowledge of the Levant."[87]

Pétis de la Croix's work was typical of the many translations that circulated in the wake of the success of Galland's *Arabian Nights*. Translators and editors pillaged stories from the wider world to produce analogues of the "Arabian" story collection with titles like *Turkish Tales* (1707), *Chinese Tales* (1723), and *Mogul Tales* (1732). The Oriental tale was also replicated in parody, pastiche, and pseudotranslation. The librarian to the French king, Jean-Paul Bignon, threw his hat into the ring with *Les aventures d'Abdalla* (1713), a novel masquerading as a translation of an Arabic manuscript found in Batavia. In this story, which replicates the *Arabian Nights* in its framing and embedded tales, the virtuous Abdalla is sent by his master, the sultan of India, to find the waters of eternal youth. The hero is a devout Muslim, but the adventures draw on some of the most common themes of European storytelling. Other literary ventures in the spirit of the *Arabian Nights* would exhibit the qualities of postmodern pastiche: Thomas-Simon Gueullette's *Thousand and One Quarters-of-an-Hour: Tartarian Tales* (1715), Jacques Cazotte's *Thousand and One Fopperies: Tales to Put You to Sleep* (1742), and Chevalier Duclos's *Five Hundred and a Half Mornings* (1756). The potential for duplicitous elaboration of the French tales of the *Arabian Nights* would be brought to its zenith at the opening of the twentieth century in the version of the story collection by Joseph Charles Mardrus. His sixteen-volume translation, which he once claimed was based on a seventeenth-century North African manuscript that turned out to be fictional, was an extraordinary collage of tales drawn from a multitude of sources and delivered with a considerable degree of imaginative invention.[88]

The inspirational quality of Galland's stylish tales has been richly documented, but a claim on behalf of the creative contributions of Diyab to this seminal translation of the *Arabian Nights* should also be considered. Like the many authors of Oriental tales in early eighteenth-century France and England, the Syrian storyteller of "Aladdin" and "Prince Ahmad" was adept at fusing the raw materials of East and West in the tales that he told to Galland and the anecdotes that he recorded in his memoir decades later. In the pages of this manuscript, we catch a glimpse of the tale of Aladdin in the sympathetic portraits of the socially marginal and the many examples of miraculous intervention. The reader may also spy elements of the splendid settings and precious objects described in the tale of "Prince Ahmad and the Fairy Peri-Banu" in Diyab's descriptions of the sumptuous palaces and ceremonies of the Paris of Louis XIV. Above all, an examination of Diyab's memoir highlights the difficulties of somehow disentangling the creative agency of Diyab and Galland in the production of the orphan tales of the *Arabian Nights*. The interplay between these imaginative responses to East and West may in part explain the continued inspiration provided by these stories three centuries after they were first recorded.

2

MARVELLOUS THIEVES

The memoir of Hanna Diyab, the Syrian storyteller of "Ali Baba" and "Aladdin," at last offers an opportunity to explore the ways in which the life and storytelling talent of this Maronite traveller shaped the famous orphan tales of Antoine Galland's French version of the *Arabian Nights*. This narrative of a young man exploring the possibilities that lay beyond the borders of his homeland contains a multitude of anecdotes that reveal the author's skills as a weaver of marvellous tales. A mixture of both travelogue and autobiography, this memoir is devoted largely to the time Diyab spent in the service of Paul Lucas, a French traveller and antiquarian, and his long return journey from Paris to Aleppo. In writing this memoir, Diyab seems to have given little thought to his own role in shaping a story collection that now has a firm place within the circuits of world literature, but he does show his attraction to the fantastical tales that were a staple of Lucas's popular travelogues.

If Diyab's memoir resembles a coming-of-age tale, it is a story in which Lucas—as master and mentor—is crucial. Diyab's journey begins in 1707 when he joins the caravan of Lucas outside Aleppo, and his account of their travels from Syria to France is dominated by the powerful personality of the Frenchman. Scholars have pointed out that Diyab's travels were not the product of an official commission and had no fixed destination, but his journey was closely connected with Lucas's goals as a collector of rare artifacts for the French court and was therefore shaped by the itineraries established by his royal patrons.[1] The lure of precious objects is thus a recurring theme in Diyab's memoir, which is full of the same stories of magic and adventure that made Lucas's own travelogues so popular among French readers. Written in Aleppo decades later, Diyab's narrative of his travels with Lucas still displays many of the motifs that define the particular spirit of the orphan tales—encounters with bandits, treasures unearthed from hidden caves, and magical elixirs that promise eternal life. If these elements are more strongly represented in the tales that Galland heard from Diyab in 1709 than in his original manuscript of the *Arabian Nights,* this may well have been the result of Diyab's immersion in a particular storytelling culture as he travelled for nearly two years at Lucas's side.

According to his memoir, Diyab met Lucas at a moment in March 1707 when the young Maronite wanted nothing more than to put Aleppo behind him. His chance of pursuing a prosperous life as part of the city's mercantile community seemed to be slipping away from him. He had been in the employ of the Rémuzat family, one of the great merchant families of the Levant, but after a quarrel, his master had dismissed him and now held a bitter grudge against him. For three months Diyab remained unemployed, and he began to despair of ever finding work in Aleppo again. When he heard there was a caravan preparing to depart for Tripoli, he decided to join it, but he knew he would have to act carefully to avoid the opposition of his older brothers. The next morning, Diyab woke early and packed his saddlebags in secret, and alone he made his way to the Khan al-Zayt, from where the caravan would depart.[2]

Lucas was posing as a physician when he arrived in Aleppo, but he was known within the merchant community of the city as a servant of the "sultan" of France. This was Lucas's second major voyage as a collector of treasures for the French court, and he had already had some success before he arrived, for he registered 250 valuable coins with the French consul in Aleppo. For Diyab, Lucas's appearance represented an exciting opportunity to pursue a fortune of his own, and he was anxious to show off the abilities he had developed by working within the merchant class of Aleppo. At the caravan's first stop, he was called by the caravan master to resolve a dispute. "I heard the Frank and the muleteer arguing without understanding each other," Diyab writes. When he intervened to settle the matter, Diyab provided Lucas with clear evidence of his facility in "the Frankish tongue."[3] The Frenchman grew curious about his new travelling companion. He had initially assumed that Diyab was a Muslim because he wore a white turban, but Diyab assured him that he was a Maronite Christian. Inviting him to dinner, Lucas pressed his new acquaintance further. Diyab explained that he had learned of Lucas in Aleppo because Lucas had been staying at the house of Master Sauron, the employer of his brother. Taking this chance to establish his own value to his new "master," Diyab portrayed himself as a sophisticated traveller who had explored the world. This lie was only the first deception in a relationship in which both Lucas and Diyab assumed a series of masks as they made their way through the fluid world of the Mediterranean.[4]

Lucas quickly saw the value that Diyab might have as a translator and as an object for display upon his arrival at the French court. If Diyab dreamed of travel, Lucas told him, then he could not have encountered a better man to facilitate that goal. He explained that his mission from the "sultan of France" was to research ancient history and collect ancient coins as well as plants and herbs, and he asked Diyab if he could read Arabic and French equally well. According to the Maronite's memoir, Lucas then made him an offer: if Diyab would return with him to Paris, Lucas would see that he was appointed by the king to the library of Arabic manuscripts. Diyab would reap innumerable rewards and live the rest of his life under the direct protection of a powerful monarch.[5] The Maronite youth clearly had some doubts about these promises, for, when the caravan reached its first destination of Tripoli, Diyab turned to a merchant acquaintance and a Christian monk for advice on whether Lucas could be trusted. Their reassurances led the young Syrian traveller to commit to the journey that would later dominate his memoir.[6]

Diyab's first outing with Lucas provides a glimpse of the nature of the expedition that the young Maronite had joined and the "master" who was called the most popular and most deceitful of eighteenth-century French travellers in the Levant.[7] On the road to Tripoli from Aleppo, Lucas heard about the ruins of an old church and convent near Kaftin and insisted on exploring them, despite a warning that bandits often frequented the site. With the addition of five hired guards, the men set off for the ruins, and Diyab watched as Lucas circled different stones, eagerly copying the inscriptions they bore. When two large skulls—of a man and a woman—were found in a tomb within the ruins, Lucas declared authoritatively that these skulls must have belonged to the former rulers of the lands. Seeking more substantial treasures, Lucas found a narrow opening into what he thought was another tomb and demanded that one of the guards enter. When the guards refused, imagining that the cave housed some wild animal, a young goatherd was recruited to do the job. He emerged from the cave with a ring and a lamp, and Lucas proclaimed the expedition a success. But Diyab's account suggests that he was not completely convinced by his master's performance. Lucas was not able to determine what material the objects were made of or find inscriptions that might indicate their importance.[8]

While Diyab's memoir records the great devotion of his younger self to his master, cracks in the image of the famous traveller are visible in this retrospective account. Lucas appears more as a tomb raider and charlatan than an antiquities expert in many of Diyab's anecdotes. It is tempting to see the tale of "Aladdin and the Wonderful Lamp" prefigured in the relationship of the two men, as Bernard Heyberger suggests in his introduction to Diyab's memoir. In "Aladdin," the older man also needs a nimble youth to descend into a cave to retrieve a precious object, and the Maghrebi magician who impersonates Aladdin's uncle might be compared to Lucas, the French traveller who masqueraded as a physician. Diyab, like Aladdin, would follow this roguish father figure in spite of his skepticism about his credentials and intentions.[9] While it may be too much to imagine that Diyab pictured himself as the protagonist of the tale of Aladdin and the magical lamp, the imprint of his travels with Lucas can still be seen within this tale of treasure and deception.[10]

Until the recovery of Diyab's own memoir, it was impossible to assess the importance of Lucas within the life of the Syrian traveller.

Lucas's second travelogue, which covers the period between 1707 and 1708 when the two men travelled together, does not even acknowledge the presence of his Maronite companion, and until recently scholars have neglected Lucas's third travelogue, which includes his reunion with Diyab in Aleppo.[11] However, reading Lucas's travelogues in conjunction with Diyab's memoir allows us to understand the context in which the orphan tales of the *Arabian Nights* were created.[12] The stories that Diyab contributed to Galland's work were products of the storytelling culture of Aleppo, but they were also shaped by his experiences on the road with Lucas. A collector of fantastic tales as well as precious artifacts, Lucas's preferences would become well known to Diyab as the two men shared their tales of fact and fiction. In his memoir and in the orphan tales of the *Arabian Nights,* Diyab's stories would carry within them a lasting imprint of the mixture of rivalry and fellowship that characterized his association with Lucas.

✦ ✦ ✦

Lucas has received little attention from scholars, but he was the most popular French travel writer of the early eighteenth century. The son of a goldsmith from Rouen, Lucas did not receive an academic education. His youthful ambition was to become a trader of precious stones. Entering the service of the Venetians, he reportedly fought against the Ottoman Empire at the famous Siege of Negroponte in 1688. From these early adventures in the Mediterranean, Lucas managed to acquire a collection of valuable coins that he sold to the French king for his cabinet of curiosities. He followed this success by launching his first great voyage of exploration to the Levant in 1699, and when he returned to France in 1703 he offered readers a rare look at Egypt in his first travelogue. With the help of his patroness, the Duchess of Burgundy, Lucas then received an official commission as an antiquarian for Louis XIV for his next two voyages (1704–1708 and 1714–1717), which were documented in two additional published travelogues.[13]

Lucas's last two voyages to the Middle East were funded by the French court for the purpose of gathering valuable artifacts and manuscripts, as well as samples of plants, minerals, and medicines that might be useful to the French kingdom.[14] Lucas received detailed instructions and itineraries from his patrons before undertaking these journeys. One list of his commissions asked him to provide information on various marbles and other stones used to build and decorate buildings; on the variety of precious stones and their sizes and cuts; on minerals and the machines used to extract them; on pearls and corals and their many uses; on different kinds of trees and the uses of their wood, bark, and gum; and on the many plant species whose seeds he was to collect for shipment to France. Lucas was encouraged by his patrons to take on the role of a physician so he might better explore different medicinal remedies and forms of drink, and to investigate the possibility of cultivating opium in the royal gardens of Versailles. With reference to art, he was asked to analyze the distinctive materials that might in future be shipped *from* rather than *to* Paris. A struck-through line in a draft of one commission prepared for Lucas states the mercantilist rationale for his voyages most explicitly: France spent too much procuring valuable commodities from the Levant. Lucas's research was intended to promote the manufacture of these goods at home.[15]

In his travelogue Lucas proudly fashions himself as a collector of classical antiquities and manuscripts for King Louis XIV. At the royal court, however, he was known more for his luck than his professional skills. Lucas did not possess the knowledge of Greek or Latin necessary to identify ancient coins or inscriptions. In 1704, the minister of the king's cabinet who commissioned Lucas's journey gave him a numismatic manual to consult—an acknowledgment of his inability to make his own judgments concerning the worth of these precious objects. Yet Lucas did make some valuable additions to the king's collection, procuring the medals that would later solve the mystery of the kings who had ruled the Bosphorus before Alexander the Great.[16] He also possessed an uncanny ability to find rare manuscripts, which earned him the sobriquet "the marvellous Paul Lucas" from Jean-Paul Bignon, the royal librarian.[17] During his second voyage to the Levant, Lucas collected twenty-two manuscripts, mostly in Arabic. This treasure trove included universal histories as well as specific histories of Aleppo, Egypt, Yemen, the conquest of Jerusalem, Tamerlane, and the Ottoman sages and emperors. Lucas also brought back works of science and medicine, treatises on the mysteries of the name of the Prophet and the theology of the Sufis, and two works of Turkish verse and fiction. Bignon would marvel at the rare instincts that allowed Lucas, who could not read Arabic, Turkish, or Persian, to acquire such a valuable collection of manuscripts.[18]

Not surprisingly, Lucas's travelogues have little in common with the emerging Orientalist scholarship of his day. Delivered with a naïve excitement, they are full of stories in which he explores strange lands, encounters mystical dervishes, and battles bandits. These publications were genuinely popular with a French reading public—each going through multiple editions—and were even translated into German. However, Benoît de Maillet, French consul general in Egypt and author of the *Description de l'Egypte* (1732), captured the academic consensus in labeling Lucas "an ignorant" and denouncing his travelogues as worthless. He criticized the "ridiculous tales" and "personal adventures" that Lucas used to please the public rather than to instruct it.[19] In the academies of France, Lucas's skills as an antiquarian may have been disparaged, but in his travelogues he plays the role of a heroic adventurer who never questions his right to pillage the precious antiquities neglected by the Ottomans.

Lucas's activities as a collector reflect an Orientalism that was defined more by a love of luxury than by academic or imperial ambitions. His correspondence with his patroness, the Duchess of Burgundy, corroborates the suggestion of recent scholarship that aristocrats at the court of Louis XIV were desperate to impoverish themselves through extravagant consumption, especially of Oriental goods. Lucas's letters to the duchess, the wife of the dauphin, boast about the beauty of the precious stones that he procured for her.[20] They also preserve the dramatic tales of banditry that obsessed Lucas. For instance, he pleaded for the duchess's aid in recovering his losses when he was robbed by men in the service of the "Pasha of Baghdad" on September 12, 1701. Lucas claimed to have lost a truly spectacular hoard on this occasion—dozens of Oriental rubies and sapphires, some thirty diamonds, 2,500 precious pearls, and countless other gems. In characteristic fashion, Lucas lamented that these specimens were all incredibly large and included a seventeen-karat ruby.[21] His description of the stolen goods in this letter rivals the descriptions of the marvellous riches of Aladdin's palace or the cave of the forty thieves. The pasha's promotion to grand vizier made it unlikely that Lucas would ever be compensated for his alleged losses, but he remained obsessed with regaining these stolen goods for fifteen years, and Diyab would certainly have heard this story repeatedly.[22]

In the two years they travelled together, Lucas gave his Maronite companion a good sense of the interests of the European collector. Coins and medals were always high on his list, but he was always looking for other kinds of artifacts. In Aleppo he would investigate the city's booksellers and venture out to the city's ancient cemeteries to search for hidden treasures. Lucas would also have sampled the city's lively storytelling culture. The French traveller was particularly intrigued by Aleppo's commerce in superstition, especially its fascination with alchemy and the Maghrebi astrologers who travelled the length of the Ottoman Empire. Lucas recorded the stories that Aleppines told about an herb that could turn the teeth of grazing lambs to pure gold, and at the end of his third travelogue, Lucas boasts of having acquired such a gold tooth as a prized curiosity in his collection.[23]

Lucas was being paid to acquire manuscripts, precious objects, and natural specimens, but his commission also allowed him to pursue his own interest in collecting popular tales. He, like other antiquarians of the king, was asked to record all the information he could about the items that he found, and this included the stories told about them by the local population. The instructions for the voyage of 1714, for instance, asked Lucas to record the coordinates and dimensions of the ruins that he explored in Egypt, but also asked him to record the names given to these monuments and any stories related to them—whether "real or fabulous."[24] Beyond these official duties, Lucas was always searching for marvellous tales to include in his successful travelogues.

Lucas's published works are a mixture of observation, fantasy, and unacknowledged borrowing from other works. He exhibits a preference for the exciting and the sensational, and he delivers accounts of distant lands that are full of piquant details. In his description of Egypt, he claims to have seen the dried blood of Saint Catherine of

Alexandria on the stone where she was decapitated; he records the torture of criminals who are skinned alive; and he offers an account of a certain class of women in Tahta who graciously place themselves at the disposal of men who "come and go." "Entering the town," Lucas writes, "I was surprised to see a dozen young women, well proportioned enough, that had nothing but shirts on, and were not ashamed to show themselves completely nude in a number of indecent postures." He provides lively descriptions of the bazaar of the goldsmiths, the slave market, and the ceremonies commemorating the birth of the Prophet, but he also has room for stories of the fantastic. Lucas's readers are presented with an account of the Orient that includes an appearance by the demon Asmodée, a description of a magical serpent that can instantly reconstitute itself when cut into pieces, and reports of ferocious attacks on swimmers in the Nile from fish with a taste for human flesh.[25]

These tales of enchanted forests, mysterious caves, and strange beasts were regarded with disdain by serious French scholars, but Lucas defended his own notion of what the reader wanted in a travelogue. Responding to those critics who objected to the fantastic stories of his second travelogue (which covers the period during which he travelled with Diyab), he declared that the principal function of travel writing was to entertain the reader, and that the foreign fable played an important part in achieving this goal. The fact that the world's different traditions are "filled with extravagance" does not make them "less curious or less interesting," Lucas writes. "Every country has its fables," and it is the task of the travel writer to describe the fabulous popular traditions of each place. In support of his position, Lucas cites a verse from Jean de La Fontaine: "If I would be told a fairy tale, / My heart would fill with extreme pleasure."[26] Aware of his reputation for credulity, Lucas blames his most fantastical claims on the misinformation provided by guides and translators. He carefully distinguishes between the erroneous reports of informants and the truth of the marvels he has witnessed himself. Given the kinds of stories related by the local population, he argues that a less scrupulous author might have included a thousand other fables about enchanted treasures lurking under fountains and the curative powers of miraculous waters.[27]

Despite this effort to defend the value of personal experience, Lucas's travelogue is riddled with fantastic stories of people and places that he claims to have encountered on his travels. Lucas's account of the marvellous caves of Cappadocia, for instance, reveals the promiscuous mixture of fact and fiction that is typical of his travelogues. Lucas claims to have discovered these caves while travelling through the mountains near Erma in October 1705. He is surprised by their beauty, but he is even more astonished by the sight of the ancient monuments on the other side of the mountain. He then describes a prodigious number of pyramids—perhaps several thousand in number. Each is made of a single rock and carved into many floors, possessing beautiful doors, staircases, and rooms lit by great windows. At first Lucas imagines them to be the homes of ancient hermits because they seem to be topped by sculptures of popes or virgins. But then he notices that some bear figures of naked women in indecent poses, masked oracles, lions, sphinxes, and birds. Through the doors Lucas catches glimpses of murals that seem to him like the remains of ancient portraits. Members of the caravan suggest that the caves are inhabited by supernatural beings, for at certain times of year the pyramids are lit with fires and an infinite number of voices speaking unknown languages can be heard. Not only do these strange structures house jinn, they are also home to a giant monster who walks alone among the pyramids and can lead men astray with the sound of his laugh.[28]

Discrepancies between the real caves of Cappadocia and Lucas's description of them reveal that his account is not based on personal observation: his pyramids are freestanding rather than carved into the mountain, they are some distance from each other rather than contiguous, and the precisely posed sculptures he describes do not exist. Lucas describes the "pyramids" as standing next to a mountain whose opposite side contains many "beautiful caves." Had Lucas seen Cappadocia for himself, he would have known that the "pyramids" and the "beautiful caves" of Cappadocia are one and the same. In episodes such as this one, Lucas integrates the accounts of others into his own narrative—reporting hearsay as fact and transforming legend into reality. These sensational images and fantastic stories would find a ready audience

Paul Lucas claims in his second travelogue that he discovered marvellous caves and fantastical pyramids as he travelled through Cappadocia in 1705. Mixing fact and fiction in his characteristic style, Lucas reports the suggestion of locals that the pyramids were inhabited by jinn. From Lucas, *Deuxième voyage du sieur Paul Lucas dans le Levant.*

among readers of the early eighteenth century and earn Lucas his reputation as the most deceitful of French travel writers.

This potent mixture of fact and fiction did not fit with the emerging standards of scholarly authority in France. Lucas's three published travelogues were the outcome of a significant editing process intended to make his observations worthy of publication. Each of the travelogues was reworked by a member of the Académie des Inscriptions to give the text a veneer of scholarly credibility. Charles Baudelot de Dairval was responsible for the first book (published in 1704); Étienne Fourmont for the second book (published in 1712); and Antoine Banier for the third book (published in 1719). This reworking of Lucas's text blurs the lines between the author's own observations and material borrowed from other authorities. References to classical sources were added by Lucas's ghostwriters so that in the final version the unlettered traveller is somehow citing Herodotus, Pliny, Pausanias, Homer, Cicero, Horace, and Virgil.[29] Other passages are copied from travelogues that preceded his—for instance that of the Capuchin missionary, Father Protais—but it is impossible to know if this was Lucas's decision or that of editors seeking to elevate the quality of the text. The ghostwriter of the second travelogue, Fourmont, was a notorious plagiarist of the work of his Chinese assistant, and such borrowings were a common part of literary production in this period.[30] The end result was a strange mixture of Lucas's preferences for the sensational and the more sober perspectives of his editors. Galland would be highly critical of these works. In his opinion, not even Fourmont's reworking of Lucas's original could bring distinction to the writing of a man with no sense of literary style and no real understanding of the significance of the sites that he visited.[31]

Lucas does not provide an explanation for his decision to bring Diyab with him on his return journey from Aleppo through North Africa and back to France. In fact, he rarely mentions his local guides, interpreters, or servants in his travelogues. Diyab's linguistic skills would have been an advantage in navigating the foreign territories on this journey, and perhaps in evaluating some of the manuscripts that he gathered. Diyab's skills in crafting stories may also have recommended him as a companion for someone with a thirst for fantastic tales. Common elements within the travelogues of Lucas and the memoir of Diyab suggest that the two men were exchanging stories during their journey together, and both authors reveal an attraction to fabulous tales that mirror features of the orphan tales.

Among the stories fit for the *Arabian Nights* in Lucas's second travelogue is a story that he claims to have heard in Jaffa, shortly after Diyab joined his party. There was a hideous sea monster, Lucas recounts, who lived in the coastal caves and terrorized the locals so that they were compelled to sacrifice their own people to the creature's dreadful appetite. When it was time for the princess to be handed over to the monster, however, the courageous young man who had fallen in love with her fought and killed the monster, thereby saving the city and the princess. Lucas claims that he asked local "Turks" when these events had taken place, but the most they would say was that it was before the time of the Prophet, in the days of the infidels.[32]

The similarity between Lucas's story of the sea monster and one of the tales told by Diyab to Galland is striking. In this story, "The Sultan of Samarkand," a giant monster prevents water from flowing into the city unless a girl is sacrificed to the monster each week. Learning that the sultan's daughter is to be sacrificed that very day, Prince Badi Alzaman sets off in a strange underground world to slay the monster, with predictable results.[33] Galland did not choose to insert this story into his version of the *Arabian Nights,* but his description of Diyab's tale reveals that the young Maronite's taste in stories resembles that of Lucas. Jaffa may have been where Diyab picked up the story elements that he would later weave together in "The Sultan of Samarkand." He may have heard a version from locals and related it to Lucas, or he may have acted as a translator for another storyteller who told the particular version inserted into Lucas's travelogue.[34] Whatever the details of this story's transmission, the repetition of these narrative elements in Lucas's travelogue and Diyab's oral performance for Galland reveals the kinds of stories that brought the two men together as they travelled.

Lucas had a talent for delivering a story that appealed to a French reading public with a taste for bandits, monsters, and heroes that matched his own. His editors, however, seem to have disapproved, and there are signs that many of these fantastic stories were cut or truncated in the published versions of Lucas's travelogues. In revising Lucas's second travelogue, Fourmont cut several hundred pages of text that appeared not long after Lucas's account of the marine monster in Jaffa. The edit is awkward and abrupt. Lucas asserts his desire to include the memories of a worthy eyewitness to twenty years of history in Carthage, but then reveals that he was prevailed on to make cuts.[35] It is unclear just how many more stories and anecdotes were cut by Fourmont to make the travelogue worthy of publication. Lucas's defense of the value of foreign fables in the prologue to his third travelogue might well have been a response to this abridgment. Unfortunately, these cuts have resulted in the loss of material that might have further illuminated the kinds of stories that Lucas and Diyab were hearing and telling during their travels. Jaffa was one of the first cities that Lucas and Diyab visited after they began travelling together, and the excised pages may have contained further accounts of the ground they covered.

On the road, Diyab performed the role of servant and translator and may have helped Lucas weave the fabulous fictions for which he was known. At the same time, Lucas was a source for some of the stories that were incorporated into Diyab's memoir, and it is likely that he influenced the creation of the orphan tales, which were told after the arrival of the two men in Paris. Certainly, Diyab shared Lucas's interest in stories with supernatural or miraculous qualities—a fact that can be seen in the way in which both writers included the tale of the philosopher's stone in their travelogues. The appearance of this tale in Diyab's retrospective memoir and Lucas's second travelogue speaks to the common frame of reference that developed during Lucas and Diyab's travels together, although it also highlights differences in the narrative strategies of the two men.

In Diyab's account, the discovery of the philosopher's stone is placed in a larger narrative that dramatizes the sense of insecurity of the young Maronite as he faces the prospect of losing his French master in a distant land. While Lucas habitually presented himself as a doctor, he seemed unable to cure himself when he fell seriously ill in Tunis. As his master lay in bed consumed with fever and unable to speak, Diyab admits that he had relinquished all hope for his recovery and was overwhelmed with anxiety about his own future. But then the faint tapping of a stick that he had left by Lucas's side drew him once more to his master, and Lucas wrote instructions that led Diyab to retrieve a small copper and ebony case from Lucas's medicine cabinet. Following his master's careful directions regarding its secret opening mechanism, Diyab found a crystal flask inside. Carefully, he added three drops of the liquid inside to two fingers of wine, and held Lucas's head so he could drink the potion. He was overwhelmed by surprise when the next morning Lucas called for him in a clear voice. Diyab found his master sitting up, and after two hours of rest Lucas was able to pace the room. Relief and astonishment gave way to anger when he realized that Lucas could have cured himself earlier by using the potion. Why, he demanded of his master, had he not spared himself so much pain, and his servant so much torment and despair?[36]

Lucas's answer was no less astonishing than the speed of his recovery. The elixir of life, he told Diyab, was only to be taken when one was certain of death. Lucas had only discovered this precious secret after decades of travel. Visiting the monastery of Saint-François, he had stumbled on the journal of a priest that finally revealed to him the mystery of the philosopher's stone. An entry in the journal indicated that a young man had approached the resident priest on the feast day of Saint-François seeking to make a confession. Asked how long it had been since he had last confessed, the man (who did not look a day older than thirty) answered matter-of-factly, "sixty years." Offended that the youth would take the holy sacrament as an occasion for mirth, the priest refused to hear his confession in the absence of proof of the statement.[37]

The youth obliged him. He explained that he had left France at the age of forty and travelled for sixty years seeking the plant that could produce the elixir of life, which he had seen sketched in the ancient books of the Greeks, who called it the "philosopher's stone." When he finally found it, he ground it into a medicinal powder, and through trial and error, he ascertained that a single dose could guarantee him another decade of youth and health. Yet over time, he had stopped caring for the fate of his immortal soul, and he now sought the sacrament of confession so that he could embrace the grace of God and die, since God had decreed that this was the fate of all men. The proof was in ten packets of the medicinal powder made from the elixir of life that he, now reconciled to death, was content to give to the priest with the promise that it would ensure him a century of youth. The priest wished to test the veracity of the traveller, and he sought out a decrepit old dog that had taken shelter in the monastery. Mixing some of the powder with its food, he was amazed to see the dog recover its youth and energy. The priest eventually disappeared, leaving only the journal to attest to his discovery.[38]

Diyab does not explain how Lucas succeeded in following the path set out in the priest's journal, but he seems to have been persuaded by his master's miraculous recovery that he did indeed possess the elixir. He attests to the power of this miraculous liquid by assuring his reader that, despite the fact that Lucas was well over sixty, he did not look a day over thirty. It is difficult to know whether the mixture of fact and fiction in this story is Diyab's or Lucas's. Lucas may have lied about his age (he was forty-three when the two men travelled through the Maghreb), and he certainly may have tried to convince Diyab that his tale of the elixir of youth was true. Given Lucas's penchant for deception, he may even have exaggerated his illness and staged his astonishing recovery to increase his hold over the imagination of his young travel companion. Lucas regularly performed the role of a healer during his journeys as a way to earn favor among locals. When Lucas returned to Aleppo in 1715, for instance, he demonstrated his ability by curing Diyab's mother with the use of an amulet—an event that made such an impression on Diyab that he related it three times in his memoir.[39] The story of finding the secret of the philosopher's stone in a priest's journal in a French monastery seems calculated to appeal to the young Maronite, who was always ready to recognize the miraculous power that might reside in the settings of European Christendom.

It is telling that when Lucas integrated the same tale type into a travelogue intended for a French audience, he situated it in a location that better satisfied metropolitan expectations of the mysterious and exotic Orient. Lucas claims that while he was in Anatolia, he turned to an Uzbek dervish to evaluate the manuscripts that he had been collecting on his journey. He was welcomed into a mosque by the dervish and three others whom he found to be persons of "greatest worth and learning," but Lucas viewed the dervish as "more accomplished than the rest, and I believe verily he spoke all the principal languages of the world." Amazed by the accumulated wisdom of the dervish, Lucas was overcome by the impression that he must have been considerably older than the thirty years that he appeared to be. "From his discourse," Lucas claims, "I was persuaded he had lived a century." Indeed, the dervish assured the French traveller that through the mastery of the occult sciences, he could aspire to live a thousand years.[40]

Lucas was initially resistant to the dervish's claim, retorting that not even the great French alchemist Nicolas Flamel had exceeded his natural lifespan. However, he reports that the Uzbek dervish "smiled at my simplicity and asked with an air of mirth:—'Do you really believe this? No, no, my friend, Flamel is still living; neither he nor his wife is dead. . . . [H]e is one of my best friends.'" The Uzbek went on to claim that he had seen Flamel three years previously in the Indies, when the alchemist would have been 375 years old.[41] Drawing on this source, Lucas was able to recount Flamel's acquisition of the philosopher's stone, which the dervish credited to the alchemist's willingness to do business with the Jews of Paris while others shunned them. When one of these Jewish merchants entrusted him with his books and papers, Flamel found in these documents the tale of an envious rabbi who had slain another rabbi in pursuit of the secret. After having a single page of this vast book translated from Hebrew, Flamel suspected that he had stumbled on a treatise on the philosopher's stone, and sought to reconstruct the work by having each page translated by a different Jew in Spain. When complete, the book revealed to him the secret of alchemy and eternal life, and earned him enormous wealth. He and his wife faked their deaths so that he might retreat into a philosophical life, sometimes in one country, sometimes in another.[42]

The parallels between the memoir produced by Diyab and the travelogues of his French master suggest that they were united in their taste for tales of miracles and marvels, but the different treatment of the story of the philosopher's stone in each work reveals the contrasting preoccupations of the two writers. While Diyab grounds the tale of the magical elixir within the more relatable drama of the illness of his cherished master and his own anxieties about the future, Lucas positions his version in an exotic world of Uzbek dervishes and secret rabbinical knowledge. For the Maronite, it is a key episode in a life story that engages his Aleppine audience's belief in the power of miracles. For Lucas, it is an extravagant tale of intrigue and fantasy for a French readership that was developing a taste for an Orient of marvels. In telling this fantastic tale, both storytellers exhibited their distance from the perspective of Galland, who regarded the genre of the fairy tale with distaste and delivered his own observations of travel in his journals with a distinct sobriety.

✦ ✦ ✦

Diyab's version of the secret of the philosopher's stone also testifies to the deceptions that characterized his relationship with Lucas. The French traveller was well known for his willingness to adopt disguises to make his way through foreign territories and collect the valuable items his royal patrons desired, and he was an accomplished liar. His claim that he was a man in his sixties was of a piece with his assertion that he was a qualified doctor—a ploy in which Diyab himself was an accomplice. As Diyab chronicles his younger self's devotion to Lucas, he also reveals many of the deceptions that Lucas employed as he navigated foreign territories, and his own attraction to the ruses of the treasure hunter's trade. Where Lucas's travelogue and Diyab's memoir cover the same territory, there is a fascinating opportunity to analyze the way in which each narrated the challenges of travelling through an environment where political boundaries were unclear and legal rights uncertain.

In 1708, Lucas and Diyab were thrown into their own adventure tale when the English ship on which they sailed encountered French corsairs near the port of Livorno on their return voyage to Europe. Like the tale of the philosopher's stone, this episode is framed differently by each writer. In Lucas's travelogue, it is the ironic conclusion to a story of travel that emphasizes his own courage and resourcefulness in the face of bandits and tricksters—all in the pursuit of the praiseworthy goal of enriching the French kingdom. When he describes his losses at the hands of the French privateers, he casts himself in the role of the aggrieved victim fighting to preserve the treasures that he has rescued from Eastern neglect. For Diyab, however, this episode is bound up with the moral ambiguities of sanctioned theft and the dangers of being caught between conflicting agents of authority.[43]

This adventure began on the island of Corsica, which was to be the launching point for the next leg of Lucas's voyage. Worried by reports of a French corsair ship with 200 sailors and twenty cannons patrolling the nearby waters, the captain of the English ship initially hesitated. But when a favorable wind appeared, he decided to risk the journey of sixty miles under the cover of night. Lucas was convinced that the conventions of piracy on the Mediterranean gave him and his precious cargo sufficient protection. It was customary for pirates to prey on foreign ships, but not on ships flying under the flag of their own country. The French consul in Tunis had advised Lucas to travel on an English ship to avoid the English corsairs, but Lucas was also convinced that he would be safe from French corsairs since he carried "the orders of the King."[44]

In narrating this encounter with pirates, Diyab demonstrates his ability to build suspense. He describes the growing alarm that spread through the ship when the wind died halfway through the voyage. Overcome with fear, the captain ordered his men to pray, but as Diyab wryly remarks, "God did not answer."[45] In the early hours of the morning, the lookouts spied a large black shape to the west that they assumed was a mountain on the Italian coast, but as dawn broke, the light revealed not a mountain but a large ship speeding directly toward them. The captain attempted to flee, but he had only six oarsmen at his command, whereas 200 men were rowing the corsair ship. Even though the desperate passengers took to the oars, the corsair ship quickly overtook the English vessel. The corsairs fired two cannon shots but the captain refused to surrender, until a third shot whizzed just above their heads and the terrified passengers pleaded for capitulation. Calls of "Submit to France!" rang out from the corsair ship, and the English vessel lowered its sails in surrender. Both Diyab and Lucas note that as the corsairs approached, the captain of their ship quickly loaded his money and possessions into a small boat and had crew members row him to safety.[46]

At this point, however, the two narratives diverge. Lucas's sense of righteous indignation fuels an account that emphasizes the barbarity of this unexpected act of piracy at the hands of his countrymen. The pillaging of the English ship by the French corsairs is described as "something horrible to behold." Lucas emphasizes "the fury and avidity of these corsairs, a hundred times more barbarous than all the Kaffirs." In Lucas's tale, he pleads with the corsairs, explaining that he is French like them and is travelling in the service of the king. He claims that the royal documents he carries give him special protection against any attempt to harm him, by French subjects or anyone else, but the corsair's captain, Joseph Bremond, does not recognize his authority and makes a point of confiscating Lucas's effects personally.[47]

If Lucas tells a story in which he depicts himself as the victim of injustice and thereby prepares the way for his claim for compensation, Diyab delivers an account in which the moral high ground remains unclear. In Diyab's version, the first encounter with the pirates occurs when the passengers of the English ship are forced to board the corsair ship. As soon as they are aboard, Lucas recognizes Captain Bremond, and the pirate and the professional treasure hunter exchange friendly greetings and words of affection. When Lucas explains to Bremond his strategy of avoiding English pirates by travelling on an English vessel, the French corsair captain hints that it was not necessarily a safe course of action. Bremond assures Lucas that he will look after his baggage and ensure that nothing goes missing, and, taken in by this ruse, Lucas is initially grateful.[48]

There is no scene of horrible, barbarous pillaging in Diyab's account. In this encounter between thieves, the booty is gathered calmly and efficiently. Bremond orders his men to transfer everything from the English ship to his own without letting anything go missing, and they obey. The following day, the atmosphere is so calm and civil that a priest is allowed to say Mass. At this point, Bremond has the contents of all the luggage and safes from the English ship arranged on the deck and recorded. He then exercises his established privilege as captain and takes the first pick of the loot. Lucas loses a pair of pistols, several purses of silver and coins, and pouches of expensive Tunisian tobacco. From Diyab's own baggage, Bremond takes his *chèche* with golden trim, announcing that "you are not going to need this in a Frankish country."[49]

According to Diyab, Lucas was furious that Bremond had dared to steal from him in what he saw as a clear violation of French law—even on the open waters of the Mediterranean. Was Bremond not aware, Lucas asked him indignantly, that he had been "sent by the Sultan of France on a voyage of exploration?" As proof, Lucas presented the corsair captain with the royal mandate recommending him to French consuls throughout the Middle East. Diyab records Bremond's irreverent response: "On this ship, I am the Sultan. . . . Go and steep your mandate and drink the juice."[50] After a long journey in which he had repeatedly assumed false identities and claimed a legal authority that he did not possess, Lucas was furious to have his treasures pilfered right before he reached his goal of European soil. When he disembarked at the quarantine station, Lucas immediately sent a letter to the French consul in Livorno to request his assistance in recovering his stolen property. According to Diyab, however, Bremond had already convinced the consul's entourage that Lucas was "one of the braggarts who run the world" and "a liar who bears with him a fake and counterfeit royal mandate."[51] In Lucas's narrative, this struggle for recognition of his claims by French authorities becomes part and parcel of the original insult. Throughout his account, he presents himself as a victim—of piracy, official negligence, and corruption.

After repeated requests, Lucas was allowed to plead his case before the consul and a group of French merchants. In Diyab's account, the case essentially revolved around the question of when and from whom it is legitimate to steal—a question that might have been raised in the minds of European readers by Diyab's tale of "Ali Baba and the Forty Thieves." When Lucas initially protested that Bremond could not steal from a fellow Frenchman, the corsair captain replied that because he had encountered Lucas aboard an enemy English ship, he was within his rights to seize Lucas's belongings. Lucas then shifted his argument to assert that Bremond had stolen from an official envoy of the king of France. With this maneuver, Lucas exposed the ambiguous position of the corsair, whose claim to be more than a common pirate lay only in the legal authority of the monarch for whom he sailed. Surely Bremond could not victimize another duly authorized servant of the French king without suffering the consequences of his criminal act. In Diyab's account, it is this perceived insult to the king himself that seems to have carried the day. Lucas told the consul of Bremond's boast that he was his own sultan aboard his ship, and, though Bremond denied it, other passengers corroborated Lucas's statement. According to Diyab, Bremond's repudiation of the French monarch's authority inclined the consul to side with Lucas.[52]

One might see this as a happy ending in which the king's authority was upheld and the wronged party vindicated. However, Diyab's narrative presents this as an ethically ambiguous decision at best, and reveals the fundamental dishonesty that characterized the French traveller. As the consul intervened to retrieve Lucas's precious possessions from

Bremond, the French collector clearly attempted to press his claim much further than it actually reached. After the corsair captain was forced to produce the goods taken in the initial capture, Lucas informed the consul that he was still missing a purse with 222 coins that he had collected for the king. The existence of this treasure could be proven because the coins had been registered with the French consul in Tunis, and their value was so great that Lucas argued that Bremond could keep all his other possessions if only he returned these coins.[53]

This was, Diyab reveals, "a ruse on [Lucas's] part to rub the captain raw." It was true, Diyab explains, that the coins existed, but Lucas had not just registered them in Tunis; he had deposited them there to be sent by diplomatic post to Marseille. Taken in by Lucas's trickery, the consul ordered that Bremond's safe be searched for the coins. When the purse but not the coins was found, Bremond swore on his life that he had neither seen nor heard of them. The consul had each of Bremond's men interrogated, but they all denied any knowledge of the coins, and in a rage he had them imprisoned. Under the threat of torture, the crew turned against the sentinel that guarded the captain's cabin. He denied the charge of having stolen the coins, ironically "swearing he had never committed any act of larceny." Unconvinced, the consul sentenced the sentinel to be hanged if he did not restore the coins. Lucas intervened at this point, Diyab reports, because he did not want anyone to "pay the price of his blood." He advised the consul to simply keep the sentinel imprisoned while they conducted a more thorough inquiry.[54]

Diyab's account of this episode pays close attention to the dangers that Lucas's manipulations posed for the ship's crew. As in his descriptions of Paris, Diyab is horrified by the potential for severe punishment to be imposed in instances where the offense was minimal—or in this case nonexistent.[55] Lucas's decision to restrain the consul's desire for "blood" seems to have won the approval of Diyab, but he leaves the reader in no doubt about the deceitfulness of his master. This assessment of Lucas's character was shared by Lucas's patrons in France. When Abbé Bignon made inquiries on behalf of his protégé regarding the possibility of recouping the value of the 222 coins "stolen" by Bremond, the official reply on September 12, 1708, called into question Lucas's honesty and integrity in reporting the affair with the corsair captain. A further reply on June 19, 1709, again questioned Lucas's ill-founded assertions, and challenged Bignon to prove Lucas's good faith in the absence of any definitive proof of his claim.[56]

Diyab's memoir provides a fascinating portrait of the ambiguous moral territory through which he and his French master moved during these years of travel. It brings to life a world peopled by rogues and thieves and filled with deceit and adventure, and it shows the undeniable attraction this life had for the young Maronite, despite his frequent sense of vulnerability. In his memoir, the description of Lucas's ruse at the expense of the corsair captain is immediately followed by a proud statement that he too had pulled off his own ruse—smuggling tobacco past the customs officials when they landed in Europe.[57] Despite the doubts he seems to have had about Lucas's character, the young Diyab did attempt to model his own life on that of his French master at some points in the narrative. In Paris, Diyab hoped to step into Lucas's role by obtaining his own commission to acquire treasures for the royal court, and Galland seems to have promised to help him achieve this goal. On his return voyage to Aleppo, Diyab adopted Lucas's familiar disguise as a physician to gain his own advantage. Just as Diyab's memoir reveals as fascination with opportunistic characters who ignore conventional moral distinctions, the orphan tales that he related to Galland in Paris were similarly filled with riches and rogues—an understandable outcome if they had been crafted in the company of Lucas.

The fact that these stories of bandits and treasure framed the relationship between Lucas and Diyab is also clear in one of the last episodes in Diyab's memoir, an account of the return of Lucas to Aleppo in 1715. When read against the account in Lucas's travelogue, Diyab's description of this visit suggests that the tale of Ali Baba might have emerged out of stories told by the young Maronite to his French master in which the caves of Aleppo were the hiding place for ruthless thieves and their treasure. Seeking out his old guide and companion on his return to Aleppo in 1715, Lucas insisted that Diyab take him to Khanaqiyyeh, the "cave of the slave," to search for its treasures. Despite the long separation of the two men, Lucas was still driven by the promise of adventure and material gain in an "Oriental tale" of thieves that was very likely told to him by Diyab. Lucas insisted on exploring the caves, clearly expecting that they would yield wonders and dangers similar to those in a story like "Ali Baba and the Forty Thieves." In his travelogue, Lucas attributes these expectations to an unnamed "guide," but the account in Diyab's memoir suggests that it was the Maronite storyteller who was instrumental in encouraging these expectations.[58]

As Diyab was once again drawn into the French traveller's pursuit of marvels in 1715, old tensions between the two men revived. Arriving in Aleppo, Lucas felt the need to reproach Diyab for leaving Paris in 1709 without notice or explanation. For his part, Diyab no doubt harbored some resentment that Lucas had not made good on his promise of employment in the royal library of Louis XIV. Writing his memoir in 1763–1764, Diyab still believed that Lucas had sabotaged his chance to receive his own commission to gather treasures for a French prince. Despite these mutual misgivings, however, the two men quickly fell back into their old habits, resuming their respective roles as master and servant. Diyab relates that he took Lucas on tours of the old city in search of coins, books, precious stones, and other artifacts, just as he used to when he was in Lucas's service.[59]

Lucas was also determined to explore the caves outside Aleppo—apparently fired by the promise of danger and material gain in an unnamed tale about a band of robbers who hoarded their wealth in caves. As he explains in his travelogue, "Of all the stories that I've been told of the people who have died in these caves, those of the robbers who hide there sometimes and who have given this place the name *Connaquie* or the 'cut-throat grotto' seem to me the most likely."[60] In his memoir, Diyab does not claim any responsibility for Lucas's original impulse to explore the cave. Rather, he presents himself as a reluctant guide trying to convince Lucas to abandon his plans to enter this dangerous environment.[61]

Clearly Lucas had taken the tale's intimation of danger seriously, for he arrived at the entrance to the cave with a full array of provisions (including string, torches, and food) and a troop of heavily armed men. This armed entourage suggests that Lucas was expecting a possible encounter with the thieves who peopled these caves in the stories he had heard, but he was deeply disappointed. Lucas admits in his travelogue that he responded by berating his guide, whom he claims had "related" to him that the depth and variety of the grottoes would yield "prodigious things"—"things more curious than he has ever encountered." His guide, he explains, had led him to believe that the caves served "as a refuge for thieves to hide after they had robbed and killed those they encountered on the plain."[62]

Diyab's memoir casts a different light on the "cave of the slave" episode and on his relationship with Lucas. He does not mention Lucas's expectation of encountering thieves or his intense disappointment at finding nothing to show for his efforts. He does, however, highlight Lucas's recklessness. When the Frenchman encounters an obstruction during his exploration of the caves, he orders his servants to load their guns and blast through the encrusted limestone, risking the collapse of the passageway on everyone. Rather than presenting the caves as an abode of bandits, Diyab simply records the explanation of their use provided by a local guide: the caves were not the refuge of versions of "the forty thieves" but were old quarries that served to hide the underground movement of soldiers.[63] Dissatisfied with this prosaic reality, Lucas would come away from this experience with a deep sense of frustration and betrayal, which he vented in a diatribe against the Maronites.[64]

This episode provides evidence that some elements of the stories that were later incorporated into Galland's *Arabian Nights* were part of the exchange of travellers' tales that occurred during the long voyage that Lucas and Diyab made together. Diyab's close relationship with Lucas during these years is more likely to have shaped the Syrian's understanding of a suitable story for a French listener than his brief meetings with Galland near the end of his stay in Paris. When Diyab told Galland the "Tale of Hogia Baba"—the basis for the story of Ali Baba in the *Arabian Nights*—it contained many affinities with the tales of marvellous treasure and disreputable bandits that interested Lucas. In Diyab's story, recorded in Galland's Paris diary, this tale is full of the kind of moral ambiguity that characterized the episode with the corsair captain, and one can easily imagine the fascination with which Lucas might have received it.

The protagonist of Diyab's tale is a poor woodcutter named Hogia Baba who lives in Persia along with his brother, a wealthy merchant named Qasim. One day Hogia Baba is in the forest as usual when forty armed horsemen ride toward him. Hidden in a tree, Hogia Baba watches as the thieves open a door set in a large boulder by pronouncing the words "Open, sesame!" and then disappear inside. Later the thieves emerge from the cave and close the door with the words "Shut, sesame!" When they are gone, Hogia Baba uses the same words to enter the cave, and finds a table set for a meal and a great quantity of silver and gold. After loading his donkeys with bags of gold from the thieves' hideout, Hogia Baba returns home.[65]

Hogia Baba's wife is astounded at what she sees on his return, and rapidly concludes that he has stolen these riches. She borrows a scale from Qasim's wife to weigh the gold, but when she returns it, her sister-in-law finds a piece of gold stuck to the bottom of the pan. When Qasim confronts Hogia Baba, he resists his questions at first, but is eventually forced to tell his brother where he has found so much money. The next day Qasim goes to the forest with two mules. Using the password, he enters the cave and gathers his treasure, but when he wants to leave with his booty he no longer remembers the magic words. The thieves return and take their revenge on Qasim—killing and quartering him.[66]

When Qasim does not come home, his wife goes to Hogia Baba to ask where her husband is. To placate her, Hogia Baba tells her that Qasim might return by nightfall and goes in search of his brother. Returning to the cave with three mules, Hogia Baba finds his brother's body inside. He loads the mules with bags that he has filled with a mixture of gold and body parts, and covers the bags with wood. At home, he tells his sister-in-law everything, and when she begins to cry, he silences her by taking her as a wife. The captain of the thieves discovers who has robbed him and attempts to sneak into Hogia Baba's home with thirty-seven of his men hidden inside empty jars. However, his plan is foiled by the clever slave girl Marjana, who pours hot oil on the hidden men. The final stratagem of the captain of the thieves—an attempt to kill Hogia Baba while in disguise—is again countered by Marjana, who stabs him while performing a seductive dance.[67]

The story of Hogia Baba, told by Diyab to Galland in 1709, drew on common story elements within the cultural environment of the Levant but also diverged in significant ways from the Syrian tales that must have been its original inspiration. According to Aboubakr Chraïbi, the core of the tale is derived from Syrian versions of the tale of the lumberjack and the magic cave, which Diyab may have heard in his youth in the coffeehouses of Aleppo. In these variants, the magical nature of the cave corresponds to the magical nature of its inhabitants, who are either ogres or jinn. By including a table set for a meal in the cave, Diyab's tale retains an element of the appetite test on which the plot of the Syrian tales turn. In the typical version, the jinn set a trap in their cave using a feast as bait. While the lumberjack is able to resist the temptation to eat, his greedy brother stops to indulge himself, forgets the password, and is caught by the jinn. In a similar tale featuring ogres, the poor brother refrains from eating from the dishes laid out in the cave, but his rich brother cannot, and is surprised and killed by the ogres. The moral of these tales implicitly associates wealth with greed and poverty with prudence. Diyab's tale maintains echoes of the appetite test by including the set table, but it does not draw a clear moral distinction. Qasim's downfall is not greed, but rather confusion. Distracted by the sight of the feast before him, Qasim forgets the only type of grain whose name will set him free from the cave—the famous password of "open sesame."[68]

Diyab's most striking improvisation in this story is his decision to replace the jinn and ogres who reside in the cave with a band of thieves. This substitution might be seen as a flaw, for it introduces a logical inconsistency into the tale. It is unclear how the thieves would have come to reside in the magical cave without supernatural beings like jinn or ogres to instruct them. In Diyab's version, Hogia Baba must also overhear the password, presumably through a clumsy mistake on the part of the thieves, rather than learn it from the jinni of the trees, as in the more traditional version of this story.[69] It is worth asking why Diyab would have made such a change, or, if such a variant already existed, why he would prefer it to the tales featuring jinn and ogres. The answer may lie within Diyab's years of travel with Lucas before he told this story to Galland in 1709.

Lucas's own travel writing is filled with real and imagined encounters with such threats, and Diyab may have adopted this framework. In fact it is encounters with thieves in various quantities that provide the narrative thread in Lucas's second travelogue, which covers his years with Diyab. Lucas introduces the threat of bandits early in this volume when he describes an exchange with a local prince in Hungary in which he bravely asserts his willingness to use violence in response to any such threat. Later, as Lucas makes his way through Anatolia in July 1705, peasants warn him that first 60 and then 200 thieves—armed to the teeth—are waiting to attack the caravan.[70] Although Lucas manages to escape this danger, his caravan finally encounters bandits in August 1705 as they travel to Eskişehir. In this instance, Lucas claims that his party of seven men was spotted at a distance by thirty robbers, but he scares them away by bluffing that forty of his own well-armed men are about to join him.[71] In the culminating event, Lucas reports that his caravan was attacked by bandits on Christmas Day 1707. With biting sarcasm, Lucas writes that when he fired a warning shot, his "illustrious companions" became frightened and fled. In this account, Lucas presents himself as behaving with exemplary courage in the face of the threat from thirty well-mounted men. He claims that he shot an advancing robber at the very moment the robber was about to pierce him with a lance, and managed an escape that could only be termed miraculous. The aftermath of this incident bears an eerie resemblance to the exemplary punishment dealt to Qasim, as the bandits spread the rumor that they killed and quartered Lucas as an example to anyone who would brave the thirty horsemen.[72]

As Diyab fell under the influence of Lucas's fabulous stories during those two years of travel, he might have been tempted to substitute the threat posed by bandits for the danger of jinn in the caves of Syria. Given that Diyab's story of Hogia Baba is the first recorded version that contains all of the key elements associated with the tale of Ali Baba—the magic cave, the clever slave girl, and the forty thieves—it is tempting to attribute the distinctive character of his story to the preferences he developed during an extended journey in which plundering artifacts and evading threats from bandits and pirates were constant preoccupations. Hogia Baba seems to breathe the air of Lucas's ambiguous moral universe where treasure was pursued unscrupulously and the threat of bandits was ever-present.

Hogia Baba's curiosity about the contents of the thieves' cave and his determination to gain his fortune by taking a share of their booty would

In his travelogue of the Levant, Paul Lucas reports that his caravan was attacked by bandits on Christmas Day 1707. Lucas claims that when he fired a warning shot, his "illustrious companions" became frightened and fled. He himself displays exemplary courage in the face of the threat from thirty well-mounted men. From Lucas, *Deuxième voyage du sieur Paul Lucas dans le Levant.*

not have disturbed either Diyab or Lucas, given their fascination with local folklore and their familiarity with the deceptions associated with hunting treasure. However, for Galland, the story that Diyab told in Paris in 1709 came with some significant challenges. As he rewrote the tale of Hogia Baba for inclusion in his French version of the *Arabian Nights,* Galland would have to make some alterations if he wanted to shore up the moral foundation for the tale. The French translator had claimed that the *Arabian Nights* stories could serve to edify their readers, but Hogia Baba's successful path to riches was difficult to reconcile with Galland's own religious principles, which associated these blessings with a virtuous life.

When Galland rewrote the tale for publication, he tried to imbue the renamed Ali Baba with some redeeming features, if perhaps unpersuasively. In his retelling, Galland suggests that Ali Baba stole only as much as he needed to provide a comfortable life for his family, and he tries to improve Ali Baba's image by creating a negative foil for him in the character of his brother, Qasim. In Diyab's summary, Qasim takes two mules to the cave to collect its treasures and Hogia Baba takes three, but Galland has Qasim setting out with "ten mules carrying large chests, which he planned to fill and he had even more chests in reserve for a second trip." It is Qasim's excessive greed that leads to his violent end, and Galland assures the reader that "he does not deserve our compassion." In contrast, Galland presents Ali Baba as a forgiving brother: "forgetting what little fraternal love his brother had shown him, he did not hesitate to perform the last rites for his brother." Despite these changes, however, Ali Baba's opportunism shines through the veneer of Galland's moralizing. Ali Baba, like the captain of the forty thieves, remains outside the law. He is content to fake a funeral for Qasim and benefit from violence and criminality to acquire his fortune.[73]

Diyab's version of the story also emphasizes the brutal efficiency rather than the moral superiority of the character who in this version has the greatest claim to being the hero of the tale—Qasim's slave girl, Marjana. While Galland rewrote this story as "Ali Baba and the Forty Thieves: Killed by a Slave," his notes record the title of the story as "Marjana's perspicacity, or the forty thieves killed by the cunning of a slave." It is an appropriate title for this variation on the "clever slave girl" narrative popular in Syrian folklore. In Diyab's tale, the quick thinking of Marjana is key to resolving the dangerous predicament of Hogia Baba, and she is willing to violate moral conventions and religious proscriptions in the process. She not only pays a cobbler to hide the state of Qasim's quartered corpse, but she also lies to the attendants of the mosque when she assures them that Qasim's body has been properly washed and prepared for burial. When she discovers the presence of the thieves hidden in the jars in Hogia Baba's courtyard, her instinct is to take the law into her own hands rather than risk the involvement of local authorities who might question Hogia Baba's newfound fortune. Once she has dispatched the thieves with hot oil, she assists Hogia Baba in burying them in the courtyard to eliminate the evidence. Similarly, when Marjana cleverly divines the presence of the disguised captain of the forty thieves in the house of her new master, she eliminates the danger personally—this time with her dagger. Marjana is rewarded for her efforts by being given to Hogia Baba's son in marriage. Over time,

Hogia Baba moves all his gold and valuables to a safe hiding spot and "they live happy and content."[74]

In his version of the story, Galland, a man of serious religious conviction, tries to explain the success of the clever slave girl by drawing on something akin to a belief in predestination. She was, it seems, destined for higher things in life. When Marjana realizes that the thieves have infiltrated Ali Baba's house by hiding in jars, she does not panic, for she is "of superior stock. . . . She grasped the need to remedy the situation swiftly and quietly, and thanks to her intelligence, she saw at once how this could be done."[75] Galland, however, cannot hide the ruthless expediency that defines her character. If Hogia Baba is defined by opportunism, Marjana is defined by her ruses. These characters might have delighted a listener like Lucas, but they were very difficult for Galland to adapt to the conventions of French literary culture. Galland would add morals to Diyab's tales, but it was a challenge to make the orphan tales read like French fairy tales or blend them seamlessly with translations of the original Arabic tales.

The story of Hogia Baba reveals the way in which the orphan tales were anchored not only in the storytelling culture of Aleppo but in the mutual exchange of stories during Diyab's journey through the Levant with Lucas. Just as Lucas picked up tales from Diyab to include in his travelogue, Diyab may have borrowed important motifs from the French traveller's own tales. At the very least, Lucas shaped Diyab's sense of what a French collector of curiosities might have liked in a story, and thereby influenced the stories that Diyab related to Galland in the spring of 1709. In integrating these stories into his version of the *Arabian Nights,* Galland would have to confront the distinct resistances that emerged from the complex intertwining of the story elements contained within them.

✦ ✦ ✦

On the basis of these neglected sources from Lucas and Diyab, one can at last piece together the contentious relationship of false promises and mutual deception that shaped Diyab's storytelling in those crucial years before he arrived in Paris and entered the history of the *Arabian Nights.*

While once regarded as only a supplier of raw material to the creator of the *Arabian Nights* in French literature, Diyab now emerges as an author in his own right. The new evidence of his memoir attests to his skill as a storyteller, and allows us to recognize the creativity of the first recorded teller of "Ali Baba." It also allows us to appreciate the forgotten role of another figure in crafting the orphan tales: the French treasure hunter whose travels and adventures exerted a distinct influence on how Diyab would narrate his stories for a European listener.

It is tempting to imagine that Lucas might have seen himself in the story of Ali Baba—the thief who steals from thieves and then escapes their clutches. Or perhaps Diyab hoped his French listener would contemplate the relative merit of master and servant in the story of the faithful and resourceful Marjana. Unfortunately, Lucas was more rogue than hero, and his relationship with Diyab ended with all his promises of advancement and prosperity unfulfilled. Six to seven years after Diyab first told the tale of Hogia Baba, the only trace in Lucas's memory seems to have been the promise of riches buried in a bandit's cave, a prize that he was certain Diyab had located in the caves outside Aleppo.

Lucas's final reference to Diyab in his travelogues is a dramatic demonstration of resentment and incomprehension. The French traveller follows his account of exploring the caves with an extraordinary tirade against Diyab and the entire Maronite community. Having enjoyed the hospitality of Diyab's family, Lucas mocks the guest rooms of the best Maronite houses and the food offered to guests. Despite the role played by Eastern Christians as intermediaries in Orientalist institutions in Paris, he proclaims them incapable of learning and scholarship. He recounts with disdain the opinion of one Maronite familiar with the freedoms of women in France (presumably Diyab) who nonetheless persists in defending the segregation of men and women within his community in Aleppo. Above all, Lucas does not understand why these Christians should be content to live meekly in a state of "captivity" in an Islamic empire.[76] As Lucas ends his travelogue, he seems consumed with anxieties about the potential for Ottoman aggression in the Mediterranean. Posters on the streets of Aleppo in September 1715 call men to the Ottoman campaign against the Venetians and promise them beautiful Christian slave women as their reward. Ottoman troop movements in Greece suggest that an army of 400,000 is ready to sweep across Europe.[77]

Although the tale of "Ali Baba" traveled from Syria to the ears of Galland in Paris through the mediation of Diyab and Lucas, this did not necessarily reflect a degree of understanding or tolerance on behalf of any of its transmitters: storyteller, interlocutor, or author. Arguably "Ali Baba" traveled *because* of the shared circumstances of mutual suspicion and personal ambition. Lucas's false promises were an important part of Diyab's decision to follow him to Paris, where he passed on the tales that Galland's edition of the *Arabian Nights* would make famous. The same kind of deceit animates Diyab's tales, in which roguish characters like Ali Baba and the Maghrebi magician of "Aladdin" carry echoes of Diyab's fascination with Lucas. Something of the context of amorality and violence that characterized Diyab's travels survives in these tales even after Galland's stylish adaptation of the stories to meet French expectations of an Oriental tale. Translators and scholars of the *Thousand and One Nights* often search for evidence that ties the development of the story collection to Moorish Andalusia and its fabled, and often exaggerated, peace between Jews, Christians, and Muslims. However, the origins of "Ali Baba and the Forty Thieves," and the story of its secret author and his audience, attest to the tensions that shaped the passage of these tales into the European corpus of the *Arabian Nights*.

3

THE EMPIRE OF ENGLISH

WORKING AGAINST THE BACKDROP of rising tensions on the northern frontiers of Britain's Indian empire, Henry Torrens, a secretary in the colonial administration, provided English readers with a grand epic of the clash between Muslims and Christians in his new translation of the *Arabian Nights* (1838). For those familiar with the countless English versions of the story collection based on Antoine Galland's French edition, this dramatic story cycle would have been a surprise. The tale of "King 'Umar ibn al-Nu'man and His Family," a complex family saga set in a period of constant conflict between Muslims, Byzantines, and Crusaders, did not appear in Galland's Arabic manuscript or in the versions of his English imitators.[1]

In this story cycle, Sharkan, the son of the king of Baghdad, is sent with his army to battle the king of Rum at the request of his father's ally, the king of Byzantium. Wandering into the lands of Rum, Sharkan encounters his enemy's daughter, the Christian princess Abriza. The bold and martial princess challenges him to wrestle, and quickly throws him to the ground since Sharkan is distracted by her "full figure of crystal, softly undulating." Entranced by Abriza's beauty, "his soul had no mastery over a single sense."[2] To win her affection, the smitten Sharkan aptly recites a poem in praise of the struggle for love:

An illustration by Mirzâ 'Ali-Qoli Kho'i from the tale of King 'Umar ibn al-Nu'man from an 1855 Persian edition of the *Arabian Nights*. Henry Torrens was the first to include this Romantic epic of the Crusades in an English translation of the story collection.

> "Fight in the holy war, Jumeel!" they say—
> What war save for the fair should I essay
> For each tradition speaks with them delight,
> And each man slain dies martyred in that fight.[3]

Through the confession of his beloved, Sharkan discovers that the Christian rulers of Rum and Byzantium have invented their feud as part of a plot to entrap him. The king of Baghdad had taken a daughter of the king of Byzantium as his concubine, and the aggrieved king plans to hold Sharkan hostage to bargain for her return. Out of love, Abriza protects Sharkan from her father's knights so he can return home safely.

Yet just as Sharkan and his men reach their own lands, they confront a band of one hundred Christian horsemen led by a knight with a face like the new moon, with "no budding hair upon his countenance." One by one the Christians engage the Muslims in single combat, until they have captured twenty of Sharkan's men. The next morning, Sharkan rides out to challenge the Christian leader, and as they battle, it is "as 'twere two mountains clashed, or two oceans dashing, together." When their duel ends in a draw, Sharkan tells his men, " 'Tis my wish that there were his like in our army, and the like of his comrades." Much to his surprise, Sharkan discovers that the formidable knight is none other than the princess Abriza and the formidable horsemen are her handmaidens. After witnessing his "prowess in the field" and "constancy in fight," the princess and her companions join Sharkan in his journey back to Baghdad.[4]

The plot of "King 'Umar" is remarkably suited to the Romantic sensibilities of an early nineteenth-century readership that thirsted after the historical novels of writers like Sir Walter Scott. This story of love against the backdrop of violent warfare contains all the action and pathos that a reader might desire—and much of the poetry for which the *Arabian Nights* was known. Arabic romances like "King 'Umar" have much in common with contemporary European romances and chansons de geste, which contain similar battles and romantic intrigues. Likely a product of the Crusades of the thirteenth century, the story cycle also employs all the stereotypes of Muslim and Christian difference to be expected within this historical context. The happy joining of a Muslim prince and Christian princess is interrupted when Sharkan is sent to become the governor of Damascus and Abriza is left behind in Baghdad. Her beauty attracts the attention of King 'Umar, and when she refuses his advances, he drugs and rapes her. Pregnant, she flees Baghdad and gives birth to her child in the desert. When she rejects the sexual advances of her slave, he kills her. Abriza's Christian grandmother swears to avenge her death by murdering King 'Umar. Instructing six beautiful girls in Muslim theology and disguising herself as a pious woman, she enters the court at Baghdad. While her protégées distract the king with their prodigious religious knowledge, she poisons him. This in turn incites Sharkan to wage a war of vengeance against the

Christian kings. The tale that begins as a romance of chivalry and love thus becomes the dramatic struggle of King 'Umar's family to unite and reconquer lands taken by their Christian foes.[5]

Torrens first came across the tale of Sharkan and Abriza while translating a newly discovered Arabic manuscript of the *Thousand and One Nights* in 1836–1837, and he was the first to include it in an English version of the story collection. Since Galland's translation of the *Arabian Nights* into French, numerous English versions of the collection had appeared, but these were largely cheap Grub Street editions based on Galland's work. Jonathan Scott's *Arabian Nights Entertainments* (1811) was a more ambitious translation of Galland's French version, with the insertion of a few additional tales from an Indian manuscript, and its success inspired other popular versions of the *Arabian Nights*.[6] Most histories of the *Arabian Nights* credit Edward Lane as the first translator to take on the challenge of producing a full English translation from an Arabic original; however, Torrens had begun the same project in colonial India a year before Lane. While Lane waited for his Egyptian collaborator to annotate sections of the Arabic edition of the *Thousand and One Nights* published in Egypt so he could proceed with his volumes of translation (published 1838–1840), Torrens had the advantage of access to a more extensive manuscript version of the tales, which had come into the possession of the Royal Asiatic Society of Bengal. As the editing and printing of this Arabic manuscript proceeded in India, Torrens produced the first volume of an English translation in 1838.[7]

Although Torrens's translation has been largely forgotten in the history of the *Arabian Nights,* its production within the context of Indian colonial history is critical for an understanding of the evolution of the story collection in English. Shaped by Torrens's own interest in the expressive qualities of Arabic poetry, the translation was fundamentally connected to the elaborate process of collecting, editing, and translating Oriental texts that was part of the apparatus of British rule. As officials of the East India Company sought to acquire and systematize knowledge of the peoples now under their control, religious and literary texts became a vital resource. Eighteenth-century Orientalists like Sir William Jones, who combined administrative positions with scholarly ambitions, promoted the study of "Indology" both within and beyond the subcontinent. At the College of Fort William in Calcutta, professors and their local assistants—known as *munshis*—systematically studied and taught classical Oriental languages such as Sanskrit, Arabic, and Persian and standardized the vernacular languages of the subcontinent. In the work of these scholars and scribes, the complex linguistic environment of India was reduced to clearly distinguishable categories, and in the process a distinct Indian culture identified with Sanskrit and Hinduism was separated from the Persian and Arabic traditions that had been an essential part of the cultural mixture of northern India.[8]

As a product of the College of Fort William and an active member of the Royal Asiatic Society of Bengal, Torrens was inevitably caught up in these colonial processes of knowledge production and in the famous debates regarding educational policy as a component of imperial rule. Torrens and his collaborator on the *Thousand and One Nights* project, William Hay Macnaghten, were counted among the "Orientalist" contingent of colonial officials who remained committed to using vernacular languages to reach their Indian subjects. Against them were ranged the "Anglicists," who, like Thomas Babbington Macauley in the famous "Minute on Indian Education," argued for an English-language education in Western literature and science. Despite the apparent victory of Macauley's approach in 1835, the "great Indian education debate" continued for decades, and Orientalists in colonial India continued to pursue their own priorities and jockey for power and resources.[9] The involvement of Torrens and Macnaghten in editing and translating the Arabic manuscript of the *Thousand and One Nights* that came to light in 1836 must be seen as part of the commitment of the Orientalist contingent to preserving texts in the classical languages of South Asia and "gifting" them to the local population as laudable examples of the distinctive cultural traditions of this colonial territory.

This rhetorical emphasis on the need for British colonial intervention to create an Indian literary canon ignored the multiplicity of overlapping writing cultures within the polyglot environment of South Asia. The *Thousand and One Nights* was already circulating in manuscript versions in Persian and Urdu; however, the printing of a new Arabic version and the publication of a new translation into English had the potential to fundamentally alter the way in which the story collection was read in colonial India. While Torrens believed the stories of the *Thousand and One Nights* spoke to certain universal passions, his translation was presented primarily as exemplifying the distinctive spirit of the Arab people and their religion and could only help solidify the categories through which the subcontinent was increasingly understood. As Orientalists within and beyond India began to identify an indigenous Indian society with Hinduism, castes, and a Hindi vernacular, the distinctive association of the *Thousand and One Nights* with an Arab, Persian, and Islamic cultural domain would register the otherness of this literary legacy. Within this context, the clear categories of religious division embodied in the Crusaders tale that Torrens included in his *Arabian Nights* paralleled the new categories of religious and cultural identity that were being created through the scholarly texts and translations produced by Orientalist scholarship in India.[10]

Torrens's translation of the *Arabian Nights* remained unfinished, and this alone might explain the neglect into which it has fallen, but it is the invisible thread that weaves through the history of the *Arabian Nights* in English. The close connection between the production of this text and the apparatus of colonial rule highlights critical features of the English translations that followed in the nineteenth century. Like Torrens, Lane translated the *Arabian Nights* with the understanding that it represented the distinctive character of the Arab people, which he associated with an Egyptian provenance. Richard Burton would follow Torrens closely in rooting his version in the distinctive culture of Arabia and the particular expressive power of Arabic poetry. He, like Torrens, came to the stories through an early education in the languages and cultures of India, and this would leave an indelible imprint on his translation. Perhaps most importantly, however, the traces of Torrens's translation of the *Arabian Nights* remain embedded in the works of Burton and his early collaborator John Payne because both felt entitled to borrow liberally from it. An *Arabian Nights* produced for the distinctive purposes of the servants of empire thus became part of a staple text of world literature in English.

✦ ✦ ✦

Torrens arrived in India in 1828 to take up a writership that would lead to a diplomatic position within the colonial administration. His life until this point had been characterized by false starts and missed opportunities, despite the raw talent that was evident to everyone who knew him. A product of a military family, he showed no inclination to follow the strict discipline of the career of his father, Major General Sir Henry Torrens. At Oxford his academic abilities were unmistakable, but according to his biographer, James Hume, "his active imagination and his animal spirits" interfered with "the staid and steady course of scholastic life which he *should* have doubtless followed." He would be sent home from Christ Church College (along with two sons of the Duke of Wellington) for painting the doors of all the buildings a bright scarlet. When he finally completed his degree, he entered the Inner Temple at the prompting of his father, but found the legal profession unsuited to "his imaginative mind and lively and sociable disposition."[11]

In India Torrens found a relatively congenial environment in which to develop his intellectual abilities and express his high spirits. Hume claims that he became "an accomplished Oriental scholar ere he had been ten years in the East."[12] Even those contemporaries who took Torrens to task for his role in launching the ill-fated British invasion of Afghanistan in 1839 acknowledged his linguistic gifts:

> Perhaps there was not in all the presidencies of India a man—certainly not so young a man—with the lustre of so many accomplishments upon him. The facility with which he acquired every kind of information was scarcely more remarkable than the tenacity with which he retained it. With the languages of the East and the West he was equally familiar. He had read books of all kinds and in all tongues, and the airy grace with which he could throw off a French canzonet was something as perfect of its kind as the military genius with which he could sketch out the plan of a campaign, or the official pomp with which he could inflate a state paper.[13]

Entering the colonial bureaucracy in India under Lord William Bentinck, Torrens showed his ability by acquiring a series of Oriental languages, including Arabic, Persian, and Hindustani. His reputation as a linguist was so great that when he toured India from 1837 to 1840 with George Eden, Lord of Auckland, the governor general, local princes and dignitaries often requested him by name to interpret for them.[14]

Torrens arrived in India with a set of political convictions that placed him among the liberal reformers who looked to Lord William Bentinck (governor general from 1828 to 1835) for leadership. A vocal contributor to political debates in British India, Torrens was also active in developing the institutional basis for an Anglo-Indian public sphere. In 1832 Torrens collaborated with Henry Miers Elliot, another Indian civil servant, to establish the first newspaper in the Upper Provinces—the *Meerut Observer.* Torrens would be a regular contributor to this newspaper, as well as several others, during his time in India—addressing political issues and sharing examples of his literary efforts, including a novel serialized in the *Calcutta Star.* Torrens's breadth of interest and ability was much admired by his contemporaries. One of the earliest accounts of periodical literature in colonial India numbers Torrens, Elliot, and the poet Henry Meredith Parker as "three of the greatest . . . that ever did credit to our Anglo-Indian periodical literature." W. F. B. Laurie judged that Torrens's "general ability, for writing on any subject . . . appears to have seldom been surpassed by those to whom literature was not a profession." He might not have been the poet that his friend Parker was, but "he had quite as much quickness and versatility of mind."[15] Torrens would develop a strong friendship with Hume, the editor of the *Morning Star* and the *Eastern Star* (both out of Calcutta), and it would be Hume who would write a biography of Torrens after his death and edit some of his work for a two-volume publication.[16]

Posted to Calcutta in 1835, Torrens threw himself wholeheartedly into public debates about freedom of the press and the use of trial by jury after the appointment of Lord Metcalfe as interim governor-general. When a new liberal Press Act was instituted by Metcalfe in August 1835, Torrens joined in the celebrations. In a speech at Calcutta Town Hall on September 5, 1835, he stressed the vital importance of freedom of the press in developing a public sphere in which "the native community" was "capable of reading the history of passing events [and] of commenting rationally on the proceedings of government." With these new freedoms,

Henry Torrens, the first translator of the Arabic manuscript of the *Thousand and One Nights* identified in Calcutta in 1836. He was a colonial official, poet, musician, actor, and satirist. From C. Grant, *Lithographic Sketches of the Public Characters of Calcutta* (1850).

the community would now enjoy "a means of self-redress, by bringing the story of their wrongs before the tribunal of the governing power and of the public at once." Applying the rhetorical skill that he had honed in his professional life, Torrens credited this victory to the influence exerted by "the progress of liberal opinions" in Europe. "The influx of popular feelings throughout so large a portion of civilized Europe has insensibly affected even our remote and semi-barbarous community," Torrens claimed. Perhaps inspired by recent revolutions in France, he celebrated "those feelings . . . actuated by which men unarmed, friendless, poor, and powerless, have by combination and by union overthrown the thrones of kings, destroyed the impiously arrogated divine right to hereditary tyranny, and demonstrated the post of chief magistrate of a people to be in truth a merely elective one, held on the tenure of the people."[17]

Torrens's speech on this occasion reveals an optimistic belief that the liberal values of an English political tradition could temper imperial power in India. He declared himself grateful that the "autocrat delegated to maintain that despotic power has been an Englishman himself, subject to the superior control of elective assemblies, and compelled to admit in his policy something of the principle which regulates the acts of his nation's rulers."[18] Well aware of the anxieties that the lifting of restrictions on the Indian press had generated within the colonial ruling class, Torrens directly addressed the concern that the native press would be "employed against the stability of our government." While sensitive to these concerns, Torrens asserted his confidence that the people of India would exercise their rights responsibly, understanding "that the advantage of the power now conceded to them must consist in its use, not in its abuse." The political significance of this freedom could not be underestimated, according to Torrens. The Indian people would now "enjoy a means of self-redress, by bringing the story of their wrongs before the tribunal of the governing power and of the public at one, and at the same time." This freedom did put a political weapon in the hands of the empire's subjects, and Torrens was sensible enough to the dangers of despotism to provide this implicit warning to the governing authorities that he himself served: "The native press may oppose hereafter the ruling power, but it will only be when the political misdeeds of that power shall have armed and given energy to the agents of opposition."[19]

Torrens remained deeply committed to his liberal principles, which he continued to express with sincerity and eloquence in the burgeoning local press of the early nineteenth century. Hume, who was most familiar with Torrens's frequent contributions to local newspapers, admits that these articles may have made him enemies. While he did not write "against the Government," Hume argues that Torrens "had a manliness of spirit that scouted the idea of being slave to any man's humours because he was a public servant." Disregarding the prerequisites for advancement in the colonial service, Torrens insisted on his own independence and repeatedly expressed what his biographer lauds as "a noble disregard for authority and great names where he thought they were doing, or giving sanction to, injustice."[20] He was also infamous for his squibs—short humorous or satirical pieces delivered at social gatherings or in the press. Hume argues that "they were full of fun, not mischief, and he could not help it," but during his time in India Torrens would use his satirical talents to skewer a wide variety of targets, from the architects of India's educational policy to the creative inventions of Orientalist philologists.[21]

Torrens found a nurturing environment for his strongly held ideals in the world of Indian Freemasonry. The Freemasons were a part of the British Empire around the globe, and in India they had enjoyed a symbiotic relationship with the governing authorities for a time. A series of governors-general, including Charles Cornwallis, Richard Wellesley, and Warren Hastings, were members. Beyond this governing elite, the members of this fraternal association were drawn from the British army and from the civil servants, lawyers, merchants, and doctors that made up the European population of the territories. Torrens seems to have joined the Lodge of Hope in Meerut sometime before 1835, along with his friend Elliot, and he continued his involvement with Freemasonry as he served at other locations in India. When he was posted to Simla in 1838, he joined with a number of other "brothers" to establish the Lodge Himalayan Brotherhood, and on his return to Calcutta in 1840 he became a member of the Lodge of Industry and Perseverance and the Lodge Anchors and Hope. He took on the responsibility of holding a series of offices within this society, and in his last lodge, the St. John Lodge in Calcutta, he served as senior warden for a number of years.[22]

Masons in India, as elsewhere, expressed a belief in the existence of a supreme being and a commitment to a cosmopolitan creed based on universal brotherhood, toleration, and benevolence. This philosophy could take on a particular edge on the frontiers of the empire. Appointed as governor-general of India in 1813, Francis Rawdon-Hastings, Earl of Moira, would happily insist that Masonry was critical to relieving "the despotism, the ferocity, the degradation of manhood in the Asiatic regions."[23] The active involvement of Freemasons in philanthropic endeavors would have been visible in Calcutta, Madras, and Bombay through press reports and public ceremonies, and these symbolic gestures even reached into the mountains of the north. In June 1839 on the Feast of the Nativity of Saint John the Baptist, the brothers of the Lodge Himalayan Brotherhood formed the first public Masonic procession ever seen on the Himalayan mountains. After attending a "Divine Service," they held a private banquet where Torrens sang a song he had composed for the occasion.[24] Torrens was an active participant in the activities of the Masons and often offered his talents as a poet and songwriter to enliven the proceedings. His collected works include several examples of verse produced for the ceremonial life of the lodge, and suggest that this social environment provided an outlet for some of Torrens's creative energy. In his song lyrics, Torrens lauded Masonry as the "spirit that set'st man's best feeling in motion" and the "truest of bonds, that stand'st firm to the test."[25]

During the 1830s, Freemasons in India would be under pressure to take their cosmopolitan tolerance as far as admitting native members who might be Muslim, Parsi, or Hindu.[26] While Torrens's involvement in these debates is unclear, one surviving piece of evidence suggests that he stood among those Freemasons who supported a firmer commitment to the principle of fraternity. The Library of Freemasonry in London still holds a copy of the lyrics that Brother Torrens wrote in tribute to Dr. James Burnes, the provincial grand master for western India. The lyrics appear to have been set to music by William Henry Hamerton, an accomplished musician and member of several Calcutta lodges.[27] Dr. Burnes, a medical officer for the East India Company, was openly supportive of admitting qualified Indians, for, he argued, it could spread "a truer knowledge of the Great Architect of the universe, and more just notions of their duty to each other" among "the natives of this mighty empire."[28] However, when Maneckji Cursetji, a respected Parsi official, sought admission to Burnes's own lodge (the Lodge of Perseverance) in Bombay in 1840, he was refused. Burnes only succeeded in imposing his view in 1843 when a new lodge was established, the Lodge Rising Star of Western India, which welcomed native members. Torrens's song in welcome of Burnes was performed at the Provincial Grand Lodge of Bengal on August 17, 1840, during the controversy regarding the admission of native members. It assures the embattled Burnes that had he "wandered among us, all penniless, poor, / With no hope on the ocean, no home on the land," he would still be as welcome in his "moment of woe" as on the present glad occasion. Within this context, Torrens's verse expresses his loyalty to Burnes and to the principles of equality that he believed were embodied in the brotherhood of Masons.[29]

Even while Torrens pursued his political interests and supported the life of the Freemasons in India, he was constantly occupied with his own literary projects. As a writer and translator, Torrens had a deep investment in Romanticism, which inspired his efforts as both a poet and a dramatist. In Calcutta he was known for adapting popular literary works for the stage, and organizing British expatriates in amateur performances. His collected writings include a series of verses meant for staging two works by Sir Walter Scott: *The Talisman,* a tale of the Crusades featuring Richard the Lionhearted and Saladin, and *Ivanhoe,* a tale of corrupt nobles and idealistic bandits set in twelfth-century England. Emily Eden, the sister of Governor-General Lord Auckland, also records a series of entertainments produced by Torrens in Simla in 1838, as British forces advanced to Kabul and their ally Shah Shuja took Kandahar. In addition to staging scenes from *Ivanhoe,* Torrens recited verses from Lord Byron's poem *The Corsair* and performed songs he had written for a version of Scott's *Kenilworth.*[30]

Torrens also made a considerable investment in honing his skills as a translator—often turning to the German Romantics for models and source material for these efforts. His collected works include a series of translations of poems by Friedrich Schiller that pay tribute to the sublime quality of the poet's art and the writer's idealistic pursuit of truth.[31] In his version of Schiller's "Hope," Torrens's idealism shows through:

No empty flattering vision this,
In madman's moping brain begot,
Hope speaks in hearts what her being is:
We all are born to a better lot;
And that which the inward voice hath told
Can never delude the hopeful-souled.[32]

Torrens also made a study of Schiller's translations of Shakespeare, and translated a piece of the fourth act of Schiller's drama *The Robbers*, whose critique of aristocratic corruption clearly appealed to his political temperament. In contrast to Galland's application of classical aesthetics in his translation of the *Arabian Nights*, Torrens approached the task of translation with the German Romantic's goal of capturing the expressive quality of the original text as fully as possible. The task of drawing out the imaginative and emotional qualities of a foreign text in another language was a source of fascination for Torrens: "It is, and to all appearance ever must be, one of the mysteries of language, the power of relative verbal affection. The sentence I repeat in one tongue makes you weep; translate it ever so exactly into another, and the words are either meaningless, or merely risible."[33] In taking on this challenge, Torrens sought to produce a translation that might somehow capture the distinctive spirit of the original source and its cultural context.

In pursuing the art of translation and defending the value of poetry, Torrens felt himself to be pushing back against the strong tendencies toward empiricism within English culture. In the "Age of Matter of Fact," which was dominated by the search for the "useful and the profitable," Torrens argued for the value of "lighter literature," which alone could "give posterity real insight into what were [a nation's] domestic manners, and familiar habits of thinking." History, with its focus on political events, often missed what was most important in a culture, and the traveller seldom stayed long enough in one place to "have imbibed something of the individuality of the people." The only alternative for someone seeking real knowledge, Torrens contended, was to turn to the "poet" and the "dramatist." Against the trend to produce novels based on "the events of the day" or the principles of "political economy," he argued for the value of translating works that were considered alien to the contemporary ethos of realism. He lamented the lack of interest in fantasy and fiction in an era dedicated to "improvement," where the "whole tribe of giants and hippogriffs, dwarfs and enchanters" had been banished to "the nursery and servant's hall."[34]

Torrens argued that within the literature of the medieval world these elements of the "marvellous" were not just silly fantasies but evidence of the barriers to cultural comprehension within that culture. For the chivalric poets, Torrens argued, these sorceries and enchantments were just a way of explaining the endless frustration of their "soldiers of the Cross" when faced with defeat at the hands of "their barbarous foeman." Instead of acknowledging the superior ability of pagan Celts or Muslim Saracens, medieval authors were forced to depict their Christian heroes as "baffled and beguiled by the blandishments of beauty, created at the will of an enchanter, or assailed by some monstrous creature, serpent, dragon or griffin, who can only be overcome by the staunchest knight, fighting for his true faith, and the lady of his love." In this spirit, the insights gained through translation were vital, and Torrens offered his translation of Matteo Maria Boiardo's *Orlando Innamorato* as an example of what a faithful rendering of a medieval text could achieve—despite the claim by others that it was untranslatable.[35]

Torrens complained about the increasing influence of Evangelical Christianity within British India, and the program of moral improvement that it brought with it. Against the puritan spirit of these reformers, Torrens defended the importance of artistic freedom. In one response to a published critique of the state of theater, Torrens denounced those "phlegmatic spirits" who out of "an innate coarseness of mind" see "sin in what to us seems innocent, . . . impiety in the aspiration of the poet, and sexuality in the nude coldness of the statuary's marble." This, Torrens proclaimed, is "not purity, but prurience, a constitutional defect of the imagination."[36] In his novel *Madame de Malguet,* he offered a rather daring meditation on issues of liberty and equality through a heroine who was explicitly defined in terms of qualities conventionally seen as masculine. In these writings, one can easily spy the translator who believed that the *Thousand and One Nights* should be translated in its entirety, in defiance of those who found the sexual content and the

"Amazonian heroine" of the Crusader tale of Sharkan and Abriza too much for their taste.[37]

In the world of colonial India, Torrens was a figure who aroused both admiration and harsh criticism. His biographer felt the need to defend him against the many detractors who saw him as vain: "Slight in figure, with long, dark, curly hair which reached his shoulders, and with a manner more foreign than English, the impression of him very commonly was that he was a fop: with those whom he knew but did not like, he was somewhat cold and reserved, perhaps haughty; but in general society he was always lively and agreeable, and with his intimates the life and soul of every meeting."[38] There is no doubt that Torrens was often frustrated by his position as a colonial civil servant, feeling himself to be better suited to an intellectual life in a more vital cultural center. Within professional circles he had serious critics, and some would blame the "Bengal clique" for Torrens's ultimate lack of success. However, even his biographer and good friend Hume could not help but point out that the persistent doubts about his judgment and discretion had some foundation. The writer who could display "an acute perception of the most delicate shades of character" was in real life "not always clear in his reading of men nor wise in his confidencies."[39]

✦ ✦ ✦

The *Arabian Nights* was already part of the common language of the colonial elite of India when Torrens began his translation. Unauthorized Grub Street translations of Galland's version had enchanted the English imagination and inspired a multitude of sequels, imitations, and parodies. The *Arabian Nights* had become the favored prism through which to view the East, and countless visitors to India would find traces of it in the exotic settings they encountered there. Emily Eden, who accompanied her brother Lord Auckland to India, would write in 1837 of narrow alleys and "wretched-looking houses" where marvellous gold brocades were sold by men who "looked as if they were cut out of the 'Arabian Nights.'"[40] On this journey "up country," Macnaghten and Torrens took on the task of translation and diplomacy for the new governor-general, Auckland, and his two sisters. The women found the formal rituals of meetings with local leaders dull, but had occasional glimpses of the Oriental worlds that they had already imagined through stories of the East. Eden records a breakfast given by the prince of Lucknow "which was quite as Arabian-Nightish as I meant it to be," with plenty of musicians, jugglers, and nautch girls presided over by a prince dressed to match the golden canopy of his throne, which boasted an embroidery of pearls and rubies.[41] Torrens became a much-valued friend to the Eden sisters on this journey by organizing social events to keep them amused and finding Emily local subjects to draw. Her many sketches from this trip represent a panorama of Indian types seen through the popular Orientalism of the English traveller.[42]

The production of a fresh English translation of the *Thousand and One Nights* in colonial India was prompted by the appearance of a new Arabic manuscript in 1836 in the estate of a Major Turner Macan, a British officer known for producing the first complete edition of the Persian epic poem *Shahnameh*. When the new manuscript was offered to the Royal Asiatic Society of Bengal for its appraisal, the chain of circumstances that led to the appearance of Torrens's first volume of the *Arabian Nights* began.[43] While this translation has been largely forgotten, the Arabic text on which it is based has continued to shape translations of the stories. The Macan manuscript—known, after editing, as the Calcutta II or the Macnaghten text—is considered by some to be the most comprehensive and the most literary version of the *Thousand and One Nights*. While Galland had been frustrated by the incompleteness of his Arabic source, the manuscript that Macnaghten edited and Torrens translated contained a full 1,001 nights of storytelling—including the lengthy crusader saga of King 'Umar. Later translators, from Burton in the late nineteenth century to Malcolm Lyons in the twenty-first century, have returned to the Arabic text that Torrens was the first to translate, but few of these translators, and virtually none of their readers, would have understood the extent to which the production of this edition of the collection was intertwined with British strategies of rule in India.[44]

The environment in which the Macan manuscript was evaluated, printed, and translated was marked by the struggle between Orientalists and Anglicists for control over educational policy in colonial India. The early dominance of the Orientalist faction was rooted in a series of institutions representing the nexus of education, scholarship, and government within British colonial rule. First among them was the College of Fort William at Calcutta, established in 1800 by Governor-General Wellesley on the principle that expertise in Oriental languages and culture was the foundation for good governance in India. Drawing on eighteenth-century precedents set by Governor-General Hastings, Orientalists associated with Fort William stressed the value of Arabic, Sanskrit, and Persian and the importance of accommodating local customs in British colonial policy. They argued that the colonial government should support the recovery and preservation of the classical culture of India and train a cadre of British civil servants who could operate in collaboration with local elites. At the beginning of the nineteenth century, Fort William was the base for a group of Oriental-language experts, including John Gilchrist, Edward Warring, William Carey, and Henry Colebrook, who collaborated with dozens of munshis to pursue translation and lexicographical projects relating to the classical and vernacular languages of India. As the source of the hundreds of textbooks and literary translations used to train a generation of colonial servants, Fort William was critical in standardizing the languages of colonial India and creating a canon of world literature that included select classical texts from these traditions.[45]

The Orientalists had another bastion of support in the Royal Asiatic Society of Bengal, which was founded by the Orientalist scholar Jones in 1784. This society had a largely amateur membership drawn from members of the British colonial elite who found time to pursue their personal interests in the history, philology, religion, and geography of the region, and to publish the results in the society's journal. Like the language specialists at Fort William, the society's members sought to make their own contributions to the systematization of knowledge about a territory they assumed was unknown by collecting and studying the coins, inscriptions, and manuscripts that they found in the course of their lives in India. Both Macnaghten and Torrens were active members of the Asiatic Society despite the many professional duties that they are juggled. Macnaghten served as a vice president until his duties took him from Calcutta, and Torrens served as the secretary of the

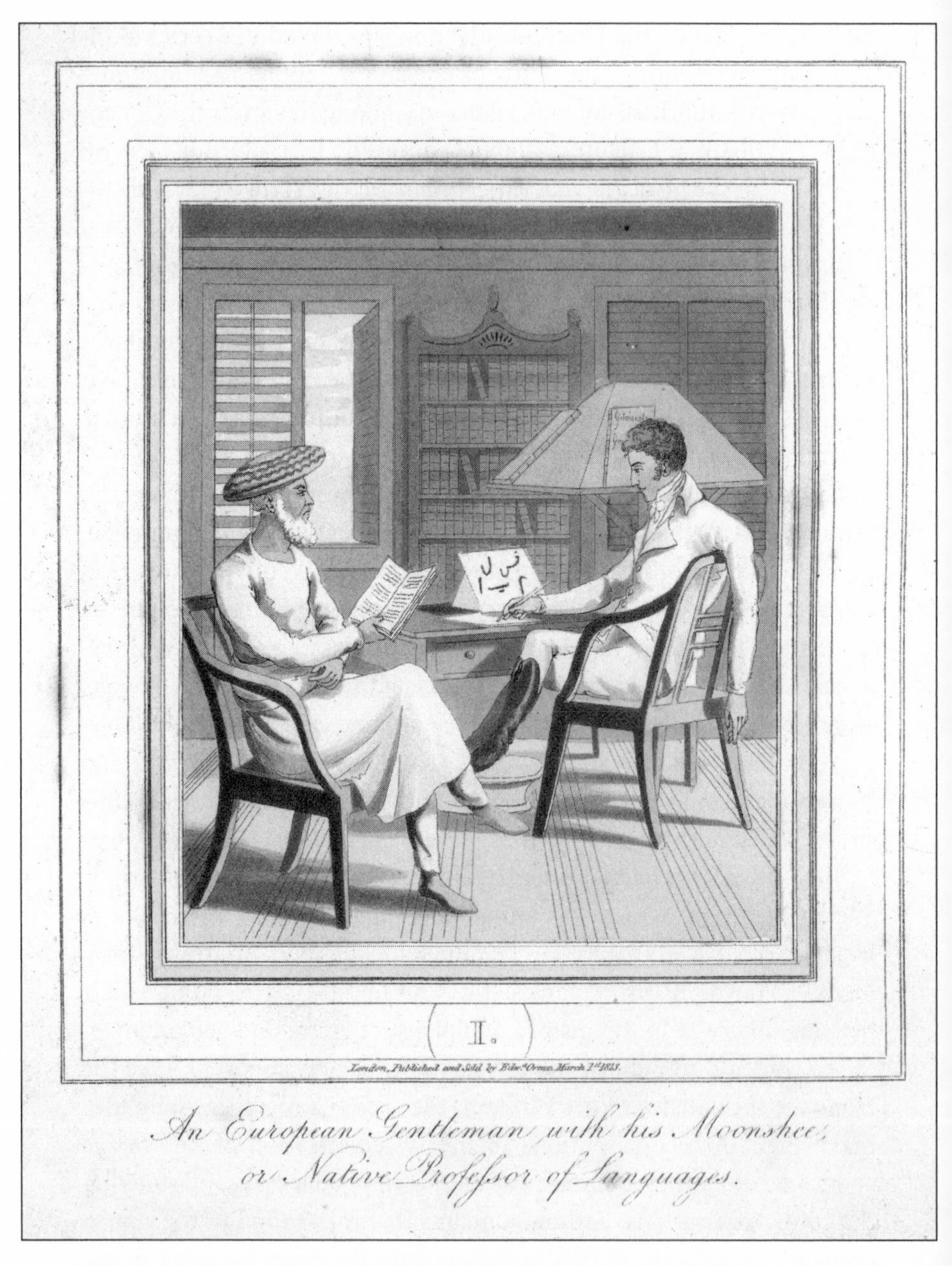

Munshis played a vital role in language teaching and translation in colonial India. This illustration is from *The Costume and Customs of Modern India* (ca. 1824).

society from 1840 to 1846, when he was finally shuffled off to a post in Mooshedabad.[46]

The commitment of the Orientalists to using native languages in the administration of South Asia and the education of its population was challenged at the end of the eighteenth century by an Anglicist faction that drew its strength from the evangelical tradition of Charles Grant. The Anglicists argued that the intellectual improvement of Britain's Indian subjects could only be secured by the introduction of Western scientific knowledge and the privileging of English in higher education. As the Anglicists gained strength, a new school for Indian civil servants, Haileybury College in England, was established so that Cambridge clergymen could ensure that the governing class destined for India took with them the moral values necessary to Christianize South Asia. The appointment of Charles E. Trevelyan to India's General Committee of Public Instruction in 1833 was a sign of the growing strength of the Anglicist faction. Trevelyan, a typical product of Haileybury, had a close association with the Church Missionary Society and a belief that spreading the English language would transform India both morally and intellectually. The mission of distributing "useful knowledge" in India was increasingly taken up by missionaries, army officers, tradesmen, doctors, and "enlightened natives." The Society for the Diffusion of Useful Knowledge took a particular interest in South Asia "as an arena in which darkness could be dispelled by knowledge of western ingenuity," and by 1839 they had a Calcutta branch. Responding to calls to abandon official support for the "erotic fantasies" of Hinduism, the government began to sponsor the translation of English classics of useful knowledge into Hindi and Urdu for use in public instruction.[47]

As colonial officials and vocal members of the Orientalist faction, both Torrens and Macnaghten were disturbed by the advances made by their rivals in the 1830s and 1840s. Backed by Governor-General Bentinck's administration in India and the Whig Parliament in Britain, the Reform Bill of 1830 legislated that English would replace Persian as the language of government in India. On March 7, 1835, Bentinck issued another resolution that followed the outlines of Macauley's "Minute on Education" by insisting that instruction in India promote "European literature and science amongst the natives of India." Funds designated for the purpose of education would now be "employed on English education alone."[48] Macnaghten would reply heatedly to this resolution, which he thought embodied the folly of the Anglicist position: "If we wish to enlighten the great mass of the people of India we must use as our Instruments the Languages of India. . . . Our object is to impart ideas, not words, and it must be much more easy to acquire these through the medium of the mother tongue than by a foreign one. They who assert that the Oriental Languages are incapable of being made the medium to conveying new Ideas must have but a superficial knowledge of those tongues."[49] For the Orientalists in India, the resolution of 1835 was a setback, and it would have immediate consequences as government funding for the study of Oriental languages and the printing of Oriental works of history and literature was cut.

Torrens had made his opposition to the increasing strength of the Anglicist contingent clear already in 1834, when he published his "Polyglot Baby's Own Book" with his friend Elliot in a Meerut newspaper. Reprinted in pamphlet form in Calcutta and Meerut, this satirical piece by "Bartolozzi Brown" ridicules the men who sought to impose English as the language of instruction in Indian schools and who supplied the improving literature of the Evangelical reformers. Inspired by an encounter with "the great Trevelyan," the work is "affectionately dedicated" to this exemplary Anglicist reformer—"the biggest baby in India." Trumpeting the advancements of a new era in which little Bengali girls "take in plain needle work" and little Bengali boys study the English grammars of Lindley Murray, Torrens and Elliot offer a new educational text that explores the complex literary influences that meet in the English nursery rhyme. What better way to prove Mr. Trevelyan's point that "English is the ocean of knowledge, and translations the rivers running *from* it"? Torrens and Elliot cannot pass over this last comment without indulging in their own instinct for sarcasm: "How noble a disregard for the laws of nature, how sincere a contempt for the dictates of common sense!" Nevertheless, they claim to welcome this effort to "abet the progress of intellectual improvement, by smoothing the threshold of the temple of knowledge, [and] clearing the tangled paths which lead to it." Inspired by knowledge of the rich textual influences that meet in "Hey, Diddle, Diddle," the authors trust that "Meerut will, like Calcutta . . . cease to be *'a divergent focus of barbarism,'* but soon become *a radiating centre,* when, to a degree infinitely greater than has yet been realized, light, and life, and intelligence might emanate to the remotest of the subordinate provinces."[50] This satirical squib provides a good sense of the spirit of Torrens's literary efforts, and strong evidence of why he was considered too "erratic in opinions, and too much a creature of impulse for the headship of any department."[51]

Serving as a junior secretary within Bentinck's administration, Torrens was assigned the unpleasant task of enforcing a resolution that he personally abhorred. In response to the news that the Bentinck government would withdraw financial support for students at the Sanskrit College in Calcutta, seventy-six Brahmin students sent a petition to the governor-general in March 1835, urging him to continue the stipends. The students defended the historical significance of Sanskrit and argued that the rulers of India, whether Hindu or Muslim, had always provided support for Brahmins to devote themselves to the study of the sacred language. As the petitioners wryly noted, the total subsidies provided by the British government for students of Sanskrit amounted to "less than the salary of many a public official." It was Torrens's duty as secretary to issue the government's reply, which stated that the allowances would not be reinstated as a matter of principle. As a champion of the pursuit of Oriental languages himself, Torrens loathed the policy he helped enforce, but as a junior civil servant within Bentinck's administration, he had little choice.[52]

Bentinck's resolution also generated a strong reaction from the leadership of the Royal Asiatic Society of Bengal, who saw this as an insult to the peoples of India—"a measure which has in the face of all India withdrawn the countenance of Government from the learned natives of the country, and pronounced a verdict of condemnation and abandonment on its literature."[53] Ironically, however, the victory of the Anglicists within the colonial administration brought a renewed importance to the activity of the Asiatic Society. The library of Sanskrit and Arabic classics that had once been housed at Fort William for the education of new colonial officials was now transferred to their care. When the colonial government, acting under the influence of Macauley's claim that "a single shelf of a good European library was worth the whole native literature of India and Arabia," cut its funding for the publication of "oriental works," it left a series of important projects unfinished.[54] The Asiatic Society quickly stepped in to take on the responsibility of finishing these projects. Exhibiting the condescension characteristic of victors, the colonial government supported these plans "to rescue the half-printed volumes of Sanscrit, Arabic, and Persian." For the leaders of the Asiatic Society, this was part of a larger campaign for knowledge pursued by "every learned Society and every scholar in Europe."[55]

The appearance of a previously unknown manuscript of the *Thousand and One Nights* in 1836 offered the Asiatic Society another chance to pursue its goal of rescuing and preserving works of Oriental literature. The *Thousand and One Nights* was already part of the linguistic apparatus of colonial India. A two-volume edition of the Arabic story collection, now known as Calcutta I, was published in 1814 and 1818 under the patronage of the College of Fort William. However, the manuscript of the *Thousand and One Nights* that was purchased by Charles Brownlow in 1836 from the estate of the late Major Macan included many more tales. The history of the manuscript's composition is somewhat mysterious, for no copy of the original used by Macnaghten to produce the published version has ever been conclusively identified. The most plausible story is that the manuscript was compiled by a scribe in Egypt before it was brought to India and the attention of the Asiatic Society.[56]

By a fascinating coincidence, the manuscript had originally belonged to Henry Salt, who was the British consul-general in Egypt when another translator of the *Arabian Nights,* Lane, first arrived in Cairo in 1825. One of the most successful collectors of antiquities in the Near East, Salt was able to build a formidable collection of ancient Egyptian artifacts during his time in Egypt. The first of these Egyptian collections was sold to the British Museum for 2,000 pounds, and a second, even more substantial collection was purchased by Charles X of France to become the core of the Louvre's Egyptian exhibit. Salt's instincts as a collector stretched into the realm of Arabic manuscripts, and he seems to have pursued the dream of every European translator of the *Thousand and One Nights:* a manuscript that actually contained 1,001 nights. Like earlier Arab compilers who used stories from various sources to create new recensions of the *Thousand and One Nights,* Salt seems to have hired an Egyptian scribe to compile a more comprehensive manuscript. This "complete" version incorporates the standard Egyptian recension, which formed the basis of the Bulaq edition used by Edward Lane for his translation, but also adds material from two other versions of the story collection. Thus the manuscript created for Salt, and later edited by Macnaghten and translated by Torrens, offered a full 1,001 nights of stories.[57]

Before Bentinck's resolution of 1835, Brownlow might have appealed to the colonial government to secure the publication of a valuable Arabic manuscript, but now he was compelled to turn to the Asiatic Society of Bengal for support. His argument emphasized the specific virtues of the *Thousand and One Nights.* "No book extant has ever enjoyed such universal popularity," Brownlow declared. He credited this both to its "vivid power of description" and its narrative of "common life" in which "a moral beauty—a knowledge of humanity" is discoverable by all readers. The value of the text lay in these universal values, but also in its importance as a portrait of the Arab nation. Quoting "an orientalist of high repute," Brownlow asserted, "We here behold a genuine portrait of the spirit and character, the common life and domestic manners, of a once powerful nation, which excelled in arts as well as in arms, in three quarters of the globe; in these tales we see the Arabs, depicted by themselves, in the tents of the desert, and in the courts of the Caliphs. We mingle among their merchants, join them in their travelling caravans, visit them in their social circles, and even penetrate into their harems." Building on the notion of literature as an expression of the essence of a nation, Brownlow argued for the value of the Arabic manuscript not only for Western scholars but for an "Eastern" readership. If European readers were already responding to the *Thousand and One Nights* in translation, "how much more emphatically must [the work] address itself to the inhabitants of the East, in the overflowing and beautiful language in which it was originally written." Brownlow thus seems to have imagined that British intervention was necessary to give this text back to the Arabic-speaking people whose spirit it represented.[58]

The most immediate goal of Brownlow and those who took up his cause in the Asiatic Society in 1836 was to establish the value of the manuscript and secure its publication in Arabic. A committee composed of senior civil servants representing both Orientalist and Anglicist opinion was quickly assembled to examine the Macan manuscript. Its most illustrious Orientalists were Macnaghten and H. T. Prinsep, with Trevelyan serving as the chief advocate of the Anglicist cause.[59] Macnaghten, a respected legal scholar and senior civil servant, had the greatest influence on the ultimate judgment of the committee. Unlike Torrens, Macnaghten rose steadily in the colonial bureaucracy to become chief secretary to the governor-general. He was by all accounts pompous and overbearing, but he possessed a remarkable linguistic genius. One of Lord Auckland's sisters described him as "*our* Lord Palmerston, a dry sensible man, who wears an enormous pair of blue spectacles and speaks Persian, Arabic, and Hindustani rather more fluently than English."[60] A product of a prominent Anglo-Indian family, Macnaghten had begun his career as a military cadet in 1809 in Madras, where he had first studied the vernacular languages of Hindustani, Tamil, Telugu, and others. In 1814, he transferred to the diplomatic service in Bengal, where he attended the college at Fort William and achieved the highest distinction for his achievements in the classical languages of Sanskrit, Arabic, and Persian. Macnaghten proves perhaps singular in the nineteenth-century history of the *Arabian Nights* in that his extraordinary command of Arabic is not merely asserted by admiring biographers, but borne out by archival evidence. In early 1817 a panel of experts was assembled to establish the officer's command of Arabic and Islamic law. Macnaghten's proficiency proved not merely "superior" but "extraordinary." As one government secretary explained to the president of the College of Fort William, college honors did not suffice for this level of achievement; rather, a "special mark of approbation" in the form of a government medal was needed.[61]

The task of the committee appointed by the Asiatic Society to evaluate the Macan manuscript was something of a strange one. They were forced to work quickly, having no more than three days to complete their assessment. Their basis for comparison was provided by a few key manuscripts and translations of the *Thousand and One Nights* circulating in Europe. Macnaghten and Prinsep compared the manuscript to Guillaume-Stanislas Trébutien's French translation of a German translation of Joseph von Hammer-Purgstall's French translation of a lost Egyptian manuscript, while Rev. William Hodge Mill added a comparison to the Arabic manuscript that Maximilian Habitch compiled in Breslau from Galland's manuscript and a series of other sources, including the forged "Tunisian manuscript." Using this source material, Macnaghten and his colleagues were not simply determining the authenticity of Macan's text. They were using comparisons to other versions to demonstrate what they saw as the distinctive virtues of the Macan manuscript as a work of literature relative to other available texts.[62] Including his own translations of "Abdallah of the Land and Abdallah of the Sea" in his report, Macnaghten argued that the version of the tale in the Macan manuscript was more complete and narratively complex than the "mutilated" French version. Applying the language of the improving literature favored by the evangelical faction within the colonial service, Macnaghten insisted that in the Macan version the story "has at least the advantage of conveying a moral." Macnaghten's assertion that the manuscript was authentic, complete, and of the greatest value was almost unanimously repeated by the other men charged with examining it.[63]

Though all five men agreed that the manuscript was a valuable work of literature, the Orientalists and Anglicists had different reasons for making this *Thousand and One Nights* publicly available. Macnaghten was primarily interested in the publication of an edited text of the Arabic manuscript as a way of enhancing the legitimacy of the colonial government. An appeal for official support should be "founded on the credit which must accrue to our nation, from presenting to the Mussulman [Muslim] population of India, in a complete and correct form in their own classical language, these enchanting tales."[64] If Macnaghten emphasized the importance of making the work accessible in Arabic, the prominent Anglicist on the committee, Trevelyan, countered that a good English translation would be even more valuable. "For one person who would read the book in Arabic," Trevelyan wrote, "five hundred would read it in English."[65] Trevelyan was more interested in the value that a translation of the work would have as part of an emerging canon of English literature to be consumed throughout the empire.

The delicate balance that was achieved between Anglicist and Orientalist opinion on this issue made it possible for the Asiatic Society to successfully appeal to the colonial administration for the financial support necessary to edit and publish the Arabic text and an English translation. The crucial intervention came in the form of a letter on October 7, 1836, from James Prinsep, secretary of the Asiatic Society, to his brother H. T. Prinsep, secretary to the government of India (and a member of the committee that had evaluated the manuscript). James Prinsep appealed to the governor-general and members of his council of directors not only as supporters of the society but as "rulers of India," and argued that "the publication of the Alif Laila [*Thousand and One Nights*] in the classical and beautiful language venerated by a large portion of its Indian subjects will reflect luster upon the British name." Such a text, Prinsep claimed, would make available to educated Muslims "a store of agreeable reading, replete with animated pictures of the vicissitudes of life, and in many cases imparting wholesome and moral instruction." Most importantly, Prinsep asserted that the publication of the *Thousand and One Nights* in Arabic would earn India's British rulers credit among the Muslim population.[66]

Prinsep's arguments neatly combined the positions of both Anglicists and Orientalists within the Asiatic Society and won the necessary support from the colonial authorities. In July 1837, the governor of Bengal not only agreed to the recommendation of the Asiatic Society, but ordered his officials to subscribe for fifty copies for public libraries and other government institutions and for use as prizes in Arabic seminaries. He also expressed "the strong desire" that a translation of the complete work into English would be undertaken soon by "some competent scholar of this Presidency" and promised that such a translation would meet with strong official backing.[67] The Arabic manuscript may have been subsidized for the sake of a subsequent English translation, but Macnaghten had achieved his goal. An Arabic edition of the *Thousand and One Nights* based on a manuscript found in Calcutta, likely pieced together by unknown scribes in Egypt, joined the growing number of teaching texts in India as exemplary of the spirit of the Arab nation. Thus secured and legitimated, the sequence of tales in this version of the *Thousand and One Nights* would be followed again and again by translators—reshaping a story collection that had previously been open and fluid.

Once Torrens was selected to translate the Macan manuscript into English, the governor of Bengal was able to make good on his promise of support for a translation of the work. At the request of the Asiatic Society, the governor committed to an order for forty copies of the first volume of an English translation for a total of 320 rupees, a crucial hedge for the society against the risk of bearing the cost of the publication alone. The educational mandate established by the Anglicists would be fulfilled at last when in 1838 the first volume of the English translation was published. Twenty copies of Torrens's translation were forwarded to the government's council of directors, and twenty were sent directly to the General Committee of Public Instruction.[68] This new translation would be put into circulation in India in the new world language of English on the understanding that it would displace versions in other languages. The Urdu version used for language exams at Fort William and the forthcoming modern Persian edition (1843) could then be relegated to the libraries of Orientalist scholars.[69] Scholars have observed that English literature as a discipline of study was codified not in Britain but in response to language policy in colonial India in the mid-nineteenth century. Evidence suggests a similar political dynamic was at work in the creation of world literature in translation.[70]

✦ ✦ ✦

The production of both the Arabic edition of the Macan manuscript and Torrens's translation reflected the Orientalist practices nurtured within the College of Fort William and the colonial bureaucracy. As editor of the Arabic *Thousand and One Nights,* Macnaghten was motivated by the goal of ensuring the preservation and circulation of the original story collection in a modern printed form, and he relied on the linguistic expertise of munshis to produce this work. In his original report to the Asiatic Society, Macnaghten suggested that his "Maulavi"—an official educated in Islamic law—"might be desired to assist in correcting" the manuscript for printing. He himself could only "aid in this duty, as far as my limited abilities and leisure might permit." Since the work on the manuscript proceeded during a time period (1839–1842) in which Macnaghten was preoccupied with his duties as a colonial officer, the real labor was clearly being provided by native officials within the Persian office.[71] In October 1837 Macnaghten left Calcutta to accompany Lord Auckland on a tour of the North-Western Provinces, where he served as a key adviser in the planning of an Afghan expedition in support of the claim of Shah Shuja to this territory. In December 1838, Macnaghten left with the British and Indian troops marching into the region, and he would remain with the occupation force in Kabul until his assassination in 1841. During this period, the preparation of the Arabic edition was in the safe hands of native language experts—the unidentified and uncredited collaborators on this crucial project.

Torrens's decision to take on the challenge of translating the *Thousand and One Nights* is perhaps surprising. Torrens was a writer of great versatility, but most of his translations seem to have been done from European languages, especially German. His linguistic training at Fort William was excellent, however, and he undoubtedly shared the Romantic assumption, espoused by the Orientalist Owen Jones, that the essential spirit of a people might be found in an authentic literary text—even more so if it was a work of poetry. In the preface to his *Arabian Nights,* Torrens repeated the sentiment that he had expressed in his translation of *Orlando Innamorato* years before: it was "the lighter literature of a people" that best captured a "national disposition." In these tales, and the interpolated poetry, one could find displayed all "the peculiarities of the Arab nationally and of the Mooslims [*sic*] at large."[72] Most importantly, Torrens was an aspiring poet who saw the *Arabian Nights* as an outlet for his own literary ambitions, and he was determined to capture the beauty of this universal text for an English readership. He would be the first English translator to render all the poetry of the *Thousand and One Nights* in verse.

As he began his translation, Torrens set out his claim that the *Thousand and One Nights* represented the essence of a distinctive Arab culture in an essay for the *Journal of the Asiatic Society of Bengal.* Leaping into an ongoing debate between the German critic August Wilhelm von Schlegel and the French Orientalist Silvestre de Sacy, Torrens attacked Schlegel's thesis that the core of the tales was of Indian origin. Writing in 1833, before the discovery of the Macan manuscript, Schlegel had portrayed the addition of tales from other cultures to this imagined Indian core as damaging to the integrity of the work, and had made the ominous prediction that "the most voluminous edition of the thousand-and-one nights will be the worst." Torrens correctly read the relevance of this contention to the Macan manuscript in the Asiatic Society's possession. Applying Schlegel's criteria, he stated that "the Macan MS. must be the worst instead of the best form of the thousand-and-one nights hitherto discovered, for it is 'the most voluminous:' the first five nights in this MS., for instance, contain the matter of the first seventeen nights of Galland's edition, and an additional tale, entirely new, besides."[73]

Taking the side of Orientalists like de Sacy, Torrens criticized Schlegel's claim that the tales could not be Arab in origin because they are crowded with supernatural beings that Muslims would consider almost polytheistic. Mockingly, Torrens suggested that Schlegel's supporters had "entirely forgotten the extreme superstition of the followers of the Prophet with respect to the existence of *jinns* (both believers and accursed), *ghols, ufreets,* and many other classes of imaginary beings, each distinguished by some peculiarity of character and habits." When these facts are considered, Torrens argued, these semideities "appear to be themselves the surest proofs of the Arabian extraction of the stories they figure in." He also refuted Schlegel's argument that the fish of four different colors in "The Tale of the Fisherman and the Jinni" represent the four Hindu castes because in Sanskrit the same word is used for "color" and "caste." Torrens countered that, in the Arabic tale, "special mention is made of the different religions of the men transmuted into fish of different colors, and it is the Arab world that encompasses Muslims, Jews, Christians, and pagans while Hindus share a single religious tradition."[74]

Torrens also argued in favor of the literary merits of his manuscript, which included better versions of tales known from other editions as well as new stories. As evidence, Torrens presented the tale of "King Sindibad and the Falcon," which does not appear in Galland's translation but forms part of the fourth night of the Macan manuscript. Including his translation of the tale in his riposte to Schlegel, Torrens praised its "power of description" and "habit of close observation." In it, a king has a hawk that "he lets not be separated from him by night nor by day," and one day the two set forth with the king's retinue to hunt. Approaching an antelope, the king proclaims that he will kill any man who lets the animal leap over him and get away. After this rash pronouncement, the antelope comes before the king, stands "firm on its hind legs, and gather[s] in its fore feet to its breast, as if about to kiss the earth before the king; so the king bow[s] his head in acknowledgment to the antelope; then it bound[s] over his head and [takes] the way of the desert." When his attendants note the irony in this outcome, the king responds aggressively, pursuing the antelope and turning his hawk loose on it. After the animal is blinded by the bird, the king attacks and kills the antelope.[75]

The first episode of violence in "King Sindibad" is followed by an even more ominous one. Looking for water to quench his thirst, the king sees "a tree dropping water, as [if] it were clarified butter." He fills a cup and places it before his beloved hawk, but "the hawk [strikes] the cup with its talons, and overturn[s] it." The king repeats his action, and once again the hawk rejects the water. When he finally places the cup in front of his horse instead, the hawk quickly overturns it again. Enraged, the king "[strikes] the hawk with his sword, and cut[s] off its wing, but the hawk begins lifting up its head, and saying by signs, 'Look at what is beneath the tree.'" Only then does the king see the poisonous snake from whom the hawk was trying to protect him, and he "repent[s] him of having cut off the hawk's wing." Returning to camp, "the king [sits] down in his chair, and the hawk on his hand, and the bird struggle[s] gaspingly, and die[s]."[76]

For Torrens new tales like "King Sindibad" justified Macnaghten's original opinion of the manuscript: "The style of the language was declared to be singularly pure, the narrative spirited and graphic, and the collection of stories enriched with many tales either perfectly new to European readers, or else given in a form very different from that under which they have been hitherto known, garbled and abridged by the carelessness of translators, or by imperfection of the MSS. whence they were translated." As a writer and a translator, Torrens particularly appreciated the descriptive detail and the more extended narrative development in the tales of the Macan manuscript. He argued that the moral quality of "King Sindibad" was reinforced by the progression of the king's offenses. It is a "spirited tale" that charts "graphically and naturally the progress of a passion (excited originally by a trifle, and ending in the blind commission of an act of ingratitude)." For Torrens this narrative coherence enhanced the emotional quality and literary value of the *Arabian Nights.*[77]

Neither Macnaghten nor Torrens was a specialist in the manuscript history of the *Thousand and One Nights,* but their evaluation of the new manuscript's literary merits was in many ways justified. The stories included in the Macnaghten edition not only are more numerous, but are at times more descriptive and complex than in other manuscripts, for when one recension includes more detailed episodes of a story, these are incorporated into a single version of the tale. As a result, tales in the Macan manuscript often display a greater narrative complexity and explore characters more fully.[78] In "The Vizier of Cairo and the Vizier of Basra," Torrens was able to exploit dramatic irony and inner monologues in the Arabic text to lend the story narrative tension and suspense. In this story, Hasan, son of the vizier of Basra, and Budur, the daughter of his brother, the vizier of Cairo, both grow into young beauties, though the cousins do not know of each other's existence. One day a female jinni becomes enamored with Hasan and grows angry with a male jinni who claims that he has seen a young girl of even greater beauty. "My sister," the male jinni declares, "surely the damsel is fairer than this youth," but he agrees that "none could be matched with her but he, for surely they are like as kindred are to one another, and the children of an uncle."[79] The dramatic irony lies in the fact that while the reader knows that Hasan and Budur are related, the jinn—and in fact the cousins themselves—do not. The tale will turn on the revelation of their kinship.

The difference between what the reader knows and what the characters know lends interest to the narrative as it develops. After the spiteful sultan orders Budur to marry a hunchback, the jinn substitute Hasan as her bridegroom. However, Budur's father is infuriated by the possibility of such a ruse. He approaches his daughter the next morning, saying "in his soul 'I will slay this daughter of mine if she has made room by her for this accursed fellow of her own accord.'"[80] The vizier's inner monologue alerts the reader to the danger that Budur, still ecstatic from the night she has spent with Hasan, will face from the wrath of her father. The more complex narrative of the tale in the Macan manuscript, as compared with the Syrian manuscript that Galland used for his translation, increases the power of the story as readers try to anticipate how these conflicts will be resolved. Not every tale in the Macnaghten text is superior to its counterpart in other manuscript versions, but when considered on a case-by-case basis, many tales in the new edition reveal specific merits.

While it may be argued that the specific qualities of Torrens's translation are rooted in the literary potential of this new edition, the literal style of translation that he used to capture the distinctive spirit of the text was also crucial. In his preface Torrens claims that this style "formed itself without any effort of my own, on the language of the original." Since his goal was to capture "the manners of a people," he needed to capture "the turn and spirit of familiar phraseology" in which the character of that Arabic culture lay. In his other efforts as a translator, Torrens always tried to mirror the distinctive voice of the author in the source language, and he proved capable of producing a bewildering range of literary styles. In approaching this same challenge in the *Arabian Nights,* Torrens believed that he needed to adhere to the original to capture the expressive qualities of the text. It was, he found, "impossible to convey an idea, such as I wished, of passions and affections, without giving also some of the spirit of the language."[81]

Above all, Torrens sought to include in his translation "the most peculiar and characteristic portion of these tales, the poetic in the form of poetry," an element of the collection which had been avoided by previous translators. In this, he clearly distinguished himself from Lane, who was simultaneously translating the *Arabian Nights* into English in London and had asserted in his ethnography of modern Egypt that Arabic poetry was "untranslatable." Lane blamed this on its propensity for puns, but Torrens felt this to be an unjustifiable belittlement of Arabic. If correct, "it would reduce the character of Arabic poetry to a most contemptible level."[82] If an Arabic text was untranslatable, Torrens argued, the problem lay in the target language, not the source. He admitted he found it trying to translate from Arabic—"a perfect language adapted to convey with metaphysical nicety, every shade of feeling, and every mood of the mind"—into an "imperfect" tongue such as English without losing the original's "terseness and force" and lapsing into diffuse paraphrase. But it was necessary. "Enough" of the original beauty of Arabic poetry could be rendered into English, even if not every pun could be translated. Learning that Lane had decided to omit the greater share of the poetry from his forthcoming translation only reinforced Torrens's conviction that his version was necessary.[83]

Torrens understood the poetry of the *Arabian Nights* not as mere embellishment, but rather as integral to the narrative structure of the story collection. In the tale of "Jafar and the Three Apples," for instance, the verses declaimed by a poor fisherman on the banks of the Tigris set the story in motion. Wandering in disguise by the river, Caliph Harun al-Rashid hears the fisherman's verses, and, taking pity on him, offers to pay one hundred dinars for whatever he catches next, which happens to be a chest containing the mutilated body of a young woman. Torrens skillfully conveys both a sense of the poem's rhyme and the sense of injustice felt by the learned sheikh reduced to fishing for his livelihood:

> "Like as the moon," they say, "showeth by night"
> "So men the light of thy learning espy:"
> "Cease such vain babbling, ye triflers," I cry,
> "None look to science, who see not the light
> Of wealth shiningly."[84]

Because Torrens valued the poetry of the story collection so highly, he was the first translator not only to render the poetry in verse without abridgment, but also to suggest that to be an author of the *Arabian Nights,* one must first be the author of its poetry.

Perceiving an intimate connection between the poetry and prose of the collection, Torrens brought a poetic sensibility to his rendering of the prose narrative as well as the verse. Although his transliterations of Arabic words and names are antiquated, his prose is much more vivid than that of recent scholarly translations of the Macnaghten edition. In the tale of "The Three Apples," the furious Harun orders his vizier Jafar to apprehend the murderer of the young woman whose body was found in a chest, or face execution himself. Torrens's poetic style heightens the narrative tension as Harun invokes his ancestry as a guarantee that he will avenge the young woman. Harun thus thunders, "Now by the accession of my lineage to this Khuleefut, this God's Vicarage, from the Sons of Ubâs, if thou dost not bring me him who slew this woman that I avenge her on him, I will hang thee at the gate of my palace, and forty thy uncle's sons with thee!" Giving up all hope, Jafar does not even attempt to find the murderer of the unknown woman, but as he waits on the gallows to be hung, a handsome young man appears and confesses to the murder. Then an old man, "stricken in years," comes forward to confess that *he* killed the young woman. In response, the young man elegantly protests, "By him who stretched out the firmament, and spread forth the earth, I am he who murdered the damsel."[85]

An explanation of this strange situation is finally provided by the young man. He claims that the murdered girl was his wife, and the old man was her father. One day, he gave his ill wife three apples from the caliph's orchard, but later he saw a black slave carrying one of the apples in the street. The slave told the young man that he had received the apple from his lover, who had received it from her husband. Enraged, the young man killed his wife, learning too late that the slave had in fact stolen the apple from one of his sons in the street. Hearing this story, Harun orders Jafar to capture the slave, or face death. Having just escaped the threat of execution, Jafar laments that "the pitcher does not scape safe every time" and "in this matter now there is no skill avails," and again makes no attempt to find the culprit.[86] Here Torrens includes a characteristically disparaging note, commenting that Jafar's conduct is "in exact consonance with the fatalist doctrines of a bigoted Mussulman."[87] Jafar only discovers the guilty slave by accident in his own household the very day he would have faced execution.

In his preface, Torrens comments that he had originally experimented with, but then discarded, a less natural style for his translation. In choosing a more literal style, Torrens created an *Arabian Nights* that sharply contrasts with the heavily stylized versions of Lane, Payne, and Burton. The latter versions are strained by the attempt to impose a single register on the entire story collection: the diction of the King James Bible for Lane, a Pre-Raphaelite style for Payne, and an exaggerated foreign-sounding style for Burton. Unconstrained by the urge to render the entirety of the work in a single style, Torrens switches tone and register to suit particular passages. In general, his style is relatively unadorned, but when quoting from the Quran he adopts a more archaic register and uses antiquated personal pronouns. He follows Galland in transforming narration into dialogue where he can, and in the process seems to give his characters a liveliness missing in the translation of his rival Lane. In the market scene of "The Porter and the Three Ladies of Baghdad," this technique enhances the flirtatiousness of the female character, and in the story of "Yunan and the Sage Duban," the wise physician seems to speak in the ringing tones of Torrens's own political rhetoric.[88] In this story, Duban cures the king's leprosy, but, responding to the evil advice of his vizier, the king decides to kill the sage on the assumption that a man wise enough to save him could also kill him. The clever physician devises a plan to kill the king with a poisoned book, but he cannot evade decapitation. His severed head declares a verdict on these extraordinary events:

> They issued savage mandates, but no long time
> Survived they in their cruelty; for lo! ye!
> 'Twas but a little, and the mandate was not.
> Had they done justice, justice were done them;
> But they did ill, and evil was their portion;
> And fortune turned against them, strongly armed
> With acts of woe and trouble; so they passed hence,
> And the mute eloquence of their condition
> Repeated to them, "This is your reward,
> Blame not the retribution."

In this verse there are echoes of Torrens's own warnings to imperial authorities that the excesses of despotic rule would provoke the resistance of their subjects, and the clarity and power of Torrens's renderings of passages like this spoke directly to his contemporaries.[89]

Burton would criticize the stylistic simplicity of Torrens's translation by claiming that it has a "hag-like nakedness," but compared to Lane's contemporary translation, and the versions by Payne and Burton composed half a century later, Torrens's translation seems the most modern in its sensibility.[90] The literary qualities of Torrens's translation were not missed by contemporary reviewers, especially when they evaluated them against Lane's first volume of the *Arabian Nights*, also published in 1838. In the *London and Westminster Review*, the commentator acknowledges that there is an "orientalism" in Torrens's style, but none of the affectations and extreme defamiliarizing techniques of Lane. Torrens's translation might have "less gravity of spirit," but he asserts that it is "more sensitive, we guess, both to mirth and to tears, and with a greater instinct of universality." If Lane resembled "an Arab full-dressed" then Mr. Torrens wore a "lighter half-apparel."[91] The *Dublin Review* praised Torrens's poetry for capturing the tender emotion in the Arabic verse of his original, as in this passage in which a woman laments the loss of her lover:

> Though thou art well, my patient heart is worn away
> For love of thee,
> My whole affections and my soul have hold and stay
> On only thee;
> Take there my spirit, take my bones, where'er thy way
> May carry thee;
> Then call my name by my cold tomb, and I'll essay
> To answer thee;
> A wailing cry shall from my bones sad greeting pay,
> Sweet voice, to thee.

The reviewer lamented the context for the poem—the affection of a lady for "an uncomely black slave"—but he could not deny the power of the translated verse.[92] In India Torrens was conscious of the pressure to produce Orientalist texts that were heavily ornamented with exotic examples of the indigenous, but he remained wedded to a method of translation that resembles that of the German Romantics that he admired so much.[93]

Reviewers were also taken with Torrens's "bold" treatment of the sexual content within the story collection, which again contrasted with contemporary translations.[94] The Orientalist in Torrens saw the *Thousand and One Nights* as embodying the "admiration of beauty inherent in the Arab, his innate voluptuousness, and his licence of expression." He acknowledged in his preface that he was obliged "to omit portions of these tales, in which the style of description, is more accurate than delicate," but Torrens was committed to capturing the sensuality of the collection because he saw it as an essential component of the poetic spirit of the Arab people.[95] The appreciation of beauty and the promise of sex weave the poetry into the fabric of the prose in many of the tales, and Torrens uses these opportunities to capture the suggestive qualities of Arabic verse in his translation. While he claims to have omitted sexual details that he found vulgar, he is successful in creating an atmosphere of sensuality.

Torrens's translation of the story cycle of "The Porter and the Three Ladies of Baghdad" is the best example of his approach to the sexual content that others considered too "objectionable" to include in English translations destined for a respectable readership. In the famous frame of this cycle, a porter from the market in Baghdad is drawn into the private domain of three ladies through a seductive encounter with one of the trio: "She stood still and lifted her short veil, and there appeared beneath it two eyes, black, with lashes like vine tendrils gentle in their earnest look, perfect in all attributes."[96] In the home of the three women, the porter engages in an extended flirtation conducted largely through the exchange of poems. It is the porter's cleverness in quoting and extemporizing poetry that convinces the women to open up their secret lives to him. Amid the sharing of much wine, the porter offers himself to the women:

> A slave among thy slaves there stands
> All at thy chamber door,
> And feels the gifts that from thy hands
> In ceaseless shower pour.
> Oh beauty's essence! may this slave
> Come in my charms to see!
> I, and my love no call can have
> To wander e'er from thee![97]

The song sung by one of the ladies also serves to create the atmosphere of frustrated desire that pervades the tale, and initiates the telling of a series of tales of love and betrayal:

The madness of my love shall last
Till all the days of time be past;
Ne'er will I shame to say
How love the curtain rent apart
That o'er my maiden face was cast,
How, when affect warmed my heart
He tore my veil away.

. . . .

Those bright-lashed eyes have caused my pain,
And I must yield my breath
By the cold edge of absence slain:
How many a prince, like simple swain,
That blade has done to death![98]

Once again Torrens's contention that the poetry of the *Thousand and One Nights* is vital to both its narrative force and its poetic atmosphere is revealed in his efforts to convey the interpolated verse.

The suggestiveness of the verse in "The Porter and the Three Ladies of Baghdad" is complemented by frank descriptions of the revelry that ensues among the ladies and the porter. It is translated by Torrens with a boldness that surprised many Victorian readers: "They kept on with dance and laugh, and songs and verses, and jingling anagrams, and the porter was going on with them with quips, and kisses, and cranks, and tricks, and pinches, and girls' play, and romping, this one giving him a dainty mouthful, and that one thumping him, and that one slapping his cheeks, and this serving perfumes to him, and he was with them in the height of joy, even as if he were sitting in the seventh Heaven among the houris of Paradise."[99] Drunk with wine and bathed in the waters of the pool, the four characters continue this sexual play by posing a series of riddles. Each of these—one posed by each of the three ladies and one by the porter—explore the power of metaphor in describing the sexual organs of man and woman. The coup de grâce is provided by the answer to the porter's riddle, which contains within it the answers to all four riddles: "The mighty mule, that feeds on the noble basil plant, and eats the peeled sesame, and lives in the khan of Aboo Munsoor."[100]

In including these elements of the story, Torrens showed his disdain for the Victorian prudery that was attributed to his fellow translator of the *Arabian Nights,* Lane. This attitude was already apparent in Torrens's earlier interventions in the literary life of colonial India, where he had always asserted the right of the artist to explore the full range of "the poetry of life."[101] Not surprisingly, the more mature subject matter in Torrens's *Arabian Nights* was a subject of some concern for English reviewers. The *London and Westminster Review* singled out "The Porter and the Three Ladies of Baghdad" as perhaps too "bold" for many readers, but acquitted Torrens "not only of all blameable intention but of any sense of an unwarrantable trespass upon the licence permitted to unusual works of scholarship, and descriptions of foreign manners." This commentator identifies the problem as Torrens's Indian location, "where the moral, and even the religious breeding of the people, gradually accustom foreigner as well as native, to toleration of ideas on certain subjects, startling even to their Eastern neighbours."[102] The association of Torrens's translation with the dangerous qualities of the colonial frontier would be a disadvantage as he competed with Lane to reach readers in the metropolis.

✦ ✦ ✦

"King 'Umar ibn al-Nu'man" is the last tale in the only published volume of Torrens's *Arabian Nights.* Sharkan and Abriza have just arrived in his father's kingdom when the volume ends, and Torrens never published the conclusion of the tale. The conventional explanation for the decision to abandon this translation was that Torrens believed that the forthcoming version of the *Arabian Nights* by Lane had made his labor unnecessary. By the time he wrote the preface to the first volume at the end of July 1838, Torrens knew of Lane's work in Cairo, but argued that the latter's intention to omit "the greater portion of the poetry of the original" made the publication of his own volume desirable.[103] However, Torrens seems to have believed that the competition Lane offered as a scholar was daunting. He admits that he had hoped to offer "a set of notes upon the habits of the Mussulmans generally," but his diplomatic duties had taken him from Calcutta to Simla, the summer retreat of the governor-general in the Himalayas. Unable to access a library in this location, he was only able to offer an occasional explanation of "an historical allusion or a local custom."[104] His notes to the stories tend to be composed of anecdotal evidence about the beliefs and customs of Indian Muslims, and they are most valuable for the insight they provide into the assumptions of British officials on the eve of the First Anglo-Afghan War. When Torrens decides to gloss the term "ghazee" (religious warrior) in the story of Sharkan and Abriza, for instance, he uses the opportunity to disparage the spirit of contemporary Muslim princes in India, whom he claims more frequently assume this title than earn it.[105]

Another explanation for Torrens's decision to abandon his translation was likely the departure of Macnaghten with the troops heading for Kabul in December 1838. It is possible that Torrens was consulting Macnaghten on the preparation of the English translation of the Arabic manuscript, but it is even more likely that Torrens was relying on Macnaghten's munshis for help in preparing his translation. This was standard practice in language learning at Fort William and probably essential for the rapid preparation of a translation from Arabic while Torrens continued with his duties as a civil servant. As both military men and civilian experts were dispatched to the north in a fateful effort to secure the Afghan territory for Britain's allies, Torrens may have been deprived of the friendship and linguistic support that he needed to pursue his challenging translation project.

Although Macnaghten wrote Torrens optimistic letters from Afghanistan, the British invasion in support of the claim of Shah Shuja and his Sikh ally Ranjit Singh was a disaster of epic proportions. Auckland's Folly, as the first British war in Afghanistan came to be called, resulted in the loss of thousands of allied Sikh and enemy Afghan soldiers and some 4,500 British soldiers and 12,000 camp followers, including servants, wives, and children. Shortly before the end of the war, Macnaghten would pay the ultimate price for his role in its planning and execution when he was killed outside Kabul.[106] The story of Macnaghten's assassination bears an unfortunate resemblance to the tales of warfare between Christians and Muslims that both he and Torrens knew from their work on the *Thousand and One Nights*. By December 1841, Macnaghten had lost any hope of rallying the British forces, and

Sir William Hay Macnaghten (*upper left*), Sir Alexander Burnes (*upper right)*, Akbar Khan (*lower left*), and Shah Shuja (*lower right*). The chief personalities involved in the debacle of the First Anglo-Afghan War (1839–1842).

hoped at best for safe passage home for his men and their families. On December 23, 1841, Macnaghten, accompanied by a few British officers and a small guard, rode out to the banks of the Kabul River, ostensibly for negotiations, and were ambushed by Akbar Khan, the son of the ousted emir, Mohammed Dost. Macnaghten's fellow officers were taken prisoner, and their captors tried to defend them from a bloodthirsty mob. Macnaghten would not be so fortunate. Akbar Khan reportedly took a pistol from his belt—one of the pistols Macnaghten had given him a day earlier—and shot him two or three times. Macnaghten's mutilated body was dragged through the streets of Kabul and his head was displayed at the city's Grand Bazaar for a year.[107]

In early analyses of the First Anglo-Afghan War, blame was placed squarely on the shoulders of advisers to the governor-general like Macnaghten and Torrens, who in the seclusion of Simla allegedly persuaded him to support Ranjit Singh and Shah Shuja, against the advice of wiser counselors. Torrens later denied that he had been instrumental in orchestrating the Afghan war, pointing to his position as a junior secretary with little power or influence. Regardless of the extent of his role, however, the embarrassment and anger produced by this disastrous colonial war overshadowed what might have been Torrens's literary legacy, and this may be the real reason why he chose to abandon his translation of the *Arabian Nights*.[108]

In his last literary effort, Torrens expressed the melancholy of a destiny unfulfilled. Visiting Egypt in 1851 in an effort to recover his health, Torrens lamented his twenty-three-year exile "on the shady side of the globe." Unable to progress in his career and earn the nest egg that might allow him to return to England and join his family, he pondered the limits the colonial context placed on his talents and took refuge in the words of his beloved Goethe. "To have done all one can," Torrens writes, "and test this by appealing to conscience for a measure for duty, and then to be patient—to avoid the useless struggle—to suffer as well as do—this is the philosophy of life, this is peace."[109]

Cairo brought Torrens a brief sense of connection to the fascinating world of the *Thousand and One Nights* that had consumed such a vital period of his life in India. He found himself "so perfectly at home among Arabs and camels" that "for the first time since I left India my spirits rose." Arriving in an unfamiliar city, Torrens nevertheless felt that he knew it: "The whole thing, city and people, were the Arabian nights in action. This is the East, not India. I could have sat in a coffeehouse all day, like a Turk, staring at every thing and nothing. I bought a silk robe for a dressing gown, and discomfited a rascally dragoman, giving my friends in English the substance of his Arabic negotiation with a shopkeeper to cheat me in the price of two Fez caps. The fellow's face was worth the journey to Cairo."[110] Torrens's experience in Egypt only reinforced his earlier conviction that a deep immersion in the life and the language of a foreign land was essential for generating any real understanding. He condemned the Romantic nonsense peddled by Western writers—Alphonse Lamartine, Victor Hugo, and Byron among them—and reiterated the position that had inspired the Orientalist camp's rather naïve sense of their colonial mission in India: "It is the people you must know, and their habits of thought. To do this you must live among them and speak, whatever it may be, their tongue."[111] His *Arabian Nights* must be seen as an expression of this spirit—born in the distinctive political context of British India.

4

THE MAGICIAN'S INTERPRETER

A LIFE-SIZE STATUE OF EDWARD WILLIAM LANE in the Turkish costume of Cairo's elite dominates room fifteen of the National Portrait Gallery in London. It was the work of his brother Richard Lane, an English artist famous for his portraits of actors and royals and a key contributor to the enduring image of Lane as an Orientalist scholar who had successfully mastered the alien codes and customs of nineteenth-century Cairo. Richard was fascinated by the exotic imagery he associated with his brother's time in Egypt. Requesting that Lane keep his mustache on his return to England in 1828, Richard produced a series of pencil-and-wash sketches and lithographs of Lane in Turkish dress against generic Egyptian backgrounds. By maintaining many of the habits of his Cairo life after his return to England, Lane cultivated the persona of al-Fackeer Mansoor, the name by which his acquaintances in Cairo addressed him.

This portrait of the Orientalist man of letters, at home in the Arab world, was taken up and elaborated by Stanley Lane-Poole, who carefully constructed a biography of Lane that would solidify his great-uncle's reputation as a pioneering Egyptologist and eminent Arabist. In Lane-Poole's portrait, Lane is "the enterprising and often daring explorer,

Edward Lane, by his brother Richard Lane, life-size plaster statue, 1829.

climbing flat-faced cliffs, swinging down a mummy-pit, crawling in the low passages of tombs and pyramids," but at the same time he is "a scholar at his desk, a learned man honoured in learned circles, the highest authority on matters Arabian to whom England or Europe could appeal."[1] This image of a clever and confident Lane was crafted by Lane-Poole in the more aggressive imperialism of the late nineteenth century and has provided the basis for the treatment of the famous ethnographer and translator in more recent academic studies. In Edward Said's *Orientalism,* Lane fits smoothly into the frame of the classic Orientalist who masquerades as a local while maintaining the "cold distance" of the Western observer.[2]

A glimpse beneath the myth of Lane as Orientalist scholar, however, reveals a more intriguing story of frustrated ambitions and suppressed voices. According to his own diary entries, Lane was decidedly unprepared for the role of Egyptian explorer when he arrived in Cairo in 1825. He could not even cross a canal without hiring a local to bear him on his back.[3] Similarly, Lane's investigations of the customs of Egyptians relied heavily on the contributions of several local associates who provided information on the issues that most fascinated him: the peculiarities of popular religious belief and the forbidden realm of Muslim domestic life. Lane's desire to dive into the mysterious world of nineteenth-century Cairo was real, but his ability to do so was entirely dependent on a series of intermediaries who guided him through the intricacies of life beyond the district of the "Franks." Foremost among these was Osman Effendi, a Scottish former slave and convert to Islam, and Sheikh Ahmad, a local bookseller with ties to the publishing house of Egypt's reformist ruler, Muhammad Ali Pasha.

Little in Lane's early life had prepared him for a career as an Arabist or Egyptologist. The pious offspring of an Anglican family, Lane was expected to become a minister like his father, but he declined in order to study mathematics at university. This plan too was shelved, however, after an eye-opening visit to his brother Theophilus at Cambridge, where heavy drinking seemed to be the norm. Instead, Lane took up the artistic vocation of his great-uncle, the painter Thomas Gainsborough, and apprenticed as an engraver with Charles Heath in 1819. His brother Richard had already been at work with Heath for three years, and Edward joined him in learning the intricacies of copperplate engraving. The apprentice engraver needed to develop the ability to incise an accurate representation of a given image onto a copper plate, which could then be used to print individual images or book illustrations. This training in the meticulous reproduction of images would be put to a new purpose when Lane travelled to Egypt.[4]

Lane's interest in Egypt was inspired by a visit to the Egyptian House in London in 1821 to view the famous exhibit assembled by Giovanni Battista Belzoni. With the help of British consul general Henry Salt, Belzoni had gathered an impressive collection of Egyptian antiquities, and in his Piccadilly showroom he displayed mummies and magical amulets among crowd-pleasing replicas of temples, pyramids, and the tomb of Seti I. The exhibit was a sensation with the English public and inspired Lane to study Arabic and set out for Egypt in 1825 at the age of twenty-four. In his first scholarly effort, the draft of his "Description of Egypt," he confesses to an interest in the language and customs of the Arabs, but most importantly a fascination with "the antiquities of that most interesting country." "I felt," Lane wrote, "even before I commenced my travels, that there was a probability of my publishing the observations that I might see; well convinced that a drawing, in many cases, is worth many pages of description."[5]

By the 1820s, Egypt was attracting gentlemen scholars who wanted to indulge their curiosity about ancient civilizations and artists who sought exotic landscapes and monuments to sketch. These enterprising antiquarians arrived in Egypt with a variety of goals largely unrelated to the formalities of scholarship and without explicit commissions. Most often these journeys were a product of personal enthusiasm and the hope for fame and fortune. Lane would be drawn into the company of these amateur Egyptologists, and a few would become good friends—most importantly Robert Hay, a Scottish aristocrat financing his own project to document the ancient monuments of Egypt. Lane did not enjoy the financial resources of Hay, but both men were operating outside the scope of scholarly institutions. Lane's own attraction to Egypt seems to have emerged from a particular nostalgia. His religious upbringing had given him a need to believe that found little purchase in an England that was growing ever more secular and industrial. In the artifacts displayed in the Egyptian Hall in Piccadilly and in the stories of the *Arabian Nights,* Lane believed he had found a world in which piety was still an integral part of life and miracles could still happen.[6]

Fascinated with the monuments of the pharaohs, Lane's objective was to capture the timeless reality of an ancient civilization that paralleled the biblical history that had shaped his early education. He brought with him to Egypt a camera lucida, an optical device that uses a prism to reflect an image onto a page, where it can then be traced with a pencil. With this realist technique, Lane attempted to record as many ancient monuments as possible and thereby preserve the essence of a time of greater purity and power.[7] During his first stay in Egypt (1825–1828), he produced hundreds of sketches in the hope of publishing them along with essays about the history, geography, and contemporary condition of Egypt. When he returned to England, however, he faced the disappointing reality of a publishing industry in crisis. John Murray II expressed interest in Lane's manuscript in 1832, but a series of delays prevented the book from going to press. Despite popular enthusiasm for the material wonders of Egypt, publishers worried about marketing a book whose tone was didactic and whose images would have made it prohibitively expensive. At that time Lane had no powerful patrons in the world of the English university or in the British social elite. His best connections came through his brother Richard, who painted the famous and powerful. In seeking recognition as a scholar of the Orient at this time, Lane was overreaching.[8]

His failure to secure the publication of his "Description of Egypt" was not just a personal disappointment for Lane; it exposed the tenuous financial basis on which his Egyptian experience rested. Lane did not have access to a family fortune like Hay's, and he did not have a formal commission that would have funded his work in Cairo. He had financed his first trip to Cairo with 400 pounds that his mother had borrowed from the estate of Mary Fischer Gainsborough, the daughter of the famous painter.[9] Lane had to find some way to make his efforts pay, so he scrambled to find another commission that would capitalize on his experience of Cairo. His prospects finally improved when the Society for the Diffusion of Useful Knowledge offered him an opportunity to return to Egypt to gather material for an ethnography of Egypt. The goal of the society was to promote self-education within the middle and working classes by producing inexpensive educational texts. Lane's ethnography—*An Account of the Manners and Customs of the Modern Egyptians*—appeared in 1836 and became part of the Library of Entertaining Knowledge created by Charles Knight. Lane's preparation of this work during his second stay in Cairo (1833–1834) demanded that he

Edward Lane arrived in Egypt with the intention of exploring the monuments of the pharaohs. He completed this watercolor sketch during archaeological expeditions in 1825–1827.

turn once again to a series of local informants that could offer him the knowledge he needed, and it established the essential methodology that would define his translation of the *Arabian Nights*.[10]

Lane's immersion in the distinctive "manners and customs" of nineteenth-century Cairo was the foundation of his legitimacy as a privileged interpreter of both contemporary Egypt and the medieval world of the *Thousand and One Nights*. When Lane finally turned to translating Shahrazad's stories in 1837, he did so in the guise of a Victorian empiricist and in the belief that the world represented in the tales was the same as the Cairo he knew—replete with its own jinn and magicians. This assertion of an essential continuity between the beliefs and social practices depicted in the story collection and those of nineteenth-century Egypt was the cornerstone of Lane's conviction that he could translate the tales for an English readership. It was also the primary justification for Lane's additions to the *Arabian Nights*—the elaborate commentary on Egyptian customs that he appended to the stories and the magnificent illustrations that merged contemporary Egyptian settings with the imagined worlds of the tales.

✦ ✦ ✦

Lane arrived in Egypt in 1825 with a basic command of Arabic and some anxiety. In an early draft of his "Description of Egypt," he confessed that as he approached the shore at Alexandria he "felt like an Eastern bridegroom about to lift up the veil of his bride, and to see, for the first time, the features which were to charm, or disappoint, or disgust him."[11] He would soon discover that he needed more than his engraver's eye to access the ancient ruins that fired his imagination and the fabric of religious belief that he believed survived in contemporary Cairo. Seeking instruction in the delicate art of being an expatriate in Egypt, Lane turned first to Osman, who was cited in the reports of many British travellers as an essential resource for Europeans trying to integrate themselves into the city. Nothing could be done without Osman, expatriates in Cairo said. The Ottoman Scot could be relied on to arrange transport and accommodation, to guide newcomers through the shops, or to procure the supplies they needed. It was Osman who facilitated Lane's first journey in Egypt, arranging for Lane's boat trip on the Nile, preparing his accommodations, and providing him with an itinerary. If Lane appears a master of cultural immersion in his brother's sculpture, it is largely due to the astute tutoring of Osman.[12]

Osman provided help with all the challenges involved in living outside the insulated bubble of the foreign quarter of Cairo. He would rent Western visitors one of his properties in a native quarter, procure the necessary residency permits, and generally help them settle in. He could provide an evening of entertainment with the city's singing girls or, for a not insignificant commission, facilitate the purchase of a slave girl in the market to provide both companionship and a defense against the suspicions raised by European bachelors. He could provide medical care in times of illness. Perhaps most importantly, Osman could teach Lane the sartorial codes that would allow him to pass as a member of the Turkish elite on the streets of Cairo. The identity of an Ottoman Turk was seen as providing the most convincing cover for an expatriate's foreign mannerisms, and this persona gave the European who adopted it a more elevated social position than that of the Egyptian Arab. Henry Westcar, an English traveller, described the impact of a trip to a local tailor in Osman's company in 1824. When dressed in European clothes, he had found himself elbowed aside by soldiers and civilians, but when he strutted out as a Turk, "all got out of the way & the Arabs who were sitting down got up as I passed & saluted me."[13]

The diary of Hay provides an intriguing description of the process by which a European traveller was transformed by adopting the Ottoman style of dress. First Hay was given a "wide pair" of silk-embroidered trousers in which "one may with little trouble lose oneself." Next came an intricate layering of silk-embroidered shirts and jackets. For travel on the street, these three layers would be covered with a loose-fitting upper jacket, fastened at the neck with a gold or silver button, with wide silk-trimmed sleeves reaching to the elbow. The head coverings were equally elaborate. First a white linen cap was fastened, to be followed by a red woolen one, and over that a turban was placed.[14] This manner of dress appears repeatedly in images of Lane in Egypt—not only those produced by his brother, but those he executed himself. Garbed with the assistance of Osman, Lane could take on the role of al-Fackeer Mansoor.[15]

The practice of dressing as a local, which Lane and other expatriates employed to ease their way through Cairo, has been interpreted as an expression of "enmity, aggression and rivalry" by Leila Ahmed, Lane's first modern biographer.[16] Some historians, however, have called for greater nuance in assessing these claims by drawing on the testimony of expatriates in Egypt. In the Cairo of Lane's time, Muhammad Ali's Westernizing reforms had increased tensions regarding the presence of Europeans in the country. An expatriate European doctor captured the feeling in the city: "Arabs despise us more for our apparel than they hate us for our creed: our tight clothes appear to them not only ridiculous, but indecent: and it is their general impression that our garments make us look like monkeys."[17] Lane certainly felt the need to blend in. This was perhaps his natural instinct, but it was also a response to the unsettled political landscape produced by Muhammad Ali's reforms. Outside Cairo, along the routes Lane travelled to explore ancient Egyptian artifacts, antireformist sentiment was strong. Lane later recalled that while sitting unnoticed in a coffee shop, he had overheard the local patrons discussing the advisability of killing all the foreigners in Egypt to send a message to the pasha about his Europeanizing reforms. Indeed, the debate was not over whether to slaughter the Europeans, but over whether to do so immediately or to wait a year. In these circumstances, having access to the expertise of someone like Osman was essential.

The blanket condemnation of Europeans seeking to embrace the customs of the Middle East has left little room to examine the importance of cultural brokers like Osman, who for decades acted as a mediator between the seemingly antagonistic worlds of Europe and the Middle East. A remarkable personality in his own right, Osman played a critical role in shaping the image of contemporary Egypt that Lane inserted into the *Arabian Nights* through his famous commentary. While some expatriates refused to socialize with a Muslim convert, Lane saw Osman as a model of how he might combine the religious beliefs of his childhood with those of Cairo. He developed a strong attachment to the Scottish convert, and this affection seems to have been mutual. As he managed his many properties, Osman reserved the apartment neighboring his own for his friend Lane, and when he died in 1836, Lane was assigned to execute Osman's will in England.[18] Despite the fact that he has been largely erased from Lane's published works, Osman's perspective on the possibility of bridging Christianity and Islam survives within them.

Osman's life story remains somewhat mysterious, but he seems to have been born William Thomson in Perth in 1784. A member of the Alexandria expedition under General Alexander Mackenzie Fraser during the Anglo-Turkish War (1807–1809), he was captured by the enemy and sold as a slave to a Mamluk master. European travellers enjoyed repeating the ghastly detail that the captive survivors of the battle at Rosetta, Osman among them, were marched through the city carrying the severed heads of their fallen comrades. There is no firm evidence of when Osman took his Ottoman name and converted to Islam. The conventional story is that he had attempted to escape, and upon his recapture, his master gave him the choice of conversion or death. According to Alexander Kinglake, the English travel writer, Osman then fought under "the orthodox standard of the Prophet in fierce campaigns against the Wahabees," returning home in triumph from these "holy wars" to become a man of property and a gentleman (hence receiving the title "effendi"). Osman's path to success was largely due to a fortuitous meeting with the famous Swiss traveller Jean Louis Burckhardt during his pilgrimage to Mecca in 1814. Burckhardt, famous for discovering the lost city of Petra and completing the Hajj, brought Osman to Cairo in 1815, and requested that the British consul-general, Salt, assist in securing his emancipation.[19]

Osman's case offers a rare glimpse into the gray area occupied by those individuals who sought to cross the seemingly impenetrable divide between Europe and the Middle East. Perceived as hostile agents of the West in Said's study of Orientalism, British expatriates who donned Turkish dress were assumed to be agents of the pasha by the British consulate and were warned not to expect any protection from their government. When asked to intervene on behalf of Osman, Salt at first refused because of his status as a convert to Islam. By 1816, however, the resistance of the British consul had been overcome and diplomatic overtures with the pasha had resulted in Osman's emancipation. From this point on, Osman cultivated a tight relationship with the consulate, working as an interpreter and providing security. By the mid-1820s he was offering indispensable services for the British expatriate community, and an English traveller reported in 1824 that Salt himself had entrusted Osman with the education of the illegitimate son born to him by his Abyssinian concubine.[20]

Once a lowly member of Fraser's regiment, Osman was now able to achieve a level of wealth and respect that he could never have achieved in his native Scotland. After receiving an initial inheritance from his Mamluk master, Osman inherited much of Burckhardt's property on his death in 1817—including the contents of his house in Cairo and all his slaves. By the time that Lane met him in 1825, he had multiplied that inheritance through his own enterprise. Osman was listed in John Gardner Wilkinson's guide to Egypt as owning four furnished houses where Europeans could rent a floor, or a set of floors, for 5 to 8 piastres a day or about 150 piastres a month. In addition to procuring slave girls for European expatriates in the city, he was also willing to lodge them on behalf of their travelling masters. Some expatriates would be privileged with an invitation to Osman's own home, where he would regale them with "humorous anecdotes of his adventures both in Arabia and Egypt."[21]

When Osman was finally emancipated in 1816, he remained a riddle for members of the expatriate circle of Cairo. According to the English traveller James Silk Buckingham, "Though [Osman] preserved all his northern peculiarities of light complexion, sandy hair, and moustaches, freckled face, light-blue eyes, and yellowish eyebrows and eyelashes, his dress, air, and manners were completely those of a Turk."[22] Some travellers insisted that Osman had only "half-converted" and therefore lived in "exile" from his true home, remaining wistful for "his own lochs or heath-covered mountains." Kinglake asserted that "the strangest feature in Osman's character was his inextinguishable nationality." In private the successful effendi of Cairo society treasured his shelves of Scottish books—"the Edinburgh Cabinet Library." It was assumed that Osman remained a Muslim only because of the social and financial position that his conversion secured him. The ease with which Osman interacted as a Muslim among Muslims was seen as an intentional deception; it

Joseph Bonomi, *Street Scene outside Mosque in Siout.* Bonomi was an English artist who accompanied Robert Hay on an archaeological expedition to Egypt in 1824. This watercolor features a European in Turkish dress matching the description of Osman Effendi, a former slave who became an indispensable resource for expatriates in Cairo.

was "absolutely necessary" for Osman, having professed to have converted, not to "undeceive" his Muslim hosts. Every aspect of his cultural immersion was judged to be calculated. He was believed to have internalized Muslim "prejudices" only to more successfully mimic them. His relocation to a Turkish quarter of the city was understood to be "necessary for the credit and sincerity of his faith." It was thought that he attended mosque just "often enough to prove that he was a true believer" and would only strictly observe the Ramadan fast or the prohibition against alcohol to maintain his public image as a genuine convert.[23]

Evidence that suggested Osman was more sincere in pursuing his "mixed religion" is discounted in this common portrait of a "half-comic, half-tragic" figure defined by his bad faith.[24] However, a report from Osman's pilgrimage to Mecca yields an intriguing image of a Muslim who would produce his family Bible from his breast pocket in an effort to convince fellow Muslims of the common ground between Islam and Christianity. In his autobiography, Buckingham related that Osman juxtaposed the two faiths' sacred texts to prove "that certain views propounded in the Koran" could not be correct "because they were at variance with other views contained in the Gospel; and vice versa that certain doctrines of the New Testament could not be of divine origin, because they were opposed to the doctrines of the Koran." In this manner he arrived at his "mixed religion." The Scot's effort to initiate theological disputations led to much mirth on at least one occasion. When Osman sought to engage patrons of a coffeehouse in Mecca with the first question of the Scottish catechism, "What is the chief end of man?," the question was interpreted in terms of anatomy, and the answer was merely a "peal of laughter."[25]

Osman's serious pursuit of a middle ground between Christianity and Islam was an important part of his bond with Burckhardt—another apparent convert to Islam. A friendship that began during the Swiss traveller's pilgrimage to Mecca in 1814 lasted until Burckhardt's death in 1817. Osman lived in Cairo as a Muslim member of Burckhardt's household, and Salt testified that when Burckhardt was dying, it was Osman who stayed beside him to the end. In his own will, Osman asked to be laid to rest with Burckhardt in the Bab al-Nasr Cemetery.[26] Burckhardt's conversion to Islam, like that of Osman, was met with skepticism by many Europeans. Some considered his adoption of the dress and social customs of the Arab world as "Ibrahim ibn Abdullah" a ruse. One commentator even dismissed the value of Burckhardt's explorations on these grounds: "Knowledge, purchased by the perpetual habit of insincerity connected with this false assumption, is not worth the price paid for it." While there is much evidence that Burckhardt was sincere in his conversion and made a serious study of Islamic law, he and his friend Osman would remain objects of suspicion within expatriate society.[27]

For Lane, the ability of Osman and his legendary patron to move between cultural worlds and religious faiths was a source of wonder. He idolized the Swiss traveller and wrote his ethnography of Egypt with Burckhardt's *Arab Proverbs* open on his desk. Among Lane's most prized possessions was a piece of the black cover of the Kaaba, the sacred shrine in Mecca toward which every Muslim prays. Burckhardt had brought it back from the Hajj and then passed it on to Osman.[28] On his arrival in Cairo, Lane had a strong desire to follow the example of Burckhardt and submerge himself in this world of strangers, to adopt their language, customs, and dress. He boasted of his success in making this transition in his letters, claiming that he had quickly surpassed his teachers' knowledge of Arabic. "When I say that I have engaged a Sheykh to teach me," Lane wrote to Hay, "they insinuate that I am to teach the Sheykh."[29] In such statements, Lane attempted to fashion his Egyptian identity as al-Fackeer Mansoor.

In Cairo, Lane believed he had found the living fabric of belief that had once existed in England, and he sought out the common ground between Christianity and Islam. Contrary to the allegations of espionage and duplicity made by recent scholars, Lane presented himself in Cairo not as an Egyptian, a Turk, or a Muslim but as an English Christian who accepted many tenets of the Quran as compatible with his system of belief. In his ethnography of Egypt, Lane acknowledged the "hand of Providence in the introduction and diffusion of the religion of El-Islam" and, in the first note to his *Arabian Nights,* he paraphrased the Quranic verses on Christ: "Jesus is held to be more excellent than any of those who preceded him; to have been born of a virgin, and to be the Messiah, and the word of God, and a Spirit proceeding from Him, but not partaking of his essence, and not to be called the Son of God." In other contexts, Lane was comfortable expressing his assent to this central element of the faith of Islam.[30]

Guided by his own religious education, Lane preferred to perceive Egypt as a land in which one could still encounter the miracles of the Old Testament. He explained his reasons in *Modern Egyptians* in 1836, stating that "if we admit that there is still such a thing as real magic, and we know from the Bible such was once the case," we should remain open to the possibility of encountering and verifying instances of this. If the Book of Exodus records the pharaoh's desire to outdo the miracles effected by God through Moses, Lane asserts, "in modern days, there have been [in Egypt], magicians not less skilled than the Pharaoh's 'wise men and sorcerers' of whom we read in the Bible."[31] Lane's notebooks reveal not the cynicism attributed to him by Said, but rather his genuine sense of "astonishment" with the potential for magic in Cairo.[32] Lane delighted in stories of jinn and the feats of street magicians. He attested to a personal encounter with a jinni that haunted the cave in which he stayed during his first explorations of the pyramids, and claimed that during his last stay in Cairo he inadvertently rented a house that was haunted by another jinni. In these last years in Egypt, Lane seriously entertained the possibility that the neighborhood seer, Sheikh Ahmed al-Leithy, was a spiritual medium gifted with clairvoyance, and he tested the man's predictions regarding Lane's family's life in London against news arriving in letters from abroad.[33]

In Cairo, Lane felt free to submerge himself in the rhythms of Islam. In his diary he wrote of the solace he found in praying alone at mosque. He gave up alcohol and pork and became addicted to the coffee and tobacco associated with the devout. He had himself circumcised so as to pass inconspicuously for a believer in public baths. In his last stay in Cairo, Lane was known to say the Bismallah before beginning work each morning, and his close collaborator Sheikh Ibrahim al-Dasūqī asserted that Lane believed in the message of Islam and swore by the prophecy of Jesus.[34] Convinced that Cairo represented a society in which religious faith defined social life on a fundamental level, Lane expressed confusion when encountering any evidence to the contrary. In one incident recorded in his diary, he confessed to being perplexed by the dancing girls loitering outside a mosque as he entered with a friend to pray. All the better to be able to sin and instantly repent, his friend assured him. But Lane remained unpersuaded. Social behavior that diverged from what Lane understood as appropriate for a Muslim society was particularly difficult for him to process.[35]

Even during his second stay in Cairo, Lane sometimes struggled to understand aspects of social life, and his method as an ethnographer, and later as a translator, depended on the contributions of local informants. Despite the success of his Arabic lessons, he seems to have had difficulty following conversations that involved metaphorical language and the use of irony. Throughout his life, he seemed more comfortable with historical and philological texts than with the ambiguities of literary forms. When he received his commission to produce an ethnography of modern Egypt, Lane found that his most productive method of research was conducting intensive interviews with a particular trusted subject. During these sessions, Lane would copy the informant's explanations of life in Cairo verbatim into his notebooks in Arabic. He would later translate these dictated observations into English and insert them—often with no modification—into the manuscript that would become *Modern Egyptians*.[36] This trick of channelling the stories of associates like Osman or the bookseller Sheikh Ahmad did not persuade all readers. Said would famously protest the strange disjunction of first-person experience and third-person voice that he detected in Lane.[37]

In *Modern Egyptians,* Lane explored contemporary Cairo through a multitude of prisms, describing its geography, religion, government, literature, industry, music, games, festivals, and domestic life. But the many "superstitions" of Cairenes were central to his portrait, and Osman was his principal informant on this subject. The most dramatic example of the practice of magic in his ethnography involved the famous Maghrebi magician Sheikh Abd al-Qadir, whose feats caused much controversy when they were published in *Modern Egyptians* in 1836. Lane recalls hearing of al-Qadir during his first trip to Egypt (1825–1828) from Salt, who had called on the magician to assist in resolving an incident of theft at the British consulate. Valuable articles of property (possibly antiquities) had gone missing from his consular residence, and although he had no proof, he was convinced the culprit was one of his servants. Catching thieves was one of the common uses of the "black lamp" with which the magician conjured the supernatural aid of jinn. It is likely that Osman, who had worked security at the consulate and who acted as al-Qadir's interpreter, made the suggestion to employ the magician. As it was related to Lane, this magical experiment was a grand success. Calling on one of the young servant boys of the household, al-Qadir drew a diagram on his hand and then added a little ink. After al-Qadir burned incense and scraps of paper on which charms had been inscribed, the boy was able to see the objects called for by the magician in the ink on his palm. When al-Qadir called for the image of the thief to appear, the boy could describe him in detail and claimed that he knew him at once. One of the laborers in the consulate's garden was immediately apprehended for the crime, and he offered a spontaneous confession.[38]

Al-Qadir's reputation preceded him in English circles. In 1833, Lane would recount how the magician could describe any man living or dead by summoning the jinn with the aid of the black lamp. One report suggested that he had described Shakespeare's person and dress in minute detail. Perhaps his most celebrated feat came in response to an English heckler who proclaimed that nothing would persuade him short of a description of his own father, known to none in the assembled company. Calling his father by name, the boy who served as the magician's intermediary was able to describe a spectacled man in European dress with a hand against his temple. In the boy's vision, the man appeared to be in the act of stepping down onto a surface, with one foot raised and another on the ground. The dumbfounded skeptic confessed the perfection of the boy's portrait. His father suffered from an almost constant migraine and had a stiff knee caused by a hunting accident. Lane specifies no source when he relates these anecdotes of the magician's power in his ethnography. Yet given the detail in Lane's account—including verbatim reproduction of the dialogue that passed from Arabic into English and back again—the source could only have been the magician's interpreter during those evenings—Osman.[39]

Stories of the magician al-Qadir fascinated Lane, and at the beginning of his second stay in Cairo in 1833 he insisted that his neighbor Osman bring the magician to him. What followed was a series of

Godfrey Thomas Vigne, *Sheikh Abdul Kadir Mugrabi, the Magician of Egypt.* Edward Lane's account of the remarkable feats of clairvoyance of this Maghrebi magician would inspire George Eliot, Wilkie Collins, and Jorge Luis Borges. Pencil, pen and ink, and watercolor, 1844.

experiments in Lane's own living room, which he would meticulously reconstruct in his ethnography. Lane describes al-Qadir as "a fine, tall, and stout man, of a rather fair complexion, with a dark-brown beard." He was dressed "shabbily" but wore a green turban to mark himself as a descendant of the prophet. Genial and unpretentious in his manner, the Maghrebi magician assured Lane that "his wonders were effected by the agency of good spirits," despite the fact that he had told others that his magic was "satanic." Al-Qadir had asked Lane to supply frankincense and coriander seed, as well as a chafing dish with some live charcoal, and the magician prepared himself by writing on strips of paper his charm and his invocation: "Tarshun! Taryooahnn! Comedown! Come down! Be present! Whither are gone the prince and his troops? . . . Be present ye servants of these names!" By burning the paper, the magician explained, he could invoke two jinn, his "familiar spirits," by name. The charm also contained a passage from the Surah Qaf in the Quran that was intended to open the intermediary's eyes "in a supernatural manner; to make his sight pierce into what is to us the invisible world." It said, "And we have removed from thee thy veil; and thy sight to-day is piercing."[40]

The successful invocation of the jinn depended greatly on the person who was chosen to be the subject of the charm. The magician requested a prepubescent boy, although he said that a virgin, a black female slave, or a pregnant woman might serve the same role. Lane himself chose a participant of eight or nine years of age from among the boys in the street. The ritual would have been a difficult, if not terrifying, experience for the boy. It was imperative for him to remain immobile throughout the invocation, and to cut his senses off from the everyday world. To this end, a seat was brought for him and the chafing dish with burning frankincense and coriander seed was placed directly before him. The Maghrebi magician took the boy's right hand firmly, and on his palm roughly drew a magic square. In its center he poured a little ink, and asked the boy to watch his reflection intently in this "mirror of ink." Dropping the strips of paper inscribed with the invocation into the chafing dish, the magician asked for the boy's vision to pierce the invisible world.[41]

The boy would likely have felt his head swim as he breathed in the fumes. Osman might have volunteered the familiar explanation—that the heat, scent, and smoke of the chafing dish would close off the boy's senses to ordinary stimuli. Sharply underlining the ingredients required for the experiment in a volume in his library years later, Richard Burton may have intuited a less innocent explanation. An experienced user of opiates and hallucinogens, he was unlikely to have missed the coincidence that frankincense and coriander seed, when heated and inhaled, possess hallucinogenic properties.[42] A boy could be expected to be more susceptible to their effects than a grown man. In the experiment staged for Lane in his living room, the boy saw nothing at first, but then reported that he saw a man sweeping the ground in the ink. Following the instructions of the magician, the boy was asked to command the jinn to bring a series of seven flags, to pitch the sultan's tent, and to arrange the ranks of soldiers around it. The boy then ordered the jinn to slaughter a bull to provide a meal for the soldiers. At this point in the boy's vision, the sultan of the jinn arrived to hold court among his armies, signalling the moment when questions could be asked through the boy.[43]

When asked whom he wished the boy to see, Lane named Lord Horatio Nelson, "of whom the boy had evidently never heard." After making his request of the sultan in the mirror, the boy described a man "dressed in a black suit of European clothes" who "has lost his left arm." But then, correcting himself, he announced, "He has not lost his left arm; but it is placed to his breast." Lane was impressed with this description—even more so when he realizes that the image in the ink has been reversed so that Nelson's missing right arm has been mistaken for his left. Next Lane asked for the boy to invoke a friend of his who was away in England. The result was reasonably convincing, but additional requests to see other absent people revealed that the boy's power of sight was fading. When another boy was brought in from the street in an attempt to repeat the experiment, the results were less impressive. The second boy could see nothing, and the magician explained that he was simply too old.[44]

Lane's description of the magician's art offers fascinating insights into one of the tales told by Hanna Diyab and incorporated into the *Arabian Nights* by Antoine Galland—"The Story of Aladdin and the Wonderful Lamp." In this tale, another Maghrebi magician seeks access to a hidden realm, and he seems to require a prepubescent boy—Aladdin—to do so. Searching for the invisible portal to an underground cave, the magician utters a magical incantation while burning incense. As dense smoke rises and the earth trembles, a door with a bronze handle is revealed. A "terrified" Aladdin seeks to flee but, like al-Qadir's young medium in Lane's description, he must remain because he is "necessary for this mysterious business."[45] Burton would later argue that knowledge of such magical practices was widespread in large parts of the Islamic world, and it is reasonable to imagine that Diyab would have known of such feats, especially given the reputation of Aleppines for welcoming magicians travelling from North Africa.[46] The role of the young boy as the key mediator between the everyday and the supernatural was thus imported into the famous orphan tale of Aladdin.

Lane's firsthand account of al-Qadir's powers of clairvoyance with the mirror of ink, published in *Modern Egyptians* in 1836, caused considerable debate in England. One English commentator in the *Quarterly Review* found this account of clairvoyance incongruous in a larger study that otherwise seemed remarkably free of exotic clichés of the East. Lane's family and friends found the public discussion of the credibility of the story, and the implicit questions about Lane's legitimacy as a scholar, embarrassing, and pressed him to retract his apparent endorsement of the performance. Lane's response was to provide additional proof in support of his claim of the magician's power: a diagram of his living room and an elaborate explanation of the physical impossibility of fraud.[47] Criticisms of Lane's credulity on this occasion brought his skills as an ethnographer into question, but even bolder accusations of deception were made against Osman. Some commentators on the event, such as Lord Nugent, seized on Osman's status as a convert as evidence of his fundamental untrustworthiness, and insisted that it was the interpreter who provided the necessary hints to make the experiment a success. Lane's account of the magical practices of al-Qadir thus put the reputations of both Lane and Osman at risk.[48]

When the account in *Modern Egyptians* is read against the evidence of Lane's own notebooks, a deliberate effort to tell this story in a way that might protect the reputation of his friend Osman, and sublimate his own nagging doubts about the magical acts that he had witnessed, can be detected. Most importantly, Lane seems to be concerned with ensuring that no accusation of collusion could be made against Osman. He thus explains in a note to the story in *Modern Egyptians* that when he called for a specific person to be described, he "paid particular attention both to the magician and to Osman. The latter gave no direction either by word or sign; and indeed he was generally unacquainted with the personal appearance of the individual called for." Lane also assured his readers that Osman had "no previous communication with the boys." It was Lane himself who chose them randomly from the street.[49]

In the description of the magical performance in his notebook, however, Lane reveals the more vital mediating role played by Osman.[50] In *Modern Egyptians,* Lane asserted that Osman had no knowledge of the appearance of the people that he wanted the boy to describe, but in his notebook he states, "I had before remarked to Osman that the boy should either describe Nelson as a man who had lost his right arm, or as having his right arm raised to his breast, since the right sleeve of his coat was usually attached to the breast."[51] A comparison of Lane's personal account of the second success of the evening also reveals that he carefully modified his published report. Lane's notebook names the missing friend as Ibrahim Salamé, an interpreter for British diplomats in Cairo, a fact that was omitted in the published version.[52] Given that Osman would certainly be familiar with someone who had worked in this profession in Cairo, the omission suggests that Lane was carefully constructing his account to deflect the suspicion that would naturally fall on Osman.

Lane's account of the Maghrebi magician raises the question of why he did not make more of the failures that occurred during most of the experiments that al-Qadir performed in his presence. Lord Nelson had been described adequately, if the explanation of the reversal of the missing arm was accepted, and Salamé appeared in recognizable form. However, subsequent attempts to conjure a distinct human form in the mirror of ink failed, and Lane expressed real disappointment that the grand feats of previous séances with European audiences had not been repeated. Why did he not question the credibility of the exercise itself? Lane's notebook reveals a startling answer. Desperately wanting to believe in the possibility of clairvoyance with the black lamp, Lane had been much more active in intervening in the experiment to ensure its success than he would ever admit in print. While he quickly explains away the boy's mistake about the arm of Lord Nelson in *Modern Egyptians,* his notes reveal that he himself provided a series of leading questions that would allow the boy to recognize his mistake and correct it.[53] Al-Qadir did not explain the reversal as being a mirror image. There was only Lane's need to believe, and his loyalty to his good friend.

When confronted later with evidence that al-Qadir was never able to replicate his success with the mirror of ink after the death of Osman in 1836, Lane was still unwilling to accept the accusation of guilt against his friend made by commentators like Lord Nugent. The most he would say is that in some cases "leading questions put *unconsciously* by Osman, as well as by others, who were persons of education and intelligence, and in other cases shrewd guesses, were the main causes of his success." However, he was certain that this was not an explanation for the magical event that took place in his own living room in February 1833. Inherently more sympathetic to Osman and his life history than Lord Nugent was, Lane remained convinced of the sincerity of his friend's engagement with the supernatural and the validity of his contributions to his own work.[54] In this relationship, there was little evidence of the bad faith that has been attributed to Lane, and perhaps too great a personal investment in the practices of magic that he sought to investigate.

When Lane embarked on his plan to translate the *Arabian Nights* in 1837, this public debate about his credibility strongly shaped his approach. Other translators of the story collection had been largely untroubled by such concerns. Galland always viewed the French appetite for fairy tales with some distaste, but he had few qualms about feeding it with fantastic stories from Diyab. Henry Torrens explored the problem of translating superstition for a more skeptical audience in his study of Friedrich Schiller's translation of *Macbeth,* but his own self-image as a man of the Enlightenment was too strong to be affected by imputations of "Eastern" weaknesses.[55] Lane's footing on this issue was far less secure because he did not just record these curious moments of magic, he experienced them directly, and, as the debate over the anecdote of the magician indicates, he often believed.

✦ ✦ ✦

Lane's translation of the *Arabian Nights* was a commission from publisher Charles Knight, who had also published his *Modern Egyptians*. Knight was trying to survive in a tough publishing market by appealing to a mass readership with cheap illustrated books delivered in affordable monthly installments. Among his other publications were the *Pictorial Bible* (1836–1838) and the *Pictorial Shakespeare* (1839–1842), and he sought to follow the same pattern with a work that was rapidly reaching the same level of name recognition. Aware of his own precarious financial situation, Lane pursued the translation of the *Arabian Nights* as a way to capitalize on his knowledge of Egypt. His "Description of Egypt" had still not been published, and he had been forced to take employment with his friend Hay, acting on his behalf in London to secure supplies and employ artists for his project to document the ancient monuments of Egypt.[56]

Lane's *Arabian Nights* would be the first English translation of the Egyptian edition that had just been published by Muhammad Ali's press in Bulaq. This version of the story collection contained much more material than the manuscript from which Galland had worked, and Lane could therefore claim that this was a comprehensive translation of the tales. Lane would also supplement the translation with notes based on his research for *Modern Egyptians* and the "Description of Egypt," and include hundreds of illustrations as an imaginative resource for readers.

An early draft of the opening of Lane's translation, written in October 1837 in a rainy London far removed from the Egyptian city that had originally inspired it, provides a singular glimpse of what he was hoping to achieve in his version of the *Arabian Nights* and some of the challenges he would need to meet to do so. For a modern scholar familiar with the awkward formality of Lane's published version of the work, this draft of "The Merchant and the Jinni," written in direct and lively English prose, is a startling discovery. Shahrazad's story begins simply enough, as a wealthy merchant suffering from the heat of the day pauses his journey to sit under a tree and eat. As he eats his snack, the merchant throws a date pit away and "immediately a Jin'nee, of gigantic stature, with a drawn sword in his hand" approaches him. Hearing that this "monster" plans to kill him, the merchant demands an explanation, and learns that when he threw the date pit, he struck the jinni's infant son on the chest and "killed him on the spot." Facing immediate execution, the merchant successfully pleads for a chance to put his affairs in order, and promises to return a year later to the same spot to receive his punishment.[57]

A year later the merchant has paid his debts and made arrangements for his family, and he returns to the scene of his crime to await the jinni in "fear and terror." As he is waiting, a sheikh leading a gazelle arrives. When the merchant tearfully explains his situation, the sheikh decides to stay with him until the jinni appears. Soon, another sheikh, leading two dogs, joins them, and then a third sheikh arrives with a dappled mule. Suddenly, "a cloud of dust [is] seen approaching them, raised, like a pillar, by a great whirlwind." When the dust clears, the jinni appears with his sword drawn and his "eyes throwing out sparks of fire." The three sheikhs—"weeping & wailing & groaning" at the plight of the merchant—offer to tell the jinni their stories in exchange for the merchant's life. The jinni promises that for each story that he finds "wonderful," he will return one-third of his claim on the merchant's blood.[58]

And so the first sheikh begins his tale: "Know, O 'Efreet, that this gazelle is the daughter of my uncle: and she is my flesh and my blood." The sheikh explains that the gazelle was his wife, but, because she remained childless during their marriage, he had taken a slave as his concubine. By this slave, he "was blest with a male child, like the full moon; with eyes & eye-brows of perfect beauty." Fifteen years later, the sheikh went on a journey, and during his absence his wife "transformed [his] son into a calf, and the slave, his mother, into a cow; and gave them in charge to the herdsman." He only discovered this horrible fact after he had inadvertently slaughtered his concubine. Luckily, the sheikh, moved to pity by the calf's weeping, had spared his son's life, and the herdsman's daughter, who had learned magic in her youth, was able to recognize the animal as her master's son under an enchantment. The sheikh was "intoxicated, without wine, by the excess of joy" that the news brought him. Using her magic, the herdsman's daughter turned the calf back into the sheikh's son and transformed the sheikh's wife into the gazelle with whom he was now travelling.[59]

In executing this first draft, Lane explicitly confronted some of the central anxieties that would shape his seminal version of the *Arabian Nights.* How could he relate these stories of marvellous beings and magical events to an English audience nurtured by the more realist ethos of the Victorian age? How was he to convey a world in which belief in magic was part of the fabric of everyday life? Even as he translated this intriguing tale of men and women transfigured, he flipped the page of his notebook to its verso and confessed his predicament: "The Arabs and other Mohammedan people enjoy a remarkable advantage of us in the composition of works of fiction: in the invention of incidents which we shd. regard as absurd in the extreme, they cannot be accused by their countrymen of exceeding the bounds of probability."[60] The challenge of bridging the seemingly incompatible cultural worlds of modern England and modern Cairo would drive Lane's translation of the *Arabian Nights,* just as it had shaped his own life from his first arrival in Cairo in 1825.

For Lane, a man whose natural instinct as an engraver and ethnographer was simply to capture the original as closely as possible, associating himself with the imaginative world disclosed by the tales of the *Arabian Nights* was not always comfortable. He had already come under criticism for his inclusion of the story of al-Qadir in *Modern Egyptians* in 1836. His solution to this predicament would be to include notes that would present both contemporary testimony and historical authority to persuade the reader to accept the tales as plausible in their own cultural context. His lament in the draft story about the difficulties of translating the "absurd" is quickly followed by a long anecdote about the possibility of such a magical transformation: "A case similar to that here described was related to me, as a fact, in Cairo. A person in that city, I was told, was suddenly surprised by the disappearance of his brother, and finding, in his place, an ass: but this animal increased his astonishment, and that of every person who beheld him, by manifesting a sagacity singularly opposed to the proverbial dullness of the generality of his species." When an old woman with knowledge of magic finally discovered this fact, "she agreed to restore the enchanted person to his proper shape." Lane carefully relates the procedure: "Having collected a number of herbs, she boiled them in a large vessel; and when the decoction had cooled, she took the vessel, and, muttering a certain spell, threw its contents over the animal, endeavoring to do so in such a manner that every part of it should be wetted." The man was restored to his "original human form, with the exception of one foot, which continued like that of an ass."[61]

This anecdote, related in the same straightforward tone as the translation of the *Arabian Nights* tale on the other side of the page, is representative of the overlapping literary and ethnographic objectives with which Lane began this translation project. For Lane, the supernaturalism of the *Arabian Nights* was merely a reflection of the world of marvels that he had sought and found in Cairo. This anecdote is presented as a story told to Lane by a local informant, likely Osman, during his time in Cairo, but he does not mean it to be understood as a foolish bit of local superstition. Lane included the anecdote in the translation because he believed there to be a direct connection between the world represented in the stories of the *Thousand and One Nights* and the city where he had lived.

Annotations such as this one were characteristic of the elaborate commentary that Lane appended to his published version of the *Arabian Nights* as a way of establishing his authority as its translator. Given that Torrens was publishing his own English translation of the story collection in the same year, it was important for both Lane and his publisher to establish the credentials of their version. The scholarly expertise asserted by Lane through his commentary was one of the main selling points of his *Arabian Nights*. Lane's preface to the tales promised that his translation would correct the misimpression inherited from Galland's version that the stories of the *Arabian Nights* pertain to the cultures of the wider Muslim world, places like Persia, Turkey, and India. In Lane's hands, the collection became an illustration of social practices specific to Cairo, "where Arabian manners and customs exist in their most refined state."[62] Implicit within this statement is the contention that Torrens, whose knowledge of the Muslim world was based on his experience of India, had no legitimate credentials to offer an accurate rendition of the work. Defining ethnographic knowledge of the Arab world as *the* prerequisite for translating the *Arabian Nights* and locating that knowledge in Cairo, the preface set Lane up as the ideal commentator and translator.

Even as he produced his first translated stories in the winter of 1837–1838, Lane was already worried about potential competition from Torrens. In a letter to Hay on January 15, 1838, Lane writes that he could not have foreseen that the *Arabian Nights* would occupy him so "overwhelmingly." He must "make the utmost haste" in his work to keep his publishers from becoming "terrible losers," for he has learned that he has competition in the form of a rival, "a very formidable one, in India."[63] There were valid reasons for Lane's anxieties regarding Torrens. The overlapping English expatriate networks of India and Egypt would have provided Lane with substantial evidence of Torrens's linguistic and literary talents. Viewed from the perspective of a rival, Torrens was everything Lane was not. More naturally gifted at translation, he flitted expertly between languages and literary genres. He was famous for his spectacular ability to improvise in different modes—poetry, drama, or political rhetoric. Above all, Torrens had a sharp wit for which he was admired and feared. By contrast, Lane admitted that he had difficulty even *following* humor and irony in Cairo.[64]

Lane's anxiety was also fed by the knowledge that his practice of translation was particularly laborious since it depended on the explanations of the text provided by Sheikh Muhammad Ayyad al-Tantawi, the scholar he referred to as "my Sheikh." An exemplary product of Cairo's prestigious college of al-Azhar, al-Tantawi was known as a skilled teacher of Arabic and had been willing to share his expertise with other European Orientalists, including the German Arabist Gustave Weil and the French traveller Fulgence Fresnel, who called his mentor "one of the most learned men of Egypt." Al-Tantawi would be recruited to teach Arabic in Russia in 1840 and would advance to the position of professor of Arabic at Saint Petersburg University in 1847. Sent to Russia by Muhammad Ali with the hope that he would learn Russian thoroughly and provide useful knowledge for his homeland, al-Tantawi produced a travelogue containing both a history of Russia and an analysis of its manners and customs. In Russia he was known for his fabulous collection of Arabic manuscripts, his ability to compose poetry in a classical style, and his respect for the methods of European scholarship.[65]

The *Thousand and One Nights* was seldom considered worthy of commentary by serious Arabic scholars, but, when Lane launched his translation, he employed al-Tantawi to do just that. In a practice that mirrored the teaching of texts in Cairo, Lane would wait in London for al-Tantawi to send him portions of the Bulaq edition covered with his handwritten annotations, and only then would he begin to render the Arabic into English. Al-Tantawi would add notes correcting the text and provide interpretations or explanations of words and passages. Lane either copied al-Tantawi's comments verbatim into his own notes or used them to resolve particular difficulties in rendering the Arabic into English. Characteristically, Lane asserted that most of al-Tantawi's notes proved "unnecessary" because they only imparted what he had already learned through his interactions with modern Arabic speakers.[66] Al-Tantawi had a more expansive sense of his contribution to the translation, stating in the colophon to the Bulaq text that his comments encompassed the "emendation of this book, its annotation, its ornamentation and its embellishment."[67] Al-Tantawi's annotations were crucial for the achievement of Lane's goal of producing a literal translation, allowing him to generate what he believed was the most accurate rendering of the Arabic.

The evidence of Lane's first draft of the frame tale and "The Merchant and the Jinni" suggests that he was capable of producing a more natural style in his translation. In this early example of his method, he even attempted to render the interpolated poetry in rhyming English verse on the verso pages of his notebook. However, as he strained to produce a single rhyming couplet, Lane no doubt recognized that the project of translating the 10,000 lines of poetry contained within the *Thousand and One Nights* was not feasible given the pressures of the publishing market.[68] He had famously claimed that the poetry of the story collection was untranslatable, but he relented and translated "select pieces, chosen either for their relative merits or because required by the context."[69] He remained convinced, however, that most of the poetry included in the story collection had little merit and was riddled with errors in meter. The third volume of his translation of tales includes a review essay in which he once again confronts the fundamental problem of untranslatability: "I must state my belief, grounded upon the great difficulty that I have often experienced in attempting to translate verses which I have perfectly understood, that, partly on account of the rhetorical figures (especially paronomasia) with which they abound, and partly from other causes, arising from the wide difference of Eastern and Western minds, and modes of life, they cannot be exactly translated into our language."[70]

Today Lane's versions of the tales are immediately recognizable for their deliberately archaic use of language—the adaptation of the register of the King James Bible to an Arabic text. Lane's decision to channel the biblical tone of his early religious education was clearly a response to the predicament he articulated as he completed his draft translation of the frame tale. Preoccupied with the foreignness of his text, he chose to pursue what reviewers would term a scriptural style. In "The Story of the Fisherman," for example, Lane's evil jinni speaks in strangely biblical proverbs: "Covet not life, for thy death is unavoidable." The response of the frightened fisherman reflects the artificiality for which Lane's translation became known: "This is a Jinnee, and I am a man; and God hath given me sound reason; therefore, I will now plot his destruction with my art and reason, like as he hath plotted with his cunning and perfidy."[71] The archaic formality of this style might be seen as an expression of Lane's belief that the tales of the *Arabian Nights* were integrally connected to the stories of miracles contained in the Old Testament. Lane may have reasoned that in England the only register that readers could accept for stories of the supernatural was biblical, but the result was a literal translation that was strangely tone deaf. By adopting this style throughout the collection, Lane was able to ignore the shifts in genre in the original—from animal fable to erotic farce to historical romance.

The cultivation of the rhetorical style of the King James Bible offered one way for Lane to cope with the challenge of "untranslatability." It not only lent the fantastic stories a veneer of authority that would facilitate their acceptance as "real," it was also less laborious than seeking equivalent idiomatic expressions in English. This archaic style adheres more closely to the word order of the original Arabic and was likely easier to produce quickly.[72] Few scholars of the *Arabian Nights* have recognized the pressures under which Lane's version of the story collection was written. Lane had promised Knight a printable manuscript of the *Arabian Nights* of 2,000 pages in the size and type of *Modern*

Egyptians. It was a formidable challenge. As Lane settled down to the task of translation a year after pocketing a 200-pound advance from the overall compensation of 1,001 pounds, he had to make a series of quick calculations about the kind of *Arabian Nights* that he could produce.[73] Given his need to make a living through his writing, Lane had to make rapid progress. Not only was he worried about the threat posed by Torrens's edition, but he also needed to receive the quarterly increments that were tied to his productivity.

The results of this approach to translation were hit and miss. "The semi-scriptural tone," remarked the *London and Westminster Review* in October 1839, "rather startled us in the humorous passages."[74] Yet the same review noted the effectiveness of the biblical style in the tales of supernaturalism. Lane would likely have gladly accepted the trade-off and the verdict. Temperamentally inclined toward the literal, humor was never going to be his strength. He was much more invested in the project of rendering the supernaturalism of the tales in a believable register, and he believed that the archaic style of his translation contributed to this goal.

The addition of commentary to the story collection was another strategy that facilitated the rapid production of pages for the publisher, and thus brought Lane closer to the completion of his commission. Even if these notes were printed in a smaller font than the translations of the tales, they were much simpler to produce for the ethnographer turned translator. Based on his belief that the story collection represented a distinctly Egyptian narrative with close links to the contemporary beliefs and social practices of Cairo, Lane could quickly insert large parts of his ethnographic research into his notes. The conversations that Lane had previously transcribed during meetings with associates like Osman were now introduced into the corpus of the *Arabian Nights* along with new references to historical and theological sources. In this way, Lane's version reproduced the voices of the men who had shaped his understanding of the city—and their words became a guide to the interpretation of the tales themselves.

Lane's emphasis on commentary justified a fundamental reorganization of the story collection. After presenting the frame tale of Shahrazad and Shahriyar, Lane dropped the organizing principle of nightly storytelling. Instead, the stories are arranged in chapters, and each chapter is followed by extensive notes. This commentary offers a flood of information on all aspects of life in Egypt, and Lane used this medium to pursue his goal of reconciling the disparate worlds of Christianity and Islam, the project he shared with Osman. As Lane proceeded with his version of the *Arabian Nights,* the translation was increasingly treated as a function of his goals as a commentator, rather than the reverse.

Just as Lane deployed a biblical register to help overcome his reader's resistance to stories of the supernatural, he hoped that notes emphasizing the affinities between the Jews of the Old Testament and the Arabs of medieval and modern Egypt would ensure acceptance of those aspects of social life that were far removed from Christian conventions. For instance, his note on polygamy goes to great lengths to explain the ending to the story of Qamar al-Zaman, in which Qamar marries the princess Hayat with the agreement of his first wife, Budoor.[75] Lane argues that Moses permitted his people "to put away their wives" and that God allowed polygamy among the patriarchs. Christians therefore should be more tolerant of "Muslim laws and tenets" that "agree with the Mosaic code and the practices of holy men." Among *"a people similar to the ancient Jews"* such practices might very well be "more conducive to morality."[76]

Tales from the Bulaq edition that did not contribute to this larger goal of building understanding between these two cultures were sacrificed by Lane. For instance, the Crusades saga "'Umar ibn al-Nu'man and His Sons," a frequent component of the story collection since the fifteenth century, was cut from Lane's version.[77] Lane claims that he omitted this extended story cycle, which composed nearly one-eighth of the Bulaq edition, because he did not want it to be mistaken for a work of history. "It is entirely a fiction," he asserts in a note to his *Arabian Nights*—a strange statement in the context of a story collection that featured jinn and a multitude of improbable plot twists. More relevantly, the tale's themes of mistrust and inevitable betrayal between Muslims and Christians were at odds with his goal of building cross-cultural understanding. The worst stereotypes of Christians and Muslims are confirmed within the tale: a young woman who perceives all Muslim men as lascivious is raped by a Muslim man, while a Muslim king who fears treachery from his Christian ally is betrayed by him. The resolution of the tale through an alliance between former enemy monarchs would not have satisfied Lane, as it rests on the unmentioned conversion of the Christian king rather than a genuine truce in the war between Christians and Muslims. While this story cycle constitutes a substantial part of the *Arabian Nights* of Torrens, it is reduced to a bare summary and hidden in the labyrinthine notes of Lane's edition.[78]

Lane's notes on magic and the jinn are among the most influential of his additions to the corpus of the *Arabian Nights*. On first reading, they seem to offer the kind of systematic analysis that one might expect from a scholar of Egyptian folklore. In his note on the jinn, for example, Lane carefully distinguishes the jinn from both angels and men, and then exhaustively surveys the position of various authorities on their typical forms, their dwelling places, their special powers, and their relationship to conventional distinctions of good and evil. He asserts that these "superstitious fancies" are prevalent among all classes of the Arabs, and among the Muslims in general, "learned" as well as "vulgar." Hiding behind a series of statements beginning with "it is said" and "it is believed," Lane obscures his own willingness to entertain the existence of these supernatural creations.[79]

The note on magic appended to "The Merchant and the Jinni" plays a similar game. Here Lane relates the anecdote about the magical transformation of the brother into an ass that he had included in his draft, but he goes on to provide a systematic treatment of the various categories of magic practiced in Cairo and referenced in the *Arabian Nights*. This explanation is framed by the distinction between "spiritual magic," which is "regarded by all but freethinkers as true," and "natural magic," which is "denounced by the more religious and enlightened as deceptive." Within these two categories, however, are subcategories and overlapping practices that quickly erode any simple understanding of the difference between magic that is accepted within Islam and magic that cannot be explained through the agency of the jinn.[80] These early notes provide the reader of the *Arabian Nights* with a basic framework to explain the multitude of references to magic in the story collection. In this way, fantastical story elements become comprehensible within a distinctive Islamic cosmology.

In his note on magic in the first chapter of his translation, Lane revisits the issue of divination with the mirror of ink in a way that might suggest a newfound skepticism about the performances of al-Qadir. Lane refers readers to his discussion of this practice in *Modern Egyptians,* but seems to signal his disdain by stating that it "is by some supposed to be effected by the aid of evil Jinn" but "the more enlightened of the Muslims" place it in the discredited category of natural magic.[81] However, anyone familiar with his description of al-Qadir's use of the black lamp would find traces of it in all the different categories of Lane's discussion of magic. Sorting through these fragments, one could construct a credible explanation for the Maghrebi magician's successes. The inscriptions on the scraps of paper that he burned might indicate the power of the names of God and passages from the Quran to render jinn subservient for the purposes of divine magic. The ability of jinn to aid in divination was explained by Lane as a function of their ability to fly to the lower heavens to eavesdrop on the angels. A seer like al-Qadir could therefore call on evil jinn to share their secret knowledge by invoking their names and burning perfumes.[82]

Lane tries to steer the discussion of magic in this note away from his own experience by replacing his description of the experiments of al-Qadir with an example drawn from a source that he regarded as authoritative: the *History of Egypt* by Cairo scholar Abd al-Rahman al-Jabarti. Lane had used this text liberally in writing his "Description of Egypt," and regarded it as a credible description of life in Cairo. In his note on magic in the *Arabian Nights,* Lane cites al-Jabarti's description of Sheikh Ahmad Saduma, a magician who, sixty years before, was famous for his ability to converse with jinn. Lane explains that when a young slave girl turned to Saduma for help in attracting the love of her owner, the Mamluk chief Yusuf Bey, the magician wrote a charm on her body. When the bey saw the magic characters, he was driven to distraction by jealousy and extracted the name of the offending magician by threatening her with immediate execution. At this point, Lane switches from al-Jabarti's account to the report of a trusted "friend" for a description of the means by which the magician resisted arrest: "Several persons, one after another, endeavored to lay hold upon him; but every arm that was stretched forth for this purpose was instantly paralyzed, through a spell muttered by the magician; until a man behind him thrust a gag into his mouth, and so stopped his enchantments."[83]

The story of Sheikh Sadoomeh is a good example of the promiscuous mixture of sources in Lane's note on magic, and in his commentary as a whole. It begins with the authority of history and then moves on to incorporate testimony from "men of intelligence and of good education [who] have related to me various most marvelous stories of his performances, on the authority of eye-witnesses whom they considered veracious." The capture of the magician is attributed to "one of my friends," and another anecdote, in which the magician conjures a garden of paradise for his friends, is also attributed to a "narrator" whose "integrity" Lane cannot doubt.[84] In this fashion, the authority of history is glossed by unattributed anecdote, and experiences of the magician's art are transformed into authoritative analysis. Lane's notes thus present an indistinguishable mixture of fact and fiction, in which the voices of associates like Osman are ever-present. When one takes into account Lane's practice of inserting summaries of tales that he chose not to translate into these same notes, the confusion of genres becomes even more apparent. Resting within this potent mixture of experience and fantasy, the feats of Osman's magicians survive as a testament to Lane's relentless search for evidence of enchantment in a changing world.

Scholars of Lane's work have seldom acknowledged just how comprehensively he prioritized the production of commentary over the literary labor of translating. Lane translated about half the stories in the Bulaq edition, and this text was already much less comprehensive than the Macan manuscript from which Torrens translated. Lane admits to cutting tales that were "on any account objectionable"—primarily on the grounds of decency—but other stories are dropped because Lane found them "comparatively uninteresting."[85] Under this rubric, Lane eliminated a series of stories that could be interpreted as variations on tale types that he had already translated and annotated. If there was nothing new to comment on, the story was not interesting enough to include in Lane's version. This strategy of scaling back the number of stories that he translated intensified as the project proceeded. Given the financial pressures under which both publisher and author labored, this may have been an attempt by both to bring the preparation of this edition of the *Arabian Nights* to a close more quickly.

✦ ✦ ✦

The production of Lane's edition of the story collection proved to be an expensive undertaking for Knight, due largely to the inclusion of over 600 illustrations. Lane's previous collaboration with Knight—his ethnography of Cairo—had included over one hundred of his own images, but the engravings of the *Arabian Nights* represented a much more elaborate attempt to situate the imagined East in an authentic material context. While illustrated versions of the story collection based on Galland's translation had appeared in Britain, Lane's version was the first to systematically ground the tales in the unique landscapes and distinct material culture of the Islamic world. In his preface, Lane explained that these engravings would "considerably assist to explain both the Text and the Notes."[86] The marvels of the story collection would rest within a distinctly realist aesthetic that would allow readers to connect imaginatively to the traditional world of medieval Cairo.

Knight had an established relationship with William Harvey, one of the Victorian masters of the art of wood engraving, and he was employed to bring the stories to life. Over forty engravers—including George Dalziel and William Linton—were employed to engrave Harvey's images onto the pieces of boxwood used in this form of intaglio printing. Lane claimed that he supervised this process and made suggestions and corrections to Harvey's images as necessary. He also provided him with a series of sources to ensure that the Arab world was authentically depicted. These included examples of "modern dresses" from Egypt, which were used as models for the costumes of the characters. Most importantly, Lane supplied a series of sketches and paintings produced by early nineteenth-century artists who had made a study of the architecture of the Islamic world. These included the images of the Alhambra produced by architect Owen Jones, who in 1836 used the new technique of chromolithography to produce arresting images of the great palace of Muslim Spain in the first installment of a twelve-part publishing project. James Cavanah Murphy's study, *The Arabian Antiquities of Spain*, published from 1813 to 1816, also offered 110 plates of images that could be used to replicate elements of Islamic design. Lane also used his connection with Hay to provide Harvey with drawings of Cairo and the surrounding region executed by Pascal Coste, an architect employed by Hay to document the antique architecture of Egypt.[87]

Lane was most excited about the opportunity to use Coste's drawings to ground the illustrations in the specific material reality of Cairo. The French architect had gone to Egypt in the service of Muhammad Ali and had spent nearly ten years on public works projects like the installation of a telegraph system and the construction of the Mahmoudiah Canal. Coste also surveyed a great number of Cairo buildings, compiling a critical body of information on the Mamluk structures of the city that could be used to develop policies to preserve these structures and design appropriate new additions to the urban landscape. His drawings translated the streets and buildings of nineteenth-century Cairo into a rational visual language that could be used by Muhammad Ali's reformers to create a modern Cairo around the historical core of the city. Hay had employed Coste and other artists in the hope of producing a book of engravings of Egyptian monumental architecture, which was to be edited and supervised by Lane, but Coste was never satisfied with the role Hay had allotted him. The French architect resented Lane's influence over the project, and he hoped to regain control of the drawings that he had originally sold to Hay so he could publish them himself. Coste did publish some of his drawings of Cairo in 1837, but he had his greatest impact on the European imagination through his contributions to the illustrations in Lane's *Arabian Nights*.[88]

The engravings produced under the supervision of Harvey provided another way for Lane to create an "authentic" version of the story collection that reflected the deep connection that he believed existed between the *Arabian Nights* and the context of Egypt. The illustrations were positioned throughout the text—sometimes as decorative head and tail pieces, sometimes within the tales themselves, and sometimes within Lane's notes. They proved to be a particularly effective technique for naturalizing the supernatural qualities of the tales. The most improbable narratives were brought down to earth through the realistically rendered objects and locations of the inserted images. Galland's

French edition of the *Arabian Nights,* in contrast, had featured a frontispiece that placed Shahrazad's storytelling in a very European bedroom. There were still some distinctly Western influences in Lane's images as well—for instance, some of the jinn bear a striking resemblance to angels.[89] However, Lane's version of the story collection would also offer English readers a closer look at the "Orient" being produced by the travelling artists of the early nineteenth century, and reinforce the translator's contention that contemporary Cairo was simply an extension of the world depicted in the *Arabian Nights.*

Strangely, Lane's own drawings are not prominently featured in the illustrations to his translation. Occasionally a specific example of a Lane sketch can be discerned—for instance, in an image of the Nilometer at the southern tip of Roda Island.[90] As he was translating the *Arabian Nights,* Lane was still hoping to publish his drawings as woodcuts in a revised version of his "Description of Egypt," and so he missed the opportunity to give this part of the translation the same personal quality that he poured into his commentary. It is difficult to determine how much he intervened in the process of creating the illustrations, but certainly he did not insist on a precise representation of the architectural styles of cities such as Damascus or Cairo. In fact it is difficult to determine the source for each of the images. While the engraver is credited in each case, the creators of the original images are not. The result is a confusing mixture of the work of many artists and craftsmen. Odd combinations often emerge from this mélange. For instance, the *mihrab* (prayer niche) of the Great Mosque of Cordoba becomes a doorway in the background of Lane's tale of "The Porter and the Ladies of Baghdad"; the tomb built for Caliph Harun al-Rashid's beloved concubine Qut al-Qulub in Baghdad seems to be modelled on Indo-Islamic mausoleum architecture; and an image of the Great Mosque of Cairo appears in "The City of Brass," masquerading as "The Palace of Kosh, son of Sheddad." Lane did, however, find a proper place for an image of pyramids in "The Story of Nur al-Din 'Ali and His Son Badr al-Din Hasan," which features a journey to Cairo.[91]

As the final installment of Lane's *Arabian Nights* appeared in 1841, Knight went bankrupt, without ever paying the translator his full 1,001 pounds for the translation. Luckily, other publishers would take over

Illustration from Edward Lane, *The Thousand and One Nights.* The three volumes were embellished with 600 woodcuts, one of the most ambitious commissions of this kind in the era. This image of a mausoleum is from "The Story of Ghanim the Son of Eiyoob, the Distracted Slave of Love."

Lane's project and produce further editions of a work that proved remarkably popular. The expensively produced illustrations may have been responsible for Knight's downfall, but they were often singled out as the most appealing part of the work as a whole. Some of the credit in this respect accrued to Harvey rather than the translator. The *Athenaeum* declared its "admiration of Mr. Harvey's tasteful and beautiful illustrations with an earnestness not altogether in keeping with the unimpassioned dignity becoming critics."[92] The *Dublin Review* placed these extraordinary images within the realist ethos that characterized Lane's project as a whole. For the "thousands who will not take the trouble to judge whether the translation is faithful, or the reverse," the illustrations "all but place the reality bodily before us, with a vividness and distinctness which all the description in the world could never reach." In this case the reviewer attributed this magical effect to Lane's direct experience of the Oriental world: "It is not the lot of every man to see, as Mr. Lane has done, with his own eyes, the streets of Cairo,—to mingle in her feasts,—to walk side by side with the sacred camel,—and to marvel over an ocular inspection of the wonders of the 'inky' magic." Out of "his own elegant and accurate taste," the reviewer argued, Lane had "selected the illuminations whence these gems are copied and altered," and it mattered little whose actual fingers traced the design or carved the block.[93] In this way, Lane received the laurels for the labor of the many artists behind the illustrations.

Lane's notes to his translation also received praise from reviewers. The *Dublin Review* described these notes as "terse, clear, and judicious" and suggested that they might "be read for amusement in an idle mood, or referred to with advantage in a studious one."[94] The *London and Westminster Review* similarly singled out the "rich and curious notes" of Lane's translation, which "promised to comprise all the most valuable information of his *Modern Egyptians*."[95] The *Athenaeum* expressed a desire to reprint excerpts from Lane's notes rather than sections from the translated tales. Its reviewer described the commentary as "a faithful and, as it were, living picture of the East."[96] Lane's translations of the stories evoked less enthusiastic responses among the critics. Attention to Lane's main text came primarily in retrospect, especially in long review essays prompted by the publication of the *Arabian Nights* of John Payne and Burton in 1885 and 1886. The most impassioned supporter of Lane's version over these later versions would be his nephew Lane-Poole, writing in the *Edinburgh Review.* And, as Robert Irwin has observed, Lane-Poole's judgment that Lane's text was more readable than Burton's does not set a high bar for a translation's fluency.[97]

Lane seems to have taken the early criticism of his translation to heart, and when his *Arabian Nights* was issued in three volumes he added a "review" at the end of the last volume to address some of the issues raised by critics. In particular, he attempts to address those reviewers who disliked his "unfamiliar style," especially when compared to Torrens's version of the collection. In aiming at "closeness and fidelity," the *London and Westminster Review* argued, Lane had "sacrificed Arab spirit to Arab letter, and consequently the greater peculiarity to the less." The reviewer could only imagine that the spirit of the original "must be far more easy, natural, impulsive, and unobstructed by a constant sense of strangeness." Lane tries to defend himself against the suggestion that he is "not duly sensible of the beauties" of the original, but still takes refuge in the virtues of "closeness and fidelity." He argues once again that the "chief value" of the *Arabian Nights* "consists in the fullness and fidelity with which it describes the character, manners and customs of the Arabs, though its *enchantment* is doubtless mainly owing to other qualities."[98] The idea that capturing the spirit of the text might require more than replicating the meaning of the words of his original was still lost on Lane.

Lane finally found the perfect outlet for his obsession with linguistic detail when he took on the task of producing his *Arabic-English Lexicon.* Begun during his last stay in Cairo, between 1842 and 1849, this lexicographical research brought Lane into an intense collaborative relationship with al-Dasūqī, whose interests in philology closely matched Lane's own. Educated at the college of al-Azhar, and familiar with a broad range of texts through his work as an editor at the Bulaq press, al-Dasūqī was an ideal partner for Lane, and the two became close friends during the seven years in which they labored on the lexicon. Arriving at Lane's home six afternoons a week, al-Dasūqī would work alongside the Englishman, transcribing the rare manuscripts that he had borrowed from the libraries of Cairo's mosques and discussing the many complexities of Arabic philology. Even after Lane returned to England in 1849, al-Dasūqī would continue to dissect words and phrases for him through their correspondence.[99] Throughout these years, Lane would try to maintain his singular control over the *Lexicon,* and hide his collaborative relationship with al-Dasūqī. As Lane fended off the advances of other Orientalists, he argued in a letter to his friend Lord Prudhoe that such a work could only be successfully pursued by "a single person" who possessed "very extensive and varied knowledge" of Arabic "obtainable only by long intercourse."[100] The *Arabic-English Lexicon* would be considered Lane's great legacy, and al-Dasūqī would be remembered in Orientalist circles merely as his assistant.

This intensive model of collaboration was Lane's ideal method of work, but it was not well suited to the production of a translation of the *Arabian Nights* under the pressures of the English publishing market. The compromises Lane made are evident in the end result. Translating about half of the Bulaq edition of the *Thousand and One Nights,* Lane managed to produce a version of the work in which the stories of Shahrazad are much reduced—in length and in importance. A close examination of Lane's method yields a clearer portrait of him as the first translator to claim authorship of the *Arabian Nights* on the basis of the composition of notes rather than the rendering of the stories. It also allows us to understand the way in which the voices of various intermediaries were inserted into the work. Rewriting and recycling material from his informants in Cairo proved more attractive to Lane than translating from Arabic, a labor he bemoaned in his correspondence with Hay.[101] Lane preferred to rewrite the accounts of his Egyptian friends, with copious cross-references to his collection of Arabic manuscripts, rather than to translate the Arabic of the tales. For him, producing two pages of commentary was less work than a single page of translation. The result was a version of the story collection in which the commentary plays a predominant role. Lane's work would be read not for the new stories that it contained, but for its beautiful illustrations and the fascinating anecdotes gathered in its commentary.

While Said's portrait of Lane in *Orientalism* is in some respects inaccurate, there is a certain amount of duplicity in Lane's reworking of the *Arabian Nights.* Already in his ethnography of Cairo, Lane had begun to assume the voices of his informants, and as he reworked the dictated notes of his sources to provide commentary for the *Arabian Nights,* he went even further in obscuring the identities of the key figures who had contributed this information. As Lane completed his edition of the story collection and turned to a new project, this instinct became even stronger. Hoping to publish a volume on Thebes composed of drawings and excerpts from his journal, he began to rewrite his diary entries to conceal the importance of those friends and acquaintances who had made his life and work in Cairo possible.[102]

In Lane's journal, it is still possible to make out the erasures through which Lane remolded his initial impressions of Osman into a more conventional form. Lane had originally written that the Scotsman had "adopted" the name Osman, thereby emphasizing his choice in the matter of his name, and his faith. But he would later erase this term, and over the rubbed-out word he would record the common traveller's perception that the Scot had "received" the name, presumably after a forced conversion of the sort attributed to him by Kinglake.[103] Traces of Osman would prove harder to erase from Lane's commentary to the *Arabian Nights,* where Lane's explorations of the religious life and the magical practices of Cairo found an appropriate setting. In these notes, Lane's voice is intertwined with those of informants like Osman, and the fictions of the *Arabian Nights* tales mingle with stories of the marvellous feats of Egypt's magicians.

5

THE WILES OF WOMEN

English readers familiar with stories of sexual transgression in Edward Lane's ethnography of Egypt might have received the news of his forthcoming translation of the *Arabian Nights* with particular interest. In *Modern Egyptians* (1836), Lane had claimed that "some of the stories of the intrigues of women in *The Thousand and One Nights* presented faithful pictures of occurrences not infrequent in the modern metropolis of Egypt."[1] Potential readers of Lane's *Arabian Nights* were certainly encouraged to expect this sexual content in the new translation. An advertisement by the publisher Charles Knight placed in several English newspapers and journals in March 1838 promised an *Arabian Nights* that would be much more than the fairy tales of Antoine Galland: "It is one of the chief objects of the translator to render these enchanting fictions as interesting to persons of mature age and education as they have hitherto been to the young."[2] While scholars now quickly categorize Lane's work as comfortable fare for a growing readership of women and children in Victorian England, this was not the original vision of the author or the publisher.

Lane's first draft of the famous frame tale, in which Shahrazad uses her gift for storytelling to circumvent the murderous plans of her husband, Shahriyar, revels in episodes of sexual transgression and dwells on the deceptive stratagems of women. Compared to the infamous "decorum" of Lane's final published version of the stories (1838–1840), the style of this first piece of translation is startlingly direct and earthy. The critical backstory is provided in full. After a long separation, King Shah Zaman of Samarkand leaves his kingdom to pay a visit to his older brother, King Shahriyar of the "Islands of India and China." En route, Shah Zaman unexpectedly decides to return to his palace to retrieve a present he had prepared for his brother, and makes a shocking discovery. "On entering his chamber in the palace," Lane's draft reads, "he beheld his wife lying in his bed, with one of his black slaves in her embraces." The world becomes "black before his eyes," and Shah Zaman kills his wife and her lover "together in the bed." When Shah Zaman finally arrives in Shahriyar's kingdom, he does not explain the cause of his strange melancholy and refuses to join his brother in the hunt organized to divert him. In the absence of his brother and his retainers, Shah Zaman becomes a witness to the even more spectacular betrayal of his powerful brother in an orgy in the palace garden:

> Now there was a window of the palace overlooking a garden; and as Sha'h Zema'n sat there, gazing at the prospect, lo, a door of the palace opened, and there came forth from it twenty females and twenty black male slaves; and in the midst of them was the queen, who was distinguished by most admirable fairness and beauty. These all proceeded to a fountain where they threw off their clothes, and sat down; both the females and the black slaves. The queen then called out "Ya' Mes'oo'd!"; and immediately a black slave ran to her; and they embraced each other, and lay down together. In like manner, also, did the rest of the women: each chose her partner from among the blacks; and they ceased not to indulge in kissing and embracing and voluptuous revelling until the approach of day.

Learning that his brother has suffered a similar betrayal, Shah Zaman's "sorrow and grief" flee from him, and he no longer refrains from eating and drinking.[3]

Upon his return from the hunt, Shahriyar compels his brother to explain the improvement in his mood and appearance, and together the brothers lay a trap to reveal the queen's betrayal. After pretending to set out on another hunt the following morning, Shahriyar witnesses the spectacle of his own cuckolding, and "reason [flees] from his head." The two brothers abandon the palace, vowing not to return until they have found "some person who has suffered as great a calamity" as theirs. On this journey they encounter a powerful jinni: "The sea became troubled, and there arose from it a black pillar, reaching to the sky, and approaching the meadow. . . . It was a Jin'nee, of gigantic stature, broad front, and lusty body." Hiding from this fearsome creature in a nearby tree, the two kings discover that this jinni had stolen a young girl on her wedding night and now holds her imprisoned in a chest. As soon as the jinni releases the young girl "of slender and beautiful form" and falls asleep, his captive threatens to betray the brother kings to the jinni unless they satisfy her: "She then told them how she desired to be gratified with their company; and, on their hesitating, through fear, she repeated her threat of awaking the 'Efree't: so they complied." After "they had remained with her as long as she desired," the young girl takes from her pocket a purse and draws out a string of 570 seal rings, explaining to the brother kings that "the owners of these rings . . . have all of them been my lovers, in spite of this Efreet." She then demands their seal rings to add to her collection. In this draft, Lane delights in the frankness of the jinni's "bride" and the astronomical number of rings that represent her sexual conquests, though he admits in a note to the draft that an equally reliable source cites the number as ninety-eight.[4]

Lane's forthright presentation of these sexual betrayals reflect his own claim, detailed at length in *Modern Egyptians,* that the women of Cairo were particularly licentious. This is made abundantly clear in the poem that appears in the draft, which was translated by Lane with a directness that is missing in his published version of the same tale:

Who trusts in woman will be ill repaid:
By sensual passion only is she sway'd:
False love & guile her heart & mind pervade.

> Regard her as in Yoo'soof's tale portray'd;
> And see in Adam's fall her wiles display'd.

In the note attached to this draft, Lane offers support for his belief that the *Thousand and One Nights* contained portraits of "the wickedness of women" that were integrally connected to patterns of life in contemporary Cairo. At first he begins by citing a saying attributed to the Prophet: "I stood . . . at the door of paradise; and lo, most of its inmates were the poor, and I stood at the door of hell; and lo, most of its inmates were women." Yet he struck it out and placed it later in his note, commencing instead with testimony from his informants in contemporary Egypt:

> The wickedness of women is a subject upon which the stronger sex among the Arabs, with an affected feeling of superior virtue, often dwell in common conversation. That women are deficient in judgment or good sense is held as a fact not to be disputed even by themselves as it rests on an assertion of the Prophet; but that they possess a superior degree of cunning is pronounced equally certain and notorious.

If Lane seems critical of the affectation of superiority that accompanies these statements, he does little to counter these contentions. Instead, he adds another authoritative source from the history of Islam to reinforce the opinions he has gathered during his stay in Cairo—a quotation from Caliph 'Umar suggesting that one "do the contrary of what [women] advise."[5]

The boldness of Lane's draft of the opening of the *Arabian Nights* is striking given his reputation for having made the stories familiar and safe for the consumption of his middle-class family readership in mid-nineteenth-century England. Indeed, in Lane's published version of the frame tale, the women of Shahriyar's court simply exchange embraces and engage in "revelling," and the two kings merely stay with the jinni's captive "as long as she required." Not surprisingly given these obfuscations, Lane chooses the lower option of ninety-eight seal rings as a more reasonable symbol of the misdeeds of the young woman, and she simply states that their owners were "admitted to converse with me, like as ye have." These alterations are explained by Lane's insistence in his preface that he believed it right to omit tales and anecdotes that might give offense. In these changes, the "scandalous decorum" that Jorge Luis Borges famously saw in Lane's version of the *Arabian Nights* is clearly visible.[6]

Yet despite the many infamous omissions in Lane's translated tales, the commentary that he provides remains remarkably consistent with the original impulse embodied in the draft of the frame tale. The published note "On the wickedness of Women," attached to his introduction, is essentially a reprise of the same assertions by his Arab informants of the moral weaknesses and sexual cunning of women, including the statement of the Prophet with which Lane contemplated beginning his draft. While he is careful to cite official authorities for most of these statements (the Prophet, Caliph 'Umar, "a learned Imam"), his own position on the subject is left ambiguous in the last anecdote in the note, in which Lane recalls being awakened from his rest near an ancient tomb near Thebes by "the cries of a young woman in the neighborhood, whom an Arab was severely beating for an impudent proposal that she had made to him." Lane's reason for accepting such an explanation for the incident is left mysterious.[7]

Through Lane's commentary, sexual transgression remains an underlying theme of his translation of the *Arabian Nights*. If the exigencies of the book market in England demanded that the most explicit sexual references of the stories be omitted in order to ensure access to the middle-class market targeted by Charles Knight, Lane was willing to move this material into the elaborate commentary that would be his primary contribution to the corpus of the collection.[8] It is also in these notes, inserted after each chapter of tales, that one can find some of the central stories of the collection, including pieces of the story cycle "The Craft and Malice of Women." Positioned in the notes, these tales are inflected by the results of Lane's ethnographic research in Cairo—the voices of the men who supplied the cultural commentary on sex, gender, and the norms of marriage. Unsuccessful in gaining entry to the intimate world of women during his stays in Cairo in 1825–1828 and 1833–1834, Lane was dependent on stories supplied by his principal informant on such matters, a bookseller named Sheikh Ahmad. Guided by these encounters with Sheikh Ahmad, Lane's notes became a labyrinthine structure of fictional tales and factual anecdotes, textual authority and misinformation.

In its many variations in Arabic, the *Thousand and One Nights* is a series of tales told by Shahrazad with the goal of ending Shahriyar's reign of terror over the young women of his kingdom. After the spectacular betrayal he suffers at the hands of his wife and his experience with the jinni's bride, Shahriyar resolves to marry a virgin every night and kill her the next morning. When he begins to run out of young women to marry, he orders his vizier to find him another bride, and Shahrazad, the vizier's daughter, volunteers for this duty. Using her knowledge of books and her gift for storytelling, she seeks to deflect her husband from his murderous plans each night by insisting that she finish her story the next day. And so begins the legendary 1,001 nights of storytelling. In his published translation of the *Arabian Nights,* however, Lane quickly abandons Shahrazad and her stories after relating the frame tale, only returning to her for a short epilogue at the end of volume three. Shahrazad is only the first of many strong female characters who disappear from Lane's version. His is an *Arabian Nights* without the rich panorama of clever slave girls and brazen female tricksters that the story collection usually offers. He not only omits many of the sexual stratagems of women, but he also eliminates many of the feats of intelligence and courage that define female agency in the tales. Given the imbalance between the notes and the tales in Lane's work, this new version of the story collection belongs in many ways to storytellers other than Shahrazad—particularly to informants like Sheikh Ahmad who created the image of licentious Cairo that pervades the text.

✦ ✦ ✦

The prominence of women within the *Thousand and One Nights*—and the reoccurring theme of the battle between the sexes—was an open invitation for Lane to include essays on these subjects in his commentary. As he struggled to finish his manuscript before the appearance of a rival translation by Henry Torrens, it was only natural that he drew on the research he had done on these subjects for his ethnography of modern Egypt. Translating the stories in England in 1837–1840, Lane turned to the journals and notes from his two previous stays in Cairo to supply material for his commentary. Lane's *Arabian Nights* reflects his previous explorations of the cultural values of Cairo, but it also indicates the limits of his ability to truly assimilate to this world. If Lane was successful in accessing popular practices of magic through the mediation of Osman Effendi, he was much less successful at finding ways to observe the lives of women. Lane's stubborn refusal to conform to the conventions of Cairo by adding a wife or a slave girl to his household represented a frustration of his dream of cultural integration and cut off his access to the realm of domestic life that was one of the chief objects of his curiosity.

Lane's boast in print that, as a confirmed bachelor of thirty-three in Cairo, he would rather risk the ire of Muslims than accommodate himself to local mores by marrying a widow or taking a slave girl justifiably earned the scorn of Edward Said in *Orientalism*. Lane may have dreamed of reconciling Islam and Christianity by following the example of converts to Islam like the Swiss explorer Jean Louis Burckhardt and the Scottish former slave Osman, but he could not attain that dream in his domestic life. Burckhardt had slaves of both sexes when he lived in Cairo, and Osman acquired his own wives and slaves, as well as inheriting Burckhardt's upon his death. Lane's household, in contrast, did not contain either a wife or a slave girl during his first two stays in Cairo, despite his desire to live as Muslims did.[9]

During these stays, Lane complained that he was continually reproached for his condition as a bachelor. During his first residency, from 1825 to 1828, Lane was surprised by how difficult he found it to rent lodging in a Muslim neighborhood. At his age, bachelorhood indicated apostasy or worse, as Lane delicately put it ("to use no harsher term"). His prospective landlords and friends sought to persuade him of the ease with which he could observe local conventions by taking in a slave girl or marrying a widow, even just for the duration of his stay. Lane took pride in being sensitive to local customs, but he proved stubborn on this point. The matter came to a head when he thought he had succeeded in renting an apartment, only to have the lease voided and his deposit returned. When he was able to negotiate a lease with Osman in the same neighborhood, even this came with a caveat: Lane could rent as a bachelor so long as he did not receive visitors wearing hats, that is, European men. Lane was exasperated at having to navigate these codes of respectable behavior. In particular, he resented the implication that he could live as he pleased as long as he made the minimum concession to convention.[10]

Lane understood the logic behind the rules preventing bachelors from renting in Muslim areas of the city. He was well aware that the governing Mamluks were credited with having made Egypt "infamous" as a relatively tolerant haven for homosexuality in the region.[11] He was also aware that European residents in Cairo were suspected of homosexuality. During festivities celebrating the wedding of Ahmad Pasha's sister in 1834, Lane observed a private performance in which Europeans were mocked as passive partners in homosexual acts: "The chief buffoon & two others, dressed as Franks [entered]; the chief with a cocked hat, & sword; & the third with a musket. After these three had danced, & performed a number of silly acts, they approached the canopy; from which several black slaves, quite naked, ran out, & attacked them." Disturbed by the memory, he abruptly interrupts the diary entry in which he recounted "the foolish & loathsome scenes exhibited during the festival."[12] Viewing Cairo's Ottomanized elite as relatively tolerant of several forms of "sexual corruption," Lane thought it particularly perverse for them to single out Europeans to mock as homosexuals. Reacting defensively against the suggestion that sexual deviance was characteristic of European residents of Cairo, Lane refused to do anything that might be interpreted as tacitly admitting that he was a homosexual seeking to conceal his activities.

One of the strangest ironies of Lane's life in Cairo was that, despite his vigorous denial of the necessity of acquiring a slave, he did in fact accept a slave girl in 1828. Lane's statement in 1836 that he was too impoverished to buy a slave for himself may have been accurate, but there was no barrier to him accepting the gift of a slave from his close friend in Cairo, the Egyptologist Robert Hay. Like other foreigners in Cairo at the time, Hay had obtained his own slave girl upon his arrival in Egypt in 1824, probably with the help of Osman. Kalitza, a young Greek girl, was renowned among Hay's friends for her beauty, and Hay openly flaunted the sexual nature of their relationship. The War of Greek Independence flooded Cairo's markets with Greek slaves, and Hay may have seen himself as liberating these young Christian girls from captivity. Other aspiring Egyptologists of Lane's acquaintance, like Joseph Bonomi and James Burton, had a less romantic understanding of their role as slave owners. On his return to England in 1828, Hay had no reluctance about resolving Kalitza's legal position by marrying her during their time in quarantine in Malta, and contemporaries believed the marriage was a success. Bonomi, on the other hand, abandoned his slave companion Fatima and their two children on his return to England, where he would pursue a successful career as a museum curator.[13]

When Hay acquired another slave girl, Nefeeseh, for his friend Lane, she too was Greek, and she developed a close bond with both Hay and Kalitza during her time as a member of their household. However, Lane's relationship with Nefeeseh was different from Hay's relationship with Kalitza from the outset. Although Kalitza looked fourteen at the time of her wedding, she was only twelve years old. Nefeeseh, in contrast, was two or three years younger, and there is no evidence that Lane had a romantic interest in her. Returning to England with Nefeeseh in 1828 created a host of problems for Lane. By the 1820s slavery in the British Empire was under attack from abolitionists and under legislative investigation. Nefeeseh's legal status on her entry into England is unclear, but Lane or his mother must have acted as her guardian. It is uncertain whether Lane had promised Hay that he would marry her when she matured, but it does seem that his friend expected him to do so. By 1832, Hay was clearly disappointed that Lane had not married her of his own accord. In a letter to his friend, he demanded that Lane either marry her or return her to his own household. The timing of this letter is crucial. Hay knew of Lane's plans to return to Cairo in 1833. If Lane was not going to marry Nefeeseh, he could have returned her to Cairo and made it possible for her to marry someone else. Under Islamic law, a master who dismisses a female slave from his household is expected to provide her with a dowry and a respectable husband.[14]

Whatever impression Lane may have initially given to Hay regarding Nefeeseh's future, he would have to contend with the opinion of his family when he returned to England. After showing his correspondence with Hay to his mother, Lane expressed, or at least feigned, astonishment at the suggestion of marriage: "I must not dismiss this subject without observing that several expressions in y^{r} letter strike me & my Mother as implying that, on my receiving N—, you considered it a *settled point* that I was to *marry* her!" The mere suggestion was an affront for Lane, as it implied Hay would "sacrifice the feelings & wishes of an old and tried friend to [his] consideration for her." Lane resented Hay's tone of moral superiority. He knew that Hay and others within the expatriate community purchased young slaves primarily for sexual purposes. On this front Lane felt himself to be above reproach, given that his interest in Nefeeseh had never been of that nature. Defiantly, Lane wrote Hay in reply that "as long as she remains under my Mother's roof, the world can say nothing; and sh^{d} I even be obliged to take her to live with myself alone, & not willing or not able, to marry her, nor base enough to take any dishonorable advantage of her, the world may say what they please, & I shall not be fool enough to mind their scandal."[15] In his correspondence, Lane clearly reveals his sexual disinterest in Nefeeseh and his unwillingness to insert himself into Orientalist narratives of harems and concubines.

When Lane returned to Cairo in 1833, he did not bring Nefeeseh with him, even though her presence in his household would have made his integration into Egyptian society much simpler. As either wife or slave, Nefeeseh might have given Lane access to new sources of information on the life of women in Cairo during the critical period in which he was completing the research for *Modern Egyptians*. Barred from social interactions with Cairo's women, Lane discovered that even Muslim men would not speak candidly to him on the subjects he desired. Lane had hoped he could get Muslim men of Cairo to talk about their harems, but not even his close friend Osman would discuss his wives. Living next to Osman from 1833 to 1834, Lane would have benefitted greatly from the opportunity to observe his harem, and he was no doubt disappointed when Osman asked his wives to leave before showing Lane into his harem.[16] Lane had wrongly imagined that his close relationship with Osman, in which they shared an interest in the supernatural, could override dictates regarding the separation of men and women within the Muslim household. Lane's difficulty in gaining the confidence of respectable Muslim men in Cairo left him vulnerable in his search for sources for his ethnography. The evidence of Lane's diaries and notebooks makes it clear that only one Muslim resident of Cairo would visit his home to engage in a discussion of women and sex—the bookseller Sheikh Ahmad.[17]

If Lane had little interest in creating a domestic life with Nefeeseh, he revelled in his social interactions with Cairo's men. His favorite site for pursuing his ethnographic research was the bookshop of Sheikh Ahmad, which was located on Cairo's main thoroughfare across from the Khan al-Khalili, the central Turkish bazaar. Lane's biographers typically draw a portrait of him seated outside the bookshop observing the hustle and bustle of street life every Monday and Thursday morning. However, Lane's own statements suggest that a great part of the attraction was the shop itself. Seated in the bookshop, he could immerse himself in the social interplay of an establishment "often frequented for the purpose of passing time in agreeable conversation."[18] In a note to his translation of the *Arabian Nights,* Lane explains the pleasures of socializing in this shop. Quoting from his own diary entry from October 27, 1834, Lane provides a rare glimpse of his lost journals from 1833–1834. In this excerpt, Lane confesses that despite the action on the street, "I am often much more amused with the persons who frequent the shop where I take my seat." Lane clearly valued the bookshop as a meeting place where people from different walks of life could socialize. For English readers accustomed to rigid class divisions, Lane explained that this distinctive social environment was a result of a culture in which even the wealthy were expected to practice a profession, and trade was considered "far more honourable." However, he also emphasized the benefits of the segregation of the sexes. Since it was indecent for women to congregate in shops, Lane argues, men from different social and economic backgrounds could mingle in an exclusively male sphere "without the risk of occasioning unequal matrimonial connections."[19]

In Sheikh Ahmad's bookshop, Lane could encounter a wide variety of people who could illuminate different aspects of Egyptian culture for him. His diary entry from October 27 provides a snapshot of the colorful characters who gathered in the shop regularly. In addition to

Sheikh Ahmad, there was his senior partner in the bookshop, who told the assembled group the story of how he had cleverly convinced two of his neighbors to sell him their shares of the house next door for a good price. There was also a "celebrated" old man who hid his great wealth to keep it from being confiscated, and a customer with a cataract in one eye who feared going to the hospital because "he had heard that many patients there were killed and boiled, to make skeletons."[20] Most importantly, the shop offered Lane reliable access to one of the principal sources in his ethnographic research: Sheikh Ahmad himself. Lane described him as "remarkable" in both "physiognomy" and "character." Sheikh Ahmad was likely in his forties but appeared rather older than this to Lane. He had a fair complexion, a reddish beard streaked with gray, and eyes that he accented with kohl on special occasions. Lane believed him to be nearly blind, and images portray him with one eye almost entirely closed. Before he had become a bookseller, "he had obtained his living exclusively by performing zikrs"—Sufi ceremonies based on the repetition of the name of God.[21]

Lane did not visit Sheikh Ahmad's bookshop twice a week just to be amused. The journal entry makes it clear that Lane relied on those who were in the shop to explain what he saw taking place on the street outside, so that he could record it for his ethnography. In the entry preserved for October 27, 1834, a funeral procession passed by the shop, and Lane asked whose it was. Surprised to hear that it was for the sheikh of the Saadeeyeh dervishes, whom he had seen just a few days earlier in perfect health, Lane was even more astonished to see the sheikh himself walking in the funeral procession. When Lane expressed confusion, he was told that the deceased was the sheikh's wife, who was a popular saint.[22] This type of confusion was characteristic of Lane's attempts to interpret the life of the city. Admirers of *Modern Egyptians* have often celebrated the liveliness and immediacy of Lane's descriptions of public life in Cairo. Lane's journal entry for this October day suggests that these qualities derive from the running commentary of local interlocutors who explained the cultural significance of the colorful processions as he witnessed them.

Lane's understanding of contemporary Cairo was shaped by the animated conversations that he encountered in Sheikh Ahmad's bookshop,

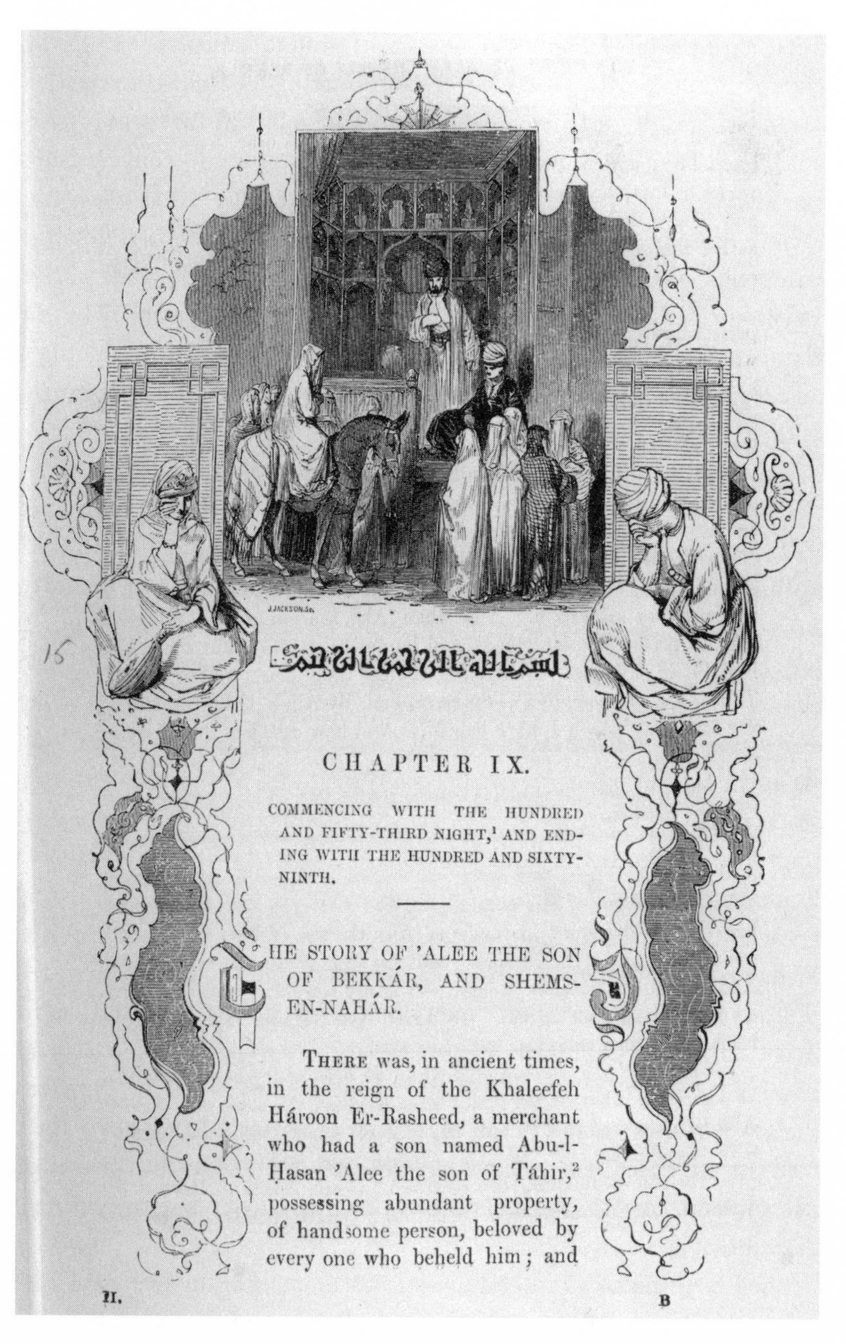

بسم الله الرحمن الرحيم

CHAPTER IX.

COMMENCING WITH THE HUNDRED AND FIFTY-THIRD NIGHT,[1] AND ENDING WITH THE HUNDRED AND SIXTY-NINTH.

THE STORY OF 'ALEE THE SON OF BEKKÁR, AND SHEMS-EN-NAHÁR.

There was, in ancient times, in the reign of the Khaleefeh Hároon Er-Rasheed, a merchant who had a son named Abu-l-Ḥasan 'Alee the son of Ṭáhir,[2] possessing abundant property, of handsome person, beloved by every one who beheld him; and

II. B

The bookshop of Sheikh Ahmad was Edward Lane's favorite place to exchange news and observe the life of Cairo. This illustration from Lane's *Arabian Nights* shows how the stores of Cairo opened onto the street.

but this verbal play could often be as confusing to Lane as the sights on the street outside. The use of irony and humor in casual conversation could be difficult for Lane to decipher, despite his skills in speaking Arabic. The use of extended metaphors to carry on entire conversations was always mystifying. As Lane admits in a note to the *Arabian Nights,* "I have more frequently been unsuccessful in attempting to divine the nature of a topic in which other persons were engaged."[23] Lane described Egyptians as "generally very lively and dramatic in their talk," but he claimed they were "scarcely ever noisy in their mirth." Recognizing a joke was difficult for a foreign observer like Lane when the amusement of the audience was registered only in "a smile or an exclamation."[24]

Lane's diary entry for October 27 provides one glimpse of the subtleties of the verbal exchanges in Sheikh Ahmad's bookshop. The man with the cataract had come to the shop to request a copy of Rifa'a Rafi' al-Tahtawi's recently published account of his stay in France. Al-Tahtawi, a product of al-Azhar college, had travelled in 1826 as a religious guide for the first group of Egyptian students sent to France for a Western education. His record of his travels, known in English translation today as *An Imam in Paris,* was printed at the pasha's press in Bulaq in 1834. As agents of that press, both Sheikh Ahmad and his partner not only stocked the work but were familiar with its contents.[25] When the customer asked about the book, he was told that during his voyage to France, al-Tahtawi got drunk on wine, ate pork, and was delighted by French girls. In short, that he "qualified himself, by every accomplishment, for an eminent place in Hell." Lane does not record who provided this answer to the customer's query, but it was clearly a satirical summary of the content of the book. In fact, al-Tahtawi continued to strictly observe the tenets of Islam in Paris. As to French women, he criticizes their lack of chastity and the absolute power they seem to have over their men. In this case, Lane either correctly read the tone of the speaker or had someone explain the meaning of this interplay later. He accurately describes it as an "ironic quizz."[26]

Sheikh Ahmad was an enthusiastic participant in the lively and humorous exchanges that were typical of his bookshop. Certainly his relationship with Lane was couched in this kind of teasing interplay, as an account of the purchase of a Quran seems to indicate. Offering Lane a copy of the holy book, Sheikh Ahmad claimed that he could only sell it to him in good conscience because he had greeted the bookseller as a Muslim and therefore could be assumed to be a believer. Surely Lane knew the Quranic command, "None shall touch it but they who are purified."[27] Yet in the midst of this formal exchange, Sheikh Ahmad tested Lane with a question the Englishman found curious: Wouldn't the king be upset by his profession of Islam? Lane laughed off the inquiry. For him, the question betrayed Sheikh Ahmad's naïve belief that every European traveller in Cairo had been sent by his king. That a man should himself incur the trouble and expense of foreign travel to acquire knowledge is alien to the Egyptian mindset, Lane observes in his notes.[28] It is a strange accusation to make against a bookseller who, as the al-Tahtawi anecdote indicates, was well connected to the emerging information networks that bound Egypt and Europe together. It is tempting to see Lane as the gullible one in this interaction—unable to identify the joke behind the question.

Lane believed that he was slowly building a relationship of trust with the bookseller that would result in another window into the distinctive social practices of contemporary Cairo. He was particularly attracted to Sheikh Ahmad's history as a Sufi dervish and was determined to impress him with the seriousness of his engagement with Islam. Toward the end of his first Egyptian sojourn in 1827, Lane proudly reported that he had convinced Sheikh Ahmad to pray with him at al-Hussein Mosque, famous for the shrine said to contain the head of Hussein, the Prophet's grandson. In Lane's account, Sheikh Ahmad first adamantly refused his request to enter the mosque and pray alongside him. Only after observing the correct manner in which Lane circled the bronze screen surrounding the shrine and settled into the right postures of prayer did Sheikh Ahmad come to pray by his side. Lane was convinced that he had gained Sheikh Ahmad's trust through such demonstrations of faith, for his friend reciprocated by speaking more openly of his life. He confessed that before he had become a bookseller (the profession of his father), he had followed the path of a dervish, joining a famous order of serpent eaters. Lane was thrilled to have come across a reliable source on one of the subjects that interested him most. In conversation, Sheikh Ahmad proved invaluable in helping Lane distinguish between the wild stories that people told about the feats of dervishes—claiming, for example, that they would lay prostrate under the advancing hooves of horses—and those acts of devotion observed by Sheikh Ahmad or an acquaintance of his—such as running a sword through one's arm in an act of mourning. For Lane, the act of seeing—in this case through the eyes of the bookseller or his friends—offered all the proof necessary to assert the credibility of such practices in his ethnographic notes.

In his published writing, Lane claims that many respectable members of Cairene society would discuss women and their harems with him, but the evidence of Lane's diaries and notebooks makes it clear that Sheikh Ahmad was his principal source of information on these topics. Lane recognized the rather dubious character of the bookseller, but he believed that this made Sheikh Ahmad all the more valuable as an informant on the forbidden areas of Muslim social life. In his notebook Lane wrote, "He has a talent for intrigue & cheating, which he exercises on every opportunity; being lax in morals, & rather so in his religious tenets." Precisely *because* Sheikh Ahmad was lax in his morals, Lane reasoned, "I find him very useful." More upstanding men, including Osman, would not be drawn into a discussion of the subjects that Lane needed to research for his ethnography, two-fifths of which concerned domesticity and the lives of women. Completing *Modern Egyptians* from information offered by Sheikh Ahmad, Lane saw no contradiction between his recognition of the bookseller as a trickster and his acknowledgment that "much of the information that I have obtained respecting the manner & customs of his countrymen has been derived from him, or through his assistance."[29]

When, in the published note to his *Arabian Nights* on "the wickedness of Women," Lane claims that this is a "subject upon which the stronger sex among the Arabs . . . often dwell in common conversation," he might more accurately have referenced the stories exchanged in the blessedly all-male environment of Sheikh Ahmad's bookshop or the tales told to him by the bookseller during his frequent visits to Lane's house.[30] These visits were a critical part of the bookseller's ritual during Lane's second stay in Cairo. At this time, there were only eight Arabic bookshops in Cairo, and their inventory was so small that when a bookseller acquired a new item, he would go around to the houses of his regular customers to inform them. In his capacity as travelling salesman, Sheikh Ahmad would go to Lane's house several times a week, and, over coffee and tobacco, he would advertise his wares. These rituals of sociability and business offered Lane the opportunity to elicit anecdotes about Egyptian women to fill out his research. Thanks to Sheikh Ahmad, Lane grew bolder and bolder in the notes he took about women. At first he had written honestly in his notebook that he should not pretend to speak of the state of women, since he had no way of ascertaining how they lived and no trusted source on the subject. The wild tales of the bookseller allowed Lane to provide the kind of portrait of Oriental women that readers in Europe expected.

With Sheikh Ahmad, Lane had at last found that social intimacy that his awkward domestic situation had made nearly impossible. Taking dictation from his one-on-one conversations with the bookseller in his own home, Lane absorbed the stories that formed the basis of his portrait of women in *Modern Egyptians* and his notes to the *Arabian Nights.* Citing his local source, Lane asserts that easy access to divorce had a "depraving" effect on the population of Cairo, particularly its women. He repeats the conventional claim that Cairene women were the most licentious of any civilized nation: "What liberty they have, many of them, it is said, abuse; and most of them are not considered safe, unless under lock and key; to which restraint few are subjected." The suggestion that Cairo's women were no better than prostitutes was reinforced by the inclusion of information about officials designated to keep a list of the city's "public women" and to tax them.[31] In his private discussions with Sheikh Ahmad, even Lane's home became a prompt for a story of sexual transgression. According to his friend, a previous tenant of Lane's house had been a famous womanizer, but when he brazenly seduced the wife of a powerful army officer, he finally sealed his fate. News of the offense inevitably reached the wronged husband, who quickly arranged for the man's execution. In this anecdote, Cairo authorities sought not only to punish the man but to signal the shame that had been brought on the house where he had lived, and so the womanizer had been beheaded immediately outside the entrance of Lane's apartment.[32]

The ease of both marriage and divorce was emphasized by Sheikh Ahmad, and this encouraged Lane to see Cairo society through the

The figure in this sketch from one of Edward Lane's notebooks matches his description of the bookseller Sheikh Ahmad in the preface to *Modern Egyptians*.

prism of sexual laxity. Lane reported that a young woman in her prime might have already married a dozen or more men consecutively, and in any given year an Egyptian man might take two or three wives. The bookseller himself claimed that he had lost count of the women he had married and divorced by the time he was forty, but there had been at least thirty.[33] In a visit to Sheikh Ahmad's home, Lane was offered a critical glimpse into life in the harem—the only one he got during this stay in Cairo. On this visit, Sheikh Ahmad's mother joined their conversation, gesturing with her hands from the opposite side of the doorway to the harem "to shew how beautifully the palm, and the tips of the fingers, glowed with the fresh red dye of the 'henna.'" This encounter, in which Sheikh Ahmad's mother tried to enlist Lane's help in convincing her son to divorce the new young wife who was causing him to neglect his first wife, would add additional color to Lane's efforts to capture the intrigues of domestic life in the *Arabian Nights*.[34]

Sheikh Ahmad taught Lane to read the behavior of women on the streets of Cairo as erotically charged. Foreigners should not be fooled by the modesty of the veils of the women of Cairo, the bookseller confided to Lane. Instead one could learn to view the almost imperceptible "twisting of the body" as a woman walked as deliberately flirtatious. If a woman was determined to catch an attractive stranger's eye, Sheikh Ahmad explained, she would "expose her face before a man when she thinks that she may appear to do so unintentionally, or that she may be supposed not to see him." After hearing this from the bookseller, Lane became convinced that he himself was the target of this provocative maneuver when a pretty young widow, believed by Lane's neighbors to be amenable to the idea of remarriage, chanced to displace her veil as she passed him in the street. Lane also claimed that "a female who cannot be persuaded to unveil her face in the presence of men, will think it but little shame to display the whole of her bosom, or the greater part of her leg."[35]

This belief seems to have inspired at least one drawing in Lane's notebook. In it, three women model Egyptian dress; one of the women is both modestly veiling her face and provocatively revealing the curve of her breast. William Harvey may have used this drawing as an example of authentic Cairene dress, but it was not among the celebrated illustrations to Lane's *Arabian Nights.* The famous wood engravings of Lane's edition treat even the most suggestive of tales with great delicacy. The orgy in the court of King Shahriyar looks like a lovers' picnic, and the revelry of "The Porter and the Three Ladies of Baghdad" seems friendly and joyous rather than libidinous. Lane's own drawing of the three women of Cairo, in contrast, captures his sense that flirtation was part of the Arab street, despite efforts to conceal the appeal of the city's fairer sex. In another version of this image, published in a recent edition of *Description of Egypt,* Lane positions the women in a market and replaces the female figure on the right with an armed guard, who is engaging at least one of the women in conversation.[36] This eroticized image of the veiled Egyptian woman, which also appeared in the first edition of *Modern Egyptians,* lies behind the portrait of women in Lane's *Arabian Nights.*

As he gathered information on the lives of women, Lane did not share with Sheikh Ahmad the fact that he was writing an ethnography of modern Cairo.[37] When Lane inquired about women, the bookseller may well have imagined that he was asking for amusing anecdotes or the kinds of entertaining tales that fill the pages of the *Thousand and One Nights* itself. The result is not always credible. For instance, Lane draws from the stories provided by Sheikh Ahmad an account of a wealthy slave dealer betrayed by his wife with a "dust-man." The unfaithful wife arranges for her lover to sneak into her quarters by means of a palm tree, but her husband discovers the affair. When brought before a judge, the clever wife somehow manages to turn the tables and convince the court that her husband is insane so that she can chain him up in their house and continue to entertain her lover right in front of him. Lane also relishes the cunning and fickleness of the army officer's wife in another story who, having smuggled her Christian lover into her home disguised as a woman, is ready to dispatch him with a bottle of poisoned water over the slightest offense. Other stories that Lane incorporates into his ethnography include the emancipated slave girl who cuckolds a wealthy slave trader, the soldier's wife who secretly has two other husbands, and the bird seller's wife who has three husbands. As Lane would comment in *Modern Egyptians,* these stories of the artifices of the women of Cairo were fit for the *Thousand and One Nights.*[38]

Watercolor from one of Edward Lane's notebooks from Cairo. Lane claimed in his ethnography of Cairo that, although the women of Cairo covered their faces, they would not hesitate to display the curve of their bosom in flirtation.

It is possible that Sheikh Ahmad was responding to Lane's prompts by intentionally recounting tales like those of women in the *Thousand and One Nights*. Perhaps he thought that the notes Lane took as he told his stories were for some collection of amusing anecdotes, or part of Lane's plan to translate the *Thousand and One Nights*. As a well-known bookseller established in a prominent location, Sheikh Ahmad would have been accustomed to catering to the tastes of European expatriates, selling them not only books but a particular image of the East. As a representative of the pasha's press in Bulaq, he was experienced in dealing with French scholars visiting Cairo and knew their taste for whirling dervishes and the erotic secrets of the harem. It is unlikely that Lane was the first European to question Sheikh Ahmad about the secret lives of Cairo's women. As the bookseller visited Lane's house, he would also have had a vested interest in enticing Lane with stories of the *Thousand and One Nights*. Lane claimed that a bookseller friend, presumably Ahmad, was supplying missing stories for a new collection of the tales, and he certainly knew that Abd al-Rahman al-Sharqawi was editing an Arabic version for publication by the Bulaq press. Before leaving Egypt in late 1834, Lane would give Sheikh Ahmad a guinea to purchase the work for him when it was printed.[39] The bookseller may have thought that by telling Lane such tales in their meetings at his home, he was merely cultivating a customer. Strangely, Lane never imagined that, with his tales of promiscuous women, Sheikh Ahmad was constructing a myth of licentious Cairo for his benefit—a myth that would be inserted into the *Arabian Nights* through his famous commentary on the tales.

✦ ✦ ✦

In the preface to his version of the *Arabian Nights*, Lane seems to suggest that he was revising the image of a sexually dissolute Cairo that he had constructed in *Modern Egyptians*. He admits to editing the collection in a way that excluded those tales and anecdotes that were "comparatively uninteresting or on any account objectionable." In some cases, he admits that certain passages "of an objectionable nature" had been "slightly varied," but suggests that they remained "perfectly agreeable with Arab manners and customs." Authenticity was an important value in Lane's version of the *Arabian Nights,* and he continued to assert that the story collection depicted the essential culture of the Arab people, as represented in its purest form in Egypt. This contention justified Lane's practice of drawing from his contemporary observations of Cairo in *Modern Egyptians* to produce his commentary to the tales.[40]

In turning to his ethnographic notes on Egypt's customs to create his elaborate commentary on the *Arabian Nights,* Lane inevitably returned to the perspectives of informants like Sheikh Ahmad. Many of the generalizations about Arab women and their "wickedness" inserted into Lane's version therefore have their origin in the humorous anecdotes and playful stories related by Sheikh Ahmad in private discussions or shared in the lively homosocial environment of the bookstore. In Lane's rush to produce his commentary to the *Arabian Nights,* he incorporated these tales and the conclusions they encouraged, along with references from religious and historical manuscripts, to create the particular discourse of women in the Orient that he had claimed that he wanted to avoid. In this way, tales of female intrigue and infidelity told to Lane by Sheikh Ahmad appear to validate the fictions of the *Arabian Nights.*

In the notes to his translation, Lane does not retract or qualify his previous claim of the unparalleled promiscuity of Egyptian women; he actually reaffirms it with more confidence and adds corroboration drawn from distinguished historians and theologians. For instance, in "The Tale of the Jewish Doctor," part of "The Hunchback's Tale," Lane includes a note containing a quotation from *Modern Egyptians* that reproduces the opinion of Sheikh Ahmad: "'The women of Egypt have the character of being the most licentious in their feelings of all females who lay any claim to be considered as members of a civilised nation; and this character is freely bestowed upon them by their countrymen, even in conversation with foreigners.'—In the work from which the above passage is quoted, I have expatiated upon this subject more than I need do in the present case." This note is offered by Lane in support of the contention that the daughter of the governor of Damascus was corrupted by her time in Cairo, where she "learnt habits of profligacy."[41] The character will later return to Damascus, seduce the Jewish doctor, insist that he sleep with her younger sister, and then murder her sibling in a fit of sexual jealousy. In notes like this one, Sheikh Ahmad becomes the author of Lane's commentary on the "wickedness" of women in the *Arabian Nights.*

Even when Lane claims that he omitted "objectionable" elements in the tales in order to protect the reputation of the women of Cairo, a close analysis of his *Arabian Nights* reveals that in many cases these silenced elements were simply moved to the notes appended to the chapters. In the "Porter and the Three Ladies of Baghdad," for instance, Lane admits to omitting "an extremely objectionable scene, which, it is to be hoped, would convey a very erroneous idea of the manner of Arab ladies." This scene, in which the porter and the three ladies engage in sexual play and exchange explicit riddles, disappears from the tale's translation, but Lane actually reinforces the implication that Egyptian women possess an unusual knowledge of sexual matters by adding to his note, "though I have witnessed, at private festivities in Cairo, abominable scenes, of which ladies, screened behind lattices, were spectators."[42] Lane uses the notes to make explicit—and ground in reality—the sexual material that he leaves implicit in the stories.

The distinctive views of Sheikh Ahmad on the loose morals of the women of Cairo also entered into Lane's notes on marriage in the *Arabian Nights.* While Lane seems to have had doubts about the bookseller's claim that he had married and divorced at least thirty wives, he nevertheless incorporated Sheikh Ahmad's assertion about the extraordinary number of marriages and divorces a typical man or woman experienced in a lifetime into his commentary.[43] In his note "On Marriage," Lane claims that Egyptians of the middle ranks generally had only one wife at a time, but they would marry and divorce dozens of times within a single decade. "There are few of middle age," he reports, "who have not had several different wives at different periods, tempted to change by the facility of divorce." Although a woman could not accumulate as many spouses as men, Lane writes that there have been "many instances of Arab women who have married a surprising number of men in rapid succession." He references the cases of Mohammad Ibn Et-Teiyib of Baghdad, who, "on most respectable authority," married over 900 women, and the Yemeni woman Umm Kharijeh, who reportedly married over forty men and had numerous children by them, "several tribes originating from her." Feeling the need to substantiate the information supplied by Sheikh Ahmad, Lane produced an even more exaggerated account of the marital habits of Arabs in his notes to the *Arabian Nights* than the bookseller had originally provided.[44]

Sheikh Ahmad had taught Lane to perceive Cairo as rife with barely concealed erotic possibility, and the notes to the *Arabian Nights* convey these lessons about the seductive powers of the Arab woman. In his note on "the opinions of the Arabs respecting Female Beauty," he shares the standard tropes from Arabic literature: a slender figure as "elegant as a twig of the oriental willow," a face "like a full moon," hair "of the deepest hue of night," dark eyes with long silken lashes "giving a tender and languid expression," and bosoms like "two pomegranates." The source for Lane's assertion that the "most bewitching age" of Arab women is between fourteen and seventeen is less certain. When Lane writes that at the age of twelve "many a maiden . . . possesses sufficient charms to fascinate every youth or man who beholds her," it is unclear if this is passed on from his own experience or represents the view of Sheikh Ahmad, who claimed to have married his second wife when she was just nine years old.[45] Lane's comments on the seductive way in which Arab women move do seem to be based on observation, guided by the assumptions nurtured by Sheikh Ahmad. In a note to "Taj al-Muluk and the Princess Dunya," Lane writes that "the gait of Arab ladies is very remarkable: they incline the lower part of the body from side to side as they step, and with the hands raised to the level of the bosom they hold the edges of their outer covering."[46]

Lane's notes, whether on the flirtatious gait of the Arab woman or the adulterous tendencies of Cairo's citizens, are recognizably those taken down during conversations with Sheikh Ahmad, rewritten with the added authority of Arabic printed and manuscript sources. Lane thus backs up the perspectives he adopts from Sheikh Ahmad with references to reputable historical and theological sources. The note "On the distribution of Virtues and Vices among Mankind" repeats the contention of Ka'ab al-Ahbar, a seventh-century Sunni scholar, that the best women in the world were "those of El-Basrah; and the worst in the world, those of Egypt."[47] In another note on women that accompanied "The Porter and the Three Ladies of Baghdad," Lane cites a passage written by an Arab historian in the late fifteenth century, the era during which Lane believed the *Arabian Nights* was composed, as "proof" that the tale of the ladies' revelry is a believable representation of female conduct in that time:

> Seeing that the women of this time deck themselves with the attire of prostitutes, and walk in the sooks (or market-streets), like female warriours against the religion, and uncover their faces and hands before men, to incline [men's] hearts to them by evil suggestions, and play at feasts with young men, thereby meriting the anger of the Compassionate [that is, God], and go forth to the public baths and assemblies, with various kinds of ornaments and perfumes, and with conceited gait; for the which they shall be congregated in Hell-fire, for opposing the good, and on account of this their affected gait . . . for they are like swine and apes in their interior nature, though like daughters of Adam in their exterior appearance.

To this virulent diatribe on the evils of Arab women in the fifteenth century, Lane simply adds, "A more convincing testimony than this, I think, cannot be required."[48] Despite occasional protestations that he is protecting the reputation of Cairo's women, these kinds of sources are inserted into his footnotes as corroboration of the anecdotal evidence of female corruption that he gathered from his conversations with Sheikh Ahmad, and they encourage a particular reading of the *Arabian Nights*.

Lane's efforts to reshape the story collection thus involved more complex methods than just the omission of stories with sexual content that might offend his readers in England. If some stories that could reflect badly on the moral standing of the women of Cairo were indeed omitted, the assumption of women's "wickedness" remains a constant in Lane's commentary on the tales. "The Porter and the Three Ladies of Baghdad" is a fascinating test case in this respect. As the encounter with the porter turns into a night of storytelling, the tales of the ladies and the three dervishes who join their party reveal a potent mix of sexuality and violence that is uncomfortable for the translator. Lane chooses to omit portions of these stories and alter others, but his notes still serve to emphasize the corruption of the female characters, ultimately producing a story that seems to legitimate assumptions about the debased sexual lives of Arab women.[49]

In the tale of the second dervish, a young prince disguised as a woodcutter discovers an underground chamber where a powerful ifrit keeps his captive bride. When the two lovers are discovered by the ifrit, the young woman displays considerable courage in refusing to kill her lover on the orders of the jinni. When the young man in turn is ordered to kill the woman, he asks the ifrit how it would be lawful to do so "if a woman, deficient in sense and religion, seeth it not lawful to strike off my head." What might have been interpreted by the reader as a desperate attempt to escape the ifrit's vengeance becomes an authoritative statement about women through Lane's intervention in the note to the tale. There, Lane explains that this comment does not refer to this specific woman, but rather "is a saying of the Prophet applied to the sex in general."[50] When the second lady, the portress, explains to the assembled company that the scars that disfigure her body are the result of her torture at the hands of a husband who unjustly believed her to have been unfaithful, Lane suggests in his note that Egyptian women "suspected of infidelity to their husbands have not unfrequently" suffered the punishment with which the second lady's husband threatens her—to be sliced in two and thrown into the Tigris River for the fish to devour.[51] For Lane's reader, this note would have lent a stark realism to these stories. Offered to his readers with clear moral criticism of its female characters, "The Porter and the Three Ladies of Baghdad" is able to take its place in Lane's *Arabian Nights* despite its sexually charged narrative.

A far more aggressive approach to reshaping the content of the *Arabian Nights* is visible in Lane's treatment of the story cycle "The Craft and Malice of Women," which stretches to almost one hundred pages in later versions by John Payne and Richard Burton. In his *Arabian Nights,* Lane reduces the cycle to a mere twenty-five pages, dramatically truncating tales or excluding them altogether. Rather than locating "The Craft and Malice of Women" in the main body of his text, Lane relegates the cycle to an endnote to "The City of Brass," burying it where his readers would not expect to find it. Like the *Thousand and*

One Nights itself, the twenty-one embedded tales of "The Craft and Malice of Women" are framed by a tale of sexual intrigue. In this frame tale, "The Story of the King and His Son and the Damsel and the Seven Wezeers," the king's favorite concubine becomes enamored of his son, the beautiful young prince. In the version in the Bulaq edition, the concubine desperately tries to seduce the prince, kissing and fondling him, and even promising to murder the king for his sake. Outraged, the prince threatens to tell the king everything she has said and done. Fearing that he will carry out the threat, the concubine tears her clothes, pulls her hair, and sheds tears, appearing before the king in this pitiable state to accuse the prince of assaulting her. The king is furious and immediately orders his son's execution, but the viziers intervene. The fate of the son will be decided by a contest of storytelling in which the seven viziers tell stories of the craft and malice of women to try to convince the king that the concubine cannot be trusted, and the concubine tells stories of the treachery of men to persuade the king of his son's guilt. With every story, the prince's life hangs in the balance.[52]

Lane chooses to include only an abstract of this frame tale rather than a complete translation, for, he claims, the tale "abounds with indecent passages and incidents." Lane's summary, however, omits the concubine's initial fabrication of an assault by the prince and then undercuts the significance of the stories that follow. In Lane's version, the viziers are trying "to divert" the king from his intention to execute his son, and the "guilty damsel endeavor[s] to counteract their influence."[53] Lane picks through the twenty-seven stories that follow, translating pieces of some tales, abstracting others, and completely omitting a substantial portion of the rest. Some of the exclusions are easy for Lane to justify based on the dictates of decency. The fourth vizier's story of "The Wazir's Son and the Hamman-Keeper's Wife," in which a bath keeper instigates a sexual encounter between his wife and the corpulent son of the vizier, "must be passed over" for its sexually explicit content, and the sixth vizier's story of "The Three Wishes," which explores a wife's interest in the size of her husband's "prickle" (in Burton's translation), is omitted because of its "abominable grossness." Similarly, the concubine's story of "The Rake's Trick against the Chaste Wife," in which a rake tries to destroy the virtuous woman who has refused his advances by placing an egg white in her bed for her husband to find, is considered "unfit for translation" by Lane.[54]

In handling this story cycle, Lane races through some of the stories in just one sentence and translates large sections of others. Printed in small font in the notes, the alterations Lane makes to the tales might be difficult for the reader to identify, but there is a distinct pattern to his exclusions and obfuscations that is not just attributable to Victorian prudishness. Of the sixteen tales told by the viziers and the prince to convince the king to spare the life of his son, Lane translates five fully and abstracts five. Six disappear with little comment. Of the ten stories told by the concubine to implicate the son in the general "perfidy" of men, Lane describes five in a very cursory fashion, abstracts one with much obfuscation, and completely omits two others. Only two stories are related more fully, but through a loose narration that includes little direct translation of the Arabic text. Though the "Craft and Malice of Women" story cycle originally provided a series of alternate viewpoints on male and female weaknesses and misdeeds, Lane produced a version in which the tales told by men are given significantly more time and weight.[55]

In fact, Lane seems to have been uncomfortable with the essential organizing principle of the story cycle—the competition to establish the greater treacherousness of women or men. He reworks the material in a way that blunts the battle of the sexes that some contemporary writers have seen as an essential part of the *Thousand and One Nights*.[56] Lane's decisions to include stories are often based on his interest in the supernatural content of the collection. "The Enchanted Spring," for example, with its wicked vizier and blameless female object of desire, provides a good example of the story type related by the concubine, but Lane chooses to relate principally the sections that involve the magical effects of a desert spring that, through the machinations of the jealous vizier, turns the young prince into a woman, and thus prevents him from marrying his intended. Lane carefully translates the next part of the story, in which the son of the king of the jinn takes the transformed prince to the Dusky Land of the jinn and allows him to drink from a second magical spring, which will change a woman into a man. This tale is filled with the marvels of magical flight and the mysteries of the parallel world of the jinn, and in translating it, Lane is able to give free rein to his fascination with the supernatural.[57] Similarly, in the tale of the fifth vizier, "The Man Who Never Laughed Again," Lane also emphasizes the supernatural rather than the competitive relationship between the sexes. In this tale, a young man, driven by his curiosity, opens a forbidden door in an old house, and is transported by a giant eagle to a kingdom of Amazonian women, where he experiences the greatest of delights as the husband of the queen. Perhaps the inversion of gender roles in this kingdom was originally intended to make the vizier's point, but the romantic vision of this faraway kingdom dominates the story as retold by Lane.[58]

When Lane abridges the tales in the "Craft and Malice" sequence to conceal their sexual content, the effect is often to minimize the violence of the male protagonists and hence to undermine the concubine's purpose in telling her stories. The tale of "Prince Bahram and the Princess al-Datma," for instance, relates the story of a warrior princess, al-Datma, who refuses to marry anyone who cannot beat her in single combat. Though she defeats Prince Bahram by dazzling him with the beauty of her visage in the final moment of their battle, he disguises himself as an old man and rapes her later in the story. Lane blunts the significance of the latter event by summarizing it: "By a stratagem, he inveigled her in her garden, and, with her consent, carried her off."[59] In contrast, Lane's abstract of "The King and His Vizier's Wife" clouds the adulterous intent of both the vizier's wife and the king, and somehow manages to make the king's refusal to follow through with his plan to seduce his vizier's wife seem noble. The king magnanimously announces, "Return, O Wezeer, to thy garden, and thou wilt be safe and secure; for the lion drew not near it." Lane also manages to make the malfeasance of the vizier's wife unclear, hence blunting the intention of the vizier who tells the tale. Ultimately, Lane is uninterested in maintaining the framework of competing tales on which the story cycle is built.[60]

In his ethnography of modern Egypt, Lane expresses fascination with the idea that women shared these stories of sexual intrigue among themselves in the confines of the harem. Both Egyptian men and women of every class indulged in immodest conversation, Lane asserts, and the most genteel woman felt no shame in discussing within the hearing of men topics that an English prostitute would refrain from mentioning.[61] Lane explains that women were allowed to listen through the screened windows of the harem to the immoral tales that men recounted on the street for money, and within the harem, when other topics of conversation had been exhausted, one of the women might herself relate some "wonderful or facetious tale" to entertain her companions.[62] Ironically, however, this portrait of Cairo's women as an essential part of the city's storytelling culture was followed by the production of a version of the *Arabian Nights* in which both the voice of Shahrazad and the agency of women are largely missing.

In Lane's introductory chapter, Shahrazad does appear in her traditional guise as a woman of intelligence and courage, determined to end the threat that King Shahriyar poses to the young women of the kingdom. In this first appearance, the famous storyteller is characterized exclusively by her love of books: "It is asserted that she had collected together a thousand books of histories, relating to preceding generations and kings, and works of the poets." Her actions and words also speak to her courage in responding to the threat represented by Shahriyar. In Lane's version, she declares, "By Allah, O my father, give me in marriage to this King: either I shall die, and be a ransom for one of the daughters of the Muslims, or I shall live, and be the cause of their deliverance from him." This is, however, an alteration of the original Bulaq manuscript, as Lane admits in a note at the end of the chapter. The original would have read, "Either I shall live, or I shall be a ransom for the daughters of the Muslims, and the cause of their deliverance from him." The difference might be subtle, but it is significant. In both versions, Shahrazad expresses the hope that she can somehow rescue all the women of the kingdom by using her stories to bring Shahriyar back to reason. However, the original implies that she has a secondary plan that is decidedly more aggressive. If she is unable to dissuade Shahriyar from his plans to kill her (and others after her) through the power of her storytelling, she intends to ensure the safety of every other daughter by killing him—ensuring her own death as a consequence.[63]

Lane made this alteration to the original text after reading the commentary on the tale provided by his "Sheikh," Muhammad Ayyad al-Tantawi, who was undoubtedly his most important collaborator in producing the translated text of the *Arabian Nights*. Al-Tantawi, a product of al-Azhar in Cairo, was an exceptional philologist and had an extensive knowledge of Arabic medieval literature. Lane depended on him to provide annotations to the Arabic tales of the Bulaq edition, which he would then use to produce a translation that he hoped would be the most accurate rendering of the original. Regarding Shahrazad, Lane's adviser remarked in the margins of the frame tale, "It would seem that she had contrived some stratagem to prevent his marrying again if he determined to kill her: otherwise, the mere killing [of] her would not be a means of rescuing the other maidens."[64] This suggestion that Shahrazad would take direct and violent action to ensure the end of Shahriyar's murderous campaign was picked up by other authors and translators, but Lane rejected it for inclusion in his main narrative.

Just as Lane refuses to suggest that Shahrazad would sacrifice her own life to secure the collective salvation of all women, he also refuses to let her narrative voice dominate the story collection as a whole. By abandoning any reference to the frame tale after the introduction and arranging the stories into chapters that disrupt the nightly rhythms of Shahrazad's storytelling, Lane deprives the character of her agency. This pattern is echoed throughout Lane's reworking of the story collection as a whole. While his notes continue to detail the dangers associated with the wiles of women, many of the female characters who possess exemplary qualities of cleverness, ingenuity, or courage appear in diminished form, or disappear altogether. As Lane scales back Shahrazad's role in the story collection, he also excludes a whole series of her analogues—women of learning and intellectual ability—from his edition of the *Arabian Nights*.

Lane's choice to expend most of his effort on his commentary rather than his translation made significant cuts to the Bulaq edition necessary, and he was likely under pressure from his publisher to finish the translation. However, there are distinctive patterns within Lane's omissions. Some of the most powerful of the female characters in the *Thousand and One Nights* disappear, and foremost among them are some of the "clever slave girls" who were such a popular part of the story collection. Lane cannot be faulted for not including Marjana of "Ali Baba" fame, for the orphan tales of Hanna Diyab had no place in the "authentic"

بسم الله الرحمن الرحيم

الحمد لله رب العالمين (والصلاة والسلام على سيد المرسلين) سيدنا ومولانا محمد وعلى آله صلاة وسلاما دائمين
متلازمين الى يوم الدين * وبعد فان سير الاولين صارت عبرة للآخرين * لكي يرى الانسان العبر التي
حصلت لغيره فيعتبر * ويطالع حديث الامم السالفة وما جرى لهم فينزجر * فسبحان من جعل حديث
الاولين عبرة لقوم آخرين (فمن تلك العبر الحكايات التي تسمى الف ليلة وليلة وما فيها من الغرائب والامثال
فقد حكي والله اعلم * واحكم واعز واكرم * انه كان فيما مضى وتقدم * من قديم الزمان * وسالف العصر
والأوان * ملك من ملوك ساسان بجزائر الهند والصين * صاحب جند واعوان وخدم وحشم وكان له
ولدان احدهما كبير والاخر صغير وكانا فارسين بطلين وكان الكبير افرس من الصغير وقد ملك البلاد
وحكم بالعدل بين العباد واحبه اهل بلاده ومملكته وكان اسمه الملك شهريار وكان اخوه الصغير اسمه الملك
شاه زمان وكان ملك سمرقند العجم ولم يزل الامر مستقيما في بلادهما وكل واحد منهما في مملكته حاكم عادل
في رعيته مدة عشرين سنة وهم في غاية البسط والانشراح ولم يزالا على هذه الحالة الى ان اشتاق الملك
الكبير الى اخيه الصغير فامر وزيره ان يسافر اليه ويحضر به فاجابه بالسمع والطاعة وسافر حتى وصل
بالسلامة ودخل على اخيه وبلغه السلام واعلمه ان اخاه مشتاق اليه وقصده ان يزوره فاجابه بالسمع
والطاعة وتجهز للسفر واخرج خيامه وجماله وبغاله وخدمه واعوانه واقام وزيره حاكما في بلاده
وخرج طالبا بلاد اخيه فلما كان في نصف الليل تذكر حاجة نسيها في قصره فرجع ودخل قصره
فوجد زوجته راقدة في فراشه معانقة عبدا اسود من العبيد فلما رأى هذا اسودت الدنيا في وجهه وقال
في نفسه اذا كان هذا الامر قد وقع وانا ما فارقت المدينة فكيف حال هذه العاهرة اذا غبت عند اخي
مدة ثم انه سل سيفه وضرب الاثنين فقتلهما في الفراش ورجع من وقته وساعته وامر بالرحيل وسار

Edward Lane's copy of the Bulaq edition of the *Arabian Nights,* with annotations by Sheikh Muhammad Ayyad al-Tantawi. Lane could not proceed with his translation until he received al-Tantawi's copious notes on the Arabic text, which he sent to Lane in England twenty folios at a time.

Arabian Nights that he was producing. However, the story of "Tawaddud" is also missing from Lane's version. This story, featuring a slave girl with extraordinary intellectual abilities, is believed to have originated in thirteenth-century Egypt and was a part of the late Egyptian recension that Lane used as the basis for his translation. In the story, Tawaddud's owner, Abu 'l-Husn, squanders his inheritance, so the slave girl convinces him to take her to the court of Caliph Harun al-Rashid and sell her for 10,000 dinars. When she is brought before the caliph, Tawaddud asserts that she is well versed in all the sciences, and Harun arranges a contest in which the slave girl competes with the most illustrious scholars of Baghdad in answering questions about law, theology, medicine, astronomy, and philosophy. Once she has bested these scholars, she successfully takes on the resident champions of chess and backgammon, and proves her musical skills. This extraordinary demonstration of her many accomplishments earns her master 10,000 dinars and a place at Harun's court.

Perhaps Lane was confused at the extraordinary compendium of scholarly knowledge incorporated into what might otherwise seem a simple fictional tale, and excluded it on these grounds. Perhaps he thought this fell within the "uninteresting" category that he marked for exclusion from his *Arabian Nights.* In any case, the omission of this remarkable demonstration of the intellectual potential of women is a distinct loss in his version of the story collection. Contemporary scholars such as André Miquel see Tawaddud's victory over the scholars of the court as an echo of the victory of Shahrazad and a "song of praise" to all women.[65] In dropping this story, Lane also sacrificed a tale that emphasizes the cultivation of science and philosophy in the capitals of the Arab world rather than just the practices of the supernatural that so fascinated him.

The story of Tawaddud is similar to a series of other tales in the Bulaq edition of the *Arabian Nights* that have likewise disappeared in Lane's version. It is perhaps unsurprising that Lane omits "Man's Dispute with the Learned Woman," in which an accomplished female preacher cites a wide range of theological and literary sources in an extended debate about the relative merits of women and men, including their value as sexual partners. Its frank discussion of pederasty did not fit in his understanding of the story collection. A greater loss is "The Man of al-Yaman and His Six Slave-Girls," in which a rich man brings his six slave girls to the caliph's court, where they demonstrate their mastery of the art of poetry and the Arabic literary tradition. Representing many different ethnicities through their skin color (white, brown, yellow, black), all the slave girls prove their amazing accomplishments and are purchased by the caliph. By embodying the common theme of the superiority of the simple slave girl over respected scholars, these stories represent a critical commentary on the gendered hierarchies of medieval Arab society. Their absence in Lane's version of the *Arabian Nights,* combined with the continued emphasis on the "wickedness" of women in the notes, reshapes a collection that is much more ambiguous on this issue.[66]

There are still traces of the story pattern of the clever slave girl in Lane's *Arabian Nights.* In his first volume, Lane tends to follow the sequence of stories in the Bulaq edition more faithfully, and in the process he delivers to English readers the story of " 'Ali Shar and Zumurrud." In this variation on the clever-slave-girl narrative, Zumurrud insists that the impoverished 'Ali Shar buy her at the slave market, and lends him the money to do so. Zumurrud proves to be exceptionally talented in crafting curtains with beautiful figures of animals and birds, and 'Ali Shar sells these at the market to support them. However, when he diverges from Zumurrud's instructions and sells a curtain to a particular Christian, a sequence of misfortunes ensues in which the slave girl is abducted not once but twice, managing to escape both times. Proving to be adept at rescuing herself from the traps of men, Zumurrud finally arrives at a city in which the king has just died, and, in accordance with local custom, she is made its ruler. At a series of monthly feasts arranged by Queen Zumurrud, she identifies her two abductors, and secures their execution. At last her old master, 'Ali Shar, appears in her city, and the couple is reunited. The narrative of the tale is driven by the courage and resourcefulness of its female character, and it is Zumurrud's active agency that brings about the happy resolution of the tale. However, Lane's intervention in his notes once again emphasizes the moral weakness of women. The tremendous skill of Zumurrud in weaving cloth leads Lane to cite the words of the Prophet's wife Aisha: "There is no woman who spins until she hath clothed herself but all the angels in the Seven Heavens pray for forgiveness of her sins."[67]

Zumurrud represents only one of the resourceful female characters in the Bulaq version of the tales, but in Lane's translation she is a more singular figure. Another version of the slave girl narrative in which the male protagonist plays second fiddle to a strong female heroine—" 'Ali Nur al-Din and Maryam the Girdle-Girl"—is cut by Lane from the main narrative. Two other stories that feature the female trickster figures of Dalila the Crafty and her daughter Zaynab are also missing, despite the popularity of this tale type in Cairo. In typical versions of this story, the widow Dalila takes up a career as a thief when she sees rogues rewarded with powerful positions at court. Through clever lies and trickery, she steals jewels, money, and goods, and manages to make a series of improbable escapes from local authorities.[68] Such female rogues play an important part in the general contest for power between men and women that contemporary writers like Hanan al-Shaykh have seen in the story collection.[69] Lane's version of the *Arabian Nights,* in which his omissions and interventions disproportionately empty the female characters of agency, demonstrates by negative example the centrality of this dynamic to the appeal of the tales.

An alternative approach to handling this dynamic in the collection might be found in the translation of the *Arabian Nights* by Lane's contemporary, Torrens. Lane remained conscious of the competition represented by Torrens's translation and was stung by critical responses that valued the poetic skill of his rival's first volume more highly than his own emphasis on accuracy. A glance at Torrens's treatment of women in his translation reveals another fundamental difference between their approaches to translating the story collection. In his version, Torrens preserves Shahrazad's interventions and makes the integral relationship between the frame tale and the interpolated tales clear throughout. The reader is conscious of Shahrazad as the narrator of the stories and the importance of the stories as a means to evade the plans of her husband. Torrens's translation also tends to give a greater voice to other female characters—pushing beyond the limits of his source text in some cases.

Torrens's treatment of the jinni's stolen bride in the frame tale is particularly revealing. As the woman collects the seal rings from Shahriyar and Shah Zaman to add to her collection, she quotes two poems to punctuate her assertion that women can achieve anything they desire. The first poem embodies the accusations against wicked women familiar from other misogynist poetry in the collection. Like Lane's translation, it cites the fates of Joseph and Adam as a warning to all men against the wiles of women. In the second poem, however, Torrens allows the jinni's stolen bride to answer the charge of promiscuity:

> But Alas! For you, who blame me,
> Fix the blamed one in his fault!
> Is the sin with which you shame me,
> Great and grievous as you call't?
> Say, I be indeed a lover,
> Have I done aught greater crime
> Than in all men you discover,
> Even from the olden time?[70]

Together the two poems in Torrens's translation capture the competing claims made by men and women throughout the story collection. A comparison of Torrens's version with Malcolm Lyons's literal translation of the same verse reveals that here the translator has stretched the limits of his original in the interest of establishing one of the key elements of the *Arabian Nights*.[71] Such a balance is distinctly missing in Lane's version of the collection, which preserves accusations of the inherent duplicity of women, but not the many moments in which a woman's voice is raised to counter these claims.

✦ ✦ ✦

Lane's inability to resolve his own domestic situation with Nefeeseh offers a fascinating counterpoint to these decisions regarding the reshaping of the *Arabian Nights*. As he labored on his translation from 1837 to 1840, the stories would likely have reminded him of the predicament of the young Greek girl whom he had brought to England. Slavery is constantly referenced in the story collection. As he worked, Lane wrote the word "slave" over 1,200 times, on average at least once a page.

Almost all the female slaves mentioned are concubines. Stories sometimes open in slave markets and often turn on a love match or intrigue through which the clever slave earns her emancipation. The narrative of Lane's relationship to Nefeeseh, however, was the reverse of the most common pattern found in stories of slave girls in the *Arabian Nights.* Unlike other Orientalists, Lane did not see her as a classic concubine, and unlike Hay, he was not attracted to the notion of taking her as a wife. Hay seemed to think that Lane stubbornly refused to consider Nefeeseh's needs at all. In a letter to Lane, he took Lane to task for only preparing her for a "lower station in life"—presumably a life as a servant. According to Lane, reading, writing, and needlework were the only accomplishments needed by slaves in Cairo. He limited Nefeeseh's education to precisely these skills, only adding arithmetic as a concession to her station as a servant in London. As he wrote Hay, he and his mother were making "full trial" of the girl and she was never idle.[72]

Clearly Lane was not caught up in the romance of the emancipation narrative constructed by Hay for his own wife, Kalitza. In fact, he was willing to question whether this form of "emancipation" was so appealing if many female Greek slaves were reported to decline it. Not "all of these," he notes pointedly, can be "supposed to have done [so] from ignorance of their parents and other relations." Greek slave girls might prefer to be kept at great expense, he muses in *Modern Egyptians,* rather than emancipated to conditions of poverty. Lane understood his legal responsibilities for Nefeeseh in accordance with Muslim laws on slavery; he detailed these at length in a note to the *Arabian Nights.* His itemized list of the expenses associated with keeping her and providing her a new wardrobe for England indicate his clear sense of the burden he was taking up by accepting Nefeeseh, and he seems to having taken little joy in it. Lane did not abandon his slave girl, but he would leave her in legal and personal limbo from about the age of seven to the age of twenty.[73]

As Lane worked on his translation of the *Arabian Nights* in London in 1838, he would have known that Nefeeseh's situation was untenable. As his mother's health deteriorated, she could no longer take charge of the girl, who was now nearing twenty. According to the Slavery Abolition Act of 1833, slaves across the British Empire (except for Ceylon and areas controlled by the East India Company) would be freed on August

1, 1838. Whatever legal right he might still have held over Nefeeseh was quickly disappearing. As Lane devoted himself to translating the *Arabian Nights* and preparing his commentaries, he continued to postpone the resolution that he knew must come. Lane would only marry Nefeeseh in July 1840, five months before he completed his translation.[74]

The marriage, however, did not seem to involve a change in Lane's feelings toward Nefeeseh. Two years later, Hay wrote to Lane expressing the wish that Lane would be possessed of the "treasure" of a child. Lane replied, "At present, I have no reason to expect it." Lane suggested in his letters to Hay that miscarriages were to blame; however, Lane does not appear to be very reliable on this subject.[75] These same letters show a peculiar insistence on controlling the flow of information on his part. Nefeeseh's letters to Mrs. Hay would have to go through him first, so that he might add some lines to her husband, and he seems to have repeatedly dissuaded her from writing to the Hays on her own. It appears that letters from Kalitza addressed to Nefeeseh also went missing. Certainly Lane made it impossible to discern the voice of Nefeeseh in his own letters and diaries. Given the limited education he was willing to offer her, it is unlikely she had an important role in shaping the stories that her husband was translating in another room of their home. If Sheikh Ahmad made a deep impact on the way in which Lane understood the tales of the *Thousand and One Nights* and explained their relevance as a portrait of the Arab world, Nefeeseh remains a mute presence throughout this work.[76]

Nefeeseh would accompany Lane to Cairo in 1842, and remain with him for the seven years in which he labored on his *Arabic-English Lexicon* alongside his Egyptian collaborator Sheikh Ibrahim al-Dasūqī. At last Lane was modelling the domestic life that was expected in Cairo. However, Nefeeseh's role in the household would be secondary to that of Lane's sister, Sophia Lane Poole, who brought her two sons to live with Lane in Cairo. During these years, Lane finally had a way of gaining an accurate sense of what life was like within the walls of the harem for the women of Cairo, but it was through his sister and not his wife. He would collaborate with his sister to produce a collection of letters entitled *The Englishwoman in Egypt,* which Poole suggested was a product of Lane's unpublished notes and the opportunities she had to obtain "an insight into the mode of life of the higher classes of the ladies in this country." The result was another example of the mingling of voices and perspectives in a portrait of Egyptian life.[77]

This publication was clearly a response to the financial insecurity that plagued Lane during all his Egyptian ventures. The *Arabic-English Lexicon* was the focus of his intellectual ambition during these years, but it did not pay his bills. There was little interest in Arabic scholarship in the hallowed halls of English universities, and Lane's overtures to the archbishop of Canterbury and the queen yielded no response. The most he could get from the East India Company was an order for forty copies of his *Lexicon*—the same number of copies they had purchased of Torrens's *Arabian Nights*. Arabic was no longer considered essential for understanding or governing the subcontinent.[78]

Although it seems that Poole made a contribution to the family's expenses, Lane still had to support a household of five and ensure an appropriate education for his two talented nephews, Stuart and Stanley. With this goal in mind, Lane and his sister took advantage of the precedent established by the Turkish letters of Lady Mary Wortley Montagu (republished in 1837) to produce a collection of letters from Cairo that represented a "woman's perspective" on the city. These letters offer a mixture of voices that is just as confusing as that embodied in Lane's commentary to the *Arabian Nights*. In taking on the role of author, Poole leaned heavily on the authority of her brother. Her preface declares that she only included letters that Lane had selected as worthy of publication. In constructing her "letters" to a fictional friend, she also drew heavily on Lane's notes for *Modern Egyptians* and his unpublished "Description of Egypt." While she did incorporate her own observations from visits to the harems of Cairo's elite and attendance at the wedding ceremony of Zayneb Hanem, the youngest daughter of Muhammad Ali, Poole also quoted verbatim from her brother in eleven of the first sixteen letters. The publisher further clouded the issue of authorship by inserting notes straight from *Modern Egyptians* at the end of the second volume and inserting notes from the *Arabian Nights* into the third volume.[79]

As a result, *The Englishwoman in Egypt* often reads more like an exercise in ventriloquism than a woman's perspective on Cairo. The book cultivates the illusion that Poole used her letters to deliver lectures on the subjects in which Lane was interested: geography, history, religious festivals, and magical practices. When it comes to the topic of domestic life, however, the letters reveal a fascinating struggle for control between Lane and his sister. Many of Lane's descriptions of marriage and domestic life are incorporated into the letters, thus putting the words of informants like Sheikh Ahmad into the mouth of Poole. However, especially in the later letters, Poole also inserts her own opinions, which are often founded in her strong commitment to Evangelical Christianity. For her, Christianity was "the only medium through which happiness may be attained by any people," and she pities the children of Muslim parents who are being educated in a "false religion."[80]

The early letters in *The Englishwoman in Egypt* highlight the comforts that wives and slaves might enjoy in the harem, echoing Lane's defense of polygamy, but as the letters continue, Poole cites more examples of corruption and violence. She decries the moral impact of Muslim men's easy access to divorce and the "habits of seclusion" cultivated in domestic life. Citing the case of "Ali," who had been married ten times, she contends that wife beating was common among the lower classes. Arab men are presented as a particular danger to European women travelling in Egypt, and Poole asserts that it is lucky they are "kept under a degree of subjection by the present government." At times, she seems to be echoing the contention of Lane, and his informant Sheikh Ahmad, that Cairo's women are particularly licentious. Without the supervisory presence of men, she claims, the harem was the setting for much improper conversation. The result, she concludes, was "that virtuous women are far more common in Christian Europe than in Eastern Hareems." In a statement that made a mockery of Lane's respect for Islam, she argued that "until enlightened by the truths of the Gospel, no important reformation can be effected in the Hareem system, nor in the general morals of the East."[81]

In this coauthored work, Lane suffers the same fate as many of the associates he had relied on in translating the *Arabian Nights*. In that work Lane had attempted to disappear into a constructed Egyptian identity based on the perspectives of his informants, but the letters of *The Englishwoman in Egypt* create a new, and largely false, portrait of him. His words would be channelled into this new forgery—constructed out of fragments of his own experience and the responses of his sister to the foreign qualities of Cairo. There is little of Lane's sympathetic account of the religious beliefs and social values of Egyptian society in this image. His defenses of polygamy and the practice of divorce in Islam, as well as his assertion of the distinct advantages in the separation of the sexes, have disappeared. His sister even rewrites Lane's account of the homosexual farce at the wedding celebration to imply that her brother's moral sensibilities were so offended that he left the event. Perhaps most significantly, Poole added a new ending to the story of the Maghrebi magician by insisting that Lane had at last recognized the deception and had denounced the falsehoods purveyed by the convert Osman.[82] A more distinctly English Lane emerges from this reworking of his legacy, one that fit more smoothly into circuits of Victorian knowledge of the Orient.

6

STEALING WITH STYLE

THE PRE-RAPHAELITE POET JOHN PAYNE (1842–1916) is a largely forgotten figure in the history of the *Arabian Nights,* demoted to a supporting character in a story dominated by the famous traveller and translator Richard Francis Burton. By the late 1870s, the mythology of Burton was well developed in the bohemian circles of London where Payne, setting aside a promising career in law, sought to establish himself as a poet and, subsequently, as a literary translator. Burton had established a formidable reputation for himself by performing the pilgrimage to Mecca and Medina in the guise of a Muslim in 1853. Extending his explorations into Africa, Burton had been the first European to enter the stone city of Harar, bringing the fulfillment of a prophecy that the city would fall after a European entered its gates. In Benin he had been honored with a crucifixion, and he had gained a reputation as one of the most renowned African explorers of his age by intuiting that the source of the Nile lay in the Mountains of the Moon in Central Africa. He had followed this up with a journey to Salt Lake City, where he met Brigham Young and defended the practice of polygamy among the Mormons.[1]

Like other artists and writers who inhabited Pre-Raphaelite and decadent circles in late Victorian London, Payne was enthralled by Burton as an explorer, adventurer, and guide to the exotic Orient. As a barrister with literary ambitions, Payne longed to be part of the overlapping bohemian circles around Leicester Square in which figures like Burton held court in the 1860s. In Bertolini's Restaurant, Dante Gabriel Rossetti and other Pre-Raphaelite poets and artists met, along with their models and muses, and Burton himself presided over meetings of his Cannibal Club. This freethinking anthropological society, founded by Burton in 1863, was notorious for its discussions of sexually transgressive subjects like hermaphroditism and phallic worship during meetings that they called "orgies," and it drew figures like the Decadent poet Algernon Swinburne.[2] Payne would have been in his early twenties at the height of the Cannibal Club's activity, but the indulgent freedom of the famous figures gathered there would shape his vision of the Baghdad of Harun al-Rashid when he set himself the task of producing a Decadent version of the *Arabian Nights* in the 1880s.

Payne's edition of the *Arabian Nights* developed in this potent atmosphere of "Decadent London" and through his engagement with Burton himself. When Payne decided to add an extra volume to his translation of the *Arabian Nights* in 1889—to offer readers a version of a newly discovered, though spurious, Arabic manuscript of "Aladdin"—he dedicated it to Burton with a poem. This dedication reveals the way in which Payne's vision of the story collection was framed by his relationship with Burton and the image of the Orient that he represented. After twelve years of immersion in the *Arabian Nights,* Payne expresses his dissatisfaction with having to return to everyday life. It was like the disenchantment that greets the sleeper who wakes from an entrancing dream of the splendors of Arabia to confront a dreary, commonplace English reality. For Payne, the opportunity to collaborate with Burton no doubt seemed a dream come true. He claimed that the sweetest fruit of his twelve years of labor on the *Arabian Nights* had been the chance to call Burton a friend.[3]

Yet by 1889, when Payne penned the dedicatory poem, he would have been aware that Burton's own translation of the *Arabian Nights* had borrowed heavily from his own work—so much so that another translator might have made an accusation of plagiarism. Burton's debt to Payne has been an open secret among scholars of the *Arabian Nights* for many decades. Mia Gerhardt observed the borrowing in her classic study of the story collection in translation; Robert Irwin remarked on the fact in his *Arabian Nights Companion;* and even the popular scholar of myth Joseph Campbell marvelled that the plagiarism was not more widely known. Given the gravity of the charge and Burton's undeniable guilt, it is puzzling that this fact is not common knowledge. The enduring fascination with Burton's life and writings in both academic circles and popular culture largely explains this lack of interest. There has been little incentive for scholars to discuss Burton's thefts from the work of an obscure poet who barely registers in print today in the Penguin book of Pre-Raphaelite verse.[4]

As glaring as Burton's plagiarism is to anyone who cares to compare the two versions, Payne's translation of the *Arabian Nights* possesses its own secrets. If it is easy to establish that Burton borrowed from Payne, it is harder to determine how Payne accomplished his translation in the first place. In 1878, Payne celebrated the success of his translation of the complete works of François Villon, a French medieval poet, by making the surprising announcement that his next project would be an unexpurgated version of *Arabian Nights.* The choice of text can be attributed to the popularity of the story collection among certain Pre-Raphaelite artists and the success of the translation of another Oriental work—the *Rubaiyat of Omar Khayyam.* However, there was a significant obstacle to the successful completion of this project: Payne was not sufficiently proficient in Arabic.[5]

Payne's biographer Thomas Wright claims that, by the age of nineteen, the poet had added to his standard knowledge of French, Greek, and Latin by teaching himself German, Italian, Spanish, Portuguese, Turkish, Persian, and Arabic.[6] However, as Irwin points out in *The Arabian Nights Companion,* an Arabic grammar did not appear in England until Thomas Wright published one in 1859–1862, so it is difficult to know how Payne mastered this language through private study in England. It is more likely that Payne began an intensive study of Arabic shortly before he started his work on the *Arabian Nights*—which was in 1877 at the earliest. Four years later, in 1881, the first volume was set for the printers. The pace of Payne's progress in 1883 and 1884 was even more unreal, and invited amazement from his correspondents. Payne had taken four years (1874–1878) to complete his translation from French of one volume of the poetry of Villon—a work that was the equivalent of just the 10,000 lines of interpolated poetry in the *Thousand and One Nights.* In 1883, Payne published three thick volumes of his *Arabian Nights,* and in 1884 he published four more. Never before or after, translating from languages he had mastered, would Payne approach this pace.[7] What was his secret?

A likely explanation appears in a review by Reginald Stuart Poole, published in the *Academy* in 1879, which responded to two anonymous essays on the *Arabian Nights* published by Payne. Poole suggested that errors in the sample translation and details in his transliterations indicated that the anonymous author was relying on other translations published in English and German to provide the substance of his version of the stories.[8] Payne's rewriting of the *Arabian Nights* was built on aesthetic principles rather than philological or ethnographic knowledge, and his use of other translations as models was justifiable in terms of this literary approach, but the expectations of translations from the Arabic had changed with the publication of Edward Lane's *Arabian Nights.* Poole, Lane's nephew, was determined to enforce these new standards, and Payne knew that he did not have the kind of intensive experience of the Orient that would shield him from such attacks. Into this vacuum stepped Burton, whose reputation as an Arabist gave credibility to the project and whose network of collaborators supplied the scholarly essays that were now seen as a critical component of any new edition of the *Arabian Nights.* This context provides an explanation for why Payne was reluctant to protest against Burton's blatant theft of his work. If Burton eventually produced his version by rewriting Payne's *Arabian Nights* (as well as Torrens's) rather than translating from the original, Payne himself had sought to use Burton to hide the source texts that lurked under his palimpsest version of the tales.

✦ ✦ ✦

Payne's path to the *Arabian Nights* was a circuitous one. An aspiring poet, Payne first chose a more conventional career as a barrister before deciding to pursue his literary ambitions in earnest in the 1870s. Payne's first encounter with the *Arabian Nights* was equally inauspicious. He claimed that he had come across Edward Lane's translation "when a boy"—"seizing upon it with all the eagerness of the youthful lover of 'The Arabian Nights.'" But he was "quickly repelled and disheartened by the cramped and unfamiliar style."[9] In 1879, at the age of thirty-seven, Payne would still blame Lane for having postponed his deeper engagement with the *Arabian Nights* for decades. Payne would only return to his youthful fascination with the collection as he sought to enter the bohemian world of Pre-Raphaelite poets and painters whose center was Dante Gabriel Rossetti and Ford Madox Brown.

The Pre-Raphaelite circle seems to have been particularly invested in the *Arabian Nights,* even by the standards of a Victorian era in which the story collection achieved enormous popularity. The Rossetti family had a tradition of regularly rereading the stories aloud and owned several different versions. It was rumored that Gabriel or his brother William possessed Percy Bysshe Shelley's copy of the work containing the poet's marginal annotations. William would recall Gabriel being enthralled as a boy by an English version of Antoine Galland's work. At the age of seven, he had written a play based on the tale of "Aladdin, or the Wonderful Lamp," opening with a scene of an African magician promising to lead the protagonist to a beautiful garden filled with fruit. When the family acquired Lane's 1838–1840 edition, the young Gabriel no doubt received it with mixed emotions. The twelve-year-old produced a series of drawings based on the *Arabian Nights,* perhaps inspired by the beautiful illustrations by William Harvey in Lane's edition. But Gabriel likely found the text of Lane's version disappointing, particularly as it did not include the tale of Aladdin, a story that had captivated his imagination from a very young age and that he would return to as a metaphor for translation in his adult years.[10]

Payne would have been attracted to the *Arabian Nights* not only through Dante Gabriel Rossetti's passion for the stories, but also through Christina Rossetti's poetic engagement with the tales. Christina had found inspiration in the tale of "The Porter and the Three Ladies of Baghdad" for an early poem, "The Dead City" (1847), which borrows its fruit imagery from the market scene in the story's opening and its theme of the enchanted city from the eldest lady's tale. But the debt to the *Arabian Nights* in Christina's poetry is deeper than previously imagined. Her most famous poem, "The Goblin Market" (1862), draws even more extensively on "The Porter and the Three Ladies." The description of the goblin market strongly resembles the long list of the purchases of the youngest lady of Baghdad in the city's market. The goblins' acceptance of a lock of hair and a tear as a payment from Laura and their refusal of Lizzie's coin recalls another market scene from the tale of the portress, in which a merchant selling silk refuses her money. Demanding a kiss instead, he bites her cheek so hard he breaks the skin. Christina draws on imagery of Baghdad's market and on the theme of the three sisters living together to weave her powerful narrative of sexual discovery.[11] Her reworking of the sexual subtext of the market scene in "The Porter and the Three Ladies" suggests that she was familiar with Torrens's translation of the tales, which included the sexual content omitted by Lane and Galland. As his biographer notes, Payne found "the finest pieces of verse" in the *Arabian Nights* "worthy" of Christina Rossetti.[12] It is possible that her eroticized use of "The Porter and the Three Ladies" gave Payne the idea of producing a version of the story collection in a Pre-Raphaelite style.

When Payne returned to the *Arabian Nights*, his youthful encounter with Lane's translation formed an important negative example. Reading and rereading Lane, Payne was persuaded that a scholarly translation was antithetical to the form of imaginative rewriting that he yearned to accomplish. This issue is highlighted in two forgotten essays that Payne published anonymously in the *New Quarterly Magazine* in 1879, which set out his essential approach to the story collection. The problem that Payne confronted in turning to the *Arabian Nights* was not just the challenge of choosing a particular style of translation, but the frustration inherent in the act of translation itself. He lamented the "inartistic expedients to which the translator is constantly driven, in the endeavor to realize his double aim of producing a book that should at once be a scientific and a popular one."[13] In these essays Payne points to an unbridgeable divide between artistry, craft, and literature, on the one side, and philology, scholarship, and translation, on the other.

If, as Payne believed, a text must be measured by its ability to capture the genius of its own place and era, Lane's version of the *Arabian Nights*

Christina Rossetti, here modelling for Dante Gabriel Rossetti, in a study for *Ecce Ancilla Domini! (The Annunciation),* ca. 1849. John Payne's fascination with the *Arabian Nights* was inspired in part by the devotion of the Rossetti family to the story collection.

was a failure. In a word, it was "unreadable." For a version of the *Arabian Nights* to be a success, Payne argued, "literary graces of style and diction" were at least as necessary as "accuracy and scholarship." Applying these standards, Payne found Torrens's version far more admirable, and expressed his belief that, had this translator completed his work, "it would not have been necessary to look further for a fairly perfect and classical version."[14] Galland's French version of the *Arabian Nights* was also valued by Payne as a model. The poet lauded Galland for imbuing the collection with his own "charming style, the fine flower of the literary manner of the eighteenth century, partaking at once of Voltaire and Diderot, of *Manon Lescaut* and *Les Bijoux Indiscrets*." The literary qualities that Payne ascribes to Galland's translation—a style that unites "simplicity and boldness, strength and grace" and that rises to "the pathetic and the majestic"—would become his own guide to translating the story collection.[15]

In these anonymous essays, Payne strongly resisted the encroachment of philology and "science" into the realm of literature. Lane's translation may have had "scientific and scholastic merit," but it lacked the "*purely* literary faculties" that Payne saw as the fundamental basis for a successful translation.[16] Rather than bringing the original text to life in a new language, Lane's literal version of the *Arabian Nights* seemed only to demonstrate that Arabic was "essentially" opposed to English. The translation was just "a matrix for the reception of crude nodules of untranslated Arabic." The cumbersome paraphrase and the excessive accumulation of notes that marked Lane's version of the story collection might have been valuable from a scholarly point of view, but Payne regarded them as "almost invariably undesirable in a work of purely literary or fictional character."[17] These forgotten anonymous essays represent Payne's only attempt to situate himself explicitly in relation to his precursors and to stake his claim to a purely literary conception of his *Arabian Nights*. In them Payne effectively acknowledged his plan to rewrite rather than translate the stories from Arabic, and he would come to rue the publication of these essays as he prepared his first volume for publication in 1882.

In his preface to his published translation, Payne is much more careful about how he presents his project. Unlike other translators before him, Payne offers no account of how he came to be interested in Arabic or the *Thousand and One Nights,* or how he produced his own version of the tales. He never states his credentials, and gives only a minimal explanation of his sources, claiming that he used the Macnaghten edition as the basis for his translation, but also collated it with two other Arabic versions—the Bulaq and the Breslau editions—to produce an improved and homogenous text. He attempts to ward off his critics by stressing the mixture that resulted from this process: "No proper estimate can, therefore, be made of the fidelity of the translation, except by those who are intimately acquainted with the whole of the latter." In fact, Payne's use of material from these different editions was likely a consequence of drawing on previous translations to produce what he claimed was "a purely literary work, produced with the sole object of supplying the general body of cultivated readers with a fairly representative and characteristic version of the most famous work of narrative fiction in existence."[18] Unlike Lane, Payne did not claim that his goal was an accurate scholarly rendition of an authentic original.

Payne's approach to translation was strongly influenced by the approach adopted by the Pre-Raphaelite poets he so admired. In 1850, Charles Dickens had criticized the Pre-Raphaelites for artificially replacing new lamps with old lamps, but in 1861 Dante Gabriel Rossetti adopted the same metaphor from the tale of "Aladdin" to defend the archaic structures and diction that were central to his practice of translation. In the preface to *Early Italian Poets,* Rossetti argued that the translator's path "is like that of Aladdin through the enchanted vaults: many are the precious fruits and flowers he must pass by unheeded in search for the lamp alone; happy if at last, when brought to light, it does not prove that his old lamp has been exchanged for a new one,—glittering indeed to the eye, but scarcely of the same virtue nor with the same genius at its summons." Rossetti advised the translator to resist the urge to simply render a foreign-language original in his "own idiom and epoch." He understood his own translations as an imaginative appropriation of an original, which reflected their source text but also demonstrated the unique creative powers of their translator. Rossetti would have no qualms about extracting from the medieval metaphysics of Dante a second Dante more akin to the Pre-Raphaelite sensibility—a poet of sensation and sensuality. This legitimation of translation as "authorship" would shape Payne's own method of "translating" the Arabic medievalism of the *Arabian Nights*.[19] If Lane had used the *Arabian Nights* as a receptacle for ethnographic commentary, Payne undertook his translation with the goal of recreating the Arabic story collection as a work of contemporary European literature.

Payne's venture into translation was also shaped by his encounter with one of Burton's associates from the Cannibal Club—the Decadent poet Swinburne, whom Payne met in 1871. Swinburne's theory of "cosmopolitan literature" would open up a new creative realm for Payne as a translator and poet. Swinburne argued that the cosmopolitan poet or critic should navigate cross-cultural networks that enabled multiple perspectives and embraced contradiction. The English writer seeking the stimulus of immersion in another culture should simply look across the Channel, where France served as the nexus of literary modernity and Charles Baudelaire was the paragon of modern poetry. This distinctly Francophile conception of cosmopolitanism offered the potential to upset the philistine narrow-mindedness of an English establishment. Swinburne admired French literature precisely for its lack of Victorian prudery. Writing about Baudelaire's "A Carcass," Swinburne praises the poet's ability to evoke the "luxuries of pleasure [not] in their simple first form but the sharp and cruel enjoyments of pain, the acrid relish of suffering felt or inflicted, the sides on which nature looks unnatural." For Swinburne, the power of the poet to create beauty from disgust demonstrated the virtues of a cosmopolitan literature in which art exists for art's sake and the medium is more important than the message.[20]

Payne's first major translation project—the work of the French Renaissance poet François Villon—was shaped by this continental orientation. Payne's literary mentors, Rossetti and Swinburne, had both translated poems by Villon (three and eleven, respectively) and strongly encouraged Payne to pursue this project as a way of completing the English discovery of a forgotten French master. Swinburne would certainly have urged Payne to include all of the sexually explicit and sacrilegious material within Villon's work as a way of unsettling an English tradition of poetry. In order to offer a complete and uncensored translation of the ribald poetry, Payne created a scheme of private subscription that would circumvent the Obscene Publications Act of 1857 in Britain. Circulating his translation to a select audience through his Villon Society, Payne established the formula that he would use throughout the remainder of his literary career—which included translations from Giovanni Boccaccio, Omar Khayyam, and Hafiz, as well as the *Arabian Nights*. His translation of Villon in 1878 received praise from Théodore de Banville and sympathetic notices in the English press, and he hoped to repeat this success by producing a version of the *Arabian Nights* that included the sexually explicit content that was missing in Lane's translation.[21]

Payne's attraction to the project of translating the *Arabian Nights* was strongly shaped by the enthusiasm with which the Pre-Raphaelite circle had embraced Edward FitzGerald's translation of *The Rubaiyat*, first published in 1859. Like Torrens's translation of the *Arabian Nights*, FitzGerald's *Rubaiyat* was made possible by the linkages established by empire. The original quatrains of the Persian poet Khayyam had been found in the library of the Royal Asiatic Society in Calcutta in 1857 by Edward Byles Cowell, FitzGerald's old Persian tutor, and sent to FitzGerald for translation. The slim volume containing FitzGerald's verse attracted little literary attention when it was first published, but became a sensation when Rossetti and Swinburne purchased a dozen copies of it in July 1861 to circulate among their friends. It was the influence of these poets that lent currency to a poem that until then had been met with indifference by the mainstream literary press and dismissal by professional Orientalists.

FitzGerald's translation of *The Rubaiyat* represented a model of Orientalist translation that dispensed with the goal of accuracy in pursuit of an intense fusion between the poet / translator and his source material. He confessed that these English quatrains emerged from his own close identification with the sensibilities of the legendary Persian poet, so that the result might be seen more as an act of ventriloquism rather than translation. Channelling the persona of Khayyam, FitzGerald could craft a decadent myth of the Orient in which sensual delight was given free rein. In a letter to Cowell in 1858, FitzGerald pressed his claim on Khayyam over that of the Orientalist scholar: "In truth I take old

Omar rather more as my property than yours: he and I are more akin, are we not? You see all [his] Beauty, but you don't feel with him in some respects as I do." For FitzGerald, translation was an exercise in empathy, not a demonstration of philological expertise. As FitzGerald wrote to Cowell, "At all Cost, a Thing must *live:* with a transfusion of one's own worse Life if one can't retain the Original's better. Better a live Sparrow than a stuffed Eagle." The creative powers of the translator were ultimately more important than his scholarly credentials. Through these acts of transformation, the translator disappeared within the avatar that his creative powers had brought to life.[22]

FitzGerald's effort to privilege style over accuracy may have produced a text with little value to Orientalist scholars, but it ensured the success of *The Rubaiyat* as a Pre-Raphaelite text. In spurring the popularity of this work in the 1860s and 1870s, Rossetti and Swinburne dictated the generic expectations that defined other highly stylized translations from Persian or Arabic such as Payne's *Arabian Nights.* The result was a critical shift in practices of reading Orientalist literature from an emphasis on ethnography and authenticity to a focus on artificiality, musicality, and the fiction of self—summed up by Swinburne as "beauty" and "pathos."[23] In executing his version of the *Arabian Nights,* Payne adhered precisely to these stylistic patterns, and hoped for the same success that FitzGerald had achieved through Rossetti and Swinburne's support. *The Rubaiyat* remained an obsession for Payne, whose study of Persian is better evidenced than his knowledge of Arabic, and he would later seek to supplant FitzGerald with his own translation of Khayyam and an original poem written in the style of *The Rubaiyat.*[24]

The expectations set by FitzGerald's *Rubaiyat* and the reception it received within Pre-Raphaelite circles are clearly visible in Payne's *Arabian Nights,* which he presents as a purely literary work. This was not an *Arabian Nights* intended to illuminate the customs and manners of Arabs. The only credentials that Payne provides in his preface are his original works of Pre-Raphaelite poetry and his translation of Villon. He included only occasional notes (in the manner of Galland), and there was no comprehensive index based on ethnographic criteria such as that produced by Lane. Also, this *Arabian Nights* was not created for a broad middle-class readership. Payne limited the printing to 500 copies to give these literary volumes the status of rare books, and he consciously set out—through lavish attention to margins, font, and illustrations (by M. A. Lalauze)—to make his prohibitively priced volumes into objects of art. Drawing on the more comprehensive collections of stories available in the Macnaghten and Breslau editions, and the seminal nineteenth-century translations of these works, Payne could offer a version of the *Arabian Nights* with a full complement of stories and all the sexual content that was considered too risqué for public consumption by other translators.[25]

In his *Arabian Nights,* Payne constructs an "Orient" that he has never seen, drawing on the standard tropes of Orientalism. The dedicatory poem in his last volume uses a classic set of oppositions to represent this translation as an attempt to take readers from "the mean workday miseries of existence" into "the dreamland of the Orient distance, / Under the splendours of the Syrian sky."

> And now, the long task done, the journey over,
> From that far home of immemorial calms,
> Where, as a mirage, on the sky-marge hover
> The desert and its oases of palms,
>
> Lingering, I turn me back, with eyes reverted,
> To this stepmother world of daily life,
> As one by some long pleasant dream deserted,
> That wakes anew to dull unlovely strife.

The Oriental dreamland constructed in this poem through contrasts between the conscious and the unconscious, the modern and the premodern, reason and all that lies beyond it, obscures Payne's lack of experience of the "untraveled East." In his version of the tales, Payne sought not the immediacy or authenticity of the traveller or ethnographer, but rather the vanishing point of the Orient in the horizon of the European imagination.[26]

Like FitzGerald, Payne sought to immerse himself in another realm of subjectivity in which the poet and his source were one. If FitzGerald imagined he could channel the voice of Khayyam, Payne sought to narrate the tales of the *Arabian Nights* by emotionally connecting with an imagined Arab essence. In his terminal essay, Payne argues that these tales are distinguished not by "the splendour of description, the showers of barbaric pearl and gold" but by the life of the people described within it: "those Arabs so essentially brave, sober, hospitable, and kindly, almost hysterically sensitive to emotions of love and pity, as well as to artistic impressions, yet susceptible of being roused to strange excesses of ferocity and brutality, to be soon followed by bitter and unavailing repentence—a people whom extreme sensibility of the nervous tissue inclines to excess of sensuous enjoyment, yet who are capable of enduring without a murmur the severest hardships and of suffering patiently the most cruel vicissitudes of fortune."[27] This rich emotional life is reflected in the mixture of genres in the story collection, which features powerful examples of "pathos," "tragic intensity," "romantic exultation," "melancholy beauty," and religious devotion. Within this culture of heightened sensuality and emotion, Payne argues, "nothing is rejected, nothing excluded as common or unclean," and he embraces the "lewdness" that Lane had hidden in its commentary. Payne acknowledges the presence of episodes of burlesque farce and bracing battle scenes in which "the text quickens into a stern and nervous energy," but as a whole the *Arabian Nights* speaks to him with the "simplicity or poignant pathos" reminiscent of "an old *Märchen*." In his hands, the story collection would become "the great Arabic compendium of romantic fiction" whose chief charm is the "grace of pathos" and "strains that linger in thought like the tones of that '*alte, ernste Weise*' [old, solemn tune] which haunts the hearing of the dying Tristan in the greatest of musical dramas."[28]

Like his English edition of the poetry of Villon, Payne's translation of the *Arabian Nights* allowed him to highlight aspects of sexual expression that were central to the bohemian lifestyle of Pre-Raphaelite circles in London. In the new publishing environment created by the Obscene Publications Act of 1857, it was common for writers to locate commentaries on sexuality in foreign lands, or in the past, or both. Tropes regarding the decadence of distant lands and times allowed late nineteenth-century writers and artists to portray sexual practices they could not associate with their own time and place. In his *Arabian Nights,* Payne seems to have adopted the typical Orientalist version of this practice by portraying Baghdad as a center of licentiousness. In his edition of the tales, Payne sees the tenth-century court of Harun al-Rashid in Baghdad through the prism of sexual permissiveness and artistic freedom. The caliph's friendship with Abu Nuwas, a "debauchee of the most debased and sensual order," becomes the most extreme symbol of this quality. By publishing his *Arabian Nights* for only 500 subscribers, Payne was able to include all the material from the stories that would otherwise earn the censor's opprobrium.[29]

Affiliating his *Arabian Nights* with Pre-Raphaelite aesthetics and the genre of romance, Payne strongly departs from Lane's ethnographic approach in the very first lines, where he chooses to replace "Allah" with "God" in rendering the opening religious invocations. A concern with producing elegant English prose shapes Payne's decisions throughout the stories. He rejects the systems for transliterating names followed by modern scholars, which might fit "works having a scientific or non-literary object," but are "foreign to the genius of the English language." The rhyming prose of the original is also explicitly rejected as a model for any English rendering. He describes the "seja or rhyming prose" in Arabic as "an excrescence born of the excessive facilities for rhyme afforded by a language whose every speaker is a versifier and the extravagant sensibility of Eastern peoples to antithesis of all kinds, whether of sound or thought." Payne betrays his own contempt for the original when he explains that "it is the summit of every Arab author's ambition to deck or disfigure" his prose with these "jingling tags." Providing a sample transliteration of the Arabic in his explanatory note to the ninth volume, he invites readers to marvel at the way in which he has adapted the original to "the genius of English prose and the exigencies of style." His method is presented as a mode of imposing order on chaos—"breaking up the endless phrases of the Arabic into convenient sentences and purging them from the excrescences of tautology and repetition that deface the text." The "original wording" is followed only where it "is consistent with English idiom."[30]

Payne found a model for his preferred method of translation from Arabic in the first volume of Torrens's edition of the *Arabian Nights*. If Lane represented the antithesis of the *Arabian Nights* author for Payne, Torrens represented the ideal. Payne's opinion that Torrens had the potential to produce "a fairly perfect and classical version" of the collection was echoed by many of his contemporaries.[31] The folklorist William F. Kirby, who collaborated with both Payne and Burton, regretted that Torrens left unfinished his "excellent" version of the work. An article in the *Cornhill Magazine* in 1875 asserted that Torrens "unfortunately, left unfinished by far the best translation which has yet appeared in any language known to the writer of this article."[32] Payne inherited his evaluation of Torrens the literary writer and Lane the scholar from a comprehensive contrast of the two translators in an 1839 review, which, having extensively established the superiority of Torrens's verse, likewise draws attention to the qualities of his prose. The author praises "the pathos of these stories, which Mr Torrens appears to us to have rendered with a more touching and affectionate earnestness, than his learned rival; more as Chaucer, or Boccaccio, might have told it." These contemporary reviews would have suggested to Payne the usefulness of Torrens's translation as a model for a literary rewriting of the story collection in a Pre-Raphaelite style.[33]

Turning to the task of translating the *Arabian Nights* in 1877, Payne would have needed this sort of model to begin the process of creating his own version of the tales. When he promised a version of the *Arabian Nights* in a notice in the *Athenaeum* in the fall of 1878, Payne had set himself a difficult task, but three years later the first volume of his edition was set for the printers and the notice soliciting 500 subscribers was issued. By 1884 Payne had published eight volumes of his translation. It was a remarkable pace for this kind of translation, leading to speculation by several contemporaries that Payne was not actually translating from Arabic but rather relying on the work of other translators.[34]

Torrens's version of the *Arabian Nights* would have offered the best means for Payne to formulate his own method of remaking the tales in a Pre-Raphaelite mode. This unfinished translation covered the first quarter of the Macnaghten edition of the tales that Payne claimed he was using as his source. After the 205th night, the Bulaq edition translated by Lane and the Macnaghten edition used by Torrens were virtually identical, and Payne could proceed by using Lane's version as his basis and consulting other German, French, or English versions when necessary. Payne himself claimed that he was collating different editions of the *Thousand and One Nights* to produce the best "effect," and he stressed the subjective nature of these editorial solutions. Even after the "laborious process of collation and comparison," the "exact sense of many passages must still remain doubtful, so corrupt are the extant texts and so incomplete our knowledge, as incorporated in dictionaries, etc., of the peculiar dialect, half classical and half modern, in which the original work is written." It is much more likely that Payne was considering the literary merits of the various European translations rather than collating the various Arabic originals at his disposal.[35]

For Payne, Torrens's translation of the tales had considerable advantages as a model. Lacking any experience of the Orient himself, Payne would have seen Torrens's time in India as a suitably nurturing context for an empathetic rendering of the *Arabian Nights*. Torrens's claim that the style of his prose "formed itself without any effort on my own on the language of the original" suggests that he had a similar belief that the spirit of the original Arab text could be channelled through an English prose style that was sensitive to its emotional qualities.[36] Payne seems to have trusted Torrens's literary instincts, and he often adopted a particular word choice or turn of phrase from his translation. Like Torrens, he believed in the importance of inserting a "beautiful word," be it archaic, French, or Irish, for emphasis or poetic effect. One example, Payne acknowledges, is Torrens's use of the neologism "ensorcelled," from the French *ensorceler*, "to bewitch." In a story collection abounding with jinn and magic charms, Payne would appropriate the word and use it in other stories. Rewriting both Torrens and Payne, Burton inherited the neologism and used it more extensively. Following Torrens, he entitled a tale in his first volume "The Ensorcelled Prince."[37]

While Payne relied on Torrens's literary instincts, he may also have made use of what he assumed was the greater precision of Lane's translation. Some of Payne's translations blend details from both the Macnaghten and the Bulaq editions of the story, and from the translations by both Torrens and Lane. The literal translation of the Macnaghten edition by Malcolm Lyons (2008) makes Payne's departures from it more visible. In the frame narrative of the two kings, for instance, Payne seems to be drawing on both Torrens and Lane as he describes their betrayal by their wives. Payne describes Shah Zaman's wife "asleep in his own bed, in the arms of one of his black slaves." Neither of these details—the couple's slumber or their embrace—appears in Lyons's version of the Macnaghten. Rather, Payne seems to have arrived at his description by combining Lane's evasive translation, in which the queen and the slave were sleeping, with Torrens's more explicit statement that they were embracing. Payne likely did not feel confident enough to reproduce Torrens at the expense of excluding Lane. Thus he incorporates both renderings, as if to err on the side of comprehensiveness.[38] A similar thought process is apparent when Payne reached the portion of the tale in which the young woman is held captive in a chest by a powerful jinni but is nevertheless resourceful enough to compel the sexual attention of Shah Zaman and Shahriyar. Torrens makes the cuckolding of the jinni by his young captive clear in his translation, where the young woman asserts that the 517 rings in her collection were "won from their owners by me, upon the horns of this Ufreet." Payne's version, in which "every one of the owners of these rings has had to do with me . . . despite of this Afrit" is closer to Lane's. Payne's dilemma in these instances seems to be that he was not translating directly from the Arabic and therefore was not certain whether Torrens's or Lane's translation was more correct.[39]

Payne's distance from the original text helps to explain the choices he made as he attempted to combine Torrens's style with Lane's accuracy. In his version of the frame tale of "The Porter and the Three Ladies," for instance, Payne follows closely Torrens's depiction of the porter's revelry with the young women. Torrens translates, "The porter was going on with them with quips, and kisses, and cranks, and tricks, and pinches, and girls' play, and romping, this one giving him a dainty mouthful, and that one thumping him." Payne created his own distinctive version of this passage by seizing on the rhythms of Torrens's translation and enhancing them with language that strongly echoes that of Christina Rossetti's "Goblin Market." Thus, in Payne's tale, "the porter fell to toying and kissing and biting and handling and groping and dallying and taking liberties with them: whilst one put a morsel into his mouth and another thumped him." Lyons's literal translation of the Macnaghten edition, which Torrens and Payne were both supposedly translating, adds that the third young woman "would *bring* him scented flowers." Payne's rendering here—the third girl "*pelted* him with flowers"—is in fact closer to Lane's wording from his translation of the Bulaq text: "and the third *beat* him with sweet-scented flowers."[40]

One of Payne's most formidable challenges was how to craft a consistent and coherent work of literature from his varied sources. Style would prove Payne's answer to this challenge. He mirrors the archaic language that is a conventional part of Pre-Raphaelite translations, and he intensifies the romantic qualities of the stories whenever possible. These qualities are particularly apparent in his version of "The Porter and the Three Ladies of Baghdad," which is filled with opportunities to explore Pre-Raphaelite tropes of beauty and pathos. The interpolated tales of the three dervishes offer many examples of the morbidly erotic that might have appealed to Payne as the author of the vampire poem *Lautrec*. The tone is set in the first dervish's tale, where he tells the porter and the three ladies about the fate of his cousin, who he has unknowingly aided in a plan to indulge his incestuous passion for his sister. Withdrawing to an underground tomb, the lovers suffer a horrible punishment, apparently at the hands of God himself. When the tomb is finally opened again, Payne draws out the pathos of the scene: "My uncle went up to the bed and drawing the curtains, found his son and the lady in each other's arms; but they were become black coal, as they had been cast into a well of fire." Again and again the stories of this cycle emphasize the tragic consequences of "passion's fatal spell," against which the characters are powerless. The only moral of such tales is contained in Payne's rendering of the verse of one of their tragic victims: "Fortune's nature is deceit, And parting is the end / of love delight."[41]

In the tale of the second dervish, Payne creates an image of idyllic beauty in a familiar Pre-Raphaelite style. The narrator, a prince disguised as a woodcutter, enters a mysterious underground chamber to find "a vaulted hall of goodly structure, wherein was a damsel like a pearl of great price, whose aspect banished pain and care and anxiety from the heart and whose speech healed the troubled soul and captivated the wise and the intelligent. She was slender of shape and swelling-breasted, delicate-cheeked and bright of colour and fair of form; and indeed her face shone like the sun through the night of her tresses, and her teeth glittered above the snows of her bosom."[42] Payne captures the typical Arabic tropes of beauty in graceful English prose that uses the deliberate archaism of the Pre-Raphaelites to create a romantic quality. By following Rossetti's advice not to exchange the old lamp for a new one, Payne imbues his *Arabian Nights* with a languid nostalgia.

Payne is perhaps at his best in translating the poetry that appears throughout the tales of "The Porter and the Three Ladies of Baghdad," where the recitation of verse becomes a way for characters to express heightened emotional states. The prince in the tale of the second dervish naturally falls in love with the beautiful damsel who has been imprisoned in the underground vault by an evil ifrit, who has stolen her to be his bride. When the lovers are discovered, the jinni demands that the young woman kill the prince, and the couple communicate their emotions without speech until the young man seizes on the sentiment of a poem:

> My looks interpret for my tongue and tell of what I feel:
> And all the love appears that I within my heart conceal.
> When as we meet and down our cheeks our tears are running
> fast, I'm dumb, and yet my speaking eyes my thought of thee
> reveal.[43]

Like Torrens, Payne translates the interpolated poetry with the goal of drawing out the emotional qualities it might contain. Rendered with remarkable naturalness, the poetry becomes an integral part of the narrative and communicates the pathos that the poet believed was the key feature of the *Arabian Nights*.

While the plots of the story collection often take the reader quickly through a series of improbable twists and turns, the interpolated poetry provided an opportunity for the Pre-Raphaelite translator to emphasize moments of pure subjectivity. The tale of the second dervish moves through a series of incredible episodes. By the end of the tale, the prince has seen the jealous jinni torture and kill his lover, he has been transformed into an ape, he has impressed a king with his skills at calligraphy and chess, and he has been transformed back into his human form after a fierce battle between a brave princess and an evil jinni. At this point, he can ponder the "misfortunes" that have befallen him:

> A vanquished man, without complaint, my doom I will
> endure, As the parched traveller in the waste endures the
> torrid glow.
>
> . . . .
>
> The wrinkles graven on my heart would speak my hidden
> pain If through my breast the thought could pierce and
> read what lies below.
>
> Were but my load on mountains laid, they'd crumble into
> dust; On fire it would be quenched outright; on wind,
> 'twould cease to blow.
>
> Let who will say that life is sweet; to all there comes a day
> When they must needs a bitt'rer thing than aloes undergo.[44]

Though he was only a minor member of the Pre-Raphaelite movement, Payne would prove one of the most talented stylists to attempt an English-language version of the *Arabian Nights.* An unpublished review of Payne's *Lautrec* reveals that Dante Gabriel Rossetti saw promise in him, but thought Payne was "wandering always in a maze of reflected styles."[45] In his translation of the *Arabian Nights,* Payne makes a virtue of his inability to find his own poetic voice by putting his talents in the service of the characters of the story collection.

✦ ✦ ✦

Payne's version of the *Arabian Nights* has undeniable literary merits, but without the legitimacy afforded by real credentials as a translator of Arabic, its author stood on shaky ground. With the appearance of the first volume in 1882, Payne had every reason to expect a hostile response from the well-established contingent of Lane supporters headed by his nephews, Stanley Lane-Poole and Reginald Stuart Poole. In the heightened imperial spirit of those years, Lane was refashioned as an English adventurer whose mastery of Egypt presaged the British occupation of

1882, and his nephews were prepared to defend his legacy. When Payne tested the waters in 1879 with his anonymous essays in the *New Quarterly Magazine,* it was Poole who issued an immediate and crushing response. No doubt motivated by Payne's condescending treatment of Lane, Poole pointed out the "anonymous" writer's lack of credentials and specialized scholarly knowledge.[46]

In this response Poole defined the criteria for a scholarly translation in a way that privileged his uncle's insistence on literal accuracy and a deep knowledge of a source language and culture. A translator of the *Arabian Nights*, Poole argued, should have knowledge of classical and modern Arabic, familiarity with Arab history and customs, the critical skill to select the best manuscript, and good English style. He seems to have found the anonymous author wanting in every category. Poole points out numerous errors of translation in the sample translations included in Payne's essays. In one instance of mistaken conjugation, the anonymous writer has the child's mother, instead of the narrator, asking the parentage of the caliph's child. In another odd reversal, a religious devotee is made to shun rather than visit men of religious learning. Poole also found the anonymous writer's mistakes regarding history laughable. The list of caliphs he provided is riddled with ridiculous errors. Somehow the essay's author had identified an orthodox Abbasid caliph—the "celebrated Egyptian Khalif, Hakim-bi-amr-Allah"—as "the founder of the Druze religion."[47]

Most importantly, as mentioned earlier, Poole suspected that the anonymous writer was not in fact translating from Arabic. He noticed that the writer transliterated using the German *s* where an English translator would invariably use *z,* and his implicit suggestion that Payne was relying on German translations to produce his versions of the stories may contain some truth. For Poole the question of English style was moot, for "if a translator cannot translate, it little matters in what form his results appear." Nevertheless, he could not resist taking a swipe at the anonymous writer's aesthetic preferences, concluding that "it may be questioned whether an Arab edifice should be decorated with old English wall-papers." With this reference to the decorative qualities associated with Pre-Raphaelite style, Poole was hinting that he knew the identity of the anonymous author.[48]

When Payne made his plans for a literary *Arabian Nights* clear in the *Athenaeum*, he had to confront another formidable opponent from the Orientalist establishment—Rev. George Percy Badger, a professor of Arabic at Oxford. Responding to the advertisement for Payne's *Arabian Nights*, Badger wrote in the *Academy* that it was regrettable and strange that "the only recommendation put forward on behalf of the translator of a voluminous and in many respects difficult Arabic book is that he has made a version [from French] of Villon's poems." Payne did not have the confidence to respond to Badger's questions directly. Instead, Payne's agents in charge of handling subscriptions printed a hostile response to Badger's inquiries. Granger Hutt of the Villon Society reproved Badger for having aired his concerns publicly and advised him that he should have privately addressed them to himself. Following this veiled legal threat, Hutt assured Badger and the reading public that Payne "has long been known to his friends and acquaintances as an accomplished Persian and Arabic scholar." Badger would not be silenced so easily, however, and made a great show of sarcastically deferring to the opinion of Payne's "friends and acquaintances." Moreover, he reiterated his previous complaint that the notice of publication "affords no clue whatever to the sources from whence the proposed 'complete version' is to be compiled." Hardly placated, Badger warned that he was looking forward to ascertaining the merits of the proposed translation himself.[49]

These public attacks on the credibility of Payne's *Arabian Nights* led him to strongly pursue an association with the one Orientalist whose reputation might shield him. Within London's bohemian circles, Burton's reputation as an expert on the Oriental world was well established, and he had made favorable noises when Payne had announced his plan to produce an *Arabian Nights* for private subscribers. Writing to the *Athenaeum* in November 1881, Burton claimed that he was encouraged by Payne's unabridged translation of Villon, which had included controversial sexual content, and expressed the hope that Payne would render the *Thousand and One Nights* word for word without giving way to any prejudice that might keep him from faithfully reproducing the original Arabic text. This might have encouraged Payne to believe that he had Burton's support, but the famous explorer had another agenda in making these statements. He was already staking his own claim to the story collection by asserting that he had made significant progress in translating it several decades before Payne had the idea. He also suggested that if Payne's version did not give the *Thousand and One Nights* "fair play," he would have to produce his own, more authentic version of this text—rendering every word of the "orgies" in the tales with absolute literalism.[50]

In these first discussions of Payne's *Arabian Nights,* Burton began to weave the myth that he would later immortalize in the preface to his own version of the story collection, where he claims that his work on the tales began in the 1850s, the decade of his famous pilgrimage to Mecca and Medina. These claims were, to use one of Burton's own neologisms, "unfacts." A more accurate view of Burton's interest in the story collection can be found in a letter to his publisher from July 1881 in which he wonders what Payne will make of the story collection and admits, "I intend to publish (at Brussels) some day all the excised parts in plain English. It will be nice reading for babes and sucklings."[51] While Payne was developing his translation, Burton was dreaming about producing something akin to what he would later call "The Black Book of the 1001 Nights"—containing the provocative sexual content of the story collection.[52] Burton may have translated a few stories earlier in his life, but he would not begin serious work on his own version of the *Arabian Nights* until 1884. His assertions in the *Athenaeum* were a bluff intended to demonstrate the antecedence and greater legitimacy of his work on the *Arabian Nights* as compared to Payne's edition.

Whether Payne understood Burton's endgame in these statements or not, his vulnerability to criticism on scholarly grounds drew him to the eminent Arabist. Almost immediately Payne wrote to Burton to propose a collaboration, on terms very much in Burton's favor. Payne most likely suggested that Burton contribute the notes and commentary while he would compose the prose, doing what Burton called the pony work. Even more generous was Payne's proposal to give Burton a portion of the royalties, which struck even Burton, who felt himself in financial difficulty, as too much. Payne's goal in making such a generous offer was his desire to borrow Burton's established reputation as an expert on the Muslim world to ensure the legitimacy of his *Arabian Nights.* Burton, however, was not interested in pursuing a real partnership. He wrote that he would be happy to help Payne in any way, but he could not accept Payne's terms for a collaboration. He explained that he did not know how much time he could devote to the work because he was a "rolling stone," but Burton most likely refused Payne's offer because he wanted to reserve the right to publish his own version.[53]

Burton would follow through on his offer to help by addressing Payne's specific need for the kind of scholarly essays on the *Arabian Nights* that were now considered essential to any translation. After Payne's first essays had been eviscerated by Poole, he lacked the confidence to tackle this challenge himself, and turned to Burton again. While Burton claimed he did not have the time to help, he did recommend three scholars who might. This list, however, would not have alleviated Payne's anxieties, for it included the famous Orientalist E. H. Palmer (who would die on a desert mission for the British military forces in August 1882), the Cambridge Arabist Robertson Smith (who would later deny that Payne translated the *Arabian Nights*), and the Reverend Badger (who was already among Payne's enemies).[54] Burton's motives in mentioning Badger are unclear. He obviously had been following Payne's progress and could not have failed to notice the very public attack the reverend had mounted on his project. Was this Burton's way of reminding Payne of his vulnerability and ensuring his absolute dependence on his help?

The result of this awkward predicament seems to have been an extension of Burton's interest in Payne's project and perhaps an implicit (or explicit) agreement to share the text that would be produced. Burton introduced Payne to a trio of researchers—the folklorists Kirby and W. A. Clouston and the Orientalist Hermann Zotenberg. While they were not acknowledged by Payne officially, all three are recognized by his biographer as having provided Payne with help on his *Arabian Nights*. They seem to have provided scholarly essays for the ninth volume and material for Payne's "Terminal Essay." All three were also contributors to Burton's edition of the *Arabian Nights* (published in 1885), and it is possible that he had commissioned them to assist Payne at the same time that he asked them to lay the groundwork for his own version. In addition to providing Payne with collaborators, Burton also read the proofs of Payne's volumes, returning them with his comments, and he allowed Payne to print in his preface that he had edited his text for ethnographic accuracy. In this way, the textual apparatuses of the *Arabian Nights* created by Payne and by Burton were already being interwoven.

Once this tenuous alliance with Payne had been established, Burton could take on a public role as a promoter of Payne's volume. He personally undertook to sell subscriptions to it, requesting in June 1882 that Payne send him "a lot of advertisements" because he could "place multiple copies." He reassured Payne that there would be no difficulty battling Poole, though it would "only be prudent to prepare for an attack." When Payne asked if Burton could do something to silence Poole's reviews of his work, Burton responded on September 29, 1882, that it would be best to let Poole "sing his song (intolerant little cad!)." He did, however, suggest that he would write to the editor of the *Athenaeum* to dissuade him from publishing reviews of privately printed works. Burton made it clear to Payne that he did not think it worthwhile to attempt to suppress negative publicity from the Lane-Poole clique, but he eagerly volunteered to take up the fight against the widely hated Poole. A public dispute, however, was the last thing Payne wanted.[55]

Burton seemed to understand the nature of Payne's predicament and was willing to come to his aid, but only in a manner that would benefit his own plans for the *Arabian Nights.* When Payne wrote to him of his trepidations, Burton responded on October 8, 1882, "Of course I don't know Arabic but who does? One may know a part of it, a corner of the field, but all! Bah!"[56] Burton may have imagined that Payne feared the Lane-Poole clique would accuse him of not having *perfect* knowledge of Arabic, while Payne seems to have feared they would accuse him of having *insufficient or no* knowledge of it. Or perhaps Burton knew that Payne lacked the Arabic proficiency to translate the *Thousand and One Nights* directly from Arabic and simply did not care, as he was himself in the habit or plagiarizing and rewriting from other sources. Whatever his understanding of Payne's predicament, Burton was more than willing to go to battle against the Lane-Poole clique that he had long loathed. He correctly anticipated that Lane's defenders would object to Payne's translation on moral grounds because he included the sexual material that Lane had omitted from his version. Payne's real concern, however, was that Poole would attack his knowledge of Arabic once again.

Drumming up subscribers for Payne's *Arabian Nights,* Burton quickly realized that there was a greater demand than could be satisfied by Payne's promised 500 copies. In December 1882, Burton asked Payne, "Is it not time to think of a reprint: are you taking any steps to open a second list of subscribers?" Payne apparently replied in the negative, perhaps citing legal considerations, given that he had promised not to reissue the unabridged text. Evidently unconvinced, Burton asked Payne on January 4, 1883, if there was no way to get around the difficulties of issuing more copies. As a solution to the problem, Burton suggested that perhaps he could reprint Payne's text. He added parenthetically that "of course" the reprint would be in Payne's interest, perhaps indicating that Burton was open to negotiations to divide the royalties from the venture.[57] However, Burton seems to have implied that he would reprint Payne's text in his own name, likely with the idea of appending his own notes and commentary. Burton's proposal seems very similar to the terms of Payne's initial offer of collaboration, in which Payne would supply the prose and Burton the commentary. But Burton now proposed to print this collaborative version solely under his own name.

Though Burton had declined Payne's offer to split the royalties and to include his name in Payne's *Arabian Nights,* he still acted for all intents and purposes as a collaborator and partner in the venture. Burton would have felt that his contributions to Payne's project justified a sense of joint ownership over it. Allowing Payne to print in his preface that Burton had edited his text for ethnographic accuracy, Burton lent Payne's *Arabian Nights* his own authority and celebrity. He also introduced Payne to Kirby, Clouston, and Zotenberg, and likely arranged, perhaps even funded, the assistance they provided him. When Payne feared that reviewers would challenge his scholarly credentials, Burton used his personal influence to ensure that negative reviews were kept out of the *Athenaeum* and experts like Badger and Smith were silenced. For all these ways in which he had helped Payne, Burton knew that Payne was in his debt. Payne's reply to Burton's proposal has not been preserved, but it is unlikely that he flatly refused. Even if he had not been keen on the idea, he would have felt that he could not say no to Burton.

Neither man seems to have returned to the matter in their correspondence until April 1884, when Payne's final volume was nearing completion.

Burton wrote to Payne matter-of-factly announcing that he would now begin his own version of the collection. Burton also made what he admitted was the somewhat indiscreet request for Payne to send him his manuscripts of the *Thousand and One Nights*.[58] Despite his claim that he had been working on a translation of the tales, Burton evidently did not possess Arabic versions of them. Once he decided to embark on his own version in 1884, he did acquire copies of the Macnaghten, Breslau, and Bulaq editions. This may indicate that initially Burton intended to, or at least considered, producing his own original translation. But even if he started with that intention, he quickly realized that he simply did not have the time, both because he was engaged in other, more pressing projects and because Payne had set an impossible precedent with the speed of his publication. For his own *Arabian Nights,* Burton replicated Payne's scheme of private subscription and even inherited some of his subscribers. In these circumstances, Burton could not fail to match Payne's rapid pace. This kind of productivity could only be achieved by implementing Burton's original idea—to reprint Payne's *Arabian Nights* as his own. Tellingly, Burton, a habitual scribbler in the volumes of his personal library, did not leave a single annotation in his copy of the Arabic edition of Macnaghten's *Thousand and One Nights*.[59]

Burton did not mention the gentleman's agreement that he seems to have struck with Payne when he returned with gusto to the theme of the precedence of his version. Though Burton had no specimens of translation that predated Payne's, he felt he could establish his antecedence by asserting that he had begun telling the stories of the *Thousand and One Nights* during his travels in Arabia. In the first draft of his preface to the collection, scrawled across his copy of Lane's edition, Burton imagined sharing the tales around a campfire with the desert Bedouin:

> The sheykhs and "white beards" of the tribe sit and squat round the camp fire whilst I reward their hospitality by reciting or reading a few pages of their favourite tales: the women and the children standing motionless outside the ring. All are breathless with attention: they seem to drink in the words with eyes & mouths as well as with ears; the wildest flights of imagina-

> tion appear to them utterly natural; they enter into every phase of feeling touched upon by the author; they take a personal pride in the chivalrous nature & knightly prowess of Taj al-Muluk. They are touched with tenderness by the self sacrificing love of Azizah and despite their gravity they roar with laughter, at times rolling upon the ground till the reader's gravity is upset by the tale of Ali & the Kurdish Sharper.[60]

It is unclear whether this scene was a recollection of one of Burton's journeys or merely an evocative image intended to establish his claim as a privileged interpreter of the *Thousand and One Nights*. In any case, this passage misrepresents his actual engagement with the project of translating the story collection.

In this first gesture, Burton began to stake his claim as the true author of the story collection, a man whose experience of the pure culture of the Arabian Desert would allow him to channel its many voices. Cultivating the belief that his *Arabian Nights* was a product of his life as a traveller, Burton resorted to a veneer of Arabic authenticity to differentiate his version from the text that he was rewriting. Professing the Romantic belief that poetry was the most characteristic expression of a people, Burton argued that to ignore the rhyme and rhythm of the *Thousand and One Nights'* poetry would be to remain deaf to the Bedouin cadences that could still be heard in the Arabic of Macnaghten's edition. Burton boasted in his commentary that he alone preserved the original rhyming prose that Lane had thought untranslatable and Payne had rejected as foreign to the genius of English. In an ostentatious statement of his method of translation, Burton claimed that he would even "Arabize" the orphan tales by translating these tales from French into Arabic and then from Arabic into English.[61]

Scholars of translation have argued that Burton adopted a method that was intentionally "foreignizing"—departing from the conventions of good English style in order to give the reader a sense of the cultural difference embodied in the source text. Lawrence Venuti argues that the strange rhythms of Burton's prose and his many archaisms, neologisms, and foreign loan words produce a foreignizing effect that subverts the prevailing regime of fluency.[62] Burton's diction did make his *Arabian*

Nights strange and somewhat unpalatable to his contemporaries, but his use of language in this work was not exactly original. Like Payne, Burton admired the translation theory of Dante Gabriel Rossetti, and Burton's style was woven from the same fabric of deliberate archaism and "beautiful" words as Payne's. Burton's best explanation of his approach appeared in 1881 in a letter to George Massey, the publisher of his translations of Luís de Camões. Burton had just published a translation of this poet's sixteenth-century epic, *The Lusiads,* and he would continue to work on translations of Camões's lyric poetry while he was creating his version of the *Arabian Nights.* Burton described his method of translation in this context as an effort "to copy tone and sound" from the original as well as meaning—adopting words such as "digno," "pergrim," "voyante," and "aspero" that connected the translation to its source. He claimed that he would only eliminate such foreignisms if the "words themselves are ugly, unpleasant, not significant."[63]

In his version of the *Arabian Nights,* Burton pushed this foreignizing aesthetic of archaic and invented words almost to the point of self-parody. In these tales, the English reader is confronted with diction that is foreign, invented, and, even in Burton's time, archaic: "solde," "betided," "bittock," "duenna," "joyance," "peregrine," "meseemeth." This extraordinary range of vocabulary recalls W. H. Mallock's satire of the vocabulary of Rossetti and his imitators from 1872: "Take a packet of fine selected early English, containing no words but such as are obsolete and unintelligible. Pour this into about double the quantity of entirely new English, which must have never been used before, and which you must compose yourself, fresh, as it is wanted. Mix these together thoroughly till they assume a color quite different from any tongue that was ever spoken, and the material will be ready for use."[64] To many of Burton's critics this would appear a precise description of his method, which seemed to reflect an idiosyncratic, if not an incomprehensible, understanding of the English language. There is an undeniable foreignness in Burton's diction in the *Arabian Nights,* although it resembles the archaic Portuguese of Camões and the deliberate archaism of Rossetti more than the Arabic original of the tales of Shahrazad.

When Burton is presented as a model of a foreignizing method of translation by theorists, the assumption is that the discordant elements of his translation of the *Arabian Nights,* particularly the use of assonance, alliteration, and rhyming prose, were an attempt to preserve the distinctive tonal qualities of the original Arabic text. Burton was undeniably attempting to disrupt literary conventions, but his choices are not about the "complete reproduction of the original," as he claimed in his preface to the story collection. He may have attempted to impose his idiosyncratic preferences on the language and rhythm of his translation, but this was a generic attempt to "Arabize" rather than a real engagement with the language of the original.[65] Despite the disruptive effects that Burton produces in the language of his stories, his translation was actually built on other English translations that had a more fluent method of translation as their goal—in particular those of Payne and Torrens. A reading of Burton's *Arabian Nights* makes it clear that while he occasionally makes use of stylistic flourishes that would be classified as foreignizing, more often than not, his version of a tale differs very little from Payne's or Torrens's.

Burton deploys his characteristic rhyming prose and exotic word choices selectively in his rewriting of the story collection, usually to mark moments of violent, sexual, or comic tension. In Burton's version of "The Sleeper and the Waker," for example, Abu al-Hasan responds with anger to a trick played on him by Caliph Harun al-Rashid with language that departs from the milder archaism of the rest of the story: "So avaunt and aroynt thee and wend thy ways!"[66] In "The Hunchback's Tale," Burton takes alliteration and rhyme to new heights to enhance the cruel humor of an episode in which a tailor and his wife entertain and playfully abuse the hunchback: "Presently the Tailor's wife took a great fid of fish and gave it in a gobbet to the Gobbo, stopping his mouth with her hand and saying, 'By Allah thou must down with it at a single gulp; and I will not give thee time to chew it.' So he bolted it; but therein was a stiff bone which stuck in his gullet and, his hour being come, he died." Nowhere else in this tale does Burton concentrate rhyming sounds and words to such a degree. Alliteration heightens the cruel humor in this central episode, and later it draws attention the tale's to implicit anti-Semitism in a way that might bring any superficial championing of the foreignizing interventions of Burton into doubt.[67]

Other passages within Burton's *Arabian Nights* reflect the greater simplicity and clarity that was characteristic of Torrens's translation of the tales. Despite Burton's attempts to denounce the "hideous hag-like nakedness" of this predecessor, a simple comparison of Burton's work with the first volume produced by Torrens reveals the unexpected link between the two versions of the *Arabian Nights.*[68] The opening of the tale of "The Hunchback" is revealing in this regard. In Torrens's version the story begins "in a city of China" with "a man that was a tailor, open-handed, that loved pleasure, and enjoyment; and so it was he went forth, he and his wife from time to time to solace themselves with amusements." Burton adds only a few foreignizing tweaks to this opening: "in a certain city of China, a Tailor who was an open-handed man that loved pleasuring and merry-making; and who was wont, he and his wife, to solace themselves from time to time with public diversions and amusements."[69] Even some of the phrasing in the alliterative sentences that Burton added to the text is reminiscent of Torrens. In the critical choking scene quoted above, Torrens renders the Arabic with a poet's attention to sound effects. The tailor's wife thus "stopped his mouth with her hand . . . and there was in it a stiff bone, and it stuck in his gullet."[70] Those who have noted Burton's plagiarism of Payne have observed that it becomes more brazen in the later volumes, as if he drops any pretense of originality. One explanation for this phenomenon might be that Burton ran out of text translated by Torrens, and therefore was unable to triangulate Payne's text with Torrens's to create the semblance of his own translation.

Burton's rewriting of Payne has been asserted by a series of scholars, but recent archival discoveries throw new light on his method. When the Royal Anthropological Institute sold Burton's library to the Huntington Library, it included a copy of Payne's *Arabian Nights* in which Burton had written on the pages of only one story. However, there have long been rumors among collectors and archivists that Burton owned a second set of Payne's work that he dismembered and used as the basis for his own edition of the story collection. A recent acquisition of the British Library now offers scholars an example of Burton's method: two small booklets made from pages cut from Payne's edition of the *Arabian Nights* and covered with Burton's handwriting. These booklets, containing three tales taken from the second and third volumes of Payne's translation, reveal the way in which Burton disassembled and reassembled portions of Payne's *Arabian Nights* to produce his own version of the stories.[71]

Burton's notes to Payne's text in these booklets are the closest thing to drafts of his *Arabian Nights* that exist, given that he did little translating from the Arabic. His emendations to Payne's tale "The Merchant of Cairo and the Favorite of the Khalif" display his method of rewriting Payne's text while making minor changes. Many of the modifications are orthographical. For instance, Burton corrects Payne's transliteration of "El Mamoun El Hakim Bi Amrillah" to "Al-Maamun al-Hakim bi-Amri'allah," and when the caliph's favorite concubine asks the merchant to build a pavilion on the island called Er Rauzeh, Burton corrects it to "Al-Rauzah, the Garden-holm." Apart from such slight changes, Burton follows Payne's text very closely. When the pavilion is finished, a rendezvous between the concubine and the merchant is arranged, but when the merchant arrives at the appointed time, he finds another young man waiting as well. After the two men join the concubine and make their way to the pavilion, they all indulge in food and drink until the young man is drunk. At this point the lady carries him into a closet, and emerges minutes later with his severed head in her hand. After the merchant disposes of the young man's body parts in the river, the lady explains that he was her former neighbor, who had forcibly taken her virginity. The merchant says that after the lady expressed her gratitude to him, "I lay with her that night and there befell which befell between us till the morning." Burton, though famed for the explicit sexual content of his *Arabian Nights,* follows Payne's euphemism word for word, only changing the spelling of "befell" to the more archaic "befel." In this and other cases, Burton relied on variant spellings to give the impression of difference from Payne's version while he left the substance unchanged.[72]

For a year, the lady continues to visit the merchant in the pavilion every month, until one day she does not appear. One of the palace eunuchs—whom Burton renames "Castratos" and "neutrals"—arrives to inform the merchant that the caliph has sentenced the lady and her "six-and-twenty" slave girls to be drowned as punishment for their

THE TWO KINGS AND THE VIZIER'S DAUGHTERS.[1]

[Aforetime] I journeyed in [many] lands and climes and towns and visited the great cities and traversed the ways and [exposed myself to] dangers and hardships. Towards the last of my life, I entered a city [of the cities of China],[2] wherein was a king of the Chosroës and the Tubbas[3] and the Cæsars.[4] Now that city had been peopled with its inhabitants by means of justice and equitable dealing; but its [then] king was a tyrant, who despoiled souls and [did away] lives; there was no warming oneself at his fire,[5] for that indeed he

[1] Breslau Text, vol. xii. pp. 384-394.

[2] The kingdom of the elder brother is afterwards referred to as situate in China. See post, p. 150.

[3] *Tubba* was the dynastic title of the ancient Himyerite Kings of Yemen, even as Chosroës and Cæsar of the Kings of Persia and the Emperors of Constantinople respectively.

[4] *i.e.* a king similar in magnificence and dominion to the monarchs of the three dynasties aforesaid, whose names are in Arab literature synonyms for regal greatness.

[5] *i.e.* his rage was ungovernable, so that none dared approach him in his heat of passion.

Page from Richard Burton's copy of John Payne's *The Book of the Thousand Nights and One Night*. His extensive annotations reveal his true practice of "translating" the work.

lewdness. "She biddeth thee to look how thou mayst do with her and how thou mayst contrive to deliver her," the eunuch tells the merchant in Payne's version. Burton follows Payne's archaic pattern of dialogue, making only a slight alteration to the reported instructions: "She sayeth to thee, 'Look how thou mayst do with me and how thou mayst contrive to deliver me.'" After purchasing "good [victuals for the] morning-meal" according to Payne, or a "right good breakfast" according to Burton, the merchant shares the meal with a boatman who happens to have been hired by the caliph to drown the lady and her slave girls. With the boatman's help, the merchant saves his lady, although her twenty-six slave girls end up in a watery grave. In Payne's version, she thanks her rescuer by saying, "Thou art indeed a friend in need." The desire to distinguish his version with alliteration leads Burton to change this simple statement of gratitude to "Thou art indeed the friend ever faithful found for the shifts of Fortune." Ironically, he adds a footnote in his overdone rewriting referring back to Payne's original wording, claiming "We say more laconically 'A friend in need.'"[73]

✦ ✦ ✦

"The translator's glory is to add something to his native tongue," Burton brashly declares in the "Translator's Preface" to the *Arabian Nights.* This philosophy of translation was Burton's own explanation for the many stylistic embellishments that he claimed would capture the "picturesque turns and novel expressions of the original in all their outlandishness," and it has proven remarkably attractive in translation studies. Less well known is the continuation of Burton's sentence, in which he specifically rejects "the hideous hag-like nakedness of Torrens and the bald literalism of Lane."[74] Within the bombast of this unnecessary denunciation of Torrens's incomplete and forgotten translation lies one more ploy by the most ingenuous of the translators of the *Arabian Nights.*

Burton's need to disparage Torrens, from whose "hag-like" and "hideous" prose he was quite content to borrow sentences at a stretch, betrays the plagiarist's anxiety of influence. Perhaps Burton reserved such venom for Torrens because he concurred, consciously or not, with the judgment of contemporaries that Torrens was the most gifted author to attempt a version of the *Arabian Nights* in nineteenth-century European letters. Possibly he still resented having spent his time in British India in the 1840s living in the shadow of men like Macnaghten and Torrens. After all, their mastery of Arabic had been recognized and even lauded by colonial authorities, and Burton, for all his ability to accumulate European and South Asian languages, had failed his exam in Arabic, a detail missing from all but one of the biographies of him.[75] Whatever the psychology at play, a plagiarist's anxiety lurks in his influential statement of the creative imperative of translation. In his *Arabian Nights,* Burton consciously deploys style to claim ownership over what he steals.

Payne proved to be particularly vulnerable to this act of thievery not only because of his lack of scholarly credentials in Arabic, but also because of the mode of distribution he had chosen for his translation. While the private sale of his *Arabian Nights* through subscriptions provided protection from the Obscene Publications Act, it did not secure Payne copyright over his work. This was a situation that Burton understood very well, for he worried that his own version of the story collection would be pirated by another publisher. He writes frankly about the matter in an essay in his *Supplemental Nights:* "England and Anglo-America . . . are the only self-styled civilised countries in the world where an author's brain-work is not held to be his private property: his book is simply no book unless published and entered, after a cost of seven presentation copies at 'Stationers' Hall'—its only aegis." Burton claimed that there was a plan afoot by a "German publisher" in London, supported by an "equally industrious" Frenchman, to pirate his *Arabian Nights* and issue it in a cheaper version. His solution was to copyright as much of his edition as he could by creating a bowdlerized version, *Lady Burton's Edition of Her Husband's Arabian Nights,* published in 1886.[76] Omitting all the sexual material that Burton had claimed was essential to any understanding of the story collection, this six-volume work successfully copyrighted 3,000 of the original 3,215 pages. Burton's wife, Isabel, was a conscious participant in this ruse: "I did not write nor translate it," she acknowledged later, "it is *Richard Burton's* 'Arabian Nights' with a coarse word or two cut out here and there . . . and my name was only put upon it to copyright and protect my husband's from piracy."

This "Household Edition" of Burton's was a sales disaster, but it served the purpose for which it was intended.[77]

The evidence that Burton plagiarized Torrens and Payne, and that Payne had rewritten other translations of the *Arabian Nights* before him, has significant implications for Burton's legacy within translation studies. His *Arabian Nights* is not really the epitome of the foreignizing and subversive translation theorized by Venuti and others, and not only because it is not in fact a translation. Burton does test, and often exceed, the limits of English in his famously "unreadable" version of the work, crammed as it is with archaisms, neologisms, and foreignisms. But the foreignizing feel of Burton's version was not intended in the sense imagined by modern scholars of translation. His stylistic excesses were largely the product of his haste and his need to differentiate his version from those of Torrens and Payne. In this respect, he adopted the same strategy as Payne, who had used the ornate style of the Pre-Raphaelites to mask the fact that he was collating other translations. In confronting the same dilemma, Burton would take this style to even greater extremes to hide his greater distance from the original Arabic.[78]

Payne would only respond to speculation that Burton had plagiarized from his version of the *Arabian Nights* in 1889 in the introduction to his edition of Omar Khayyam's *Rubaiyat.* He did so not to level charges against the famous Orientalist, but to challenge the notion that was "becoming daily more prevalent that [Burton's] translation of the Arabian Nights must of necessity be more accurate" than Payne's own, especially "considering Sir Richard Burton's long practice in *colloquial* Arabic." In refuting this claim, Payne argues for the value of a translation based on literary rather than ethnographic skills. He states that it is a common error that "the *colloquial* knowledge of a language is sufficient, without other literary equipment, to enable a possessor to deal with difficult literary enterprises of translation." As proof Payne points to the translation of the *Arabian Nights* by Lane, which he claims is "swarming with errors and mistakes of all kinds" because Lane undertook it "when he had little or no *literary* knowledge of the Arabic language." Similarly, Payne contends, "Capt. Burton's knowledge of literary Arabic . . . was, (as he himself, like the high-minded and honourable man he was, freely admitted on becoming acquainted with my work,) much inferior to my own," and therefore his translation is "*far less accurate* than mine."[79]

Having never journeyed farther south than France, Payne knew he could not compete with Lane's or Burton's reputations as travellers of the East with firsthand knowledge of Arabic. He could, however, try to shift the field of competition to aesthetic grounds. Given the status of the *Thousand and One Nights* as a popular story collection rather than a work of high literature, Payne's defense of his own achievement as founded on a greater sensitivity to the literary qualities of the stories betrays the weakness of his understanding of their place in the Arab world, but it did allow him to finally address the connection between his version of the stories and Burton's. Careful to express no resentment toward his friend, Payne presents himself as an essential contributor to Burton's translation. Burton had the "immense advantage," Payne writes, "of the use of my previously-issued translation of the whole of the *Thousand and One Nights*, which he followed, in the main, closely and from which he again and again borrowed whole pages in difficult passages, such as are of frequent occurrence in the work."[80] Payne cleverly characterizes Burton's plagiarism, which some might see as an act of betrayal, as a form of flattery through imitation. In this instance, the hidden collaborator announces himself, but cleverly screens his own practice of translation behind the elaborate screen of his own "age of aesthetics."

7

THE FALSE CALIPH

In 1853 a man bearing the name of Mirza Abdullah disembarked at the port of Alexandria with the aim of making the pilgrimage to Mecca. He would describe the brilliance of the city that day as a "matter of fable." The stucco on the city's walls was so exquisitely tempered and polished that the inhabitants of Alexandria had to wear masks to protect themselves from the blinding light. The man who arrived on this day would become a matter of fable himself. Mirza Abdullah was not in fact his name, nor was he a Muslim. The assumption of this disguise was simply part of Richard Burton's plan to complete the pilgrimage of the hajj while avoiding the scorn shown to the convert—the *Burma*, in the pejorative term used by Turks, "one who has twisted," "one who has turned." The insult would have perhaps struck too close to the bone. Burton was a man of twists and turns who had delighted in adopting foreign disguises since his itinerant childhood as the son of an impoverished military officer in Italy and France. Burton claimed that he had assumed the identity of a Persian merchant named Mirza Abdullah when, as a British soldier in India in the 1840s, Charles Napier had asked him to explore the brothels of Karachi. Making his way through the crowds of Alexandria in 1853, Burton recreated this "old character

The Pilgrim, an illustration from Richard Burton's *Personal Narrative of a Pilgrimage to El-Medinah and Meccah* featuring Burton in disguise. Burton prided himself on the detailed cultural knowledge required to bring "Sheikh Abdullah"—an Afghani born and raised in India—to life.

of a Persian wanderer." He claimed that the disguise was so successful that the Egyptian servants saw him simply as an *Ajami*, a Persian rather than an Arab Muslim; and at least one Armenian dragoman passing on the street in Alexandria recognized the "devilish" Persian disguise.[1]

Before setting out for the holy cities of Islam, "Mirza Abdullah" took some time in Cairo to settle into his new role. The first volume of Burton's account of his pilgrimage, *A Personal Narrative of a Pilgrimage to El-Medinah and Meccah,* is devoted to this time in Egypt, during which the author seems to be self-consciously walking in the footsteps of Edward Lane. Lane's ethnography, *Modern Egyptians* (1836), with its sensationalist portraits of the Egyptian magician Sheikh Abd al-Qadir and the Sufi dervish Sheikh Ahmad, had defined the city for a generation of English readers. The image of Lane clothed in Ottoman garb and his story of clairvoyance with a black lamp more fabulous than Aladdin's had already passed into Victorian lore of the Middle East. Fixating on this mythology, Burton seized on the topic of clairvoyance aided by a mirror of ink in his early travelogues of Sindh, seeking to ground Lane's famous account of the Maghrebi magician in a broader understanding of cultural exchange between South Asia and the world. He argued that the presence in India "of the Egyptian practice of seeing figures shifting over the ink poured into a boy's hand" must point to a pre-Islamic, and likely Indian, genesis for this mode of divination.[2] Writing in 1851, Burton attributed these insights to credible "informants," but as he cultivated his own self-image as a cosmopolitan traveller and translator, Burton seems to have made the decision to erase the mediators in this process of knowledge production. In manuscript revisions of his travelogue of Sindh, he struck out the reference to informants and insisted that he himself had witnessed the operation of the mirror of ink.[3] Arriving in Alexandria in 1853, he would go even further in fashioning himself as cultural informant.

In his time in Egypt, Burton was trying not just to outdo Lane, but to take on the roles of the informants who had made possible Lane's ethnography of Cairo and his commentary on the *Arabian Nights.* In Alexandria, Mirza Abdullah set out to refashion himself as dervish and magician—as both Sheikh Ahmad and al-Qadir. Under the sun's glare, he emerged brightly decked out in the dervish's costume of gown, short shirt, and large blue pantaloons, and he sought to establish his credentials as a magician through acts of divination. Burton was convinced no character in the Muslim world was so fitting for disguise as that of the dervish, for "no one asks him—the chartered vagabond—Why he comes here? Or Wherefore he goes there?" The consummate outsider, Burton preferred to don disguises that captured an element of foreignness that was not easy to place, rather than trying to fit into a known social category, as Lane had done in styling himself as a member of the Ottoman elite. Burton noted the distinct advantages of the dervish disguise, which accommodated any social background (a disgraced nobleman or an idle peasant) and permitted those of a "choleric temperament," like himself, "to ignore ceremony and politeness." Burton delighted in the less savory elements of the dervish's reputation, for "the Darwaysh's ragged coat not unfrequently covers the cut-throat." This character also allowed Burton to manifest all the qualities of Lane and his informants: "a little knowledge of medicine, a 'moderate skill in magic and a reputation for caring for nothing but study and books.' "[4]

Through the character of Mirza Abdullah, Burton was able to reenact the most famous episode in Lane's ethnography by performing acts of clairvoyance with the aid of a magic mirror. After these performances, Burton boasted "even respectable natives . . . opined that the stranger was a holy man, gifted with supernatural powers, and knowing everything."[5] In case readers missed the slight to Lane, Burton added a long note in the account of his pilgrimage to Mecca that belittled Lane's knowledge of the black lamp and asserted the greater comprehensiveness of his own cross-cultural frames of reference. With little grace, Burton disparaged the expertise of the famous ethnographer by observing that "there is scarcely a man in Cairo who does not know something about it [divination with the mirror of ink]." Lane's "fair and dispassionate recital of certain magical, mystical, or mesmeric phenomena" would have caused less of a sensation "throughout the civilized world" if London, Paris, and New York had been more attentive to their own "dozens studying the science." Drawing on the wider knowledge that Burton's life as a traveller provided, he explained common variations of the magical practice for his English readers. The Greeks poured oil rather than ink in the palm of the boy's hand, while in Persia ink was rubbed into the thumbnail of the seer. Burton also drew attention to the agency of Lane's close associate Osman Effendi in these performances by disingenuously defending him against accusations of fraud. In these passages, he reminded readers of his predecessor's need to rely on others for his famed cultural immersion and distinguished himself by assuming Osman's role of convert and pilgrim. What Lane accomplished with the help of others, Burton would do by himself.[6]

Yet the stranger had miscalculated. Mirza Abdullah found himself unwelcome in Cairo due to the prejudice against Persians, who were thought to be "clever and debauched." Throughout his journey to Mecca and Medina, Burton claimed that he was not able to avoid "the uncomfortable consequences of . . . having appeared in Egypt as a Persian." "Although I found out the mistake, and worked hard to correct it," he lamented, "the bad name stuck to me; bazaar reports fly quicker and hit harder than newspaper paragraphs." To salvage his trip, Burton decided to dispense with one identity and reemerge as a Pathan—an Afghani born and raised in India. Mirza Abdullah thus became Sheikh Abdullah. In the *Personal Narrative,* Burton elaborated on the fine adjustments necessary to inhabit this new identity. Even the simple act of drinking water as a Muslim raised in India rather than Persia required "no fewer than five novelties." Now he would have to clutch the tumbler "as though it were the throat of a foe," proclaim the mercy and compassion of God, swallow rather than sip the water, give praise to God before setting down the cup, and wish his drinking companion blessings and health. In this discussion of the refinements necessary to pass as a Muslim pilgrim on the road to Mecca, Burton takes on the narrative voice of the cultural informant himself—"the silent friend [who sought] to aid with advice future adventurers."[7]

This tour de force—taking on not one but two distinct Muslim personae in quick succession—would make Burton famous. Few readers would remember that the account of the pilgrimage in the next two volumes was filled with episodes that fluctuated between triumph and self-sabotage, between enthusiasm and ennui. Shortly after his chameleonlike feat of self-invention in Alexandria, Burton ruined the goodwill he had accrued as Sheikh Abdullah in a single night of boozing and brawling with an Armenian friend, prompting him to rush his departure from the city. As he continued his journey, Burton would find it impossible to overcome his sense of himself as an outsider. He experiences a brief sense of communion at the first sighting of Medina: "It was impossible not to enter into the spirit of my companions." When the party remounted, however, he found that "the traveler returned strong upon me." Later, surrounded by the intense emotion of pilgrims circling the Kaaba in Mecca, Burton's consciousness of having a different agenda returns in force: "Theirs was the high feeling of religious enthusiasm, mine was the ecstasy of gratified pride." The *Personal Narrative,* with its many borrowings from the account of Swiss traveller Jean Louis Burckhardt's pilgrimage of 1814, sometimes reads as just one more failed disguise in the life of the famous traveller.[8]

Despite the many instances in which the mask of Sheikh Abdullah slipped, Burton's self-portrait as a pilgrim, with his long beard and newly shorn hair, captured the imagination of his contemporaries. The quick succession of disguises adopted at the outset of his journey seemed to symbolize the extraordinary capacity for feats of cultural immersion that he demonstrated in his travels to the seminary of Brigham Young in Salt Lake City, the imperial court of Dom Pedro II in Rio de Janeiro, and the forbidding landscapes of Central Africa. Throughout these travels, Burton proved to have been uniquely capable of shedding the assumptions and beliefs associated with the Englishman abroad. He returned from his travels defending the practice of polygamy among the Mormons and the tolerance of homosexuality among the Arabs, but also, more problematically, supporting the practice of slavery in Brazil and Central Africa.[9] When he sat down to translate the *Arabian Nights,* Burton brought this brand of cosmopolitanism to the project. He would boast that only he, from his unique position as the eternal exile, could truly relinquish the nineteenth-century prejudices of his contemporaries and therefore offer the dissonant world of the *Arabian Nights* to an English readership.

✦ ✦ ✦

Like Henry Torrens, Burton's path to the *Arabian Nights* began in colonial India, which provided an intensive education in both foreign languages and the management of cultural difference. It was the catastrophe of William Hay Macnaghten's Afghan campaign of 1839–1842 that prompted him to seek a military commission in the East India Company after being expelled from Oxford's Trinity College. Inspired by romantic ambitions to participate in a British campaign to retake Kabul from Akbar Khan, Burton prevailed on his father to help him secure this post. He claimed to be haunted by reports of the return of one solitary survivor from the retreat from Kabul—out of the original force of 13,000—but may also have shared the belief of other new recruits that the decimation of the British colonial force offered an excellent chance for rapid advancement in India. En route to Bombay in 1842, Burton readily admitted to sharing the general disappointment when a government pilot boarded and informed the excited young men bound for military service that the avenging army had already returned through the Khyber Pass. "At his answer all hopes fell to zero," Burton recalled with irony. "There was no chance of becoming Commanders-in-Chief within the year." The cadets promptly voiced their frustration in terms "unfit for ears polite."[10]

Burton claimed that on this voyage to Bombay, he had already hit on another scheme for advancement: language acquisition. By studying Urdu, and making good use of the native servants on board, he would be able to land in India with "*éclat*" and "to astonish the throng of palanquin bearers that jostled, pushed and pulled at me at the pier, with the vivacity and nervousness of my phraseology."[11] Here and elsewhere in his autobiographical reflections, Burton suggests that his superior curiosity about people from different cultures yielded quick dividends. Biographers have generally indulged this line of interpretation, seeing in Burton's attraction to language study a desire to be close to the people amongst whom he travelled. They are quick to imbue Burton's relationships with his various language teachers with a spirit of friendship, and even romance. However, Burton's report of "making the three native servants who were on board, talk with me" has also invited a dissenting interpretation from Simon Digby, who suggests that it represents the superior and "bullying manner that Burton would adopt throughout his Indian years." Digby is more inclined to believe that Burton fashioned a grand narrative of arrival in Bombay out of little more than the customary curse words.[12]

Richard Burton claims that he was haunted by the story of William Brydon, who arrived at Jalalabad as the sole survivor of the British contingent of 13,000 that was forced to evacuate Afghanistan in 1842. Burton hoped to arrive in time to join the British forces sent to take back Kabul from Akbar Khan. This painting by Elizabeth Butler depicts Brydon's arrival. *The Remnants of an Army,* oil on canvas, 1879.

In India, Burton would take advantage of the apparatus of language learning that had been the chief strength of the "Orientalist" camp. He did not have access to the program in classical and vernacular languages that had been offered at Calcutta's Fort William to Torrens, but he did regard the linguistic achievements of this institution as offering a model for his own advancement in the service of empire. For Burton, the career of Macnaghten was a particularly powerful spur to his own ambitions. He envied Macnaghten's rapid advance through the Indian civil service on the basis of his superior language skills, but he also vilified him for his role in the British debacle in Afghanistan. Macnaghten, Burton claimed, was "a mere Indian civilian," and "had fallen into the dodging ways of the natives." Attracted to Macnaghten's example but also determined to distinguish himself from it, Burton would strike out to master the languages of the subcontinent while cultivating his own sense of superiority over the "cunning" of the natives.[13]

Before departing for India in 1842, Burton had been briefly introduced to Hindustani by Duncan Forbes, author of the *Hindustani-English Dictionary,* but once in India, he learned the local languages from a series of munshis, employed by the British administration as teachers and scribes.[14] Paramount among them was Dosabhai Sohrabj, well known to British military officers stationed in Bombay. Burton's sketch of Sohrabj was included in the biography of him edited and finished by Isabel Burton after his death:

> With him, as with all other Parsees, Gujarati was the mother tongue, but he also taught Hindostani and Persian, the latter with the usual vile Indian article. He had a great reputation as a teacher, and he managed to ruin it by publishing a book of dialogues in English and these three languages, wherein he showed his perfect unfitness. He was *very* good, however, when he had no pretensions, and in his hand I soon got through the Akhlak-i-Hindi ["Indian Ethics"] and the Tota-Kahani ["Tales of a Parrot"]. I remained friends with the old man to the end of his days, and the master always used to quote his pupil, as a man who could learn a language running.[15]

Sohrabj and other munshis introduced Burton to vernacular tales that, like the *Thousand and One Nights,* were connected to the popular storytelling traditions of the wider Islamic world. Like Lane in Cairo, Burton wrote of his language teacher with both warmth and condescension, taking pleasure in exposing his "unfitness" and implying a reversal in the role of master and pupil.

Munshis were integral to the remarkable feats of language acquisition and cultural immersion by which Burton built his reputation during his time with the East India Company. His ability to switch between languages, dialects, and identities, as demonstrated on his arrival in Alexandria in 1853, became the stuff of legend. However, like other aspects of Burton's personality, his astounding ability to achieve fluency in foreign languages has been the subject of some mythmaking. According to his widow Isabel's biography of him, Burton passed official examinations in Arabic, Hindustani, Sindhi, Persian, Turkish,

This young officer being tutored by a munshi bears a striking resemblance to Richard Burton. Given Burton's fame in the wake of his 1853 pilgrimage to Mecca and the publication of his South Asian travelogues, the resemblance may not be accidental. From George Atkinson's *"Curry & Rice" on Forty Plates; or, The Ingredients of Social Life at "Our Station" in India.*

Armenian, and four other South Asian languages in the course of his seven years in India. Documentation is available for only six of these—Marathi, Sindhi, Gujarati, Persian, Hindustani, and Punjabi—and the chronology of Burton's munshis does not support the most boastful of his claims.[16]

Burton maintained that he had mastered Persian in the two months at the end of 1844, in addition to learning some Arabic and Punjabi, and he would turn to Sindhi the following year. In his "Terminal Essay" to the *Arabian Nights,* he claims that in 1845 he was the only one among Napier's officers who could converse in Sindhi. Yet another autobiographical fragment states that Burton was studying those same four languages in 1847 and 1848. An analysis of the various munshis who were teaching Burton during this time lends the later date more credibility. After his Persian munshi Mohammad Hosayn returned to Shiraz in 1846, Burton engaged a young Abyssinian named Hajji Jawhar to teach him Arabic. In Sindh Burton would engage Munshi Nanda to teach him Sindhi, and Shaykh Hashim to continue his study of Arabic and instruct him in Quranic recitation. Burton improbably claims that once he finished a language examination he had no further need for instruction, and would immediately hire a new munshi to teach him a new language, but Walter Abraham, a fellow officer who knew Burton in Sindh in 1847, recalled Burton's study habits differently. According to him, Burton employed a team of munshis "who relieved one another every two hours, from ten to four."[17]

During his time in India, Burton began to cultivate the native identities for which he became known with the aid of munshis and other native informants. He claimed that while he was posted to Gujarat, he learned Sanskrit along with Gujarati and Marathi under the tutelage of a munshi from a prominent subcaste in Gujarat, the Nāgār Brāhmins. His progress was so phenomenal, he bragged, that in a short time his Hindu teacher "officially allowed" him to wear the Brahminical thread, the *Janeo,* with the right and obligation to recite the secret mantras of the Brāhmins.[18] There is no hard evidence that Burton learned Sanskrit, but at least one biographer takes him at his word and imagines what the ceremony of initiation into these sacred rituals would have entailed.[19] This image of Burton as capable of exceptional acts of cultural assimilation was an important element of his self-fashioning in India and might be seen as a deliberate attempt to avoid acknowledging his dependence on local teachers. Doubting the trustworthiness of such local intermediaries, Burton would attempt to style himself as an informant.[20]

Despite the close association between Burton and the *Arabian Nights,* he does not appear to have received credit for proficiency in Arabic from the colonial authorities. The exam was arranged while Burton was returning from his pilgrimage to Mecca and Medina, and he sat it in Aden in 1854. Burton would dispute the fairness of the result, and indeed Rev. George Percy Badger, who subsequently reviewed the papers, thought that the examiners had been too harsh in their judgment. There is no doubt that the pattern of language study that Burton practiced in

India was effective. Burton's competence in languages, from Persian to Sindhi, is clear from the fact that he passed several of his exams in first place. Yet he was not a self-sufficient linguistic genius able to absorb native speech patterns with miraculous ease. He relied on a steady diet of round-the-clock tutoring by local language teachers who took the time to explain the many particularities of the texts he was studying.[21] While Lane spent a lifetime pursuing his knowledge of Arabic and seeking to submerge himself in one cultural identity, Burton pursued a basic facility in a series of languages on the understanding that he would receive concrete benefits from being accredited as an interpreter of those languages.[22]

Burton's tendency to spend long hours with his local teachers earned him criticism from his colleagues and the "ominous soubriquet" of "The White Nigger."[23] While in some cases the munshi was merely a stepping-stone to linguistic proficiency, Burton did develop some more sustained relationships. Mirzā Mohammed Hosayn Shirazi, whom Burton engaged between 1844 and 1846, both deepened his understanding of Persian language and literature and became a good friend.[24] Burton's notebooks reflect his preference for Persian among the Oriental tongues and attest to his ambition to translate the work of canonical Persian poets into English. When Burton began his translations of the Portuguese Renaissance poet Luís de Camões, he would look for traces of influence from Persian poetry, and the terminal essay to his version of the *Arabian Nights* (1885) would include a declaration of his admiration for the Persian people. "The gifted Iranian race," Burton opined, "physically the noblest and the most beautiful of all known to me, has exercised upon the world-history an amount of influence which has not yet been fully recognized."[25] When Burton began to adopt Oriental disguises, he would often fashion himself as Persian or half-Persian, as he did on his arrival in Alexandria.

Some biographers of Burton have taken up suggestions made by the famous traveller that his extraordinary acquisition of languages in the subcontinent was aided by a succession of local mistresses who doubled as "walking dictionaries." Biographers extrapolate from Burton's observation that all the "boys" in India entered into such morganatic marriages to argue that he must have had one or more of these local helpmates.

She was "all but indispensable to the student," Burton wrote. "She teaches him not only Hindostani grammar, but the syntaxes of native Life. She keeps house for him, never allowing him to save money, or, if possible, to waste it. She keeps the servants in order. She has an infallible recipe to prevent maternity, especially if her tenure depends on such compact."[26] Scholars find further evidence in a passage in Burton's 1865 poem *Stone Talk,* in which the narrator, Frank Baker, yearns nostalgically for a South Asian lover with jet-black eyes and hair, and a form like "the tam'risk's waving shoot." This poem, however, is satirical, and Burton's reference to English officers speaking the Urdu they have learned from their mistresses is disparaging. Burton's sense of superiority is evident when he claims that an officer in his regiment spoke of himself as a woman, that is, in the feminine form, because "he had learnt all his Hindostani from his harem."[27]

Burton invited speculation regarding his romantic misadventures in South Asia by inserting stories of romance into his travelogues of Sindh and Goa. Yet these episodes are more akin to the incredible tales embedded in the travelogues of Hanna Diyab and Paul Lucas than a credible part of Burton's own experience in India. In one he engages in a flirtation with a Persian beauty visiting Karachi through letters delivered by her young servant, only to have her party suddenly decamp without notice.[28] It seems to belong with the other clichés of romance in these early travelogues, which include the British officer who abandons his career to live with a nautch girl and the Maratha trooper who falls desperately in love with a Brahman widow and tries to rescue her from the funeral pyre of her husband, only to lose her to an archer's arrow. In another story, told by a Goan servant named Salvador, a British officer attempts to kidnap a pretty young Latin teacher from a convent in Goa—only to find he has entered the wrong room and seized the wrong woman. Some commentators have interpreted this as representing Burton's own experience: the Goan servant has the same name as Burton's servant in India, and the officer could be seen as an avatar of the author. The story, however, is simply a variation on a pattern that can be traced back to the tales of Giovanni Boccaccio and other sources. There is also a strong similarity between Burton's inserted tales and the fantasies peddled by the *Oriental Annual,* which

In his travelogues, Burton dropped tantalizing hints about encounters with beautiful women in India, a mythology embraced by his biographers. But some of these escapades were borrowed from Giovanni Boccaccio and the *Oriental Annual,* which included this 1834 portrait of the "Queen of Candy."

suggests that these stories were fabrications for the purposes of entertaining the reader and cultivating a romantic mystique for its author. Despite the hints of his widow, Isabel, and his niece Georgiana Stisted that he had had a relationship with a Persian princess during his South Asian years, Burton had a clear preference for the company of his munshis.[29]

Burton was anxious to find ways of mixing with the people of Sindh, and experimented with various disguises to overcome the obstacles to gaining greater intimacy with locals. "The European official in India," he lamented, "seldom, if ever sees anything in its real light, so dense is the veil which the fearfulness, the duplicity, the prejudice and the superstitions of the natives hang before his eyes." If Burton wanted to gain the kind of insights into Sindhi life that would set him apart from his fellow officers, he would have to craft a local identity. It was in this context that Mirza Abdullah was born—the travelling merchant who combined both Persian and Arab qualities.[30] The hybrid nature of Burton's preferred disguise was not coincidental. On a practical basis, this mixture served to explain the lingering strangeness of Burton, who still spoke both Persian and Arabic with an odd accent. In keeping with his own self-perception, Burton gravitated to a disguise that represented his own outsider status.[31]

Just as Burton began to forge his most successful disguises from the cultural resources available in Sindh, he also completed his first experiments in translation from non-European languages in this colonial context. A manuscript notebook bearing the date 1847 contains *Pilpay's Fables*, Burton's first effort to prepare a translation from Hindustani for publication. This work is a translation of *Akhlak-i-Hindi*—a version of the Sanskrit fables known as *Panchatantra*—complete with preface and annotations. A Hindustani version of this story collection had been produced in 1803 by the College of Fort William and was used for language examinations of British officers, and Burton had studied it with his first munshi, Sahrabj. The fact that Burton turned to a teaching text that had already been glossed for him by his munshi reveals the roots of his method of translation in conventions of Indian language study.[32] For Burton, the practice of translation was part of the politics of knowing and governing other cultures.

The debate between Orientalists and Anglicists regarding the role of native languages in educational policy had been resolved in favor of the Anglicists in Bengal in 1835, but in the Bombay presidency where Burton was stationed, these issues continued to be debated. Like Orientalists such as Torrens, Burton advocated the use of local languages in primary education, and pushed for instruction in the Sindhi language using the Perso-Arabic script of the Muslim population.[33] Burton's understanding of language as a critical tool of colonial power shaped his translation of *Pilpay's Fables,* which he presented as a way of promoting the kind of knowledge necessary for imperial rule. Speaking to the British rulers of this territory, Burton invokes the "duty laid on us as a nation, accurately to know the condition of so many of our fellow subjects in the East." So far, Burton contends, the actions of the servants of the East India Company had tended to "lower us" in the opinion of the surrounding natives, and it was therefore necessary to remedy "European ignorance of, and contempt for" local manners. Burton offers his commentary on this translation of *Pilpay's Fables* as a way of promoting understanding of local customs to avoid giving offense or attracting ridicule "by misplaced attention and impoliteness." In an early example of a pattern that appears again and again in his *Arabian Nights,* Burton uses his commentary to distinguish his own insights from the erroneous assumptions that pass for knowledge in Europe—the "impious bigotry" and invented "calumnies" that result from ignorance of the Arabic language.[34]

Burton's notes for *Pilpay's Fables* reveal the way in which his Parsi munshi in Bombay had initiated him into the intricacies of the Hindustani language. Contemplating the word *Sawab*—often translated in English as "a spiritual reward for a pious act and life"—Burton stresses the inherent resistance of Arabic to translation: "It is the remark of my old teacher, Moonshee Dossabhai that the English language has no word which singly expresses the meaning of the Arabic '*Sawab.*'"[35] Burton thus introduces what would become a familiar form of philological commentary in his notes to the *Arabian Nights*—the idea that the English version of a Hindustani or Arabic word cannot do justice to its original resonance within a distinctive culture. "Vain are regrets, whate'er the pen of destiny / Assigns to mortals, that, and only that can be," Burton translates. But he cannot simply translate *Kaza* as destiny without stopping to explain that his readers should not "suppose that Islam is a religion of predestination."[36] A version of this observation made it into his *Arabian Nights,* and readers of his commentary to the tales will come across nods to the limits of translation so often that they might assume it to be a convention of European Orientalism. In fact it is a conviction that Burton shared with his first munshis in Hindustani, Persian, and Arabic.

Burton's first forays into translation in India reveal the approach to translation that he would pursue through much of his life. His translation of *Vikram and the Vampire; or, Tales of Hindu Devilry* (1870) is purportedly based on a Hindustani text from the College of Fort William. However, according to one estimate, less than 5 percent of Burton's version actually constitutes translation. Burton directed his energy primarily to the production of an elaborate commentary that he inserted into the text to provide explanations of local customs and settings. He may well have used his student notebooks with the comments of his munshi to create this apparatus, but there are also traces of articles from the *Journal of the Asiatic Society of Bengal* and William Ward's *View of the Hindoos.* Digby traces elements of the translated text to an anonymous English translation published in India, which Burton characteristically considered fair game to plagiarize. Burton attempted to deflect attention from his method by claiming that his version was not intended to be a literal translation: "It is not pretended that the words of these Hindu tales are preserved to the letter. . . . I have ventured to remedy the conciseness of their language and to clothe the skeleton with flesh and blood."[37]

Burton's method and metaphor here anticipate a passage in the preface to his *Arabian Nights* in which he complains of the naked quality of Torrens's translation of the story collection—another "Indian" text that he felt entitled to borrow and flesh out through added commentary.[38] Certainly, these early experiments in translation reveal patterns that would reoccur as Burton prepared his *Arabian Nights* in 1885. Just as he relied on his munshis in India to do the essential work of translating and interpreting the text, Burton was content in later years to delegate these basic tasks to an uncredited collaborator while he provided the poetic flourishes and the commentary. Appropriating the linguistic labor of others was only the first step toward producing a translation whose real purpose lay in the ethnographic insights of its attached commentary and the critical stance of their author.

The intensive program of translation and publication pursued by colonial officials in India provided a treasure trove of texts for aspiring authors like Burton to draw on. Within this expanding library of Oriental literature, the *Thousand and One Nights* would take its place as a tool of colonial knowledge production. An Arabic version of the story collection containing 200 nights (Calcutta I) was edited and printed by munshis for use at Fort William as a teaching text, and references can also be found to an Urdu translation that was used on language exams. Burton was no doubt familiar with the *Thousand and One Nights* before he arrived in India, but his immersion in the array of vernacular texts available in Bombay gave him a deeper sense of the syncretic qualities of the story collection. When he translated *Pilpay's Fables* in 1847, he was attentive to the possible connections between these two cycles of tales, and he adds a note comparing one story from the Indian collection to the tale of the bath keeper and his wife in the *Thousand and One Nights* story cycle "The Craft and Malice of Women."[39]

When he launched his "translation" of the *Arabian Nights* in Trieste in the 1880s, Burton turned to versions of the Arabic story collection circulating in India to solve the problem of how he could "foreignize" the orphan tales. Burton seems to have completely discounted any authentic influences from Diyab in these stories, and was determined to make them less European. Burton had suggested that he would integrate the orphan tales into his story collection by translating them first into Arabic and then back into English, but another solution presented itself when James Fuller Blumhardt, a teacher of Indian languages, showed him two versions of these tales in Hindustani and agreed to collate and translate them into English, annotating as necessary.[40] Archival evidence also reveals that Burton heavily annotated a copy of the tale "The Adventures of the Caliph Harun al-Rashid," which he had found in a version of Jonathan Scott's edition of the *Arabian Nights' Entertainments* published in Lucknow.[41] This was another of Diyab's tales, and this annotated copy seems to indicate that Burton simply avoided all the steps that he proclaimed were necessary to produce a suitably Oriental *Arabian Nights,* instead rewriting an existing English version. In this way the orphan tales were reshaped in unexpected ways within the cycles of translation and publication that characterized Britain's Indian empire.

While academic studies of Burton present him as the ultimate cosmopolitan determined to "go native" in different cultural contexts, his writings from India reveal a distinct anxiety about this prospect and a continued commitment to the duty to rule. In some instances, he clearly portrayed linguistic fluency as a tool of power. In his travelogue of the Sindh, he argued that familiarity with "the literary effusions of a semi-barbarous race" were not a means of "amusement or improvement" but rather "valuable weapons in our hands."[42] However, the fate of Britain's Afghan venture was presented as clear evidence of the failure of efforts to ground imperial rule on intensive knowledge of native languages and cultures: "The Macnaghtens, the Burneses, and generally those who devoted their time and energies, and who prided themselves most on their conversancy with native dialects and native character, are precisely the persons who have been the most egregiously, the most fatally, outwitted and deceived by the natives."[43] Burton thus presented the Orientalist's primary tool—fluency in native languages—as a sign of his vulnerability to the manipulations of the local population. In accordance with this perspective, Burton asserts that Macnaghten "distinctly deserved his death."[44]

While critical of Orientalists who had assimilated too fully to the cultures they ruled, Burton was also adamantly opposed to the wave of initiatives to civilize and anglicize these Indian subjects. He criticized the efforts of colonial officials who insisted that their local subjects assimilate to English manners, laws, beliefs, and dress. From his earliest publications on Sindh, Burton defined his perspective against that of the stereotypical embodiment of the English nation, John Bull, to whom he often sarcastically addressed his ethnographic observations. To those who would anchor English identity in romantic evocations of rural belonging, Burton retorted, "I regret to say, that the Scindians . . . having no word to explain your 'home,' attach none of those pretty ideas to the place in question."[45] In India Burton would define his own distinctive perspective in opposition to that of the Orientalist and the Anglicist—fashioning himself a "semi-Oriental" who was "neither European nor oriental but an artful though mongrel mixture of the two."[46]

In these years, Burton established the image that he would cultivate his entire life—the solitary traveller who could immerse himself in the life of the natives but who possessed the broader perspective necessary for true understanding. For Burton only the traveller, or the cosmopolitan imperialist, at one remove from either European or native perspectives, could ascertain the right balance between the accommodation of local mores and the assertion of colonial power. Burton believed that General Napier, the conqueror and governor of Sindh, was mistaken in his quest to rid the territory of traditional practices such as sati, but he was also remiss in not applying his knowledge of local customs to create new strategies of governance. For instance, Burton suggested that the English colonial administrator could keep his Muslim subjects in line if he was willing to threaten them with cremation, an unthinkable punishment that would have precluded an afterlife, according to Muslim belief. Burton believed that other servants of the British Empire were either too English or not English enough to effectively govern this Indian territory, too native or not native enough.

✦ ✦ ✦

In an overlooked draft of his preface to the *Arabian Nights,* likely written in 1884 or early 1885, Burton retrospectively weaves his work on the story collection into the narrative of his famous pilgrimage to Mecca. Writing in pencil over the preface in his copy of Lane's *Arabian Nights,* Burton claims that it is impossible to open the pages of the collection without reviving "a host of reminiscences which are not the common property of travellers": "I found myself even more under the diaphanous Arabian sky, in air pure as aether, into a breeze that [whispering the pulse true {thus}] & who raises the spirits of man like a sparkling wine. I saw the evening star hanging like a diamond from the front of the Western sky; the low black tents dotting the boundless waste of golden [yellow] clay; and the campfire dotting the 'village center' like a glow worm."[47] Burton scribbled the word "METEMPSYCHOSIS" in large capitals over Lane's preface as a way of explaining the extraordinary sense of connection he felt with the tales of the *Arabian Nights*. There was such a "perfect harmony" to his time in the desert that he sometimes felt as if he was reliving the experiences of a past life. In the "Terminal Essay" to his version of the tales, Burton would return to this dream. While others might desire "to have wealth, to have knowledge, to have a name," Burton claimed that he yearned for the life of an Arab, where the only goal "was to be—to be free, to be brave, to be wise."[48]

The origins of Burton's *Arabian Nights* were considerably more complex than this example of preternatural connection might suggest. In producing his version of the famous story collection, Burton was not channelling the spirit of the desert, but rather borrowing and combining the translations offered by very different authors. Embedded in Burton's version are traces of the story collection that Lane positioned within the distinct belief system of Egyptian Cairo, the literal translation produced by Torrens in colonial India, and the romantic tales woven by the Pre-Raphaelite poet John Payne. As in his earlier relationships with his munshi teachers in India, Burton exhibited no qualms about rewriting the raw material that these authors of the *Arabian Nights* provided him—using this opportunity to place himself in the position of the cosmopolitan informant by erasing the narrower vision of his predecessors.

Burton's biggest challenge in establishing his own reputation as a translator of the *Arabian Nights* was Lane. When Burton turned to the story collection in the mid-1880s, Lane was receiving renewed attention as a guide to understanding an Egyptian territory now occupied by British forces. Lane's nephews would ensure that his *Arabian Nights* was reissued in 1883 and dedicated to the memory of E. H. Palmer, the eminent scholar of Arabic who had been killed while on a mission for the British army among the Bedouin of the Arabian Peninsula. In a new preface that effaced Lane's own effort to highlight the connections between contemporary Egypt and the ancient traditions of Christians and Jews, Stanley Lane-Poole emphasized the political usefulness of Lane's ethnographic notes on the foreign manners and customs of Cairo for Britain's new policy of rule in Egypt.[49]

When Burton cited the journey of the hajj as the basis for his translation of the *Arabian Nights,* he attempted to supplant Lane as the recognized authority on the Arabic culture of the story collection. His claim in the preface to his edition that he was somehow empathetically linked to the culture of the Bedouin through metempsychosis represented an intensified version of the imaginative affinity expressed by both Torrens and Payne.[50] However, Burton was never content with just claiming his deep investment in Arab lifeways, or his sympathetic link to some kind of Arab essence. Instead Burton presented himself to readers in the guise of Mirza Abdullah, someone who moved fluidly within the world of the Orient. If Lane had staked his credentials to translate the stories on his knowledge of Muslim Cairo, Burton's edition of the tales would be nurtured by a traveller's knowledge of innumerable lands and cultures.

Even during his later years as a British diplomat (1861–1890), Burton refused to associate himself with any conventional notion of English identity or any "civilizing" mission pursued by the agents of empire. In West Africa, he strongly denounced the work of missionaries who broke up polygamous marriages and dressed up locals in travesties of English style. He disapproved of the principle of converting "pagans" and Muslims to Christianity with such vehemence that in 1864 the House of Commons struck a parliamentary committee to investigate the claims made against him by the missionaries of Sierra Leone. As British consul in Damascus, Burton's failure to serve the interests of the local British populace, especially the many missionaries among them, doomed his career as a diplomat in the Middle East.[51] When Burton turned to translating the epic of the Portuguese poet Camões, he would find an alternative model for empire. Respect for local customs, such as the Dutch had shown in Java, and the encouragement of local manufacturing were the cornerstones of Burton's plan for reform in India.[52]

The most important literary statement of Burton's views on British imperialism is contained in a long satirical poem, *Stone Talk,* published in 1865. This poem, whose subtitle identifies it as *Some of the Marvellous Sayings of a Petral Portion of Fleet Street, London, to One Doctor Polyglott, Ph.D.*, is reminiscent of the satirical squibs that Torrens used to criticize imperial policy during his service in India. The two characters in Burton's poem are both versions of the author. Dr. Polyglott clearly possesses Burton's linguistic talents, as well as a tendency to overindulge that lands him on Fleet Street in a drunken stupor. Here he encounters a second avatar of the author—a talking paving stone that represents the reincarnated spirit of a Hindu Brahmin. It is the stone that clearly gives voice to Burton's viewpoint. Speaking through a character as fabricated as his own persona of Mirza Abdullah, he launches his attack on the hypocrisy of British imperialism:

> Thieves of the world, that spoil wholesale
> And plunder on the largest scale!
> Who so unblushed ye that you dare
> To all the globe your crime declare?
> . . . .
> You arm yourselves with fire and steel,
> High raising the ennobling cry
> Of Cotton and Christianity;
> And, armed with these, each man of sense
> Ascribes his course to Providence,
> Favouring your pre-eminence,
> And purposing to occupy
> The globe with Anglo-Saxon fry—
> One marvels how! One wonders why![53]

Searching for a vehicle to deliver uncomfortable truths to an English readership, Burton seized on the tactic of ventriloquism. By this time, he had left India and his army career behind, and was attempting to pursue advancement in the British diplomatic corps through the political connections of his wife, Isabel. In an attempt to salvage that new career, Isabel would buy up all the copies of *Stone Talk* she could find and destroy them.[54] This poem would be the least read of all Burton's work, but it is an important example of his efforts to use a foreign persona—in this case the Hindu Brahmin—to express a political perspective forged at the edge of British influence.

Against the benefits of immersion in any one culture, Burton consistently asserted the importance of the cognitive expansion that extensive travel provided. It was no less important in the literary realm than in the political. Burton interwove the cognitive benefits of travel and literary translation most cogently in a letter to the *Athenaeum* in February 1872. "Let us not be behind our neighbours in the race for a truly cosmopolitan literature," he entreated his fellow readers. In launching his program to create a fund for translations from all languages, Burton cites William Makepeace Thackeray's assertion that French literature was the "wisest" because it was "the most cosmopolitan—cosmopolitan because most given to translating!" Translation, Burton argued, gave French literature "the enormous advantage of being capable of comparing native with foreign ideas and views of the world." Within a national culture, this comparative perspective could produce the same broadening of the imagination generated by the cognitive dissonance of travel in a foreign culture.[55]

In his commentary to the *Arabian Nights,* Burton returns to this parallel between the cognitive dissonance experienced by the explorer in uncharted realms and the unsettling impact produced by an encounter with a translated text, using it to describe the reader's experience of the magical tales of the *Arabian Nights.* For Burton, the collection's chief virtue lay in its ability to offer a disruptive education in uncertainty, the unknown, and the unexplored. The magical tales of the *Arabian Nights,* with their "outraging probability" and "outstripping possibility," work a "strange fascination" on the European reader who, surrendering to the spell, feels "almost inclined to enquire 'and why may it not be true?' " The European reader encounters the tales of magic in the *Arabian Nights* as the traveller would "the sudden prospect of magnificent mountains seen after a long desert-march: they arouse strange longings and indescribable desires; their marvelous imaginativeness produces an insensible brightening of the mind and an increase of fancy-power, making one dream that behind them lies the new and unseen, the strange and unexpected—in fact, all the glamour of the unknown." Drawing on the thrill of exploration that he had experienced many times in his career, Burton asserted that the pleasure in a magical tale rests "in the natural desire to learn more of the Wonderland which is known to many as a word and nothing more, like Central Africa before the last half century."[56]

Claiming that the cognitive value of the stories of the *Arabian Nights* could only be properly understood through the cosmopolitan perspective of the traveller, Burton wove his experiences of the pilgrimage to Mecca into his translation of the tales. This connection is emphasized in over a hundred footnotes to the tales as Burton bound his translation to his *Personal Narrative*. Burton pointed the reader to his account of the pilgrimage in notes dealing with customs of women's mourning, the Festival of the Sacrifice, wine drinking, the right to revenge, the mihrab, and the pomegranate. However, the frequency of these citations tapered off sharply after the third of the ten volumes produced by Burton. The excitement of reliving the pilgrimage would fade—replaced by a recognition of the plight of the cosmopolite who belongs to no land.[57]

For Burton, the donning of disguises and the blending of the roles of ethnographer and informant represented a cognitive disruption, but not quite a cognitive gain. In the *Personal Narrative,* Burton wrote of the traveller's imperative to wander as a curse rather than a gift. After "a long and toilsome march," he might enjoy the pleasures of domesticity for a time, but soon "a paroxysm of ennui [comes] on by slow degrees, [he] loses appetite, he walks about his room all night, he yawns at conversations, and a book acts upon him as a narcotic. The man wants to wander, and he must do so, or he shall die."[58] As a traveller he lost his sense of ease with himself and his culture, but he never truly made up for that loss by embracing a new identity or source of belonging. Jean-François Gournay has interpreted Burton's "frenzy" of translations as another series of disguises that Burton assumed as he pursued this elusive quest for identity.[59] This psychological predicament was strongly evident as he sought to articulate the relationship between his own life and his work on the *Arabian Nights.* "This work," Burton wrote, "laborious as it may appear, has been to me a labour of love, an unfailing source of pleasure, during my long exiled life in the luxuriant and deadly deserts of Western Africa and in the dark and uninteresting half-clearings of South America & long a solace and a talisman against ennui & despondency."[60] Understood as loss and unbelonging, Burton's cosmopolitanism runs counter to the version presented in the work of Kwame Anthony Appiah, where the cosmopolite inhabits concentric circles of belonging.[61]

Searching for a means of expressing the sensibility of exile, Burton turned to pseudotranslation before he turned to the *Arabian Nights.* In

1880, he published the *Kasidah,* a long poem supposedly translated from the Persian by Frank Baker, the same pseudonym used by Burton for *Stone Talk.* Clearly hoping to replicate the success of Edward FitzGerald's *Rubaiyat of Omar Khayyam,* which was closer to an adaptation of the work of the Persian poet than a translation, Burton created his own original author—Haji Abdu El-Yezdi, a Sufi from a desert city in central Persia. Just as FitzGerald imagined he could channel the spirit of Khayyam, Haji Abdu served as the perfect mouthpiece for Burton, who had always identified with the figure of the wandering Sufi dervish. Like Burton, the Sufi author of the *Kasidah* is "of No-hall, Nowhere," and his message seems to embody a cosmopolitanism born of travel:

> All faith is false, all Faith is true:
>   Truth is the shattered mirror strown
> In myriad bits; while each believes
>   His little bit the whole to own.[62]

Defending his decision to take on the role of the Sufi wanderer to critics in England after the publication of the *Personal Narrative,* Burton stressed this figure's openness to many belief systems. Searching for terms an English audience would understand, he described him as "an Oriental Freemason"—a representative of unitarianism in a world of difference. This philosophy is richly expressed in Burton's *Kasidah,* where he fulfills one of Appiah's criteria of cosmopolitanism: the ability to recognize and learn from cultural difference.[63]

When Burton turned to the *Arabian Nights* he imagined that it represented an ideal literary vehicle to carry these ideas. While Lane had defined the story collection in terms of an essential Egyptian corpus, Burton embraced the expansive nature of the collection and the syncretism that lay within its tales. His text would be as inclusive as possible, including late additions made in Arabic in the sixteenth and seventeenth centuries and those made by Antoine Galland in the eighteenth. Burton had no desire to take on the labor of collating and editing the many different versions of the *Thousand and One Nights* that were now available to scholars: "Even if lightened by the aid of Shaykhs, Munshis and copyists, the labour would be severe, tedious and thankless; better leave the holes open than patch them with fancy work or with heterogeneous matter."[64] In fact, Burton would rely on the collated text prepared by Payne and would borrow large parts of his translation from him as well. Burton's own cosmopolitan perspective would be most visible in the commentary that he appended to the stories. While Lane's notes on manners and customs were meant to ground the reader's understanding in one distinct culture, Burton's notes were intended to represent the cognitive advantages of a life lived beyond national borders and inclusive of a diverse range of cultural practices. At its best, this practice of commentary had the potential to destabilize the certainties of the target culture.[65]

The orphan tales were a particular challenge for a translator determined to use the *Arabian Nights* to make readers aware of the great diversity of cultural practices beyond their borders. Burton introduced one element of foreignness by using a Hindustani source for some of these stories (translated into English by his collaborator Blumhardt), but he would use his notes to push this further. In the tale of Aladdin, for example, Burton accentuated what he felt to be the familiar tale's overlooked esoteric contexts. The uncommon oil said to fuel the wonderful lamp reminds Burton of the eternal flame of the Rosicrucians and the practice of burying sepulchral lamps that still prevailed throughout Syria. The magician's signet ring prompts a discussion of the Muslim cosmology of the jinn and King Solomon's dominion over them. The swords wielded by Aladdin's guards lead to an explanation of how one could protect oneself against the evil eye. When Aladdin's princess seeks the help of a holy woman and she lays a hand on the head of Aladdin, Burton finds an excuse to explain the path of Sufism and the practice of mesmerism for his readers. If Lane's commentary explored the distinctive practices of Cairo as a framework for interpreting the *Arabian Nights,* Burton found ways of asserting his broader knowledge of cultural practices throughout the Islamic world.[66]

In some cases, Burton's commentary seems an odd fit with the text of the story that it is meant to elucidate. When Aladdin is served coffee with ambergris, for example, Burton takes this opportunity to educate the reader on the subject of aphrodisiacs, which "in the East would fill a small library." Distinguishing between medicinal, mechanical, and magical aphrodisiacs, Burton amplifies his consideration of just one of these categories by mentioning practices of scarification and "the application of insects as practiced by certain savage races." The relative modesty of the reunion scene between Aladdin and Princess Badr al-Budur serves as an excuse for Burton to direct the reader to the reunion of the "immodest" Queen Budur with Qamar al-Zaman, where, dressed like a man, the queen seeks to draw her unsuspecting husband into a homosexual encounter. Most bizarre is Burton's treatment of an episode of miraculous healing by a holy woman. Insisting that the recovery of the ill citizens was entirely due to the power of imagination, he then explains an incident "during the debauched days of the Second Empire" when a crowd believed that a public sexual display by a young man was due to his own imaginative power, only to discover that manual stimulation was involved. In these examples, Burton's interventions in the text reflect an agenda that has little to do with issues of interpretation posed by the tale itself.[67]

The clearest evidence of Burton's attempt to challenge existing conventions lies in his handling of the sexual content of the tales. His interest in diverse expressions of human sexuality is well established, and among like-minded associates at the London Anthropological Society and the Cannibal Club he could draw on his travels in vigorous discussions of polygamy, prostitution, eunuchism, circumcision, phallic worship, and same-sex love. Burton's correspondence with Payne indicates that he thought of his version of the *Arabian Nights* largely in terms of this agenda. Not only did he produce an "unexpurgated" edition of the story collection—relying on the inclusive versions of Payne and Torrens—but he insisted on increasing the range of sexual experience contained in the stories by drawing on the personal knowledge he derived from his extensive travels. The Orient is imagined by Burton as possessing superior sexual knowledge, which offered a necessary corrective for Western societies marked by the unhealthy repression of their sexual instincts. In his correspondence with Payne, Burton argued that the sexual content of the *Arabian Nights* material was particularly essential for his female readers. The "fair sex needs to get all the *Nights,*" he declared in October 1882.[68] Adopting the same opinions on female sexuality that Lane had attributed to the Cairenes, Burton asserted that women were by nature more sexually desirous than men, and he argued that they needed access to erotic literature.[69]

Following the model of Payne's Villon Society, Burton had joined with Forster Fitzgerald Arbuthnot in the early 1880s to create the Kama Shastra Society, a fictive organization used to print and circulate texts whose sexual content was prohibited under the Obscene Publications Act of 1857. Their first success came in 1883 when they printed an English translation of *The Kama Sutra.* Usually attributed to Burton, this version of the classic Sanskrit erotic guide was actually a translation by Bhugwuntlal Indraji, an authority on classical Sanskrit. This publication was quickly followed by another Sanskrit sex manual, *Ananga-Ranga,* in 1885 and *The Perfumed Garden,* a notorious Arabic text in the same vein, in 1886.[70] Burton's translation of the *Arabian Nights* in 1885 was intended to fulfill a similar purpose as these works by introducing readers to material that might otherwise be classified as pornographic. Rewriting Payne's text, Burton added little salacious detail to the tales themselves; however, his notes would "abound in esoteric lore, such as female circumcision and excision; different forms of eunuch manufactury, etc."[71] With the craft of a pornographer, Burton uses these notes to create an index to guide the reader, especially the female reader, to the "forbidden" topics within the collection. Burton almost always marks provocative passages in the tales with notes, which are then cataloged by topic in a final index, thus allowing the reader to explore her interests with ease.

Over a century before, Galland had felt it necessary to tame the foreign qualities of his original Arabic manuscript and to add morals to the orphan tales of Diyab. In 1885 Burton viewed these efforts to remake the stories in the image of the West as a violation of the cosmopolitan mission of translation, which should pursue the goal of unsettling the reader's sense of what is right or even what is possible.[72] In Burton's view, the *Arabian Nights* had shown its power to challenge the assumptions of its European readers from the moment of its arrival. With the appearance of the first European translations, he claimed, "France was a-fire with delight at something so new, so unconventional, so entirely without purpose, religious, moral or philosophical."[73] For Burton the virtue of the tales of the *Arabian Nights* remained their ability to frustrate the conventions of the European fairy tale. As the author of his own version of the story collection, Burton sought to enhance this cognitive disorientation through the fascinating and provocative notes that he inserted into the fabric of the tales.

✦ ✦ ✦

As he attempted to reshape the *Arabian Nights* in accordance with his own ambitions, Burton found in the figure of Caliph Harun al-Rashid an analogue for his own restlessness. His deep identification with the figure of the famous Abbasid caliph was already evident when he was planning his pilgrimage to Mecca. Determined to distinguish his journey from that of other European pilgrims, Burton had boasted that he would follow the historical route of Harun across the Arabian Desert in completing the hajj—using the wells established by Harun's wife, Zubeida. Like Payne, Burton believed that Harun was the principal protagonist of the *Arabian Nights,* and he saw in the legend of the caliph who wandered his capital in disguise a symbol of his own endless wanderings. Extending this idea in his "Terminal Essay" to the *Arabian Nights,* Burton cast himself as heir to the cosmopolitan inheritance of the legendary Baghdad of Harun, which he imagined as a model of religious syncretism and sexual tolerance.

In developing Harun al-Rashid as a central character within his *Arabian Nights,* Burton had to contend with the two very different versions of Harun that appear in the story collection.[74] In the older, "core" tales, Harun is portrayed as a pious pilgrim and a just sovereign. This is the character who appears in "The Porter and the Three Ladies," where the disguised caliph listens to the extraordinary stories related by the ladies and the dervishes and acts where he can to restore justice. Other tales, which are later additions to the *Thousand and One Nights,* offer a very different Harun. They show the caliph carousing with figures such as Abu Nuwas, his court poet and cup companion, and feature bawdy humor and the stratagems of tricksters. As fictional portraits, both "Harun the Just" and "Harun the Reveler" reflect the distinct mythology of the caliph that developed as the Abbasid Caliphate entered a period of decline and fratricidal warfare. In the literary legends that emerged from this historical crisis, Harun presided over the apogee of Arab Islamic civilization and his capital of Baghdad was imagined as a place of wealth and indulgence.[75]

In his Pre-Raphaelite version of the *Arabian Nights,* Payne seized on the character of Harun as the central character of the story collection—explaining his significance in fifty pages of commentary in the "Terminal Essay." Lingering tones of German Romanticism can be seen in Payne's version of Harun, who is characterized by "fits of gloomy depression" and "chronic restlessness" that send him into the city to seek distraction and consolation.[76] Unfamiliar with the caliph of history, Payne relied on a popular Orientalist stereotype of Harun as a quintessential tyrant. His "Terminal Essay" argues that the caliph combined the vices of the worst European despots and added "a bloodthirsty savagery, peculiarly his own." While other interpreters might stress the political significance of Harun's nocturnal travels in disguise, Payne argued that these were the wanderings of Harun's tortured conscience "pursued . . . by spectres of his own crimes." Payne's attempt to extract a coherent character from two very different sets of tales was problematic. The outcome of this struggle was a version of the character that possessed "strains of exalted morality" and "traits of heroic faith," but also demonstrated his "selfish sensuality" and "fiendish treachery."[77]

In Payne's *Arabian Nights,* Harun is presented as embodying all the passionate energy and sensuality that he attributed to the Arab people as a whole. The caliph possesses an "almost hysterical" appreciation of music, poetry, and conversation and draws the land's most talented poets, musicians, and artists to his court. Baghdad is a city devoted to sensual pleasures—a "città cortigiana" in which the "men and women seemed to vie with each other in refinements of luxury and dissipation." These tales of licentious pleasure might be "redeemed by touches of pathos, poetry or romance," but Payne was not as forgiving of a caliph that he saw as the ultimate hypocrite—a ruler who observed the dictates of piety in public while secretly violating every religious and moral taboo. The worst of Harun's crimes in Payne's eyes was his execution of his vizier Jafar. For Payne, Jafar was the true hero of the *Arabian Nights*—the talented and loyal vizier who was responsible for the ideals of governance mistakenly attributed to Harun. His execution could only be seen as an act of "unreasoning paroxysm of savage ferocity" unworthy of a caliph.[78]

In emphasizing the cosmopolitan character of the rule of Harun in his version of the *Arabian Nights,* Burton explicitly answered the interpretation of Payne. In his "Terminal Essay," Burton adopts Payne's belief that Harun is the central protagonist of the story collection, but he presents the caliph as the ruler of an empire that embraced the diversity prized by the cosmopolite, not as a vicious despot. Although certain tales might portray the caliph as "a headstrong and violent autocrat," Burton proclaimed that the historical Harun was "not more tyrannical or more sanguinary than the normal despot of the East, or the contemporary Kings of the West: in most points, indeed, he was far superior to the historic misrulers who have afflicted the world from Spain to furthest China." Drawing out the political significance of the *Arabian Nights* within his own Victorian age, Burton contrasts the "civilised and well regulated rule" of Harun's Baghdad with the "barbarity and turbulence" of contemporary Christian nations. While London and Paris were mired in "quasi-savagery," Harun's court enjoyed the luxurious life of a wealthy, cosmopolitan capital.[79]

By emphasizing the mythical Baghdad of Harun as the center of gravity in a cosmopolitan *Arabian Nights,* Burton established the value of his own distinctive perspective on the tales. In his "Terminal Essay," he casts himself as the privileged interpreter of the cosmopolitan inheritance of this capital. Countering Payne's portrait of a city in decline, Burton presents Harun's Baghdad as the apogee of Arab Islamic civilization. For Burton, the city's many vices grew up like "weeds in a rich fallow." They were simply one manifestation of "the cosmopolitan views" that suggest themselves in "a meeting-place of nations." Within the many exchanges of the empire's capital, Burton stresses the importance of those that led to religious syncretism. During this period, he argues, Islam was enriched by borrowing the "whole of its supernaturalism" and "all manner of metaphysical subtleties" from Persia. At the same time, Babylonian beliefs made their way into Muslim cosmography through the mediation of the Jews. The result, Burton contends, is that the Muslim's "soul and spirit, his angels and devils, his cosmogony, his heaven and hells, even the Bridge over the Great Depth are all either

Talmudic or Iranian." Sufism and other varieties of mysticism were similarly nurtured by a mix of these "Mesopotamian and Persic influences," as well as by strong injections of Platonism and Gnosticism.[80] For Burton, Harun's execution of Jafar and the Barmakids represented a betrayal of the cosmopolitan moment that had produced this extraordinary syncretism, and it was a cautionary tale for those in Britain who would seek to enforce their own provincial values in defiance of the diverse traditions of the territories they governed.

In his "Terminal Essay" of 1885, Burton draws out the political significance of the example of the cosmopolitan caliph. From his first appearance in Galland's French translation, Burton argues, the figure of Harun wandering his city in disguise was experienced as a sharp challenge to the principles of monarchical rule in Europe. Absolutist France was shocked by a cycle of tales in which the ruler leaves the safety of his palace to walk its streets in flowing robes—discovering and righting wrongs in the lowly guise of a merchant. Drawing from this example, Burton claims provocatively that the ideals of fraternity and equality might be better represented in "Eastern despotisms" than in the republics of Europe. By pointing out in his preface to the *Arabian Nights* that Britain is now the "greatest Mohammedan" empire, Burton suggests that these lessons might have particular relevance for the rulers of this other great empire.[81]

Harun was a figure that validated both Burton's enthusiasm for disguise and his desire to exercise power as a single solitary figure capable of penetrating the deceptions of the subjects of empire. As he pursued his diplomatic career, he seems to have acted the part of Harun on a number of occasions. There is evidence that when he served as British consul in Damascus he often dressed in the costume of an Arab sheikh to mingle with locals. One Arab acquaintance reported that "his attempts to pose as a native were a constant source of amusement to all with whom he came in contact."[82] In some cases, Isabel would also participate in these excursions, walking in Arab dress in the streets of Damascus or venturing into the desert. Isabel seems to have found it all very romantic and exciting, but for Burton, for whom this was a lifelong obsession, these impersonations seemed to fill a deeper need. Imagining himself in the role of Harun, he could dream of exercising the power that he never succeeded in achieving and associate himself with the subversive cosmopolitanism that he saw as characteristic of the Islamic world.

In the *Arabian Nights,* Burton used the tales of Harun as a vehicle to express his own vision of a more diverse and tolerant imperial space. Among these stories, "The Sleeper and the Waker" offers a particularly useful vantage point to examine the distinctive mixture of cross-cultural perspectives and political objectives that come together to produce the Harun of Burton's *Arabian Nights.* Originally two independent tales, this story includes both of the Harun characters—the just sovereign and the jocose reveler. The first part represents a variant of the "dreaming man" tale in which Harun fulfills the political function of restoring order and justice. The second half of the story, in which Harun is the victim of a trick played by his drinking companion, is more akin to tales added later to the *Arabian Nights* featuring Harun and the notorious trickster Abu Nuwas. This second anecdote has been attributed to either Abu Dulama, a black poet and jester who performed in the court of three Abbasid caliphs in the eighth century, or, alternatively, a poet in the tradition of Abu Nuwas himself.[83]

In the first part of "The Sleeper and the Waker," Harun meets the merchant Abu al-Hasan while wandering Baghdad in disguise, and joins him for an evening of drinking. As a character, Abu al-Hasan represents a variation on the profligate son who squanders his fortune—a frequent opening for a tale in the *Thousand and One Nights.* Unlike other versions of this character, however, Abu al-Hasan had buried half of his fortune before wasting the rest in entertaining his friends, so he has the chance to put things right again. Resolving to change his ways, he vows to only entertain strangers, and then for only one night. When Harun takes on the role of his companion for an evening of drinking and feasting, he enjoys Abu al-Hasan's company so much that he asks him what wish he would like fulfilled. Unaware of his guest's true identity, Abu al-Hasan answers that he would like to be caliph for a day so he could punish his neighbors—an imam and four sheikhs from the local mosque who disapprove of his drinking and carousing. When Harun grants Abu al-Hasan his wish by drugging him, transporting him to the palace, and installing him as caliph, Abu al-Hasan takes advantage of his opportunity. He orders that the imam and sheikhs be given 1,000 lashes (in Payne's version, 400) and paraded through the streets tied to donkeys, their noses to the tails.[84]

This first part of "The Sleeper and the Waker" seems to reveal some of the critical potential that lies within the stories of Harun in disguise. This story invites a political reading in which the imam and four sheikhs are interpreted as representing religious orthodoxy and the four schools of Islamic jurisprudence. In ordering their punishment, Abu al-Hasan can be seen as defending himself against religion and law in an attempt to live his life as he pleases. Aboubakr Chraïbi suggests that Harun's decision to give the merchant supreme authority for a day might be seen as a clever ploy to check the power of certain groups while maintaining traditional religious restraints on the caliph's power. The characterization of Abu al-Hasan as a prudent though profligate son is significant, for it seems to mark him as a good candidate to take on the responsibilities of government for one day while still serving the political ends of the caliph.[85]

Given Burton's comments about the subversive potential of the political examples contained in the *Arabian Nights,* one might expect him to comment on the significance of an episode that seems to be aimed at checking the influence of orthodox imams. However, Burton is strangely uninterested in a political reading of this story and seems to see it through the more familiar prism provided by a classic text of European literature—*Don Quixote.* Burton's note to the story thus presents Abu al-Hasan as a variation on Sancho Panza, depicting him as a comic squire in the service of Harun. Abu al-Hasan's reign as caliph is likened to Sancho's governorship over an insula in the novel by Miguel de Cervantes.[86] As variations of the "king for a day" tale, the stories of Abu al-Hasan's caliphate and Sancho's governorship do share certain features. In Cervantes's tale, Sancho is appointed as the governor of a small village as part of a trick played by a duke and duchess. To the surprise of all concerned, he proves to be a wise and just governor. However, he is also subjected to various torments—starvation and beating—for the duke and duchess's entertainment. Resigning his governorship, Sancho makes a claim for maintaining the status quo: "Each man is fine doing the work he was born for." The political implications of Sancho's brief governorship are more conservative than those that Chraïbi sees within Abu al-Hasan's reign as caliph. By affiliating this story with *Don Quixote,* Burton rejects a reading that would highlight the generation of justice from below or that would acknowledge that wise leadership might be exercised by someone other than the caliph. For Burton, the political lessons of the *Arabian Nights* are primarily embodied in the cosmopolitan rule of the singular leader, whom he sees as an analogue for his own elevated position in a world marked by ignorance and intolerance.[87]

Burton's cosmopolitan approach to developing this episode is primarily contained in the comparison that he makes to Cervantes. Burton decides to draw out the humor in Abu al-Hasan's situation in an effort to develop his affinity with Sancho, that "sprightly Arab with grave Spanish humour." When Abu al-Hasan as caliph orders the punishment of the imams and sheikhs, Burton prefers the figure of 1,000 rather than 400 lashes, because it struck him as more comical. Harun's role as a trickster is highlighted, and he is shown fully enjoying the farce that he has constructed for his own entertainment, laughing at the drunk Abu al-Hasan as he is placed before him.[88] Burton enhances the cruel humor in this episode by adopting Payne's translation of Abu al-Hasan's request that a slave bite his ear to determine if he is dreaming. The rhyming prose that scholars associate with Burton, which is actually lifted directly from Payne, heightens the comedic potential of the scene: "So he closed his teeth upon Abu al-Hasan's ear with all his might, till he came near to sever it; and he knew not Arabic, so, as often as the Wag said to him, 'It doth suffice,' he concluded that he said, 'Bite like a vice,' and redoubled his bite and made his teeth meet in the ear." As Abu al-Hasan cries out for mercy, "the Caliph [loses] his senses for laughter."[89] In this story, Burton stresses his understanding of the *Arabian Nights* as a form of entertainment characterized by low, bawdy humor, and sought to connect these qualities to other key texts in an emerging canon of world literature.

Burton felt that such cross-cultural comparisons represented the strength of his version of the *Arabian Nights*—in contrast to a work of translation done in a narrower Orientalist framework—and he followed this line of inquiry even when he knew that there was little hard evidence to support it. In the case of "The Sleeper and the Waker," Burton had sent the folklorist W. A. Clouston on a fruitless quest to find parallels between this story and the figures of Sancho in Cervantes and Christopher Sly in Shakespeare. He knew that his interpretation lay beyond what scholarship deemed plausible, but with characteristic stubbornness, Burton printed his notes regarding Abu al-Hasan's resemblance to Sancho in the same volume as Clouston's skeptical essay on the subject, confident that the force of the parallels that he saw would override the objections noted by the scholar. Where syncretism did not exist, Burton would create it.[90]

If Burton is unwilling to derive a more substantial political meaning from the first part of "The Sleeper and the Waker," he does embrace the subversive potential that lies in Harun's other role as a participant in the sensual pleasures of Baghdad. The second part of "The Sleeper and the Waker" represents this spirit more directly, casting Harun as the victim of a prank by Abu al-Hasan, the caliph's cup companion. This section of the tale reflects other late additions to the Harun tales of the *Arabian Nights,* which Burton regarded as evidence of a key cosmopolitan virtue of Harun's capital—an openness to different forms of sexuality. These tales of trickery and debauchery had already become an issue of dispute between Payne and Burton as they discussed the possibility of collaborating on a version of the *Arabian Nights.* After reading the proof of Payne's version of "The Sleeper and the Waker," Burton rebuked him for his portrayal of the sexual escapades at court. In a letter from Trieste dated May 12, 1883, Burton wrote, "You are 'drawing it very mild.' Has there been any unpleasantness about plain speaking? Poor Abu Hasan is (as it were) castrated. I should say be bold or audace etc only you know better than I do how far you can go and cannot go. I should simply translate every word." When Payne pushed back in his reply, Burton reaffirmed the imperatives that governed his construction of the story collection: "It is these 'offences against nature' . . . that give the book much of its ethnolog[ical] value." For Burton, the subversive potential of the collection for an imperial metropolis like London lay in these characters and episodes.[91]

In accordance with this belief that the transgressive sexuality of the *Arabian Nights* was central to the value the stories had for an

English reading public, Burton introduced into his edition an unexpurgated version of "Abu Nuwas with the Three Boys and the Caliph Harun al-Rashid." The tale begins when Abu Nuwas prepares a grand feast and sets out to find company, setting his sights on "three youths handsome and beardless . . . differing in complexion but fellows in incomparable beauty." The three youths would go their separate ways, but Abu Nuwas holds their attention with a poem that promises them a feast of "luxury" and the occasion to frolic with each other and with him. The youths, "beguiled by his verses, consented to his wishes."[92] At this luxurious feast the youths appeal to Abu Nuwas to decide which of them is the fairest, a game in which the court poet earns kisses for his verses to each youth. Burton is at his comedic best describing the "deboshed state" in which Harun finds Abu Nuwas: "The drink got into his noddle, drunkenness mastered him and he knew not hand from head, so that he lolled from side to side in joy and inclined to the youths one and all, anon kissing them and anon embracing them leg overlying leg."[93] When the caliph teases his friend with the news that he has appointed him to the office of *Kazi* (judge) of pimps and panderers, the poet, without missing a beat, simply inquires if Harun has a case to petition before his court. Offended, the caliph orders for the poet to be beheaded after crawling naked in an ass's saddle through the slave girls' quarters. Yet Abu Nuwas's good humor during this punishment and his interrogation by the vizier Jafar earns him a pardon and monetary compensation from the caliph.[94]

Burton cites these tales of the caliph's nighttime revelry with Abu Nuwas as his justification for including an extensive historical and socio-anthropological discussion of homosexuality (or pederasty, in the terminology of his time) in his "Terminal Essay" to the *Arabian Nights*. For those familiar with Burton's own explorations of the forbidden realms of Victorian sexual experience, this inclusion is unsurprising. Fawn Brodie, whose 1967 biography of Burton remains the most psychologically incisive in many respects, proposed that Burton's constant compulsion to explore new regions of the world was driven by the repression of his latent homosexuality. However, Burton's tendency to wander the world was more likely a product of his own insatiable sexuality than the result of some stereotype of Victorian repression. His travelogues and letters suggest that he left few areas of sexual expression unexplored. Burton wrote frankly about his preference for the male form, and there were always rumors about homosexual liaisons. Isabel likely destroyed evidence of these relationships upon his death, but at least one letter by Algernon Swinburne, also rumored to be among Burton's lovers, refers to a "lost love of Burton's, the beloved and blue object of Central African affections," in terms that make it clear that he enjoyed men sexually. Evidence contained in Burton's unpublished diary of his sea voyage to Canada in 1860 also suggests that he relished the opportunities that travel offered to have sexual encounters with other men. In this account, Burton records an extended flirtation with an English widower and his deep disappointment when his efforts at seduction fail.[95]

Burton's personal interest in promoting greater acceptance of homosexuality partly motivated his treatment of the stories of Abu Nuwas and the caliph, but few scholars have recognized that Burton's most important intervention on this subject in the *Arabian Nights*—his discussion of homosexuality in the "Terminal Essay"—was also shaped by Payne's role as Burton's hidden collaborator. The correspondence between the two men on the challenges of translating the work was instrumental in prompting Burton to articulate his conception of Harun's Baghdad as a haven of sexual tolerance. When Burton met with Payne in 1881 to discuss a potential collaboration, he may not have had substantial notes on the *Arabian Nights,* but he had already done substantial research on the subject of homosexuality. Payne appears to have been aware of the nature of its contents and to have been curious about, if alarmed by, the prospect that some of it might make its way into print, even after Burton's death. Other correspondents and associates of Burton had participated in more open discussions in which Burton expressed his theory that homosexuality was universal, and therefore no less common in Britain than in the Orient, but Payne, who stood "poles" apart on this issue, seems to have prompted Burton to produce a more focused defense of homosexuality.[96]

The correspondence between Payne and Burton suggests that Burton's infamous hypothesis of a "Sotadic Zone" in which homosexuality was more prevalent globally may have been a strategy that Burton used to interest Payne in a joint project to reprint Payne's translation with the more critical inflection provided by Burton's commentary. On May 22, 1883, Burton wrote Payne about his existing essay on the Sotadic Zone, which showed "the geo(graphical) limits of sodomy." It was, he suggested, "a broad band across Europe and Asia widening out into China and embracing all America." Payne could not fail to notice that the heart of this region was formed by the Mediterranean and the Middle East: "Port Spain S. France Italy Greece Turkey Persia China America." On the edge of this band, Burton positions "N. Africa" and "Cashmere." The geographical determinism of this theory seems to have been deployed by Burton in this instance as a line of argument that might be expected to elicit more sympathy among classically educated gentlemen well aware of the prevalence of same-sex love in ancient Greece. Payne represented a test case for the response of such an audience. In Burton's published "Terminal Essay," this theory would rest uneasily alongside other suggestions that homosexuality was as common in the cities of Paris, Berlin, and London as in the so-called Sotadic Zone.[97]

In this section of the "Terminal Essay," Burton revisits the Oriental identity that he had developed during his time in Sindh and deployed during his pilgrimage to Mecca. He slyly inserts evidence of homosexual practice among the British in India, as well as others within the Sotadic Zone, by recounting his investigation of the brothels of Karachi in the 1840s. According to Burton, the governor of Sindh, Napier, had asked him to corroborate or refute reports that British soldiers serving under him were frequenting such establishments. The scandalous fact was not that such brothels existed but that they catered to British servicemen. Burton claims that he visited the brothels over several nights as Mirza Abdullah al-Bushiri, a merchant from the northern shore of the Hormuz Strait, and that he was accompanied by his Persian munshi, Shirazi. Burton stresses that it was his fluent Sindhi that had recommended him for this commission, but a mission to the brothels of Karachi would not seem to require such talent. The presence of Burton's friend and language teacher is also a strangely discordant note in a tale that is meant to impress us with Burton's exceptional ability to become the native himself.[98]

Inserted into Burton's "Terminal Essay," the Karachi episode can be interpreted as a fable cleverly constructed to draw aspects of an extraordinary life together into a statement on the realities of British sexual life on the frontiers of empire. Revisiting this episode, Burton disappears into the persona of Mirza Abdullah once more, but in this narrative he combines the functions of both Harun and Abu Nuwas into one. As a self-professed cosmopolite observer, Burton's goal was to reveal that practices rejected and criminalized in England were not as foreign to the self and the homeland as was imagined. Portraying himself as both a participant in the sexual transgressions of the colonial frontier and a tolerant cosmopolite, Burton sought to apply the subversive potential of the *Arabian Nights* to an issue of pressing concern in Britain.[99]

✦ ✦ ✦

Burton's "Terminal Essay" to the *Arabian Nights* reflects his own understanding of the potential that lay within the story collection to provide a disruptive education in alternative beliefs and social practices. His portrait of Harun and his discussion of homosexuality were united by his belief in the virtues of a cosmopolitan perspective generated by crossing cultural boundaries through both travel and translation. It is this perspective that distinguishes his version of the story collection from those with which it shares a common textual basis. It is perhaps ironic that Burton, the archetypal cosmopolitan, borrowed so heavily from the Pre-Raphaelite Orientalism of Payne, but he went much further in insisting that the tales in his *Arabian Nights* reflect the distinctive spirit of his traveller's perspective. It was as a commentator rather than a translator that Burton exercised his own subversive instincts.

The notes that Burton scrawled over the pages of the "Terminal Essay" in his copy of his own translation of the *Arabian Nights* reveal his dissatisfaction with the many compromises this first version contained, and his plan to publish a new edition that would give more attention to homosexuality in Europe. In these annotations, long considered unreadable by scholars, Burton would sketch a passionate defense of cross-class sexual encounters that resonated with his own experience and that he chose to locate in the utopia of sexual tolerance of Harun's Baghdad. Whatever professional price he thought he had paid for the reports that he produced on homosexual encounters in the brothels of Karachi, these notes show that Burton was now convinced that sex was perhaps the only realm in which individuals from different worlds could establish a connection that transcended their social circumstances. In his marginalia, Burton lyricized the ability of homosexual encounters to eclipse "differences of degree": "Master & valet, millionaire and miserable, gov't officer and ex-convict meet in terms of social equality."[100] These notes also suggest that Burton intended to replace the limited focus on the Sotadic Zone in the "Terminal Essay" with a frank account of homosexuality in Paris. Only the specter of prosecution under the new Criminal Law Amendment Act of 1885 would have stopped Burton from detailing the homosexual circles and haunts in London in a similar way. If his notes had been published, the subversive potential of the cosmopolitan vision cultivated by Burton would finally have been directed at the true heart of the imperial capital.

Burton's optimism regarding the potential of transcending divisions of class, and perhaps race, through sexual connection speaks to both the appeal and the limitations of his cosmopolitan vantage point in the *Arabian Nights*. Burton revelled in the violation of taboos through sexual acts, starting with his literary improvisations on the interracial affair of Shahriyar's queen in the frame tale. His diary account of his passage to Canada embodies his genuine conviction that homosexual sex was the one realm in which different kinds of men could meet as equals. Yet this is a vision emptied of any radical political force. Despite his intensely critical position on imperial modes of governance and sexual conventions, Burton lacked Torrens's passion for checking political authority. The experience of equality in sex did not make Burton rethink the privilege of his cosmopolitan stance. The sexual utopia Burton offers in his proposed revisions to the *Arabian Nights* promises at best solidarity among sophisticates at the expense of valets, servants, guides, and slaves, whose only "equal" value rests in their status as available and willing sexual partners.[101] Burton's is very much an elite cosmopolitanism from above. It is fitting that Burton projected his desire to subvert European norms onto the figure of the caliph in disguise. The image of Harun selectively intervening as an agent of justice or offering a beneficent tolerance to sexual outsiders was a perfect analogue for Burton's own perspective.

What Burton's sexual tolerance and openness share more broadly with his much-vaunted cosmopolitan stance is the need to obscure the other individuals who partook in the experiences that formed this distinctive perspective. A common thread in Burton's travel writing throughout his life is the erasure of sources that had been acknowledged in earlier and shorter drafts, and the appropriation of their knowledge and experiences as his own. His famous attempt to take credit for the discoveries of his travel companion John Hanning Speke in their search for the source of the Nile is only the most prominent of many instances in which the guides and collaborators who enabled Burton's explorations were erased from the public record.[102] Fashioning himself as the cultural insider necessitated blotting out the actual insiders who enabled him to go native again and again, to inhabit new cultural realms, and to "collect" new identities. Theorizing the cognitive benefits of travel, Burton characteristically conceived of these journeys as a solitary act and persistently cultivated the distance that was so apparent on his pilgrimage to Mecca. The cosmopolite sensibility was something to be pursued and developed as an individual, or perhaps as the basis for a league of extraordinary gentlemen, not the grounds for a broader empathy or community of solidarity.

In shaping his version of the *Arabian Nights,* Burton would draw on his own understanding of the virtues of cosmopolitanism. Using his extensive experience as a traveller in lands well beyond the reach of his English readers, Burton took on the role of the local informant who could explain the strange worlds that one encounters in the story collection. If Lane's commentary to the *Arabian Nights* represents a collage of many voices, Burton's commentary is dominated by his own distinctive personality, which seems to have been uniquely capable of adopting a series of different personae to tell wondrous stories of universal truths and particular curiosities. While Lane and Payne positioned their *Arabian Nights* as Orientalist constructions that privileged scholarship and aesthetics, respectively, Burton transformed the collection into a vehicle for the cosmopolitan wanderer to speak of endless journeys and to provoke the disorientation that passing through these worlds could produce.

At the greatest remove from any notion of authenticity, Burton's version of the *Arabian Nights* exerted a particular appeal on writers such as James Joyce, Salman Rushdie, and Orhan Pamuk. If Joyce responded to the formal innovation offered by the structure of framing and embedded tales, Rushdie's concern was with the challenges of a cosmopolitan heritage in the context of postcolonial India, reflected in the recurring image of a boy discovering Burton's version of the *Arabian Nights* in the library of a family patriarch. The enduring power of the *Arabian Nights* to shape the responses of contemporary writers lies in both the original stories and the additional tales and commentaries added in French and English.

Pamuk's relationship to the story collection reveals both the challenges and the creative potential offered by the *Arabian Nights*. Pamuk confesses that he had difficulty reconciling the French tales of Galland to the realities of his childhood Istanbul. In his early twenties, Pamuk encountered but did not relate to a Turkish version of the collection that stressed the original Arabic core. Burton's commentary inspired Pamuk to return to the *Arabian Nights* in his novel *The Black Book*.[103] In his use of the motif of Harun al-Rashid's nocturnal wanderings through the city and the doubling of the caliph, apparent in stories such as "The Sleeper and the Waker," Pamuk adapts the concerns of Burton's *Arabian Nights* to fashion a critique of authoritarian rule in Turkey in the 1980s.

For a writer like Pamuk, the distance of Galland or Burton from an original Arabic text opens up a space for new variations on the tales of the *Arabian Nights*. In *The Black Book*, the protagonist explains to the owner of "Aladdin's Shop" that Aladdin's tale "was never actually told to Galland by Scheherazade but by a Christian scholar from Aleppo called Youhenna Diab. . . . But . . . if truth be known, it was impossible to know what was what as to the origins of any story any more than the origins of any life."[104] Pamuk's novels show the possibility of reconciling Middle Eastern sources with European elaborations, for writers who continue to be inspired by the tales of Shahrazad.

NOTES

INTRODUCTION

1. Unless otherwise attributed, all translations from foreign-language works are my own.
2. The term "orphan tales" was coined by Mia Gerhardt to refer to the stories without Arabic originals in Galland's work. See Mia Gerhardt, *The Art of Storytelling: A Literary Study of the Thousand and One Nights* (Leiden, Netherlands: Brill, 1963), 14.
3. Jean-Paul Sermain, "Présentation," in *Les mille et une nuits: Contes arabes,* ed. Jean-Paul Sermain, trans. Antoine Galland (Paris: Éditions Flammarion, 2004), 1:xvii–xxxii.
4. Hanna Diyab, untitled memoir, Biblioteca Apostolica Vaticana, Sbath.254. The memoir has been published in French as Hanna Diyab, *D'Alep à Paris: Les pérégrinations d'un jeune Syrien au temps de Louis XIV,* ed. and trans. Bernard Heyberger et al. (Paris: Sinbad, 2015).
5. The research project led by Chraïbi in Paris traced the evolution of the story collection across the whole of the Arabic-speaking region encompassing the Middle East, North Africa, and Spain during the millennium that stretches from the ninth to the nineteenth century. See Aboubakr Chraïbi, ed., *Arabic Manuscripts of the Thousand and One Nights: Presentation and Critical Editions of Four Noteworthy Texts; Observations on Some Osmanli Translations* (Paris: espaces&signes, 2016).
6. Ibid., 15–64; Roy P. Mottahedeh, "*'Ajā'ib* in *The Thousand and One Nights,*" in *The Thousand and One Nights in Arabic Literature and Society,* ed. R. G. Hovannisian and G. Sabagh (Cambridge: Cambridge University Press, 1997), 29–39.
7. Abdelfattah Kilito, *Arabs and the Art of Storytelling: A Strange Familiarity,* trans. Mbarek Sryfi and Eric Sellin (Syracuse, NY: Syracuse University Press, 2014),

116–125, first quotation from p. 120; Abdelfattah Kilito, *Thou Shalt Not Speak My Language,* trans. Waïl Hassan (Syracuse, NY: Syracuse University Press, 2008), 27.

8. It is said to be "incomplete" because it breaks off in the middle of the story of "Qamar al-Zaman and Budur."
9. Ulrich Marzolph and Richard van Leeuwen, eds., *The Arabian Nights Encyclopedia* (Santa Barbara: ABC-CLIO, 2004), 635–636, 581–582.
10. Muhsin Mahdi, *The Thousand and One Nights* (Leiden, Netherlands: Brill, 1995), 92–101.
11. John Dryden, "Dedication of the Aeneïs," in *The Works of Virgil, Translated into English Verse,* ed. John Carey (London, 1819), 1:319.
12. François Pétis de la Croix, *Les mille et un jours: Contes persans* (Paris: Ricoeur, 1710–1712); [Jean-Paul Bignon], *The Adventures of Abdalla, Son of Hanif,* trans. William Hatchett (London, 1729).
13. Srinivas Aravamudan, *Enlightenment Orientalism: Resisting the Rise of the Novel* (Chicago: University of Chicago Press, 2012), 51.
14. David Damrosch, *What is World Literature?* (Princeton: Princeton University Press, 2003), 288–297.
15. Emily Apter, "Translation with No Original: Scandals of Textual Reproduction," in *Nation, Language, and the Ethics of Translation,* ed. Sandra Bermann and Michael Wood (Princeton, NJ: Princeton University Press, 2005), 159.
16. "Huntington Acquires Newly Identified Portrait by Major French Artist of the 17th Century," Huntington Library, Art Collections and Botanical Garden website, May 12, 2010, http://www.huntington.org/uploadedFiles/Files/PDFs/pr_champaigne.pdf.
17. Jorge Luis Borges, "A History of Angels," in *Selected Non-fictions,* trans. Suzanne Jill Levine et al. (New York: Viking, 1999), 17.
18. Bram Stoker, *Personal Reminiscences of Henry Irving* (London: Macmillan, 1906), 1:360–361.
19. Kwame Anthony Appiah, *Cosmopolitanism: Ethics in a World of Strangers* (New York: W. W. Norton, 2006), 1–8.
20. Emily Apter, *Against World Literature: On the Politics of Untranslatability* (London: Verso, 2013), 293.
21. On literary texts as collaborative events, see Jerome McGann, *The Textual Condition* (Princeton, NJ: Princeton University Press, 1991).
22. Lawrence Venuti, *The Translator's Invisibility: A History of Translation* (London: Routledge, 1995), 268–273.
23. Robert Irwin, *The Arabian Nights: A Companion* (London: Tauris, 2004), 237. Also see Marina Warner, *Stranger Magic: Charmed States and the Arabian Nights* (London: Vintage, 2012).
24. Jorge Luis Borges, "The Translators of the Thousand and One Nights," in *Selected Non-fictions,* 92.

25. Paulo Lemos Horta, "'A Covenant for Reconciliation': Lane's *Thousand and One Nights* and Eliot's *Daniel Deronda*," in *Scheherazade's Children*, ed. Philip Kennedy and Marina Warner (New York: New York University Press, 2013), 154–171.

1. THE STORYTELLER AND THE SULTAN OF FRANCE

1. Antoine Galland, journal entry for March 25, 1709, in *Le journal d'Antoine Galland, la période parisienne*, ed. Frédéric Bauden and Richard Waller (Paris: Peeters, 2011), 1:290; Germain Brice, *Description de la ville de Paris et de tout ce qu'elle contient de plus remarquable* (repr., Paris: Minard, 1971), 3:181–182.
2. "Lettre de M_ écrite à un de ses amis au sujet des curiosités qui se trouvent dans le cabinet de M. Paul Lucas, à Paris," in *Mercure de France*, December 1732, 1:2720–2724. Lucas's cabinet was auctioned after his death and a thirteen-page catalog produced. *Mémoire des antiques et autres pièces rares et curieuses, du cabinet du feu Sr Paul Lucas* (Paris: Imprimerie de V. Rebuffe, 1738).
3. Antoine Galland, "M. Diyab quelques contes Arabes fort beaux," in *Journal*, 1:290.
4. Diyab told Galland stories on May 5, 8, 10, 13, 22, 23, 25, 27, 29, and June 1 and 2. Galland, *Journal*, 1:321, 326, 329, 331, 343–346, 347–367, 373–376. Diyab told Galland fifteen tales. (I follow Marzolph in counting the embedded tales in "The Caliph's Night Adventure" separately.) Galland claims to have received "Aladdin" in writing, but no authentic manuscript has ever been found. See Ulrich Marzolph, "Les Contes de Hanna," in *Les mille et une nuits*, ed. É. Bouffard and A.-A. Joyard (Paris: Institut du monde arabe, 2012), 87–91.
5. Galland on Lucas in letters from July 12, 1709, and February 20, 1714, in Mohamed Abdel-Halim, "Correspondence d'Antoine Galland" (PhD diss., Université de Paris, 1964), 602, 657. Galland's visit on March 25 was the latest in a flurry motivated by a desire to see Greek and Latin coins that Lucas had brought back from the Levant. See journal entries for February 18, March 10, March 17, and March 18, 1709, in Galland, *Journal*, 1:264, 282, 286, 287.
6. Janine Miquel-Ravenel, *Antoine Galland: Inventeur des "Mille et une nuits"* (Paris: Geuthner, 2009); Raymond Schwab, *L'auteur des "Mille et une nuits": Vie d'Antoine Galland* (Paris: Mercure de France, 2004); Sylvette Larzul, *Les traductions françaises des "Mille et une nuits": Études des versions Galland, Trébutien et Mardrus* (Paris: Harmattan, 1996); Georges May, *Les "Mille et une nuits" d'Antoine Galland, ou, Le chef-d'œuvre invisible*, Écrivains (Paris: PUF, 1986). On Galland's acts of "creation" rather than "adaptation," see Sylvette Larzul, "Further Considerations on Galland's *Mille et une nuits:* A Study of the Tales Told by Hanna," *Marvels and Tales* 18, no. 2 (2004): 270.
7. Jean-Paul Sermain, *Les mille et une nuits entre Orient et Occident* (Paris: Éditions Desjonquères, 2009), 89–92; Jean-Paul Sermain, "Notice," in *Les mille et une*

nuits: Contes arabes, ed. Jean-Paul Sermain, trans. Antoine Galland (Paris: Éditions Flammarion, 2004), 3:i–xiv.

8. Hanna Diyab, untitled memoir, Biblioteca Apostolica Vaticana, Sbath.254 (hereafter Diyab memoir), 128r; Hanna Diyab, *D'Alep à Paris: Les pérégrinations d'un jeune Syrien au temps de Louis XIV*, ed. and trans. Bernard Heyberger et al. (Paris: Sinbad, 2015). I would like to acknowledge Frédéric Bauden for directing me to this source in December 2009, and Paule Fahmé-Thiéry for sharing the French translation of Diyab's memoir prior to its publication.
9. On Diyab's biography, see Bernard Heyberger, introduction to Diyab, *D'Alep à Paris*, 8–10; Johannes Stephan, "Spuren fiktionaler Vergegenwärtigung im osmanischen Aleppo: Narratologische Analysen und Kontextualisierungen des *Reisebuchs* von Hanna Dyāb (1764)" (PhD diss., Universität Bern, 2015), 19–21. Lucas's promise can be found in Diyab memoir, 171r; Diyab, *D'Alep à Paris*, 434.
10. Heyberger, introduction, 9; Stephan, "Spuren fiktionaler Vergegenwärtigung," 21–22. For eighteenth-century Aleppo, see Bruce Masters, "Aleppo: The Ottoman Empire's Caravan City," in *The Ottoman City between East and West* (Cambridge: Cambridge University Press, 1999), 48–58.
11. Diyab memoir, 80r–80v, Diyab, *D'Alep à Paris*, 224–225; Stephan, "Spuren fiktionaler Vergegenwärtigung," 43–50. On the missing first five folios, see Heyberger, introduction, 7, 53.
12. Nicholas Dew, *Orientalism in Louis XIV's France* (Oxford: Oxford University Press, 2009), 1–40, 173–175; Ina McCabe, *Orientalism in Early Modern France: Eurasian Trade, Exoticism, and the Ancien Régime* (London: Berg, 2008), 293.
13. Mohamed Abdel-Halim, "Le Premier Voyage (1670–1675)," in *Antoine Galland: Sa vie et son oeuvre* (Paris: A. G. Nizet, 1964), 29–50.
14. Charles Olier, Marquis de Nointel, letter of July 1672, in Henri Omont, *Missions archéologiques françaises en Orient aux 17e et 18e siècles: Documents publiés par Henri Omont* (Paris: Imprimerie Nationale, 1902), 175, 180. For Galland as a classicist, see Frédéric Bauden, introduction to Galland, *Journal*, 1:7–21.
15. See the contemporary description by the Hellenist Jacob Spon in *Voyage d'Italie, de Dalmatie, de Grèce et du Levant, 1678*, ed. R. Étienne, A. Duchêne, and J.-Cl. Mossièrre (Paris: Honoré Champion, 2004), 194–196; also see Omont, *Missions archéologiques françaises*, 196.
16. Antoine Galland, *Voyage à Constantinople (1672–1673)*, ed. Charles Schefer (Paris: Maisonneuve et Larose, 2002), 1:120–144; Larzul, *Les traductions françaises*, 268.
17. Jean-Baptiste Colbert, "Mémoire des observations que l'on peut faire dans les voyages de Levant, remis à M. Galland, lors de son voyage, par M. Colbert" (1679), in Omont, *Missions archéologiques françaises*, 203–207.

18. Galland to Spon, October 18 and 23, 1682, in Omont, *Missions archéologiques françaises*, 218–219.
19. Galland, letter of March 21, 1701, in Omont, *Missions archéologiques françaises*, 203.
20. Galland, *Voyage à Constantinople*, 2:45–46. The tale is from the late fourteenth- or fifteenth-century Turkish collection *Ferec ba 'd el-shidde*, itself likely of Persian origin. Ulrich Marzolph, "A Scholar in the Making: Antoine Galland's Early Travel Diaries in the Light of Comparative Folk Narrative Research," *Middle Eastern Literatures* 18 (2016): 300–317.
21. Aboubakr Chraïbi, ed., *Arabic Manuscripts of the Thousand and One Nights: Presentation and Critical Edition of Four Noteworthy Texts; Observations on Some Osmanli Translations* (Paris: espaces&signes, 2016). Delio V. Proverbio provides the analysis of Turkish translations in this volume (see 367–429).
22. Nicholas Dew, "The Order of Oriental Knowledge: The Making of D'Herbelot's *Bibliothèque Orientale*," in *Debating World Literature*, ed. Christopher Prendergast (London: Verso, 2004), 233–252.
23. Eastern Christians served as librarians, translators, and copyists in a number of European countries in the seventeenth century. Bernard Heyberger, *Hindiyya, Mystic and Criminal (1720–1798): A Political and Religious Crisis in Lebanon*, trans. Renée Champion (Cambridge: James Clarke, 2013), 83.
24. See, for instance, Galland's diary entries for May 7 and May 10, 1709, in Galland, *Journal*, 1:325–327.
25. Abdel-Halim notes this discrepancy in *Antoine Galland*, 203. James Montgomery is skeptical of Galland's contention that there is a connection between Sinbad and Odysseus: J. Montgomery, "Al-Sindbad and Polyphemus: Reflections on the Genesis of an Archetype," in *Myths, Historical Archetypes and Symbolic Figures in Arabic Literature*, ed. A. Neuwirth, B. Embalo, and S. Gunther (Beirut: Steiner in Komm., 1999), 437–466.
26. Richard Hole terms "Sinbad" the "Arabian *Odyssey*" in *Remarks on the Arabian Nights' Entertainments: In Which the Origin of Sindbad's Voyages and Other Oriental Fiction Is Particularly Considered* (London: Strand, 1797).
27. In a letter to Pierre-Daniel Huet dated February 25, 1701, Galland claims to have completed his "Sinbad." MS Paris Bibliothèque nationale de France, fr. 6138, ff. 130–143. Munich's Staatsbibliothek preserves the unpublished *Histoire arabe de Sindabad le Marin mise en français par F. Pétis de la Croix* (Paris, 1701), Cod.gall. 799.
28. Abdel-Halim, *Antoine Galland*, 265–267.
29. Ibid., 198–201; Larzul, "Further Considerations," 262.
30. Antoine Galland, "Avertissement," in *Les mille et une nuits: Contes arabes*, 1:22; Larzul, "Further Considerations," 262.
31. Sermain, *Les mille et une nuits entre Orient et Occident*, 61–76.
32. Galland, "Avertissement," 1:21; Abdel-Halim, *Antoine Galland*, 200.

33. Sylvette Larzul, "Les *Mille et une nuits* de Galland; ou, L'acclimatation d'une 'Belle étrangère,'" *Revue de littérature comparée* 3 (1995): 312–318; Larzul, "Further Considerations," 262–264.
34. Larzul, "Further Considerations," 260.
35. An Arabic manuscript source has also been found for "The Ten Viziers," a story that Diyab told to Galland, but that he did not include in his *Arabian Nights*. Galland mentions a written version of "Aladdin," asserting that he finished the tenth volume of his *Arabian Nights* based on that text. See Galland, entries for November 3, 1710, and January 10, 1711, in *Journal*, 2:302. However, no authentic Arabic manuscript of the tale has ever been found.
36. Sermain, *Les mille et une nuits entre Orient et Occident*, 61–76; Larzul, "Further Considerations," 264–270.
37. Abdel-Halim, *Antoine Galland*, 235, 280–282; Larzul, "Further Considerations," 261.
38. The only other scholar who has considered this issue is Stephan, in his dissertation from December 2015. See Stephan, "Spuren fiktionaler Vergegenwätigung," 33.
39. Abdel-Halim, *Antoine Galland*, 283.
40. Galland, *Journal*, 1:8–21. For the argument that Diyab was narrating his stories in French, see Ruth B. Bottigheimer, "East Meets West: Hannā Diyāb and *The Thousand and One Nights*," *Marvels and Tales* 28 (2014): 302–324.
41. Galland, *Voyage à Constantinople*, 2:45–46.
42. Madeleine Dobie, "Translation in the Contact Zone: Antoine Galland's *Mille et une nuits: Contes arabes*," in *The Arabian Nights in Historical Context: Between East and West*, ed. Saree Makdisi and Felicity Nussbaum (Oxford: Oxford University Press, 2008), 30–32.
43. The Abbé is Pierre Cureau de La Chambre, French theologian and member of the Académie française. Galland is quoted in Michèle Longino, "The Reluctant Diarist, Antoine Galland (1646–1715)," in *French Travel Writing in the Ottoman Empire* (New York: Routledge, 2015), 156.
44. Diyab memoir, 128r; Diyab, *D'Alep à Paris*, 334.
45. Stephan, "Spuren fiktionaler Vergegenwätigung," 20–23; Heyberger, introduction, 7–47; Galland, entry for May 27, 1709, in *Journal*, 1:358.
46. Alexander Russell and Patrick Russell, *The Natural History of Aleppo* (London: G. G. and J. Robinson, 1794), 1:148–149.
47. Jonathan Scott restated this observation in his *Arabian Nights' Entertainments* (London: Longman, Hurst, Rees, Orme, and Brown, 1811), i–ii, and it is widely reproduced in several reviews of his translation in 1812. It is also quoted in Richard Burton's translation: Richard Francis Burton, "Terminal Essay," in *The Book of the Thousand Nights and a Night* (London: Privately circulated by the Burton Club, 1885), 10:78.
48. Heyberger, introduction, 32.

49. Ulrich Jasper Seetzen, *Tagebuch des Aufenthalts in Aleppo 1803–1805* (Hildesheim, Germany: Olms, 2011), 231.
50. Heyberger, introduction, 27, 36; Marzolph, "Les Contes de Hanna," 87–91.
51. Heyberger, *Hindiyya;* Dana Sajdi, *The Barber of Damascus: Nouveau Literacy in the Eighteenth-Century Ottoman Levant* (Stanford, CA: Stanford University Press, 2013); John-Paul Ghobrial, "The Secret Life of Elias of Babylon and the Uses of Global Microhistory," *Past and Present,* no. 222 (February 2014): 51–93; Stephan, "Spuren fiktionaler Vergegenwätigung," 43–67.
52. Heyberger, introduction, 13–14. On Diyab and travel literature in Aleppo, see Stephan, "Spuren fiktionaler Vergegenwätigung," 43–89.
53. Hilary Kilpatrick, "Between Ibn Battūta and al-Tahtāwi: Arabic Travel Accounts of the Early Ottoman Period," *Middle Eastern Literatures* 11, no. 2 (August 2008): 233–248.
54. Heyberger, introduction, 36. Diyab memoir, 59r–60v, 73r–74r; Diyab, *D'Alep à Paris,* 181–184, 209–212.
55. Diyab memoir, 1r–7r; Diyab, *D'Alep à Paris,* 53–65.
56. This mirrors common elements in travelogues from this period. See Stephan, "Spuren fiktionaler Vergegenwätigung," 66.
57. Diyab memoir, 58r; Diyab, *D'Alep à Paris,* 179.
58. Diyab memoir, 79r–81v; Diyab, *D'Alep à Paris,* 223–227.
59. Diyab memoir, 81v–83v; Diyab, *D'Alep à Paris,* 227–231. See Galland's record of Diyab's storytelling session of May 22 (Galland, *Journal,* 1:343–347) in the context of Bauden's note to Galland's journal entry of May 20 (ibid., 1:342).
60. Diyab memoir, 105r; Diyab, *D'Alep à Paris,* 282.
61. Diyab memoir, 105v; Diyab, *D'Alep à Paris,* 284.
62. Diyab memoir, 105v; Diyab, *D'Alep à Paris,* 284.
63. Galland, *Journal,* 1:373.
64. Diyab memoir, 131r–132r; Diyab, *D'Alep à Paris,* 340–343.
65. Diyab memoir, 129r–132v; Diyab, *D'Alep à Paris,* 336–344.
66. The Marquise d'Huxelles quoted by Bauden in Galland, *Journal,* 1:321n461.
67. Diyab memoir, 124v–128r; Diyab, *D'Alep à Paris,* 323–333.
68. Diyab memoir, 122v; Diyab, *D'Alep à Paris,* 320–321.
69. Diyab memoir, 122r; Diyab, *D'Alep à Paris,* 320.
70. Diyab memoir, 111v; Diyab, *D'Alep à Paris,* 299.
71. Paul Lucas, *Voyage du sieur Paul Lucas dans le Levant: Juin 1699–juillet 1703* (Saint-Étienne, France: Publications de l'Université de Saint-Étienne, 1998), 213–249.
72. Diyab memoir, 94r; Diyab, *D'Alep à Paris,* 258.
73. Diyab memoir, 95r–95v; Diyab, *D'Alep à Paris,* 261–262.
74. Diyab memoir, 96v; Diyab, *D'Alep à Paris,* 264–265.
75. Diyab memoir, 96v; Diyab, *D'Alep à Paris,* 264–265.

76. Galland, *Les mille et une nuits: Contes arabes,* 3:291.
77. Diyab memoir, 98r–99r; Diyab, *D'Alep à Paris,* 267–270; Galland, *Les mille et une nuits: Contes arabes,* 3:50–51.
78. Diyab memoir, 96r; Diyab, *D'Alep à Paris,* 263.
79. Diyab memoir, 100r–101r; Diyab, *D'Alep à Paris,* 272–273.
80. Diyab memoir, 113r–115r; Diyab, *D'Alep à Paris,* 302–305.
81. Galland, entry from May 22, 1709, *Journal,* 1:345–346.
82. Galland, *Les mille et une nuits: Contes arabes,* 3:76–77; Ursula Lyons, trans., "The Story of Aladdin, or The Magic Lamp," in *The Arabian Nights: Tales of 1001 Nights,* trans. Malcolm C. Lyons with Ursula Lyons (London: Penguin, 2008), 3:796–797. On the building of Versailles, see Diyab memoir, 100r; Diyab, *D'Alep à Paris,* 272.
83. Lyons, "The Story of Aladdin," 3:796, 806.
84. Larzul, "Further Considerations," 267–268.
85. Diyab memoir, 125v–126r; Diyab, *D'Alep à Paris,* 327.
86. "Huntington Acquires Newly Identified Portrait by Major French Artist of the 17th Century," Huntington Library, Art Collections and Botanical Garden website, May 12, 2010, http://www.huntington.org/uploadedFiles/Files/PDFs/pr_champaigne.pdf.
87. François Pétis de la Croix, *Les mille et un jours: Contes persans,* ed. Paul Debag (Paris: Bourgois, 1980); Galland, letter of June 16, 1710, translated and quoted in Larzul, "Further Considerations," 263.
88. Jean-Paul Bignon, *Les aventures d'Abdalla, fils d'Hanif* (La Haye, France, 1713); J. C. Mardrus, *Le livre des mille nuits et une nuit* (Paris: Éditions de la Revue Blanche 1899–1904). Also see Srinivas Aravamudan, *Enlightenment Orientalism: Resisting the Rise of the Novel* (Chicago: University of Chicago Press, 2012), 50–55.

2. MARVELLOUS THIEVES

1. Bernard Heyberger, introduction to Hanna Diyab, *D'Alep à Paris: Les pérégrinations d'un jeune Syrien au temps de Louis XIV,* ed. and trans. Bernard Heyberger et al. (Paris: Sinbad, 2015), 17; Johannes Stephan, "Spuren fiktionaler Vergegenwärtigung im osmanischen Aleppo: Narratologische Analysen und Kontextualisierungen des *Reisebuchs* von Hanna Dyāb (1764)" (PhD diss., Universität Bern, 2015), 17–18.
2. Hanna Diyab, untitled memoir, Biblioteca Apostolica Vaticana, Sbath.254 (hereafter Diyab memoir), 7r; Diyab, *D'Alep à Paris,* 66.
3. Diyab memoir, 7v; Diyab, *D'Alep à Paris,* 67–68.
4. Diyab memoir, 8r; Diyab, *D'Alep à Paris,* 69. Stephan argues that Diyab's story takes on the qualities of a picaresque narrative through these deceptions. See Stephan, "Spuren fiktionaler Vergegenwärtigung," 88.
5. Diyab memoir, 8v; Diyab, *D'Alep à Paris,* 69–70.
6. Diyab memoir, 10r; Diyab, *D'Alep à Paris,* 74.

7. Jean-Marie Carré, *Voyageurs et ecrivains français en Egypte* (Cairo: Institut français d'archéologie orientale, 1956), 47.
8. Diyab memoir, 9r–9v; Diyab, *D'Alep à Paris,* 72. Stephan suggests that Lucas inserted this episode into his third travelogue. See Stephan, "Spuren fiktionaler Vergegenwärtigung," 38n77.
9. Heyberger, introduction, 28–29.
10. See particularly the case of "Ali Baba and the Forty Thieves," discussed in this chapter.
11. Stephan is the only other scholar who has recognized the importance of the third travelogue in analyzing the relationship between the narratives of Diyab and Lucas. See Stephan, "Spuren fiktionaler Vergegenwärtigung," 39–40.
12. The travelogues are Paul Lucas, *Voyage du sieur Paul Lucas dans le Levant: Juin 1699–juillet 1703* (Saint-Étienne, France: Publications de l'Université de Saint-Étienne, 1998); Paul Lucas, *Deuxième voyage du sieur Paul Lucas dans le Levant: Octobre 1704–septembre 1708* (Saint-Étienne, France: Publications de l'Université de Saint-Étienne, 2002); Paul Lucas, *Troisième voyage du sieur Paul Lucas dans le Levant: Mai 1714–novembre 1717* (Saint-Étienne, France: Publications de l'Université de Saint-Étienne, 2004).
13. Carré, *Voyageurs et ecrivains,* 44. References to Lucas can be found in Christopher Drew Armstrong, "Progress in the Age of Navigation: The Voyage-Philosophique of Julien-David Leroy" (PhD diss., Columbia University, 2003); Dirk van der Cruysse, *Le noble désir de courir le monde: Voyager en Asie au XVIIe siècle* (Paris: Fayard, 2002); Olivier Salmon, *Alep dans la littérature de voyage européenne pendant la période ottoman (1516–1918)* (Aleppo: El-Mudarris, 2011). See previous note for the travelogues.
14. Several of the instructions for Lucas are preserved. "Instruction pour le sr. Paul Lucas pendant son voyage en Levant," April 1, 1704, is a seven-page document from Louis XIV to the adventurer, delineating his route and focusing on the antiquities to be procured. An undated memorandum from A. Jullien, a professor of botany at the royal garden, details Lucas's remit in the field of natural history. Several drafts show the revisions of general instructions for Lucas, in particular, Correspondance et papiers de Paul Lucas (1701–1725), NAF 801, manuscrit en français, Richelieu, Bibliothèque nationale de France (hereafter Lucas correspondence).
15. "Recherches a faire dans les Païs Étrangers," Lucas correspondence.
16. Armstrong, "Progress in the Age of Navigation," 131.
17. Jean-Paul Bignon, letter to M. Mesnard, April 8, 1725, in Henri Omont, *Missions archéologiques françaises en Orient aux 17e et 18e siècles: Documents publiés par Henri Omont* (Paris: Imprimerie Nationale, 1902), 378–379.
18. Pétis de la Croix, *Catalogue raisonné des manuscrits Orientaux afforés par le sieur Paul Lucas,* August 9, 1712, in Lucas correspondence. Bignon's letter is from September 25, 1727. See Omont, *Missions archéologiques françaises,* 380.

19. Carré, *Voyageurs et ecrivains,* 47, 58; Irini Apostolou, *L'orientalisme des voyageurs français au XVIIIe siècle: Une iconographie de l'Orient méditerranéen* (Paris: Presses de l'Université Paris-Sorbonne, 2009), 181; de Maillet quoted in Omont, *Missions archéologiques françaises,* 772.
20. See, for instance, Lucas to the Duchess of Bourgogne, November 8, 1701, Lucas correspondence.
21. Lucas presented his account to the Marquis de Ferriol, the king's extraordinary ambassador to the Ottoman port, in a document dated 1702, Lucas correspondence; Lucas to the Duchess of Bourgogne, November 8, 1701, Lucas correspondence.
22. *Mémoire de ce qui a été pris par les corsaires des envoys faits du Levant à Monseigneur le Comte de Pontchartrain par Paul Lucas,* Acquisitions patrimoniales menées par Paul Lucas (1703–1708), 2011 / 091 / ACMA01 / 030 Mitterrand 1, Bibliothèque nationale de France.
23. Lucas, *Troisième voyage,* 330.
24. Apostolou, *L'orientalisme des voyageurs français,* 372–374.
25. Carré, *Voyageurs et ecrivains,* 45–46; Lucas, *Voyage du sieur Paul Lucas dans le Levant,* 91.
26. Paul Lucas, preface to *Troisième voyage,* 19.
27. Ibid., 17–18.
28. Lucas, *Deuxième voyage,* 87–88.
29. Omont, *Missions archéologiques françaises,* 318–319n1; M. de Boze, "Éloge de M. L'Abbé Banier," *Histoire de l'Académie royale des Inscriptions et Belles Lettres* 16 (1751): 304.
30. Father Protais and his missionary brother Father Charles-François d'Orléans are credited with providing the first modern description of Thebes. On Fourmont, see Urs App, *The Birth of Orientalism* (Philadelphia: University of Pennsylvania Press, 2010), 191–197; Cecile Leung, *Étienne Fourmont (1683–1745): Oriental and Chinese Languages in Eighteenth-Century France* (Leuven, Belgium: Leuven University Press, 2002).
31. Galland, letters to Gijsbert Cuper on Lucas dated July 12, 1709, and February 20, 1714, in Mohamed Abdel-Halim, "Correspondence d'Antoine Galland" (PhD diss., Université de Paris, 1964), 602, 657.
32. Lucas, *Deuxième voyage,* 166.
33. Antoine Galland, entry for May 22, 1709, in *Le journal d'Antoine Galland, la période parisienne,* ed. Frédéric Bauden and Richard Waller (Paris: Peeters, 2011), 1:343–352.
34. Ulrich Marzolph argues that these tales are variations on common tale types. Lucas's tale is type 550, and Diyab's is a combination of type 550 and 301. Marzolph and Richard van Leeuwen, *The Arabian Nights Encyclopedia* (Santa Barbara: ABC-CLIO, 2004), 417; and Marzolph, personal communication.
35. Lucas, *Deuxième voyage,* 220.
36. Diyab memoir, 59r; Diyab, *D'Alep à Paris,* 181.
37. Diyab memoir, 59v; Diyab, *D'Alep à Paris,* 182.

38. Diyab memoir, 59v; Diyab, *D'Alep à Paris,* 182, 183–184.
39. Diyab memoir, 29v, 137r–v, 171v–172r; Diyab, *D'Alep à Paris,* 120, 354, 435.
40. Lucas, *Deuxième voyage,* 65. The translation of this excerpt is from Arthur Edward Waite, *Lives of Alchemystical Philosophers* (London: George Redway, 1888), 115–116.
41. Ibid., 66. The translation is from Waite, *Alchemystical Philosophers,* 117.
42. Ibid., 66–68.
43. Lucas, *Deuxième voyage,* 220–224; Diyab memoir, 62v–70v; Diyab, *D'Alep à Paris,* 187–202.
44. Diyab memoir, 62r–62v; Diyab *D'Alep à Paris,* 187–189.
45. Diyab memoir, 62v–63r; Diyab, *D'Alep à Paris,* 188.
46. Diyab memoir, 63v; Diyab, *D'Alep à Paris,* 190.
47. Lucas, *Deuxième voyage,* 222.
48. Diyab memoir, 64r–v; Diyab, *D'Alep à Paris,* 191–192.
49. Diyab memoir, 64v; Diyab, *D'Alep à Paris,* 192.
50. Diyab memoir, 65r; Diyab, *D'Alep à Paris,* 192–193.
51. Diyab memoir, 65v; Diyab, *D'Alep à Paris,* 194.
52. Diyab memoir, 66r–67r; Diyab, *D'Alep à Paris,* 195–196.
53. Diyab memoir, 67r; Diyab, *D'Alep à Paris,* 197.
54. Diyab memoir, 67r–68v; Diyab, *D'Alep à Paris,* 197–199.
55. The theme of judgment and punishment is one of the recurring patterns identified by Stephan in Diyab's travelogue. See Stephan, "Spuren fiktionaler Vergegenwärtigung," 187–188.
56. Documents dated September 12, 1709, and June 19, 1709, in Omont, *Missions archéologiques françaises,* 339, 342–343.
57. Diyab memoir, 68v–69r; Diyab, *D'Alep à Paris,* 200–201.
58. Diyab memoir, 171r–174r; Diyab, *D'Alep à Paris,* 433–440. Lucas, *Troisième voyage,* 101–107.
59. Diyab memoir, 171r–171v; Diyab, *D'Alep à Paris,* 434–435. On the sabotage of Galland's plan to secure Diyab a commission as a collector, see Stephan, "Spuren fiktionaler Vergegenwärtigung," 36–37.
60. Lucas, *Troisième voyage,* 101.
61. Diyab memoir, 172r; Diyab, *D'Alep à Paris,* 436.
62. Lucas, *Troisième voyage,* 101, 103–107.
63. Diyab memoir, 173r–174; Diyab, *D'Alep à Paris,* 438–440.
64. Lucas, *Troisième voyage,* 103–107.
65. Galland, entry for May 27, 1709, in *Journal,* 1:359–363.
66. Ibid.
67. Ibid.
68. Aboubakr Chraïbi, "Galland's 'Ali Baba' and Other Arabic Versions," *Marvels and Tales,* 18, no. 2 (2004): 159–169.
69. Ibid.
70. Lucas, *Deuxième voyage,* 47, 69.

71. Ibid., 74.
72. Ibid., 151.
73. *Les mille et une nuits: Contes arabes,* ed. Jean-Paul Sermain, trans. Antoine Galland (Paris: Éditions Flammarion, 2004), 3:186–190. The quotations are from the translation of Galland produced by Ursula Lyons, "Ali Baba and the Forty Thieves," in *The Arabian Nights: Tales of 1001 Nights,* trans. Malcolm C. Lyons with Ursula Lyons (London: Penguin, 2008), 1:936–938.
74. Galland, entry for May 27, 1709, in *Journal,* 1:363.
75. This English translation is from Lyons, "Ali Baba and the Forty Thieves," 1:949. The original is Galland, *Les mille et une nuits,* 3:203.
76. Lucas, *Troisième voyage,* 103–107.
77. Lucas, letter of September 25, 1715, Lucas correspondence.

3. THE EMPIRE OF ENGLISH

1. Henry Whitelock Torrens, trans., *The Book of the Thousand Nights and One Night,* from the Arabic of the Egyptian manuscript, ed. W. Hay Macnaghten (Calcutta: Thacker, St. Andrews Library; London: W. H. Allen, 1838), 445–492. The story cycle of "King 'Umar ibn al-Nu'man and His Family" also appeared in the Tübingen manuscript (dated to the fifteenth century), the Egyptian manuscript brought to Paris by Benoit de Maillet in 1702, and the Reinhardt manuscript (dated 1831–1832) brought to Strasbourg by a German diplomat. See Ulrich Marzolph and Richard van Leeuwen, *The Arabian Nights Encyclopedia* (Santa Barbara: ABC-CLIO, 2004), 434–435, 635–636.
2. Torrens, *Thousand Nights and One Night,* 457.
3. Ibid., 473.
4. Ibid., 490–491.
5. Wen-Chin Ouyang, "The Epical Turn of Romance: Love in the Narrative of 'Umar al-Nu'man," *Oriente Moderno* 19, no. 1 (2002): 490. See also Wen-Chin Ouyang, "Romancing the Epic: 'Umar al-Nu'man as Narrative of Empowerment," *Arabic and Middle Eastern Literatures* 3, no. 1 (2000): 5–18.
6. Jonathan Scott, *Arabian Nights' Entertainments* (London: Longman, Hurst, Rees, Orme, and Brown, 1811); Robert Irwin, *The Arabian Nights: A Companion* (London: Tauris, 2004), 19–22.
7. 'Abdarrahmān al-Safati al-Sharqāwī, ed., *Alf Layla wa-Layla,* 2 vols. (Cairo: Bulaq, 1835 [1251 A.H.]); W. Hay Macnaghten, ed., *The Alif Laila or Book of the Thousand Nights and One Night* (Calcutta, 1839–1842).
8. Aamir R. Mufti, *Forget English! Orientalisms and World Literatures* (Cambridge, MA: Harvard University Press, 2016), 99–130.
9. "Minute Recorded in the General Department by Thomas Babington Macaulay, Dated 2 February 1835," in Lynn Zastoupil and Martin Moir, *The Great Indian Education Debate: Documents relating to the Orientalist-Anglicist Controversy,*

1781–1843 (Richmond, UK: Curzon, 1999), 161–173. For the debate concerning colonial education policy, see Zastoupil and Moir, introduction to *The Great Indian Education Debate,* 1–80; Norbert Peabody, "Knowledge Formation in Colonial India," in *India and the British Empire,* ed. Douglas M. Peers and Nandini Gooptu (Oxford: Oxford University Press, 2013), 83–84.

10. On the complexity of writing cultures in India, see Mufti, *Forget English!,* 104–105, 121–126. Ronald Inden argues that India is defined in terms of a number of reinforcing "essences": caste, Hinduism, sacred kingship, and idyllic village communities. See Ronald Inden, *Imagining India* (Oxford: Basil Blackwell, 1990).
11. James Hume, "Biographical Memoir," in *A Selection from the Writings, Prose and Poetical of the Late Henry W. Torrens,* ed. James Hume (London: R. C. Lepage, 1854), 1:viii–ix.
12. Ibid., 1:iv.
13. John Kaye, *History of the War in Afghanistan* (London: W. H. Allen, 1874), 314.
14. Hume, "Biographical Memoir," xcix. Lord Auckland (George Eden) was joined in India by his two unmarried sisters, Fanny and Emily Eden.
15. W. F. B. Laurie, *Sketches of Some Distinguished Anglo-Indians* (London: W. H. Allen, 1887), 312–313.
16. Hume, "Biographical Memoir," i–cxiii. For biographical information on Hume, see Gary Simons, "The Squab and the Idler: A Cosmopolitan-Colonial Dialogue in the *Calcutta Star* between William Thackeray and James Hume," *Victorian Literature and Culture* 42 (2014): 388–390.
17. Torrens quoted in Hume, "Biographical Memoir," xv–xvi.
18. Torrens quoted in ibid.
19. Torrens quoted in ibid., xix.
20. Hume, "Biographical Memoir," xix, xx.
21. Ibid., lxvii; Henry Whitelock Torrens [and Henry Miers Elliot], "Polyglot Baby's Own Book" and Henry Whitelock Torrens, "An Essay on the Jungle Poetics," in *Selection from the Writings,* 1:3–22, 238–248.
22. On Meerut, see Hume, "Biographical Memoir," cx. The information regarding Torrens's membership in various lodges comes from the Freemason Library and Archive in London, Annual Returns Anchor and Good Hope Lodge Calcutta (no. 284), 1833–1844, Box C8, AS B 4 1/6, Document 284 Calcutta, and Initiations and Certificates, 6.2.6, June 8, 1841; Annual Returns St. John's Lodge (no. 715), 1833–1844, Box C19, AS B 4 1/7; Annual Returns Lodge Hope, Meerut (no. 596), 1833–1840s, Box C16, AS B 4 1/6.
23. Jessica Harland-Jacobs, *Builders of Empire: Freemasons and British Imperialism, 1717–1927* (Chapel Hill: University of North Carolina Press, 2007), 174. The Earl of Moira (later the Marquess of Hastings) had served a twenty-three-year term as English grand master before he was posted to India. Ibid., 4–5, 171–175.

24. Walter K. Firminger, *The Early History of Freemasonry in Bengal and the Punjab; with Which Is Incorporated "The Early History of Freemasonry in Bengal" by Andrew D'Cruz* (Calcutta: Thacker, Spink, 1906), 231–232.
25. Henry Whitelock Torrens, "Masonry," in *Selection from the Writings,* 1:182. Also see Henry Whitelock Torrens, "A Welcome: To the R. W. Br. Burnes, K. H." and "A Bumper of Claret," in *Selection from the Writings,* 1:181–182, 183.
26. Harland-Jacobs, *Builders of Empire,* 220–232.
27. *Masonic Lyrics/Inscribed with Fraternal Regard to the Free-Masons of India by Brother W. H. Hamerton* (1840), Library and Museum of Freemasonry, London. Torrens's verse is reprinted as the poem "A Welcome," in *Selection from the Writings,* 1:181–182.
28. Harland-Jacobs, *Builders of Empire,* 222.
29. Ibid., 222–223; Torrens, "A Welcome," 181–182; *Freemason Quarterly Review,* March 1841, 116.
30. Henry Whitelock Torrens, "Tableaux from the Talisman" and "Tableaux from Ivanhoe," in *Selection from the Writings,* 1:177–181, 261–262; Emily Eden, journal entry from May 31, 1839, in *Up the Country* (London: Richard Bentley, 1867), 509–510.
31. Henry Whitelock Torrens, trans. "The Sharing of the Earth," "Pegasus at the Plough," "Poetry of Life," "The Play of Life," and "Hope," in *Selection from the Writings,* 1:229–230, 231–233, 234–235, 235–236, 237–238.
32. Torrens, "Hope," 1:238.
33. Henry Whitelock Torrens, trans. "The Robber's Song," in *Selection from the Writings,* 1:236–237. Quotation from Henry Whitelock Torrens, "The Witches of Shakespeare and of Schiller," in *Selection from the Writings,* 1:219.
34. Henry Whitelock Torrens, introduction to *Orlando Innamorato,* by Matteo Maria Boiardo, trans. Henry Whitelock Torrens, in *Selection from the Writings,* 1:28–30.
35. Ibid., 30–33.
36. Henry Whitelock Torrens, "The New Histriomastix," in *Selection from the Writings,* 2:206.
37. Henry Whitelock Torrens, *Madame de Malguet: A Tale of 1820* (London: Longman, Brown, Green, and Longmans, 1848); "New Translations of the Arabian Nights," *London and Westminster Review* 33 (October 1839): 69n.
38. Hume, "Biographical Memoir," xcix.
39. Ibid., cv.
40. Emily Eden, *Letters from India* (London: Richard Bentley and Son, 1872), 1:319.
41. Eden, *Up the Country,* 111.
42. Torrens appears as Mr. C in Emily Eden's journal. See Eden, *Up the Country,* 152, 280, 294, 308, 323, 470, 521, 579.
43. Charles Brownlow, letter to the Asiatic Society of Bengal dated September 5, 1836, *Journal of the Asiatic Society of Bengal* 5 (1836): 514.

44. Muhsin Mahdi, *The Thousand and One Nights* (Leiden, Netherlands: Brill, 1995), 101–106; John Payne, *The Book of the Thousand Nights and One Night* (London: Printed for the Villon Society by private subscription and for private circulation only, 1882–1884); Richard Francis Burton, *The Book of the Thousand Nights and a Night* (London: Privately circulated by the Burton Club, 1885); Malcolm C. Lyons with Ursula Lyons, trans., *The Arabian Nights: Tales of 1001 Nights* (London: Penguin, 2008).
45. Mufti, *Forget English!*, 100–130; David Kopf, *British Orientalism and the Bengal Renaissance* (Berkeley: University of California Press, 1969), 45–94.
46. O. P. Kejariwal, *The Asiatic Society of Bengal and the Discovery of India's Past, 1784–1838* (Delhi: Oxford University Press, 1988), 162–220; Hume, "Biographical Memoir," lv–lvi.
47. Zastoupil and Moir, introduction, 25–31; C. A. Bayly, *Empire and Information: Intelligence Gathering and Social Communication in India, 1780–1870* (Cambridge: Cambridge University Press, 1997), 215–220.
48. "Minute Recorded by Thomas Babington Macaulay," 161–173; W. C. Bentinck, "Resolution of the Governor-General of India in Council in the General Department, Dated 7 March 1835," in Zastoupil and Moir, *The Great Indian Education Debate*, 194–196.
49. W. H. Macnaghten, minute from March 24, 1835, quoted in Kopf, *British Orientalism*, 250–251.
50. Torrens [and Elliot], "Polyglot Baby's Own Book," 3–22.
51. Hume, "Biographical Memoir," civ.
52. Ibid., viii.
53. James Prinsep, "Preface," *Journal of the Asiatic Society of Bengal* 4 (1835): vii–viii.
54. "Minute Recorded by Thomas Babington Macaulay," 165.
55. James Prinsep, "Preface," *Journal of the Asiatic Society of Bengal* 4 (1835): vii–viii.
56. Mahdi, *The Thousand and One Nights*, 101–126.
57. Ibid.
58. Charles Brownlow, letter to the Asiatic Society of Bengal dated September 5, 1836, 514–516.
59. Also on the committee were Dr. Mill, a Unitarian preacher and professor of Oriental languages, and John Russell Colvin, private secretary to the governor-general. Report of the Committee of Papers on Alif Laila, *Journal of the Asiatic Society of Bengal* 5 (1836): 589–599.
60. Emily Eden, *Miss Eden's Letters*, ed. Violet Dickinson (London: Macmillan, 1919), 299.
61. Trotter, on behalf of the Chamber of the Council of Directors, to I. H. Harington, President and Members of the Council of the College of Fort William, March 8, 1817, India Records Office Collection, British Library.
62. Report of the Committee of Papers on Alif Laila, 589–599.
63. Ibid., 590–596.

64. Ibid., 596.
65. Ibid., 599.
66. James Prinsep, Secretary of the Asiatic Society, to H. T. Prinsep, Secretary of Government, India, October 7, 1836, and H. T. Prinsep to James Prinsep, November 2, 1836, both in Public Department Collection 11 #32, 12567, Draft 556–1039, British Library, Bengal (hereafter Public Department Collection).
67. Bengal Public Letter #14, July 5, 1837, Public Department Collection.
68. As noted retrospectively in an extract from Bengal Public Letter #5, April 4, 1839, Public Department Collection. The public letter specifies that the forty copies had been disbursed along with a letter to Secretary Melville dated November 28, 1838.
69. Ulrich Marzolph, "The Persian Nights: Links between the *Arabian Nights* and Iranian Culture," *The Arabian Nights in Transnational Perspective,* ed. Ulrich Marzolph (Detroit: Wayne State University Press), 221–244.
70. Gauri Viswanathan, *Masks of Conquest: Literary Study and British Rule in India* (New York: Columbia University Press, 1989); Mufti, *Forget English!*
71. H. T. Prinsep also makes it clear that Macnaghten would be using the *maulavis* of the Persian office to complete this work. Report of the Committee of Papers on Alif Laila, 596–597.
72. Torrens, *Thousand Nights and One Night,* iii. On Jones, see Mufti, *Forget English!,* 67–72.
73. Henry Whitelock Torrens, "Remarks on M. Schlegel's Objections to the Restored Editions of the Alif Leilah," originally printed in *Journal of the Asiatic Society of Bengal* 6 (March 1837): 161–168; reprinted in *Asiatic Journal and Monthly Register,* 2nd ser., vol. 25 (1838): 72–77. Citations refer to the 1838 reprint. Schlegel quoted on p. 72.
74. Torrens, "Remarks on M. Schlegel's Objections," 72–74.
75. Ibid., 75–76.
76. Ibid., 75–76.
77. Ibid., 72, 77.
78. David Pinault, "Bûlâq, Macnaghten, and the New Leiden Edition Compared: Notes on Storytelling Technique from the *Thousand and One Nights,*" *Journal of Semitic Studies* 32 (1987): 125–157.
79. Torrens, *Thousand Nights and One Night,* 213.
80. Ibid., 226.
81. Ibid., iii.
82. Ibid., ii, vi. Lane quoted by Torrens on p. vi.
83. Ibid., v, viii.
84. Ibid., 184. Compare to Lyons and Lyons's translation:

> They said to me: "Among mankind
> You with your wisdom are a moonlit night."
> I said: "Do not say this to me;
> There is no wisdom without power." (Lyons and Lyons, *Arabian Nights,* 1:123)

85. Torrens, *Thousand Nights and One Night,* 185–187. Compare to Lyons and Lyons's translation: "By the truth of the One God Who raised up the heavens and spread out the earth, it was I who killed her" (Lyons and Lyons, *Arabian Nights,* 1:125).
86. Torrens, *Thousand Nights and One Night,* 191.
87. Ibid., xx, n92.
88. Ibid., 74–75, 45–51.
89. Ibid., 50; "New Translations of the Arabian Nights," 67–68.
90. Richard Francis Burton, "Translator's Preface," in *The Book of the Thousand Nights and a Night,* 1:xiv.
91. "New Translations of the Arabian Nights," 66.
92. Torrens, *Thousand Nights and One Night,* 66; "*The Arabian Nights' Entertainments,*" *Dublin Review* 8 (February 1840): 122.
93. See Torrens's satire, "An Essay on the Jungle Poetics," in *Selection from the Writings,* 1:238–249.
94. "New Translations of the Arabian Nights," 69.
95. Torrens, *Thousand Nights and One Night,* iii.
96. Ibid., 74.
97. Ibid., 81.
98. Ibid., 91.
99. Ibid., 82.
100. Ibid., 85.
101. Torrens, "The New Histriomastix," 206.
102. "New Translations of the Arabian Nights," 69.
103. Torrens, *Thousand Nights and One Night,* vii–viii.
104. Ibid., ii–iii.
105. Ibid., xlvi, n236.
106. This story is told in a series of historical works. See, for example, William Dalrymple, *Return of a King: The Battle for Afghanistan* (London: Bloomsbury, 2013).
107. Ibid., 347–354.
108. Kaye, *History of the War in Afghanistan,* 312–316, 352–353, 494–497.
109. Henry Whitelock Torrens, "Idle Days in Egypt," in *Selection from the Writings,* 2:359–366.
110. Ibid., 372–373.
111. Ibid., 382–385.

4. THE MAGICIAN'S INTERPRETER

1. Stanley Lane-Poole, "Lane: Biographical Sketch," in Edward William Lane, *An Arabic-English Lexicon* (London: Williams and Nortgate, 1863), xiii.
2. Edward Said, *Orientalism* (New York: Penguin, 2003), 162.

3. Lane writes casually of crossing Bahr Yussef canal "on the back of an Arab who waded through the stream." Diary from Lane's first trip to Egypt (1825–1828), MS 1.1.2, fol. 36, Edward William Lane Collection, Griffith Institute, Ashmolean Museum, University of Oxford (hereafter Lane Collection).
4. Jason Thompson, *Edward William Lane, 1801–1876: The Life of the Pioneering Egyptologist and Orientalist* (Cairo: American University of Cairo Press, 2010), 12–16.
5. Maya Jasanoff, *Edge of Empire: Lives, Culture, and Conquest in the East, 1750–1850* (New York: Vintage, 2005), 269; Edward William Lane, manuscript draft of "Description of Egypt," MS 6.1, fol. 2, Lane Collection, quoted in Jason Thompson, "Edward William Lane's 'Description of Egypt,'" *International Journal of Middle East Studies* 28 (1996): 566.
6. Jasanoff, *Edge of Empire,* 287–299; Jason Thompson, *Sir Gardner Wilkinson and His Circle* (Austin: University of Texas Press, 1992); Selwyn Tillett, *Egypt Itself: The Career of Robert Hay, Esquire, of Linplum and Nunraw, 1799–1863* (London: SD Books, 1984), 13–89.
7. Thompson, *Edward William Lane,* 91–93; Thompson, "Lane's 'Description of Egypt,'" 567–569.
8. Thompson, "Lane's 'Description of Egypt,'" 567–569.
9. Mary Fischer Gainsborough was entrusted to the care of Lane's mother due to mental illness. See Thompson, *Edward William Lane,* 10–11, 22–23.
10. Thompson, *Edward William Lane,* 284–288; Valerie Gray, *Charles Knight: Educator, Publisher, Writer* (Aldershot, UK: Ashgate, 2006), 46–68.
11. Lane, manuscript draft of "Description of Egypt," quoted in Jason Thompson, "Editor's Introduction," in Edward William Lane, *Description of Egypt,* ed. Jason Thompson (Cairo: American University in Cairo Press, 2000), x.
12. John Gardner Wilkinson, *Topography of Thebes, and General View of Egypt* (London: John Murray, 1835), 568; Anne Katherine Elwood, *Narrative of a Journey Overland from England* (London: Colburn and Bentley, 1830), 1:137–164; Thompson, *Edward William Lane,* 44–52.
13. Jason Thompson, "Osman Effendi: A Scottish Convert to Islam in Early Nineteenth-Century Egypt," *Journal of World History* 5, no. 1 (Spring 1994): 99–123; Westcar diary entry from June 25, 1824, quoted in ibid., 109.
14. Robert Hay diary typescript, pp. 31–33, Archives of the Griffith Institute, Ashmolean Museum, University of Oxford.
15. Thompson, *Edward William Lane,* 237–240 and inserted plates.
16. Leila Ahmed, *Edward W. Lane: A Study of His Life and Works and of British Ideas of the Middle East in the Nineteenth Century* (New York: Longman, 1978), 95–96. See also Timothy Mitchell, *Colonising Egypt* (Berkeley: University of California Press, 1988), 27; Rana Kabbani, *Imperial Fictions: Europe's Myths of Orient* (London: Pandora, 1994).

17. Robert Irwin, "Life! Life!," review of *The Arabian Diaries, 1913–1914,* by Gertrude Bell, ed. Rosemary O'Brien, *Times Literary Supplement* (London, England), July 27, 2001, 4.
18. Fulgence Fresnel to Lane [on Osman's death], November 13, 1835, MSS 5.1.16, Lane Collection.
19. Thompson, "Osman Effendi," 99–123; Alexander William Kinglake, *Eothen: Traces of Travel Brought Home from the East,* introduction by Barbara Krieger (Evanston, IL: Northwestern University Press, 1992), 161.
20. Katharine Sim, *Desert Traveller: The Life of Jean Louis Burckhardt* (London: Gollancz, 1969), 413; Thompson, "Osman Effendi," 103; Deborah Manley and Peta Ree, *Henry Salt: Artist, Traveller, Diplomat, Egyptologist* (London: Libri, 2001), 182.
21. Thompson, "Osman Effendi," 104; John Gardner Wilkinson, *Modern Egypt and Thebes: Being a Description of Egypt, including Information Required for Travelers in That Country* (London: John Murray, 1843), 1:204; quotation from James Augustus St. John, *Egypt and Mohammed Ali; or Travels in the Valley of the Nile* (London: Longman, Rees, Orme, Brown, Green, and Longman, 1834), 2:187–188.
22. James Silk Buckingham, *Autobiography of James Silk Buckingham* (London: Longman, Brown, Green, and Longmans, 1855), 2:291.
23. Kinglake, *Eothen,* 160–162; John Carne, *Recollections of Travels in the East: Forming a Continuation of the Letters from the East* (London, 1830), 325–331; William Holt Yates, *The Modern History and Condition of Egypt: Its Climate, Diseases, and Capabilities; . . . with an Account of the Proceedings of Mohammed Ali Pascha, from 1801–1843* (London, 1843), 1:285–293.
24. Sim, *Desert Traveller,* 328.
25. Buckingham, *Autobiography,* 2:296.
26. Fresnel to Lane, November 13, 1835, MSS 5.1.16, Lane Collection.
27. "Memoir of the Late Rev. C. Burckhardt," *Christian Herald and Seaman's Magazine* 7 (1820): 451. In her biography of Burckhardt, Katharine Sim takes seriously the idea that he had truly accepted "the principles of the Muslim religion." See Sim, *Desert Traveller,* 257–258.
28. Thompson, *Edward William Lane,* 328, 311.
29. Lane to Hay, October 15, 1842, Department of Western Manuscripts, Bodleian Library, Oxford University, MS Eng. lett. d. 165 (hereafter Hay correspondence).
30. Edward William Lane, *An Account of the Manners and Customs of the Modern Egyptians* (London: John Murray, 1860), xv; Edward William Lane, trans., *The Thousand and One Nights* (London: C. Knight, 1839), 1:17n1; Ibrāhīm al-Dasūqī, "Essay," in Ali Mubarak, *al-Khitat al-Tawfiqiyya al-jadida* (Cairo: Bulaq, 1887–1888), 12.
31. Lane, *Modern Egyptians,* 263.
32. In particular in the notebooks pertaining to *Modern Egyptians:* MSS 4.1, 4.2, 4.3, 4.4, 4.5, and 4.6, Lane Collection.

33. Sophia Lane Poole, *The Englishwoman in Egypt: Letters from Cairo, Written during a Residence There in 1842, 3 & 4 with E. W. Lane,* 5th ed. (London: Charles Knight, 1844), 1:199–205; al-Dasūqī, "Essay," 12.
34. Thompson, *Edward William Lane,* 53–59, 78, 83–85; al-Dasūqī, "Essay," 12.
35. Quoted in Jason Thompson, "Small Latin and Less Greek: Expurgated Passages from Edward William Lane's *An Account of the Manners and Customs of the Modern Egyptians," Quaderni di Studi Arabi,* n.s., 1 (2006): 7–28.
36. "Many of their communications I have written in Arabic, at their dictation, and since translated, and inserted in the following pages." Edward William Lane, "Author's Preface," in *Modern Egyptians,* xx.
37. Said, *Orientalism,* 157–167.
38. Lane, *Modern Egyptians,* 267.
39. John Gardner Wilkinson, *A Handbook for Travellers in Egypt* (London: John Murray, 1867), 138–141; Lane, *Modern Egyptians,* 274.
40. Lane, *Modern Egyptians,* 268–269.
41. Ibid., 270–271.
42. Annotations in Burton's copy of Ja'far Sharif, *Qanoon-e-Islam; or, The customs of the Mussulmans of India,* trans. G. A. Herklots, 2nd ed. (Madras, India: J. Higginbotham, 1863), Kirkpatrick 1998, Richard Francis Burton Library, Manuscript Collection, Huntington Library, San Marino, CA.
43. Lane, *Modern Egyptians,* 270–271.
44. Ibid., 271–272.
45. Ursula Lyons, trans., "The Story of Aladdin, or The Magic Lamp," in *The Arabian Nights: Tales of 1001 Nights,* trans. Malcolm C. Lyons with Ursula Lyons (London: Penguin, 2008), 3:745.
46. See discussion of Burton in Chapter 7.
47. Review of *The Manners and Customs of the Modern Egyptians,* by Edward Lane, *Quarterly Review* 59 (1837): 165–203; "Note on Egyptian Magic," *Quarterly Review* 59 (1837): 203–208.
48. George Nugent-Grenville, or Baron Nugent of Carlanstown, was a British politician and traveller. His report concerning the magician is in George Nugent-Grenville, *Lands, Classical and Sacred* (London: Charles Knight, 1846), 1:133–141.
49. Lane, *Modern Egyptians,* 273n1.
50. MS 4.2.36r–40r, Lane Collection.
51. MS 4.2.39r, Lane Collection.
52. Ibid., 4.2.40r.
53. "I afterwards placed myself before him, & putting my left hand to my breast, said—'Was it thus the person whom you saw was standing, or'—putting my right hand to my breast—'was it in this attitude?'—He answered that it was in the latter attitude. This made his description perfect: but when I told him that he had said first that it was the left arm which was raised, to the breast, & afterwards that the

attitude was the same as that which I assumed when I raised my right arm, he seemed to be afraid of being blamed for making a mistake, & again said that it was the left." Ibid.

54. Lane, *Modern Egyptians*, 275n1. Emphasis in the original. Lane's sister, Sophia Lane-Poole, claimed that he finally understood that he had been duped by Osman, but she is not a trustworthy source on the subject. See discussion in Chapter 5.
55. See discussion in Chapter 3.
56. Thompson, *Edward William Lane*, 242–250, 255–261.
57. Manuscript of *Thousand and One Nights* translation, 6.2.13r–14r, Lane Collection.
58. Ibid., MS 6.2.14r–15r.
59. Ibid., MS 6.2.16r–18r.
60. Ibid., MS 6.2.15v.
61. Ibid., MS 6.2.15v–16v.
62. Lane, *Nights* (1839), 1:viii–ix; Lane's original preface is only excerpted in later editions of the translation. For comparison see Edward Stanley Poole, "Editor's Preface," in Edward William Lane, trans., *The Thousand and One Nights, Commonly Called, in England, the Arabian Nights' Entertainments*, ed. Edward Stanley Poole (London: Routledge, Warne, and Routledge, 1865), 1:ix–x.
63. Lane to Hay, January 15, 1838, Hay correspondence.
64. See discussion of Lane's difficulty following humor in Chapter 5.
65. Svetlana Kirillina, "Arab Scholars from the Ottoman Empire in Russian Universities in the Nineteenth and Early Twentieth Centuries," in *Frontiers of Ottoman Studies: State, Province, and the West*, ed. Colin Imbe, Keiko Kiyotaki, and Rhoads Murphey (London: I. B. Tauris, 2005), 2:166–172.
66. Lane's original preface, quoted in Poole, "Editor's Preface," 1:xii.
67. Lane's annotated copy of the Arabic tales is ʿAbdarrahmān al-Safati al-Sharqāwī, ed., *Alf Layla wa-Layla*, 2 vols. (Cairo: Bulaq, 1835 [1251 A.H.]), Adv. B. 88, 78, 79, Rare Books, Cambridge University Library. Tantawi's colophon appears on 2:620. The translations and analysis of al-Tantawi's comments were provided by Krisztina Szilagyi.
68. Manuscript of *Thousand and One Nights* translation, MS 6.2.9v, Lane Collection.
69. Lane quoted in Poole, "Editor's Preface," 1:xiii.
70. Edward William Lane, "Review," in *The Thousand and One Nights, Commonly Called, in England, the Arabian Nights' Entertainments*, trans. Edward William Lane (London: C. Knight, 1841), 3:745.
71. Lane, *Nights* (1839), 1:82, 1:82–83.
72. Tarek Shamma assumes that Lane deliberately sought to replicate the syntax, rhythms, and colloquial expressions of the Arabic of his Bulaq edition for a foreign-sounding effect. Tarek Shamma, "Translation and the Manipulation of Difference: Translating Arabic Literature in Nineteenth-Century England" (PhD diss., Binghamton University, 2006). Yet the comparison between Lane's polished

draft and his rushed versions for print suggests necessity rather than design was at play.

73. Thompson, *Edward William Lane,* 401.
74. Leigh Hunt, "Review of Lane's *Arabian Nights' Entertainments,*" *London and Westminster Review* 33, no. 1 (October 1839): 112.
75. Edward William Lane, trans., *The Thousand and One Nights, Commonly Called, in England, the Arabian Nights' Entertainments* (London: Charles Knight, 1840), 2:148.
76. Edward William Lane, "On Polygamy, &c.," in ibid., 2:234n84. Emphasis in original.
77. "Tale of King 'Umar ibn al-Nu'mân and His Sons Sharrkân and Daw' al-Makân," in *The Arabian Nights Encyclopedia,* ed. Ulrich Marzolph and Richard van Leeuwen (Santa Barbara: ABC-CLIO, 2004), 430–436.
78. Lane, *Nights* (1839), 1:604n1.
79. Ibid., 1:65–70n15.
80. Ibid.
81. Ibid., 1:67–68n15.
82. Note on magic in ibid, 1:65–70n15; note on the jinn in ibid., 1:29–38n21.
83. Ibid., 1:69–70n15.
84. Ibid., 1:69n15.
85. Ibid., 1:xvii.
86. Ibid., 1:xxi; Kazue Kobayashi, "The Evolution of the *Arabian Nights* Illustrations: An Art Historical Review," in *The Arabian Nights and Orientalism: Perspectives from East and West,* ed. Yuriko Yamanaka and Tetsuo Nishio (London: I. B. Tauris, 2006), 171–193; Marina Warner, "'The Reality Bodily before Us': Picturing the *Arabian Nights,*" in *Fictions of Art History,* ed. Mark Ledbury (New Haven, CT: Yale University Press, 2013), 154–155.
87. Lane, "Translator's Preface," in Lane, *Nights* (1839), 1:xxi; Percy Muir, *Victorian Illustrated Books* (London: B. T. Batsford, 1971), 5–7, 28–33; Robert Irwin, *Visions of the Jinn: Illustrators of the Arabian Nights* (Oxford: Oxford University Press, 2010), 61–65.
88. Eva-Maria Troelenberg, "Drawing Knowledge, (Re-)Constructing History: Pascal Coste in Egypt," *International Journal of Islamic Architecture* 4 (2015): 287–313; Caroline Williams, "Nineteenth-Century Images of Cairo: From the Real to the Interpretive," in *Making Cairo Medieval,* ed. Nezar AlSayyad, Irene A. Bierman, and Nasser Rabbat (Oxford: Lexington Books, 2005), 97–99; Pascal-Xavier Coste, *Architecture arabe ou monuments du Kaire: Mesurés et dessinés, de 1818 à 1825* (Paris: Firmin Didot, 1839). Hay's book of illustrations finally appeared in November 1840, a beautifully produced volume that no one bought. See Robert Hay, J. C. Bourne, and Owen B. Carter, *Illustrations of Cairo* (London: Tilt and Bogue, 1840).

89. Frontispiece to Galland's *Thousand and One Nights* in Irwin, *Visions of the Jinn,* 14; illustration to "Qamar al-Zaman" in Lane, *Nights* (1840), 2:94.
90. Lane, *Nights* (1840), 2:612, 634n5.
91. On the Great Mosque of Cordoba, see Irwin, *Visions of the Jinn,* 65; the image is in Lane, *Nights* (1840), 2:120. On the Great Mosque of Cairo, see Warner, "The Reality," 155; the image is in Lane, *Nights* (1841), 3:123. For pyramids, see Lane, *Nights* (1865), 1:232.
92. Review of *The Arabian Nights' Entertainments: With Copious Notes by E. W. Lane, Athenaeum* 572 (October 13, 1838): 737.
93. "*The Arabian Nights' Entertainments,*" *Dublin Review* 8 (February 1840): 127.
94. Ibid., 126–127.
95. "New Translations of the Arabian Nights," *London and Westminster Review* 33 (October 1839): 114.
96. Review of *The Arabian Nights' Entertainments: With Copious Notes by E. W. Lane,* 739.
97. Robert Irwin, *The Arabian Nights: A Companion* (London: Tauris, 2004), 24.
98. "New Translations of the Arabian Nights," 113; Lane, *Nights* (1841), 3:746.
99. al-Dasūqī, "Essay," 10–12; Ahmad Amin, "Al-Shaikh al-Dasuqi and Mr. Lane," in *Faid al-Khatir* (Cairo: Maktabat al-nahdah al-misriyah, 1965), 39–50; Paulo Lemos Horta, "Heterotopia as a Site of Cross-Cultural Collaboration: Ibrāhīm Al-Dusūqī and Edward Lane," *Middle Eastern Literatures* 15, no. 3 (2012): 273–285; al-Dasūqī to Lane, December 21, 1849, and January 1850, MS 5.1, Lane Collection.
100. Lane to Lord Prudhoe, July 22, 1843, Add. 8843/1/5, Cambridge University Library, Department of Manuscripts and Rare Books, Additional Manuscripts. Algernon Percy, Lord Prudhoe, became the Duke of Northumberland in 1847. He was a traveller, antiquarian, conservative politician, and trustee of the British Museum.
101. Lane to Hay, May 5, 1840, fols. 113–114, Hay correspondence.
102. On the Thebes project, see Thompson, "Lane's 'Description of Egypt,'" 572. Lane's other translation from these years, *Selections from the Kur-an,* was a barely concealed theft of a translation by George Sale from 1734. Lane's major contribution to reshaping the text was to insert Sale's notes directly into the translated verses of the Quran. The result was a largely indigestible version of this sacred text that shows little sensitivity to the quality of the original. See Edward William Lane, *Selections from the Kur-an, Commonly Called in England, the Koran: With an Interwoven Commentary: Translated from the Arabic, Methodically Arranged, and Illustrated by Notes, Chiefly from Sale's Edition: To Which Is Prefixed an Introduction Taken from Sale's Preliminary Discourse, with Corrections and Additions* (London: James Madden, 1843). For a discussion of this work see Ahmed, *Edward W. Lane,* 178–189.
103. Diary from Lane's first trip to Egypt (1825–1828), MS 1.1.7, Lane Collection.

5. THE WILES OF WOMEN

1. Edward William Lane, *An Account of the Manners and Customs of the Modern Egyptians, Written in Egypt during the Years 1833, -34, -35, Partly from Notes Made in a Former Visit to That Country, 1825, -26, -27, -28,* 5th ed. (London: John Murray, 1860), 296.
2. "The Translator's Advertisement [March 1838]," *Bent's Literary Advertiser and Register of Engravings, Works on the Fine Arts, Etc., from January to December, 1838* (London: Robert Bent, 1838).
3. Manuscript of *Thousand and One Nights* translation, MS 6.2.1r–4r, Edward William Lane Collection, Griffith Institute, Ashmolean Museum, University of Oxford (hereafter Lane Collection).
4. Ibid., MS 6.2.5r–7r, and note on 6v. Burton would also prefer the higher number, as for him it heightened the satirical force of what he took to be a comic scene.
5. Ibid., MS 6.2.7r (poem), 2v–3v (note on the "wickedness of women").
6. Edward William Lane, trans., *The Thousand and One Nights* (London: C. Knight, 1839), 1:6, 1:8, 1:xvii; Jorge Luis Borges, "The Translators of the 1001 Nights," in *Selected Non-fictions,* trans. Suzanne Jill Levine et al. (New York: Viking, 1999), 92–109.
7. Lane, *Nights* (1839), 38–39n27.
8. On Charles Knight, see Chapter 4.
9. Edward Said, *Orientalism* (New York: Penguin, 2003), in particular 160–173; Katharine Sim, *Desert Traveller: The Life of Jean Louis Burckhardt* (London: Sterling, 2001), 413.
10. Lane, *Modern Egyptians,* 155.
11. Ibid., 295.
12. Diary from Lane's second trip to Egypt (1833–1835), MS 1.21.27–28, Lane Collection.
13. See Robert Hay diary typescript, 1827, Archives of the Griffith Institute, Ashmolean Museum, University of Oxford. Kalitza is discussed in Jason Thompson, *Edward William Lane, 1801–1876: The Life of the Pioneering Egyptologist and Orientalist* (Cairo: American University in Cairo Press, 2010), 114, 167, 176, 224–234.
14. Hay's letter to Lane is not extant. This information is from a letter from Lane to Hay, January 30, 1832, Department of Western Manuscripts, Bodleian Library, Oxford University, MS Eng. lett. d. 165 (hereafter Hay correspondence). Lane, *Modern Egyptians,* 185.
15. Lane to Hay, January 30, 1832, Hay correspondence.
16. Thompson, *Edward William Lane,* 323–324. Thompson makes this argument based on the experience of Alexander Kinglake. See Alexander William

Kinglake, *Eothen: Traces of Travel Brought Home from the East,* introduction by Barbara Krieger (Evanston, IL: Northwestern University Press, 1992), 161.

17. Lane claims differently in his preface to *Modern Egyptians,* but this does not conform to other evidence. See Lane *Modern Egyptians,* xv.
18. Edward William Lane, trans., *The Thousand and One Nights, Commonly Called, in England, the Arabian Nights' Entertainments* (London: Charles Knight, 1840), 2:70n4.
19. Ibid., 2:70–71n4.
20. Ibid., 2:72.
21. Lane, *Modern Egyptians,* xvi–xix.
22. Lane, *Nights* (1840), 2:72.
23. Lane, *Nights* (1839), 1:608–609n18.
24. Lane, *Modern Egyptians,* 206.
25. Rifa'a Rafi' al-Tahtawi, *Imam in Paris: Account of a Stay in France by an Egyptian Cleric (1826–1831),* trans. Daniel L. Newman (London: Saqi, 2004). Al-Tahtawi's understanding of the challenge of translating between French and Arabic is discussed in Shaden M. Tageldin, *Disarming Words: Empire and the Seduction of Translation in Egypt* (Berkeley: University of California Press, 2011), 108–151.
26. Lane, *Nights* (1840), 2:72.
27. Quran 56:78, quoted in Lane, *Modern Egyptians,* xix.
28. Lane, *Modern Egyptians,* xix.
29. Diary from Lane's second trip to Egypt (1833–1835), MS 1.21.5, Lane Collection; Lane, *Modern Egyptians,* 181.
30. Lane, *Nights* (1839), 1:38n27.
31. Lane, *Modern Egyptians,* 179–182, 295–297, 118–119.
32. Ibid., 299n3.
33. Ibid., 181, 295.
34. Ibid., xviii.
35. Ibid., 186–187, 177.
36. Edward William Lane, watercolour, MS 3.6.1, Sackler Library, Bodleian Libraries, Oxford University; "Garden of Shariyar's Palace," Lane, *Nights* (1839): 1:6; "The Porter and Ladies Carousing," Lane, *Nights* (1839): 1:140–141; Edward William Lane, *Description of Egypt,* ed. Jason Thompson (Cairo: American University in Cairo Press, 2000), fig. 18; Edward William Lane, *An Account of the Manners and Customs of the Modern Egyptians* (London: C. Knight, 1836), 47–55.
37. Lane, *Modern Egyptians,* xxi.
38. Ibid., 296–301.
39. 'Abdarrahmān al-Safati al-Sharqāwī, ed., *Alf Layla wa-Layla,* 2 vols. (Cairo: Bulaq, 1835 [1251 A.H.]); (Lane, *Nights* (1839), 1:11–12; Thompson, *Edward William Lane,* 407.
40. Lane, *Nights* (1839), 1:xvii.
41. Ibid., 1:428n54.

42. Ibid., 1:214–227n22.
43. Thompson, *Edward William Lane*, 295.
44. Lane, *Nights* (1839), 1:319n39.
45. Ibid., 1:28–29n19.
46. Ibid., 1:617n65.
47. Ibid., 1:125n20.
48. Ibid., 1:226–227n22, 1:227n22.
49. Krisztina Szilagyi observes that Lane's "Sheikh," al-Tantawi, does not provide his usual density of comments for these pages dealing with "The Porter and the Three Ladies of Baghdad." Perhaps he is as uncomfortable as Lane with the erotic context in this story cycle. Personal communication, November 4, 2015.
50. Lane, *Nights* (1839), 1:232n59.
51. Ibid., 1:249n94.
52. Edward William Lane, trans., *The Thousand and One Nights, Commonly Called, in England, the Arabian Nights' Entertainments* (London: C. Knight, 1841), 3:158–159n51.
53. Ibid.
54. Ibid., 3:166n51, 173n51, 160n51.
55. Ibid., 3:158–182n51. Lane completely omits another story cycle—"Jali'ad of Hind and His Vizier Shimas"—in which tales are told to a corrupt king to teach him to turn away from the wicked counsel of women. Burton skewers Lane for his judgment that the tale is "extremely puerile," and instead argues that it is a "most characteristic tale"—one of the oldest in the collection. See Richard Francis Burton, *The Book of the Thousand Nights and a Night* (London: Privately circulated by the Burton Club, 1885), 9:32.
56. See the literary adaptation by Hanan al-Shaykh, *One Thousand and One Nights* (London: Bloomsbury, 2011), and the adaptation for the stage by Hanan al-Shaykh and Tim Supple, *One Thousand and One Nights* (London: Methuen Drama, 2011).
57. Lane, *Nights* (1841), 3:162–166n51.
58. Ibid., 3:169–173n51.
59. Ibid., 3:173–174n51.
60. Ibid., 3:159–160n51.
61. Lane, *Modern Egyptians*, 295.
62. Ibid., 297, 188.
63. Lane, *Nights* (1839), 1:226–227n22, 1:227n22.
64. Ibid., annotation by Tantawi, 1:5.
65. Miquel's theories are discussed in Ulrich Marzolph and Richard van Leeuwen, eds., *The Arabian Nights Encyclopedia* (Santa Barbara: ABC-CLIO, 2004), 409.
66. Robert Irwin, *The Arabian Nights: A Companion* (London: Tauris, 2004), 159–177. The stories can be found in Burton, *Thousand Nights and a Night*, 4:245–260, 5:154–163.
67. Lane, *Nights* (1840), 2:434–470, 472–473n19.

68. See Burton's version of "Dalilah the Crafty" in Burton, *Thousand Nights and a Night*, 7:144–171.
69. Al-Shaykh, *One Thousand and One Nights*. Also see the discussion of sexual politics in Fedwa Malti-Douglas, "Shahrazād Feminist," in *The Thousand and One Nights in Arabic Literature and Society*, ed. Richard G. Hovannisian and George Sabagh (Cambridge: Cambridge University Press, 1997), 40–55.
70. Henry Whitelock Torrens, *The Book of the Thousand Nights and One Night*, from the Arabic of the Egyptian manuscript, ed. W. Hay Macnaghten (Calcutta: Thacker, St. Andrews Library; London: W. H. Allen, 1838), 7–8.
71. Ibid.; Malcolm C. Lyons with Ursula Lyons, trans., *The Arabian Nights: Tales of 1001 Nights* (London: Penguin, 2008), 1:6. In the Lyonses' literal translation, the line "Is the sin with which you shame me" is missing.
72. Lane to Hay, January 30, 1832, Hay correspondence.
73. Thompson, *Edward William Lane*, 226. Lane's letters reveal an odd preoccupation with the "improvement" of Nefeeseh (never specifying what improvement he expected). See Lane to Hay, January 7, 1831; Lane to Hay's sister, April 27, 1831; Lane to Hay's sister, February 18, 1832; Lane to Hay, July 1, 1832; Lane to Hay's sister, October 15, 1832; and Lane to Hay, May 13, 1833; Lane to Hay, February 14, 1832, all in Hay correspondence.
74. Thompson, *Edward William Lane*, 458–460.
75. Lane to Hay, October 16, 1843, Hay correspondence.
76. Thompson, *Edward William Lane*, 460, 466; Lane to Hay, March 29, 1841, and Lane to Hay, October 16, 1843, Hay correspondence.
77. Sophia Lane Poole, *The Englishwoman in Egypt: Letters from Cairo, Written during a Residence There in 1842, 3 & 4 with E. W. Lane*, 5th ed. (London: Charles Knight, 1844), 1:v.
78. Correspondence regarding the *Arabic-English Lexicon* in the Cambridge University Library, Department of Manuscripts and Rare Books, Additional Manuscripts: Samuel Lee to Edward Lane, April 23, 1845, Add. 8843/2/22; William Howley to Lord Prudhoe, March 14, 1844, Add. 8843/1/20; Samuel Lee to Lord Prudhoe, July 3, 1844, Add. 8843/2/14; Lord Prudhoe to Richard Lane, January 2, 1844, Add. 8843/1/15; Richard Lane to Lord Prudhoe, January 9, 1844, Add. 8843/1/16; John Cotton to Mountstuart Elphinstone, February 26, 1844, Add. 8843/1/17; Edward Lane to Samuel Lee, March 17, 1845, Add. 8843/2/21.
79. Mary Wortley Montagu, *The Letters and Works of Lady Mary Wortley Montagu*, ed. Lord Wharncliffe, 2 vols. (Paris: A. and W. Galignani, 1837); Poole, *Englishwoman in Egypt*, 1:v–vi; Thompson, *Edward William Lane*, 571, 589.
80. Poole, *Englishwoman in Egypt*, 2:74–75, 3:43. For this text as a site of struggle, see Jill Matus, "Collaboration and Collusion: Two Victorian Writing Couples and Their Orientalist Texts," in *Literary Couplings: Writing Couples, Collaboration, and the Construction of Authorship*, ed. Marjorie Stone and Judith Thompson (Madison: University of Wisconsin Press, 2006), 175–181.

81. Poole, *Englishwoman in Egypt,* 2:74, 2:117–118, 2:161, 3:7, 3:12.
82. Ibid., 3:61–77, 2:162–170. Poole's rewriting of Lane's views of the magician were echoed by Lord Nugent in George Grenville Nugent, *Lands, Classical and Sacred* (London: Charles Knight, 1846), 1:133–141.

6. STEALING WITH STYLE

1. The state-of-the-art biography of Burton in his time is Dane Kennedy, *The Highly Civilized Man: Richard Burton and the Victorian World* (Cambridge, MA: Harvard University Press, 2007); the best fictionalized biography is Iliya Troyanov, *The Collector of Worlds* (London: Faber and Faber, 2009); and the most skeptical study is Jon R. Godsall, *The Tangled Web: A Life of Richard Burton* (London: Matador, 2013). Fawn M. Brodie, *The Devil Drives: A Life of Sir Richard Burton* (New York: W. W. Norton, 1967), remains relevant. New biographies of Burton are forthcoming from David Paul Nurse and Jason Thompson.
2. Kennedy, *Highly Civilized Man,* 165–170; Deborah Lutz, *Pleasure Bound: Victorian Sex Rebels and the New Eroticism* (London: Norton, 2011).
3. John Payne, *Alaeddin and the Enchanted Lamp; Zein Ul Asnam and the King of the Jinn: Two Stories Done into English Prose from the Recently Discovered Arabic Text* (London: Printed for subscribers only, 1901), iii, v.
4. Mia Gerhardt, *The Art of Storytelling: A Literary Study of the Thousand and One Nights* (Leiden, Netherlands: Brill, 1963), 77–87; Robert Irwin, *The Arabian Nights: A Companion* (London: Tauris, 2004), 26–31; Joseph Campbell, "Editor's Introduction," in *The Portable Arabian Nights* (New York: Viking, 1952), 31–32. For Payne as a Pre-Raphaelite, see Dinah Roe, ed., *The Pre-Raphaelites: From Rossetti to Ruskin* (London: Penguin, 2010).
5. John Payne, trans., *The Poems of Master Francis Villon of Paris* (London: Printed for the Villon Society for private distribution, 1878). Edward FitzGerald's version of *The Rubaiyat* was originally published in 1859, and it is available in multiple editions. See Edward FitzGerald, *Rubáiyát of Omar Khayyám*, ed. Daniel Karlin (Oxford: Oxford University Press, 2010).
6. Thomas Wright, *The Life of John Payne* (London: T. F. Unwin, 1919), 12. Between the ages of fourteen and nineteen, Wright claims, Payne had translated the second book of Goethe's *Faust,* Gotthold Ephraim Lessing's *Nathan der Weise,* Calderón de la Barca's *El Mágico Prodigioso,* and "the whole of Dante." Ibid.
7. Irwin, *Arabian Nights,* 26; Wright, *Life of John Payne,* 58; John Payne, *The Book of the Thousand Nights and One Night* (London: Printed for the Villon Society by private subscription and for private circulation only, 1882–1884).
8. Reginald Stuart Poole, "Specimens of a New Translation of the 'Thousand and One Nights,'" *Academy,* April 21, 1879. Payne had praised Gustav Weil's version as the finest completed version. [John Payne], "The Thousand and One Nights," pt. 2, *New Quarterly Magazine,* April 1879, 397.

9. [Payne], "The Thousand and One Nights," pt. 2, 397.
10. Deanna Victoria Mason, "'The Perennial Dramas of the East': Representations of the Middle East in the Writing and Art of Dante Gabriel Rossetti and William Holman Hunt" (PhD diss., Queen's University, 2009), 24–26, 33–63.
11. Christina Rossetti, "The Dead City" and "The Goblin Market," in *The Poetical Works of Christina Georgina Rossetti,* ed. William Michael Rossetti (London: Macmillan, 1904), 99–103, 1–8.
12. Wright, *Life of John Payne,* 87.
13. [Payne], "The Thousand and One Nights," pt. 2, 397.
14. Ibid., 398.
15. [John Payne], "The Thousand and One Nights," pt. 1, *New Quarterly Magazine,* January 1879, 154.
16. [Payne], "The Thousand and One Nights," pt. 2, 398.
17. Ibid., 400–401.
18. John Payne, "Prefatory Note," in *Thousand Nights and One Night,* 1:viii–ix.
19. Charles Dickens, "Old Lamps for New Lamps," *Household Words,* June 15, 1850, 1:12–14; Dante Gabriel Rossetti, "Preface," in *Dante and His Circle* (London: Ellis and White, 1874), x.
20. Algernon Swinburne, "Charles Baudelaire: *Les Fleurs du Mal,*" *Spectator* 6 (1862): 998–1000.
21. Wright, *Life of Payne,* 57–63.
22. FitzGerald quoted in Marina Warner, "Ventriloquism," review of *Rubáiyát of Omar Khayyám,* by Edward FitzGerald, ed. Daniel Karlin, *London Review of Books* 31 no. 7 (April 2009): 13–14. Warner sees this as a distinct pattern among European writers of the nineteenth century, starting with Goethe's ventriloquisms of the Persian poet Hafiz. Ibid.
23. Swinburne to Clement Shorter, March 4, 1896, in *The Swinburne Letters,* ed. Cecil Y. Lang (New Haven, CT: Yale University Press, 1962), 6:96.
24. John Payne, *The Quatrains of 'Omar Kheyyam of Nishapour* (London: Printed for the Villon Society for private circulation, 1898); John Payne, *The Quatrains of Ibn et Tefrid* (London: Printed for private circulation, 1908).
25. Payne, "Prefatory Note," 1:x.
26. John Payne, dedicatory poem dated February 5, 1885, in *Alaeddin and the Enchanted Lamp,* v.
27. John Payne, "Terminal Essay," in *Thousand Nights and One Night,* 9:373–374.
28. Ibid., 9:376–378; Payne, "Prefatory Note," 1:vii.
29. [Payne], "The Thousand and One Nights," pt. 1, 169–172.
30. Payne, "Terminal Essay," 9:382.
31. [Payne], "The Thousand and One Nights," pt. 2, 398.
32. "The Arabian Nights," *Cornhill Magazine* 32, no. 192 (December 1875): 720.
33. "New Translations of the Arabian Nights," *London and Westminster Review* 33, no. 64 (October 1839): 69.

34. Notice under "Literary Gossip," *Athenaeum,* no. 2661 (October 26, 1878): 533.
35. Payne, "Prefatory Note," 1:ix; Poole, "Specimens of a New Translation."
36. Henry Whitelock Torrens, trans., *The Book of the Thousand Nights and One Night,* from the Arabic of the Egyptian manuscript, ed. W. Hay Macnaghten (Calcutta: Thacker, St. Andrews Library; London: W. H. Allen, 1838), iii.
37. "The Ensorcelled Prince," in ibid., 59; Payne, *Thousand Nights and One Night,* 3:104, 5:36; Richard Francis Burton, *The Book of the Thousand Nights and a Night* (London: Privately circulated by the Burton Club, 1885): 1:30, 36, 69, 73, 77, 133, 186. These are only the references in Burton's first volume.
38. Payne, *Thousand Nights and One Night,* 1:2; Malcolm C. Lyons with Ursula Lyons, trans., *The Arabian Nights: Tales of 1001 Nights* (London: Penguin, 2008), 1:3; Edward William Lane, trans., *The Thousand and One Nights, Commonly Called, in England, the Arabian Nights' Entertainments,* ed. Edward Stanley Poole (London: Routledge, Warne, and Routledge, 1865), 1:4; Torrens, *Thousand Nights and One Night,* 3.
39. Payne, *Thousand Nights and One Night,* 1:6; Torrens, *Thousand Nights and One Night,* 7; Lane, *Nights* (1865), 1:9. Torrens misstates the number of rings.
40. Torrens, *Thousand Nights and One Night,* 82; Payne, *Thousand Nights and One Night,* 1:76; Lyons and Lyons, *The Arabian Nights,* 1:55; Lane, *Nights* (1865), 1:124–125. All emphasis my own.
41. Payne, *Thousand Nights and One Night,* 1:94, 102.
42. Ibid., 1:99–100.
43. Ibid., 1:105.
44. Ibid., 1:120–121.
45. Dante Gabriel Rossetti, review of John Payne's *Lautrec,* draft manuscript from 1878, Catalog Number 23296, Troxell Collection, Princeton University.
46. Poole, "Specimens of a New Translation."
47. Ibid.
48. Ibid.
49. The debate took place in three issues of the *Academy,* April 26, 1879, November 29, 1881, and December 7, 1881.
50. Richard Francis Burton, "The Arabian Nights," *Athenaeum,* November 26, 1881, 703.
51. Burton to Massey, July 30, 1881, Add MS 88876, Western Manuscripts, British Library.
52. Handwritten draft entitled by Burton on the wrapper "Translator's Preface" and "The Black Book," fols. 19–33, Add MS 88873, Western Manuscripts, British Library.
53. Burton to Payne, letter #2, March 20, 1882, RFB 313, box 26, Sir Richard Francis Burton Papers, Huntington Library, San Marino, CA (hereafter Burton Letters to Payne). The deliberation with which Burton pursued his plan to plagiarize Payne is described most clearly in C. Knipp, "The 'Arabian

Nights' in England: Galland's Translation and its Successors," *Journal of Arabic Literature* 5 (1974): 45.

54. Burton to Payne, letter #2, March 20, 1882, RFB 313, box 26, Burton Letters to Payne.
55. Burton to Payne, letter #5, London, June 3, 1882, letter #9, Trieste, September 29, 1882, and letter #10, Trieste, October 2, 1882, in RFB 313, box 26, Burton Letters to Payne.
56. Burton to Payne, letter #11, Trieste, October 8, 1882, RFB 313, box 26, Burton Letters to Payne.
57. Burton to Payne, letter #14, Trieste, December 23, 1882, and letter #15, January 4, 1883, RFB 313, box 26, Burton Letters to Payne.
58. Burton to Payne, letter #23, Trieste, April 17, 1884, RFB 313, box 26, Burton Letters to Payne.
59. Burton's copy of *The Alif Laila, or Book of the Thousand Nights and One Night,* ed. W. H. Macnaghten (Calcutta, 1839–1842), with no annotations, Kirkpatrick 679, Richard Francis Burton Library, Manuscript Collection, Huntington Library, San Marino, CA (hereafter Burton Library).
60. Burton's copy of Edward William Lane, *The Thousand and One Nights* (London: Charles Knight, 1839–1841), with extensive overwriting in Burton's hand, Kirkpatrick 682, Burton Library.
61. In the advertisement to subscribers for the *Supplemental Nights to the Book of the Thousand Nights and a Night,* Sir Richard Francis Burton Papers, Huntington Library, San Marino, CA.
62. Lawrence Venuti, *The Translator's Invisibility: A History of Translation,* 2nd ed. (London: Routledge, 2008), 265–273.
63. Burton to Massey, April 7, 1881, Add MS 88876, Western Manuscripts, British Library.
64. W. H. Mallock, *Every Man His Own Poet; or, The Inspired Singer's Recipe Book* (Boston: A. Williams, 1880), 22.
65. Richard Francis Burton, "Translator's Preface," in *The Book of the Thousand Nights and a Night* (London: Privately circulated by the Burton Club, 1885), 1:xiv.
66. Richard Francis Burton, *Supplemental Nights to the Book of the Thousand Nights and a Night with Notes Anthropological and Explanatory* (London: Printed by the Burton Club for private subscribers only, 1886), 1:20.
67. Burton, *Thousand Nights and a Night,* 1:255. Burton describes the Jewish doctor as motivated by "greed of gain" on 1:257.
68. Burton, "Translator's Preface," 1:xiv.
69. Torrens, *Thousand Nights and One Night,* 257–258; Burton, *Thousand Nights and a Night,* 1:255.
70. Torrens, *Thousand Nights and One Night,* 258.
71. Burton's copy of John Payne, *The Book of the Thousand Nights and One Night* (London: Printed by the Villon Society for private circulation, 1882–1889), Kirkpatrick 685, Burton Library; printed pages cut from John Payne's translation, *Tales from the Arabic of the Breslau and Calcutta (1814–18) Editions of the Book*

of the Thousand Nights and One Night, vol. 3, heavily annotated pages from "The Merchant of Cairo and the Favourite of the Khalif El Mamoun El Hakim Bi Amrillah," and "The Two Kings and the Vizier's Daughters," 1884, fols. 1–18, Add MS 88873, Western Manuscripts, British Library. Another section of the third volume of Payne's *Tales from the Arabic* titled "Shehrzad and Shehriyar (Conclusion)" is mislabeled in the British Library's catalog as "corrected proofs of pp. 183–196 of a supplement to Burton's translations of *The Thousand Nights and a Night,* 1885, and the *Supplemental Nights,* 1886–8," fols. 64–70, Add MS 49380, Western Manuscripts, British Library. There are extensive corrections written between the lines and in the margins of all three of these stories.

72. Annotated pages from Payne's "The Merchant of Cairo," fols. 1–18, Add MS 88873, Western Manuscripts, British Library. Compare to Burton, *Supplemental Nights,* 2:282–284.
73. Annotated pages from Payne's "The Merchant of Cairo," fols. 1–18, Add MS 88873, Western Manuscripts, British Library; Burton, *Supplemental Nights,* 2:284–285, 286n4.
74. Burton, "Translator's Preface," 1:xiv.
75. Jon R. Godsall, "Fact and Fiction in Richard Burton's Personal Narrative of a Pilgrimage to El-Medinah and Meccah (1855–6)," *Journal of the Royal Asiatic Society* 3, no. 3 (November 1993): 331–351.
76. Burton, *Supplemental Nights,* 6:451–452; Isabel Burton and Justin H. McCarthy, *Lady Burton's Edition of Her Husband's Arabian Nights: Translated Literally from the Arabic,* (London: Waterlow, 1886–1887).
77. Isabel Burton, *The Life of Captain Sir Richard F. Burton* (London: Chapman and Hall, 1893), 2:286. Emphasis in the original. For the collusion between Isabel and Richard in this matter, see Jill Matus, "Collaboration and Collusion: Two Victorian Writing Couples and Their Orientalist Texts," in *Literary Couplings: Writing Couples, Collaboration, and the Construction of Authorship,* ed. Marjorie Stone and Judith Thompson (Madison: University of Wisconsin Press, 2006), 182–189.
78. Venuti argues for the subversiveness of Burton in a section entitled "Call to Action," in *The Translator's Invisibility,* 268–273.
79. Payne, *Quatrains of 'Omar Kheyyam,* lix–lxi. All emphasis in the original.
80. Ibid., lix.

7. THE FALSE CALIPH

1. Richard Francis Burton, *Personal Narrative of a Pilgrimage to El-Medinah and Meccah* (London: Longman, Brown, Green, and Longmans, 1856), 1:11.
2. Richard Francis Burton, *Sindh, and the Races That Inhabit the Valley of the Indus* (London: Wm. H. Allen, 1851), 180–181.

3. The deliberate erasure of previous references to informants is evident in Burton's manuscript revisions in his own copy of *Sindh, and the Races That Inhabit the Valley of the Indus* (London: Wm. H. Allen, 1851), Kirkpatrick 3, Richard Francis Burton Library Manuscript Collection, Huntington Library, San Marino, CA (hereafter Burton Library).
4. Burton, *Pilgrimage,* 1:14–15.
5. Ibid., 1:12.
6. Edward William Lane, *An Account of the Manners and Customs of the Modern Egyptians, Written in Egypt during the Years 1833, -34, -35, Partly from Notes Made in a Former Visit to That Country, 1825, -26, -27, -28* (London: John Murray, 1860); Burton, *Pilgrimage,* 1:15, 18, 2:177–181.
7. Burton, *Pilgrimage,* 1:10–18.
8. Ibid., 1:280, 2:160–161. Burton's extracts from Burckhardt's descriptions of the Bait Ullah are in *Pilgrimage,* 3:149–185.
9. For Burton's biography, see Dane Kennedy, *The Highly Civilized Man: Richard Burton and the Victorian World* (Cambridge, MA: Harvard University Press, 2007); Jon R. Godsall, *The Tangled Web: A Life of Richard Burton* (London: Matador, 2013); and Fawn M. Brodie, *The Devil Drives: A Life of Sir Richard Burton* (New York: W.W. Norton, 1967).
10. Isabel Burton, *The Life of Captain Sir Richard F. Burton* (London: Chapman and Hall, 1893), 1: 94–95, 99. Also see Richard Burton, "Richard Burton's Little Autobiography," in ibid., 1:153.
11. Burton, "Little Autobiography," in Isabel Burton, *Life of Burton,* 1:154.
12. Isabel Burton, *Life of Burton,* 1:98; Simon Digby, *Richard Burton: The Indian Making of an Arabist* (Jersey, Channel Islands: Oriental Monographs, 2006), 18, 50.
13. Isabel Burton, *Life of Burton,* 1:95. Also see Richard Francis Burton, *Scinde; or, The Unhappy Valley* (London, 1851), 2:3.
14. Isabel Burton, *Life of Burton*: 1:93–94.
15. Ibid., 1:101.
16. Ibid., 1:159; Godsall, *The Tangled Web,* 34–37, 129.
17. Digby, *Richard Burton,* 18–21; Walter Abraham, letter to the *Times of India,* October 31, 1891, quoted in Isabel Burton, *Life of Burton,* 1:182–183.
18. Isabel Burton, *Life of Burton,* 1:123.
19. Mary Lovell, *A Rage to Live: A Biography of Richard and Isabel Burton* (New York: Norton, 2000), 39.
20. On Burton's doubts about local informants, see Kennedy, *Highly Civilized Man,* 43.
21. Godsall, *The Tangled Web,* 129.
22. On Burton's understanding of the power of languages in colonial India, see Kennedy, *Highly Civilized Man,* 34.
23. Isabel Burton, *Life of Burton,* 1:123.

24. Burton's biographers sometimes confuse Mirzā Mohammed Hosayn Shirazi with his near namesake Mirzā Hosayn Mahallātī, the Āghā Khān's brother, whom Burton also befriended in the mid- to late 1840s, resulting in far-fetched speculations regarding the nature of the rapport between Burton and his munshi. Edward Rice concludes the two were pawns of the great game between Russia, Persia, and Britain and asserts that Burton secretly converted to the Ismaili sect. See Edward Rice, *Captain Sir Richard Francis Burton: The Secret Agent Who Made the Pilgrimage to Mecca, Discovered the Kama Sutra, and Brought the Arabian Nights to the West* (New York: HarperCollins, 1990), 122–139.
25. Richard Francis Burton, "Terminal Essay," in *The Book of the Thousand Nights and a Night* (London: Privately circulated by the Burton Club, 1885), 10:127.
26. Isabel Burton, *Life of Burton,* 1:135. On the value of these relationships in colonial India, see C. A. Bayly, *Empire and Information: Intelligence Gathering and Social Communication in India, 1780–1870* (Cambridge: Cambridge University Press, 1997), 55, 94, 178.
27. Richard Francis Burton [Frank Baker, pseud.], *Stone Talk . . . Being Some of the Marvelous Sayings of a Petral Portion of Fleet Street, London, to One Doctor Polyglott, Ph.D.* (London: Robert Harwicke, 1865), 10; Isabel Burton, *Life of Burton,* 1:109.
28. Burton, *Scinde; or, The Unhappy Valley,* 1:72–78.
29. Richard Francis Burton, *Goa, and the Blue Mountains; or, Six Months of Sick Leave,* introduction by Dane Kennedy (Berkeley: University of California Press, 1991), 65–67, 73–89; Digby, *Richard Burton,* 35–38, 60–61n126; Thomas Bacon, *Oriental Annual, containing a Series of Tales, Legends and Historical Romances* (London, 1840); Georgiana Stisted, *The True Life of Captain Sir Richard F. Burton* (London: H. S. Nichols, 1896).
30. Richard Francis Burton, *Falconry in the Valley of the Indus* (London: J. van Voorst, 1852), 99; Kennedy, *Highly Civilized Man,* 43–44.
31. Parama Roy, *Indian Traffic: Identities in Question in Colonial and Postcolonial India* (Berkeley: University of California Press, 1998), 8.
32. Richard Francis Burton, "Alhlak I Hindi or a Translation of the Hindustani version of Pilpay's Fables," typescript, written in Bombay, 1847, Kirkpatrick 104, Burton Library. This work has been published as *Pilpay's Fables* (Tucson: Asian Ethnographer Society Press, 1997).
33. Kennedy, *Highly Civilized Man,* 39.
34. Burton, "Alhlak I Hindi," 22.
35. Ibid., 17.
36. Ibid., 22.
37. Richard Francis Burton, preface to *Vikram and the Vampire; or, Tales of Hindu Devilry* (London, 1893), xxxi. For the evidence of plagiarism, see Digby, *Richard Burton,* 62.

38. Richard Francis Burton, "Translator's Preface," in *Thousand Nights and a Night,* 1:xiv.
39. Burton, "Alhlak I Hindi," 67.
40. Prospectus for Burton's *Supplemental Nights to the Book of the Thousand Nights and a Night,* inserted in volume 4, Kirkpatrick 94a, Burton Library; Richard Francis Burton, "Foreword," in *Supplemental Nights to the Book of the Thousand Nights and a Night with Notes Anthropological and Explanatory* (London: Printed by the Burton Club for private subscribers only, 1886), 3:viii. "Aladdin" was, however, taken from the forged manuscript of Michel Sabbagh.
41. Burton's copy of [Jonathan Scott], *The Arabian Nights' Entertainments* (Lucknow, India: Newul Kishore Press, 1879–1880), Kirkpatrick 684d, Burton Library.
42. Burton, *Sindh, and the Races,* 364.
43. Burton, *Scinde; or, The Unhappy Valley,* 2:3.
44. Isabel Burton, *Life of Burton,* 1:95.
45. Burton, *Scinde; or, The Unhappy Valley,* 1:182.
46. Ibid., 2:288.
47. In Burton's copy of Edward William Lane, *The Thousand and One Nights, Commonly Called, in England, the Arabian Nights' Entertainments* (London: Charles Knight, 1839–1841), Kirkpatrick 682, Burton Library. Brackets in the original.
48. Ibid.; Burton, "Terminal Essay," 10:265.
49. Stanley Lane-Poole, "Advertisement," 1882, reprinted in Edward William Lane, *The Thousand and One Nights,* ed. Edward Stanley Poole (London: Chatto and Windus, 1912), 1:v–vi.
50. Burton, "Translator's Preface," vii. Burton had little direct experience with the Bedouin, apart from experiencing Bedouin raids of pilgrims during the hajj, but he claimed knowledge gained from the reports of others in a performance of expertise. See Burton, *Pilgrimage,* 2:101–118.
51. Lovell, *Rage to Live,* 427; Kennedy, *Highly Civilized Man,* 181–185.
52. Richard Francis Burton, *Camões, His Life and His Lusiads: A Commentary* (London: Bernard Quaritch, 1881), 1:274.
53. Burton, *Stone Talk,* 34–36.
54. Kennedy, *Highly Civilized Man,* 170–171.
55. Richard Francis Burton, "Translators," *Athenaeum,* no. 2313 (February 24, 1872): 241–243.
56. Burton, "Terminal Essay," 10:113, 102, 114. See James L. Newman, *Paths without Glory: Richard Francis Burton in Africa* (Washington, DC: Potomac, 2010).
57. Burton, *Thousand Nights and a Night,* 1:74n1, 28n2, 97n1, 101n1, 166n1, 134n1; Burton, *Pilgrimage,* 2:25.
58. Burton, *Pilgrimage,* 2:16.
59. Jean-François Gournay, *L'appel du proche-orient: Richard Francis Burton et son temps, 1821–1890* (Paris: Didier-Erudition, 1983), 124.

60. Burton's draft preface in his copy of Edward William Lane, *The Thousand and One Nights, Commonly Called, in England, the Arabian Nights' Entertainments* (London: Charles Knight, 1839–1841), with extensive overwriting in Burton's hand, Kirkpatrick 682, Burton Library.
61. Kwame Anthony Appiah, *Cosmopolitanism: Ethics in a World of Strangers* (New York: Norton, 2006), xi–xxi.
62. Richard Francis Burton, *The Kasîdah of Hâjî Abdû al-Yazdî* (New York: Alfred A. Knopf, 1924), 63.
63. Richard Francis Burton, "Preface to the Third Edition," in *Personal Narrative of a Pilgrimage to Mecca and Medina* (Leipzig: Bernhard Tauchnitz, 1874), 1:xvii; Appiah, *Cosmopolitanism,* 4–5.
64. Burton, "Terminal Essay," 10:168.
65. In this sense it had the potential that Thomas Bender identifies with cosmopolitan experience, which should lead to disorientation and self-reflection. Thomas Bender, "The Cosmopolitan Experience and Its Uses," in *Cosmopolitanisms,* ed. Bruce Robbins and Paulo Horta (New York: New York University Press, forthcoming).
66. Burton, *Supplemental Nights,* 3:72n1, 72n2, 146n1, 185n1, 189n1.
67. Ibid., 3:133n3, 176n1, 182n1.
68. Burton to Payne, letter #12, Trieste, October 21, 1882, RFB 313, box 26, Sir Richard Francis Burton Papers, Huntington Library, San Marino, CA (hereafter Burton Letters to Payne).
69. Burton, *Thousand Nights and a Night,* 3:241. Rana Kabbani argues that Burton replicates Orientalist stereotypes of a sexualized Orient and justifies patriarchal authority. See Rana Kabbani, *Europe's Myths of Orient* (London: Macmillan, 1986), 7, 66.
70. *The Perfumed Garden* was actually translated from a French manuscript in the absence of an Arabic version. See Kennedy, *Highly Civilized Man,* 215–218.
71. Burton to Payne, letter #12, Trieste, October 21, 1882, RFB 313, box 26, Burton Letters to Payne.
72. Burton, *Thousand Nights and a Night,* 3:265.
73. Burton, "Terminal Essay," 10:99.
74. Neither of these Haruns reflects the Abbasid caliph of history (r. 786–809), who turned against his vizier Jafar and his Barmakid relatives in a spectacular fashion in 803.
75. "Harun al Rashid," in *The Arabian Nights Encyclopedia,* ed. Ulrich Marzolph and Richard van Leeuwen (Santa Barbara: ABC-CLIO, 2004), 585–586. On the real Abu Nuwas, see Philip F. Kennedy, *Abu Nuwas: A Genius of Poetry* (Oxford: Oneworld, 2005).
76. John Payne, "Terminal Essay," in *The Book of the Thousand Nights and One Night* (London: Printed for the Villon Society by private subscription and for private

circulation only, 1882–1884), 9:331; [John Payne], "The Thousand and One Nights," pt. 1, *New Quarterly Magazine,* January 1879, 169–172.

77. Payne, "Terminal Essay," 9:320, 331, 378.
78. Ibid., 9:377.
79. Burton, "Terminal Essay," 10:120–124.
80. Ibid., 10:156, 115, 116.
81. Ibid., 10:63; Burton, "Translator's Preface," *Thousand Nights and a Night,* 1:xxiii.
82. Salih, "Burton at Damascus," *Bookman,* October 1891, 24; Kennedy, *Highly Civilized Man,* 89–90.
83. Ulrich Marzolph, "The Story of Abū al-Ḥasan the Wag in the Tübingen Manuscript of the Romance of ʿUmar ibn al-Nuʿmān and Related Texts," *Journal of Arabic Literature* 46 (2015): 44.
84. Burton, *Supplemental Nights,* 1:1–38. Compare Payne on lashes in *Tales from the Arabic of the Breslau and Calcutta (1814–18) Editions of the Book of the Thousand Nights and One Night* (London: printed for subscribers only, 1884), 1:14.
85. Chraïbi's argument is discussed in Marzolph, "The Story of Abū al-Ḥasan," 54.
86. Burton draws the comparison to Cervantes and Sancho in *Supplemental Nights,* 1:1, 16.
87. Ibid.
88. Burton, *Supplemental Nights,* 1:4.
89. Ibid., 1:24.
90. W. A. Clouston, "Appendix: Variants and Analogues of Some of the Tales in the Supplemental Nights, Vols. I. and II., The Sleeper and the Waker," in Burton, *Supplemental Nights,* 2:291–295.
91. Burton to Payne, May 12, 1883, Burton Letters to Payne.
92. Burton, *Thousand Nights and a Night,* 5:64–65.
93. Ibid., 5:66–67.
94. Ibid., 5:67–68.
95. Richard Francis Burton, *Abeokuta and the Camaroons Mountains: An Exploration* (London: Tinsley Brothers, 1863), 1:110–111; letter from Swinburne to Theodore Watts, August 30, 1875, in *The Swinburne Letters,* ed. Cecil Y. Lang (New Haven, CT: Yale University Press, 1959–1962), 3:61; Richard Burton, notebook leaves relating to his crossing of the Atlantic and arrival at Halifax, 1860, Add MS 49380, British Library. Burton's journal entries for his trip across the Atlantic are interpreted as a spoof by Lovell in her biography of Burton and his wife, Isabel. This interpretation is necessary for her to uphold her argument that Burton had no "homosexual tendencies," in defiance of the opinion of his closest companions. See Lovell, *Rage to Live,* 343–345.
96. Handwritten draft entitled by Burton on the wrapper "Translator's Preface" and "The Black Book," fols. 19–33, Add MS 88873, Western Manuscripts, British Library. On this issue see Kennedy, *Highly Civilized Man,* 206–247.

97. Burton to Payne, May 22, 1883, Burton Letters to Payne. For the Sotadic Zone, see Burton, "Terminal Essay," 180–212. For homosexuality in northern Europe, see ibid., 213–217.
98. Burton, "Terminal Essay," 10:178–179.
99. Ibid.
100. Handwritten note in blue ink atop of page 251, in Burton's proof copy of his *Arabian Nights,* vol. 10, Kirkpatrick 91a, Burton Library. The passage is an adapted, abbreviated, and idealized summation of a passage from A. Coffignon's *Paris Vivant: La Corruption à Paris*: "The *shared vice* effaces all social differences. The master and the manservant are on the same footing; the millionaire and the beggar fraternize; the functionary and the repeat offender exchange their *ignoble caresses.*" Purged of Coffignon's terms of judgment—*"shared vice," "ignoble caresses"*—Burton's is altogether a more optimistic vision.
101. See Burton's manuscript notes, mainly taken from Coffignon, across the top of pages 248–255 of Burton's proof copy of his *Arabian Nights,* vol. 10, Kirkpatrick 91a, Burton Library.
102. For Burton's African ventures, see Newman, *Paths without Glory.*
103. Orhan Pamuk, "To Read or Not to Read: The Thousand and One Nights," in Pamuk, *Other Colors: Essays and a Story,* trans. Maureen Freely (New York: Alfred A. Knopf, 2007); personal communication.
104. Orhan Pamuk, *The Black Book,* trans. Güneli Gün (New York: Farrar, Straus and Giroux, 1994).

ACKNOWLEDGMENTS

Research into how texts are reshaped outside their cultures of origin demands collaboration. Early in the conception of this book, Wen-Chin Ouyang, my co-conspirator on an edition of *The Arabian Nights* for Everyman's Library, challenged me to make use of my vantage point in the Middle East to seek new material to supplement the usual sources for studies of Antoine Galland, Edward Lane, and Richard Burton. I would like to acknowledge the scholars who made that research possible and who supported the writing of this book in Abu Dhabi, London, Paris, Toronto, and Cambridge, Massachusetts.

My first debt is to the preeminent scholars of the *Arabian Nights* who have welcomed me into their company and shared their knowledge and critical insights during the past five years. Aboubakr Chraïbi's work on the story collection in Arabic and French has offered an inspiring example of literary research, and I thank him for his encouragement and advice. I am also deeply indebted to Ulrich Marzolph, who generously shared his expertise in narrative traditions in Arabic, Persian, and Western languages, and who provided invaluable feedback on a draft of this book. I benefitted greatly from Chraïbi's invitation to join his *Mille et une nuits* project in 2010, through which I was able to present my research at the universities of Seville, Granada, Copenhagen, Rome, Bologna, and Harvard. During these sessions, I was fortunate to receive feedback from Ibrahim Akel, Francesca Bellino, Nathalie Bléser, Abdallah Cheikh-Moussa, Anne Duprat, Ferial Ghazoul, William Granara, Beatrice Gruendler, Robert Irwin, Dominique Jullien, Abdelfattah Kilito, Peter Madsen, Delio Proverbio, Carmen Ramirez, Joseph Sadan, Jean-Paul Sermain, Evanghélia Stead, Richard van Leeuwen, and Ilaria Vitali.

For discussions on Hanna Diyab, I am particularly indebted to Frédéric Bauden, Ruth Bottigheimer, Bernard Heyberger, Johannes Stephan, and Paule Thierry. Bauden first pointed me in the direction of Diyab's manuscript in the Vatican Library in 2009; Thierry graciously made her French translation available to me prior to its publication; and Stephan generously double-checked my references to Diyab's manuscript memoir, which will be the subject of his own book-length study. Bottigheimer's analysis of the grammar of Galland's diary entries relating to Diyab's storytelling confirmed the need to explore the importance of Diyab's storytelling in French. I would also like to thank Richard van Leeuwen for inviting me to Berlin's Literaturhaus to present material from this book and chair a panel of European translators of the *Arabian Nights* that included Amund Bjørsnøs (Norway), Claudia Ott (Germany), and Ellen Wulff (Denmark). Wulff replicates the rhyming prose of Arabic in her version and notes that Burton used rhyme for passages that in the Arabic have none, a critical insight into Burton's practice of rewriting.

My interest in the *Arabian Nights* is long-standing, but this book could not have been conceived without the stimulus provided by the Harvard Institute for World Literature, and the seminar that I taught for the institute in Istanbul in the summer of 2012. I would like to thank David Damrosch for the invitation to participate in the program, and my hosts in Istanbul, Murat Belge and Jale Parla. Discussions with fellow faculty members at the institute, including Amir Mufti, Orhan Pamuk, Martin Puchner, and Bruce Robbins, were critical to my study of hidden collaborations and the making of the *Arabian Nights* as a work of world literature. For their generosity, and the welcome offered by so many others at Bilgi University, Koç University, and the German Orient Institute, I must offer my sincerest thanks. My two weeks in Istanbul soon became four, and four soon became six, and in the cafés of Cihangir the first draft of this book was born.

My project was also nurtured by a series of panels and conferences on world literature that I have organized along with Aboubakr Chraïbi and Dominique Jullien over the past five years. Through these discussions, I have benefitted from the insights of, among others, Pierro Boitani, Stefan Helgesson, Efrain Kristal, Suzanne Jill Levine, Francesca Orsini, and Mads Rosendahl Thomsen. I have also gained important feedback on this work through talks given at the kind invitation of Jullien, Margaret Litvin, Jan Loop, and Karla Mallette.

At NYU Abu Dhabi, I have benefitted tremendously from conversations with scholars associated with the Library of Arabic Literature, published by NYU Press. Among the editors, translators, and fellows associated with this project, I must single out Marilyn Booth, Michael Cooperson, Philip Kennedy, Jan Loop, James Montgomery, Maurice Pomerantz, Justin Stearns, and Shawkat Toorawa for their constructive responses to my research. At NYU, Toral Gajarawala Jacques Lezra, Cyrus Patell, and Jini Kin Watson provided helpful feedback on an early draft, and Thomas Augst and William Germano gave me critical advice that reshaped the book. In the literature program at NYU Abu Dhabi, Awam Amkpa, Una Chaudhuri, Phillip Mitsis, Robert Stam, and Robert Young provided invaluable support and encouragement. While I was writing this book, I enjoyed a summer at the University of Toronto's Centre for Diaspora and Transnational Studies, where I learned from the stimulating perspectives of Ato Quayson and was able to reconnect with my valued mentors Suzanne Akbari and David Shaw. I finished a draft of the book while a visiting scholar in Comparative Literature at Harvard in 2015, and I would like to acknowledge the collegial welcome of David Damrosch, Martin Puchner, and Karen Thornber. Reaching back in time, I would also like to thank my colleagues in the program of world literature at Simon Fraser University—Azadeh Yamini-Hamedani, Melek Ortabasi, and Ken Seigneurie—and the kind mentorship of Derryl MacLean in the history program.

My work would not have been possible without the advice of amazing archivists and researchers at the Huntington Library, the British Library, the Cambridge University Library, the Bodleian Library and the Sackler Library at the Griffith Institute of Oxford University, both the Richelieu and Mitterrand branches of the Bibliothèque nationale de France, the Bibliothèque des Sciences religieuses at the Sorbonne, the Vatican Library, and London's Library and Museum of Freemasonry. I owe special thanks to Nicholas Martin of the Special Collections at NYU Abu Dhabi, Gayle M. Richardson at the Huntington Library, Susan Snell at the Library and Museum of Freemasonry, and Catherine Warsi at the Griffith Institute. I have also benefitted from a treasure trove of research assistants, including S. Ahmad (who helped procure sources on Lane in Cairo), Mohammad al Mubarak, Alistair Blacklock, Carmen Germaine, Katherine Delia James, Brendan Marriott, and Krisztina Szilagyi.

I would like to thank the entire team at Harvard University Press, including the authors of the peer-review reports, the Board of Syndics readers, the design team, Senior Editor Louise Robbins, Assistant Editor Heather Hughes, and, in particular, Executive Editor-at-Large Sharmila Sen. Thanks also to Brian Ostrander and Ashley Moore at Westchester Publishing Services, proofreader Joanne Galli, and Murphy Indexing.

My greatest thanks are due to my family, who have served as my most constant interlocutors on the *Arabian Nights,* from my mother, Lia, who first told me the stories (that she had herself read in her childhood), to my father, Guilherme, and sisters, Lis and Elza, who also share with me a love of literature and inquiry. My thanks also to my brother-in-law Marco, whose wit and example helped seal my decision to pursue an academic career. *Marvellous Thieves* contains echoes of our countless conversations in Trieste, where Burton produced his translation of the *Arabian Nights,* and Brazil, where the same Victorian adventurer inspired the emperor Dom Pedro II to study Arabic and attempt his own translation of the *Arabian Nights* into Portuguese. My parents first took me to Istanbul as an infant, and they raised me among the objects they had gathered from their own sojourn in the Middle East. It is fitting that I should return to compose this book in their honor.

If the book's flaws are my own, many of its strengths are due to my wife, Nadine, whose inspiration and editorial advice are just a small part of the magic she has worked on this volume. As a marvellous thief, I have taken the most from her. I dedicate this book to our beautiful boys, Gabriel and Rafael.

ILLUSTRATION CREDITS

9 Philippe de Champaigne, *Portrait d'un Turc.* Reproduced with the permission of the Huntington Library, Art Collections, and Botanical Gardens.

12 Sketch by Edward Lane. © Griffith Institute, University of Oxford.

29 Illustration from "The Ebony Horse." Reproduced with permission from Ulrich Marzolph's archive of Persian lithographed illustrations.

34 View of the city of Aleppo. Reproduced from Alexander Drummond, *Travels through Different Cities of Germany, Italy, Greece and Several Parts of Asia, . . .* (London: Printed by W. Strahan for the author, 1754), between 184–185. British Library filename c13253-10, shelfmark 457.e.2. © The British Library Board.

50 From score of Jean-Baptiste Lully's opera *Atys* (1709). Reproduced with the permission of the Bibliothèque nationale de France, département Musique, VM2-28.

65 The pyramids of Cappadocia. From Lucas, *Deuxième voyage du sieur Paul Lucas dans le Levant.* Reproduced with the permission of the Bibliothèque nationale de France.

83 Attack by bandits. From Lucas, *Deuxième voyage du sieur Paul Lucas dans le Levant.* Reproduced with the permission of the Bibliothèque nationale de France.

89 Illustration from the tale of King 'Umar ibn al-Nu'man. Reproduced with permission from Ulrich Marzolph's archive of Persian lithographed illustrations.

96 Henry Torrens. From C. Grant, *Lithographic Sketches of the Public Characters of Calcutta* (1850). Photo reproduction courtesy of the University of Toronto.

106 A munshi. Reproduced from *The Costume and Customs of Modern India* (ca. 1824) plate 1. British Library filename 073742, shelfmark X 380. © The British Library Board.

129 Sir William Hay Macnaghten, Sir Alexander Burnes, Akbar Khan, and Shah Shuja, by Lowes Cato Dickinson. National Portrait Gallery, reference collection NPG D38122. © National Portrait Gallery, London.

133 Edward Lane, by Richard James Lane. National Portrait Gallery, primary collection NPG 940. Given by the sitter's grand-nephew, Stanley Lane Poole, 1893. © National Portrait Gallery, London.

137 Sketch by Edward Lane. © Griffith Institute, University of Oxford.

143 Street scene by Joseph Bonomi. © Griffith Institute, University of Oxford.

149 *Sheikh Abdul Kadir Mugrabi,* by Godfrey Thomas Vigne, 1844. Reproduced with the permission of the Victoria and Albert Museum. Museum number SD 1148. Purchased with the assistance of The Art Fund, the National Heritage Memorial Fund, Shell International, and the Friends of the V&A.

170 Illustration from "The Story of Ghanim the Son of Eiyoob, the Distracted Slave of Love," in Edward Lane, *The Thousand and One Nights: Commonly Called The Arabian Nights Entertainments* (London: Chatto and Windus, 1912). Reproduced with the permission of the Special Collections Division of New York University Abu Dhabi.

187 Illustration of a store in Cairo, from Edward Lane, *The Thousand and One Nights: Commonly Called The Arabian Nights Entertainments* (London: Chatto and Windus, 1912). Reproduced with the permission of the Special Collections Division of New York University Abu Dhabi.

192 Sketch of a bookseller by Edward Lane. © Griffith Institute, University of Oxford.

195 Watercolor from one of Edward Lane's notebooks from Cairo. © Griffith Institute, University of Oxford.

207 Edward Lane's copy of the Bulaq edition of the *Arabian Nights,* with annotations by Sheikh Muhammad Ayyad al-Tantawi. Photo reproduction courtesy of the University of Cambridge Library.

223 Christina Rossetti, study for *Ecce Ancilla Domini! (The Annunciation),* by Dante Gabriel Rossetti (1828–1882), ca. 1849. Tate reference number T00287. © Tate, London 2016.

250 Page from Richard Burton's copy of John Payne's *The Book of the Thousand Nights and One Night.* Photo reproduction courtesy of British Library Imaging Services.

256 *The Pilgrim,* from Richard Burton's *Personal Narrative of a Pilgrimage to El-Medinah and Meccah.* Photo reproduction courtesy of the University of Toronto.

262 *The Remnants of an Army,* by Elizabeth Butler (1846–1933), 1879. Tate reference number N01553. © Tate, London 2016.

264 Young officer being tutored by a munshi. From George Atkinson's *"Curry & Rice."* Photo reproduction courtesy of the University of Toronto.

268 "Queen of Candy," from *Oriental Annual, or Scenes in India* (London: Edward Bull, 1834). Reproduced with the permission of the Special Collections Division at New York University Abu Dhabi.

INDEX